Anonymus

The Monthly Magazine of the Holy Rosary

Volume 1, August 1872 - July 1873

Anonymus

The Monthly Magazine of the Holy Rosary
Volume 1, August 1872 - July 1873

ISBN/EAN: 9783742825964

Manufactured in Europe, USA, Canada, Australia, Japa

Cover: Foto ©Thomas Meinert / pixelio.de

Manufactured and distributed by brebook publishing software
(www.brebook.com)

Anonymus

The Monthly Magazine of the Holy Rosary

THE

MONTHLY MAGAZINE

OF THE

HOLY ROSARY,

ϳfor Catholic Households and Readers of all Classes.

Under the Direction of the Dominican Fathers.

I. ANNUAL VOLUME.

NEW SERIES.

AUGUST, 1872—JULY, 1873.

With Copious Index.

Sancte Pater Dominice, ora pro nobis.—LIT. SS.

LONDON:

BURNS, OATES, AND COMPANY,

17, PORTMAN STREET, W.; AND 63, PATERNOSTER ROW, E.C.

1873.

PREFACE.

S. PAUL says, "Brethren, I would not have you ignorant;" and then proceeds to say of what he would not have his brethren ignorant—"how our fathers were all under the cloud, and all passed through the sea," &c. (1 Cor. x. 1). When S. Paul wrote these words he established a principle or rule to remain in force for the Christian people as long as tho world should last, namely, that they should always seek diligently for knowledge about all things pertaining to their faith.

To Hebrews this knowledge inculcated by the Apostle was becoming on the double ground of both nationality and faith. It was not only their own national history that they were required to know, but the history of the dealings of God with their nation. To the Christian people of the nations, however, this knowledge could only be becoming on the second ground, because it would be shameful in them not to know the great works of God, by which He had prepared the way for their faith in the mission of Jesus Christ and in His redemption of the world by His sacrifice of Himself on the Cross.

But these works of God upon earth have never ceased, and never will cease upon the earth. "The God who keepeth Israel," says the psalmist, "neither slumbers nor sleeps." If the wise king speaks of the powerlessness of men in his time either "to add to or to take away from the works which God had done that He may be feared" (Eccles. iii. 14), the reasons remain unchanged why God should continue to make Himself feared by His works. He is the selfsame God now, as regards power, that He was in the days of Moses. The difference, therefore, between an intelligent and well informed Christian and a supposed well informed Infidel, will consist in this—besides the departments of knowledge possessed by both in common—that the Infidel will see in the world nothing but the strife of men and what he calls the operations of the powers of nature, whereas, the Christian will see and recognize in the world the present action and interposition of God.

If, unhappily, Catholics are to be found to whom the Apostle's rule is little else but a dead letter, and who are quite satisfied with the state of ignorance which the Apostle condemns,—should such as these chance to come into the company of the infidels, it will most likely not take a great deal to make them feel ashamed of themselves and of their faith. Who does not see, however, that it is the very reverse that ought to be the case? It is the infidels who ought to feel abashed and ashamed in the presence of those who believe, but, then, it · is impossible for us not to suffer in the way that our neglect of Apostolic rules, whatever it may be, justly brings upon us. God certainly never intended that His people should be abashed in the presence of any infidels.

The object, then, of our Magazine of the Holy Rosary is to offer to all our fellow Catholics, and particularly to members of the Confraternity of the Rosary, in conformity with the Apostle's rule, such select information about the works of God, in the midst of which we live, as our space permits, varied with passages from the past history of the lives of Saints, and other similar matters of current interest   And while we hope to be able to continue a labour the need for which can never cease as long as faith continues upon earth, we hope also, as regards our past efforts, that they have proved not altogether unacceptable.

Hinckley
    Feast of SS. Peter and Paul.
        A.D. 1873.

CONTENTS.

CONTENTS.

THE

Monthly Magazine of the Holy Rosary.

NEW SERIES.

No. 1.]　　　　　　AUGUST.　　　　　[A.D. 1872.

THE FEAST OF S. DOMINIC.—4TH August, 1872.

ADDRESS TO OUR READERS.

In resuming our labours, which were interrupted by the un-
foreseen death of the late Very Rev. P. MACKEY, in the issue of
the present New Series of our *Monthly Magazine of the Holy
Rosary*, to which we have boldly determined to give an en-
larged form and a cheaper price, we may be permitted to
cherish a happy augury for its future, in the circumstance
that it begins its new career in the month of August, under
the immediate shadow of the Feast of S. Dominic. What
more fitting tribute of gratitude for having given us the Holy
Rosary can we offer to him, or what more likely to obtain
his patronage and to draw down his benediction, than the
dedication to his honour and memory of the opening pages of
a publication whose end is one that he had so much at heart,
and to accomplish which he so patiently and zealously
laboured!

In reading the Life of our great Saint, we cannot fail to
observe that he was given to the Church, not only to do a
great work in his own lifetime, but to maintain and assert a
principle of action, which was to survive him, and to become
a strong and permanent motive power with those who were
to come after him.

Called, as he was, to labour in a period of the Church's
history when social life was disorganized to its very centre,
by the long continued miseries of civil strife, and in a portion
too of her vineyard sadly devastated by ignorance and heresy the
natural results of such calamities, S. Dominic's first efforts
were directed to bring back to the minds and hearts of the
people the knowledge and love of those Divine truths well-
nigh forgotten, which alone could heal and save society.
This he accomplished by means of the "Holy Rosary," and
to quote Father Lacordaire, his efforts were " blessed with a

success of the most perfect kind—success, that is, among the
people.   The people of Christ have clung to it, from age to age,
with incredible fidelity; the confraternities of the ' Rosary,'
have been infinitely multiplied; there is scarce a Christian
in the world who does not possess in that which he calls his
string of beads, or chaplet, a portion of the ' Rosary.'   Who
has not heard," he continues, "at evening in the country
churches, the deep voices of the peasants reciting in true
chorus the angelical salutation?   Who has not met processions of pilgrims, moving between their fingers the beads of
the Rosary; and beguiling the length of the road with the
alternate repetition of the name of Mary?   As often as
anything attains to perpetuity and universality, it must
necessarily possess some mysterious agreement with the
wants and destinies of man.   The shallow rationalist does
but see long lines of men pass by, continually repeating
the same word; those who have more sense will easily
understand that love has but one word, and that to be
continually repeating that word is no idle repetition."*
   Again, by the foundation of his Order, and in the constitution which he gave to it, he has asserted and established the
principle that it is by means of the gifts of knowledge and the
love of truth that the Church of God carries on the mission
of enlightening and saving mankind, as a learned Benedictine†
remarks in his recent life of S. Thomas Aquinas: "From the
very first, knowledge was taken by the Dominicans, as a
principle of power; not knowledge buried in seclusion or
antiquated in its form, but knowledge which would tell upon
mankind and raise up humanity from the egotism of nature
to the standard of the Cross."   Inspired by a motive such as
this, S. Dominic drove back the mist of ignorance in his
own times, and by the institution of a teaching Order—the
" Order of Truth," as a good Pontiff called it—rekindled in
the world the torch of Divine truth.   The great design he
had in view is embodied in that passage of the constitutions
where it is said that "the Order of Preachers was principally
and specially designed for preaching and teaching, in order to
communicate to others the *fruits of contemplation*, and to
procure the salvation of souls."
   The "Egotism of Nature" is an evil not less rife in the pre-

* "Life of S. Dominic." By Father Lacordaire.
† The Very Rev. B. Vaughan, "Life of S. Thomas Aquinas." Vol. i.
p. 115.

sent day than in the times of S. Dominic, and the same principle of action must ever continue to be opposed to it, if the
Church is to succeed in overcoming the pride of intellect, which
is eating its way, like a canker, into the very heart of social,
political, and religious society. The surface of society is not
wanting in certain unmistakable indications that there are
those who suspect its inability by itself to solve the problem of
the restlessness by which it is agitated. There are signs of its
becoming more and more conscious of the evils of which ignorance of God is the fruitful parent, and while there is a manifest craving and demand for indiscriminate knowledge, it will
daily become more and more the duty of those who labour for the
cause of God to meet it by an adequate supply of the right sort.
Whence can the supply safely come, except from the hands of
those who have received the mission to teach in the Church of
God?   The Church alone has the duty laid upon her of teaching the nations of the earth; and they have to learn knowledge at her hands; yet it is not knowledge of any kind, much
less the "knowledge that puffeth up," that can regenerate
a people, but the knowledge of God, taught and preached
under the standard of the Cross. As of old, in the hour of ·
the Church's need in the thirteenth century, so now too
may S. Dominic help us, by his spirit and by his prayers. In
furtherance of the good end he had at heart, our little
magazine goes forth under the invocation of his name, and
in the hope of being prospered by his blessing.

It has before itself the hard and laborious work of the
"Friar preacher," to be done, not in the spirit of strife and
contention, nor in the way of rivalry with any undertaking of
a kindred character, but in the spirit of true penance and sorrow of heart for the wide-spread evils of ignorance, cowardice,
feebleness of faith, decay of morals, contempt of God and
His truth that desolate the vineyard of Christ. Its vocation
is to appear as a teacher bound to bear faithful witness to
eternal truths, that even the very people of the Church may
be led to forget, deceived as they are liable to be by the
glitter and fascination of the world of unbelief in the midst
of which they live.

In the garden of the Church grow and flourish many different beautiful flowers of devotion, for all of which there is
abundant room, and if our flower of predilection is the devotion of the "Holy Rosary," so dear to the Holy Mother of
God, no one will be angry with us on this account; for we are

nothing more than labourers in the garden of our common Lord, whose joy on this earth it must be to see His garden cover itself with every kind of rich bloom, and abound in every sort of sweet perfume, waiting "for the north wind to arise and the south wind to blow through the garden, that its sweet perfumes may be spread around" (Cant. iv. 16) for the general good and benefit of all.   D. Trenow.

OBITUARY NOTICE OF THE VERY REV. FATHER PETER MACKEY,

Late Editor of the Magazine.

Peter Mackey was born on the Feast of the Purification, 1843, at Erdington, near Birmingham, of Catholic parents. He was sent to school at Sedgley Park, in 1853, and after leaving it in the summer of 1856, he studied art with his father; and in the early part of 1857 entered us a student at the Birmingham School of Design, where he gained several prizes for excellence in drawing. At home he was a great favourite, being very unselfish, thoughtful for others and punctual in all he did. In a small missal given to him at this time we find written, "For regular service at the altar." It was in the course of the year 1857 that he first began seriously to reflect upon the words of the Apostle, "The form of this world passes away," and to turn his thoughts to embracing the discipline of the religious life. In November, 1858, the opportunity he had long waited for first occurred, in the preaching of a mission at Erdington by Dr. Gonin, the present Archbishop of Port of Spain, and Dr. Aylward. He was allowed to go to Woodchester, in January, 1859, and was clothed with the habit of the Friar Preachers on 13th February, the Feast of S. Catherine of Ricci. He made his profession the same day in the following year, and remained at Woodchester, pursuing his studies under the rule of the noviciate, until September, 1866, when he was ordained priest.

Touching this period of his life, we will quote the words of his former novice master, Dr. Gonin, who, writing since the death of Fr. Mackey, says, " Of all my novices at Woodchester he is certainly one of those who had made the best impres-

sion upon me.   I do not think we have any occasion to regret
his removal from this world, as far as he himself is concerned, for I do believe he was a very pure soul, and ripe for
heaven."

It was at the latter period of his sojourn at Woodchester
that he experienced his first and a very severe attack of heart
disease, from which he suffered ever afterwards.   This disease
brought out very forcibly a special feature of his character,
his complete resignation to God's will.   The following remarks, taken from his diary, are a sample how he habitually
thought and spoke: "I had also vivid thoughts of death,
and how I might easily be taken off in one of these attacks,
but I was not disturbed or frightened.   Deo gratias, I slept
soundly until morning."   No disappointment ever seemed to
ruffle the evenness of his mind; he would smile and say, "The
will of God must be our rule in all things."   On occasion of
a Novena in honour of S. Walburga being made for his recovery, he wrote, "I place the matter entirely in God's hands.
—I know and firmly believe that He can and will cure me by
the merits of S. Walburga, if He so please, and if it be for my
good; and I beg that His holy will may be done.   I only wish
for health in perfect conformity to His blessed will.   After
the little devotion which we had in the noviciate chapel, I
took a little of the oil of S. Walburga, on a small piece of
bread; I have no doubt but that it will do me good, if not
corporally, at least spiritually."

A deep sense of gratitude to Almighty God was another
marked feature of his character.   He wrote once upon his
birthday, "Thanks to God for all His mercies to me hitherto,
and I trust that He will enable me to be truly grateful for
them, and to persevere faithfully to the end."

On the occasion of his first mass he wrote, "At 10½ I
sang my first mass,—I shall never forget it,—the solemnity,
and my unworthiness!"   His state of health, combined with
the desire to enable him to pursue his studies with greater
advantages, caused his Superiors to send him to Rome, shortly
after his ordination.   He left England, in November, 1866,
and lived in Rome until the July following, during
which time he received the degree of Lector of Sacred Theology.

Shortly after his return to England, he was assigned to the
Priory newly opened at Haverstock Hill, where he taught
philosophy and theology, and took a part in the parochial

duties of the mission. In the fall of 1870 he was removed
from London to the house in which he had spent his novice-
ship at Woodchester, and where, until his death, he taught
as he had done in London.

Shortly after his arrival he was appointed to the offices of
Sub-prior and Librarian, and at the end of the same year he
undertook the Editorship of the *Rosary Magazine*, which some
time after changed its name to that of *Rosarian*. To these
various charges he added, from July, 1871, until his death, the
duties connected with the chaplaincy at Woodchester Park,
and a small chapel and mission a mile from thence.

Dying as he did immediately after Easter, one of his sweetest consolations on his deathbed was that all in his little
congregation had made their Paschal Communion by Easter
day. On Good Friday he caught a slight cold, which, although it did not at all impede his missionary duties upon
Easter Sunday, yet developed, upon his return to the monastery on Easter Monday, into a severe attack of his old heart
complaint, followed by congestion of the lungs. His state became so alarming by Thursday that, with the advice of the doctor, the last Sacraments were administered; he rallied slightly
afterwards, but no decided change took place until Monday
night, when he was so much worse that the last blessing was
given, and the prayers for the dying recited. His last moments were an epitome of his former life; full of faith, hope,
and love, contrition, gratitude, and resignation. He joined,
at least mentally, in all the prayers which were continually
said around him, making various suggestions, at one time
requesting that the Passion should be read, and showing particular anxiety that everything prescribed by the ritual of the
Church and of the Order should be observed; he kept his eyes
constantly fixed upon the Crucifix, bowing his head towards it
each time the Holy Name was uttered, and requiring it to be
brought near to his lips at the conclusion of each form of prayer.
The Rosary was also recited many times in addition to the
prayers with which the Church assists the dying.

When he was told that all human hope was past, and he
was asked whether he would like that recourse should be had
to any supernatural means, he replied, with his habitual resignation, " I wish for nothing but God's Holy Will." Upon this,
the Prior made use of the water of Lourdes, and of the well of
S. Winefrid, and blessed him with some relics, which he kissed
with much faith and reverence, many times expressing his

gratitude for the gift of faith, and for his vocation to religion, while he protested his unworthiness, and that he had done no good. Thus he lingered on, attended by his brother, Dr. Mackey, and nursed by his religious brethren, until just before midday on Tuesday, April 9th, when he died most placidly (having never lost his consciousness throughout the whole of his protracted agony), whilst the entire community were singing round him the sweet words of the "*Salve Regina*."

His body was brought into the choir by 1 o'clock, and laid upon the bier, dressed in the full habit of his Order, with the stole upon his shoulders. From this time, except during the recitation of the divine office, the Psalter was said beside him by his religious brethren, until the solemn dirge and mass upon Thursday morning.

The obsequies were performed by the Very Rev. Father King, Provincial of England, and the body was buried in the quadrangle of the Convent, amidst the prayers and tears of all. For eight days after, the Community gathered round the grave, according to the custom of the Order, and sang the "*Libera me, Domine,*" for the everlasting rest of their brother's soul.—R.I.P.

No. IV.—THE SCIENCE OF THE HOLY ROSARY.

With reference to the papers on the "Science of the Holy Rosary," of which three numbers have already appeared in our former Series, our new circle of readers, to whom they may not be known, will probably be glad to be put briefly in possession of the main point of view from which the writer is treating his subject.

In common, then, with many others, he deplores the widespread calamity of a certain lamentable ignorance under the reproach of which great multitudes of the Catholic people, sad to say, are content to pass their lives; and his object is to show that the cultivation of the devotion of the Holy Rosary is by no means limited to the work of benefiting the Catholic people by providing them with a form of private and social prayer, most pleasing as it is to God and the Holy Virgin; but that it is in its true nature also a system of Christian doctrine, and that it must always be diligently taught and learned as "a popular body of Christian doctrine," as well as a form of de-

vont prayer.   It is only when the Holy Rosary is thus actively
and effectively taught, as a form of sound doctrine for every one
to understand and know in connection with its devout observance as a beautiful pious exercise of prayer, that it comes
to be placed in the true way of spreading its full measure
of blessing far and wide in the bosom of the Christian Society.
Those who are content to go on in their dull lifeless way, without caring to make any sensible effort to acquire for themselves a becoming Christian knowledge of the 15 Mysteries, will
necessarily suffer in consequence, by remaining incapable of
entering into the full spirit of the Rosary as an exercise of
prayer.

The following passage, which we quote from the last paper
(No. III.), will suffice to give our new readers a sufficient
key to all that has preceded :—

"One of the characteristic notes of the handiwork of God is 'simplicity,' and if the Holy Rosary, as we have asserted, contains in itself a
system of popular theology competent to be, everywhere throughout the
world, the corrective of the ignorance which is, in like manner everywhere
throughout the world, the enemy of faith, we shall be entitled to expect
that it will present itself under some short form, which will both surprise
us by its extreme simplicity, and, at the same time, startle us by the
depth of knowledge which the simple form conceals. Such was the way
in which it pleased the wisdom of God to deal with the former people
of the Mosaic Covenant. What could be a more succinct and simple form
of enunciating the faith of the former people of God than the words
which Moses was commissioned to utter : 'Hear, O Israel, the Lord our
God is one Lord' (Deut. vi. 4), and yet the Christian Apostle, contemplating what God had done for the Hebrew people, could say : 'O, the
depth of the riches of the wisdom and knowledge of God' (Rom. xi. 33).

"The Holy Rosary will not be found to disappoint the above just and
well founded expectations. Its system of theology could not be essentially popular except it were found to exist in the shape of some singularly
simple formula or statement, and it would not be a system of theology at
all unless the Christian mind, intelligently contemplating it, should be
constrained to say with the Apostle : 'O, the depth of the riches of the
widom and knowledge of God.'"

The writer then briefly sketches out the course intended to
be followed in the Series, and shows in outline in what way
the four words, "Mysteries," "Joyful," "Sorrowful," and
"Glorious," when they come to be properly understood, contain in themselves a complete formula of the popular knowledge of God.—(Note of the Editor.)

No. IV.—THE POPULAR THEOLOGY OF THE WORD MYSTERY.

S. PAUL assures us that "without faith it is impossible to please God" (Heb. xi. 6), and how displeasing want of faith can be in the sight of God appears from the case of Zacharias, who made a very marked demur to believing the message of the angel, whom he nevertheless could not have failed to know to have been an angel, from his appearing in the very sanctuary at the right hand of the Altar of incense. The consequence to Zacharias of this demur was that he was not allowed to bear his testimony to the Divine Wonder accomplished in the Blessed Virgin, when she came to be a guest in his house for three months. And though as Priest of the temple and as father of the future precursor of Christ, nothing could have been more natural and becoming than that he should have given his testimony, he had unhappily ruined his title to do so by his backwardness in believing the communication of the angel. Hence we have not a word from him during the whole three months that the Blessed Virgin was a guest in his house.

S. Peter is an example of the contrary. He by his faith and by his outspoken confession of it, "Thou art the Christ, the Son of the living God," obtains a blessing and an exaltation which has no parallel in its own kind. "Blessed art thou, Simon Bar Jona. . . . And I will give to thee the keys of the kingdom of Heaven." (Matt. xvi. 17.)

Now, on coming to study the nature of S. Peter's confession, we find our Lord making this comment upon it, "Blessed art thou, Simon Bar Jona," and why? "for flesh and blood hath not revealed it to thee, but my Father who is in Heaven." Comparing the substance of S. Peter's confession with a passage in S. Paul's Epistle to Timothy, we are able to learn that what was especially pleasing to our Lord in S. Peter's confession was, that he had given in his formal adhesion to the truth of a MYSTERY, and, indeed, to the truth of a very great and wonderful MYSTERY. S. Paul's words are, " And evidently great is the mystery of Godliness, which " was manifested in the flesh, was justified in the spirit, ap- " peared unto angels, hath been preached to the Gentiles, is " believed in the world, hath been taken up into glory."

(1 Tim. iii. 16.)   It would thus be as if S. Peter had said, " I
acknowledge and confess openly this great mystery of Godliness—God manifest in the flesh—Thou art the God manifest
in the flesh.   In Thee is this great mystery of Godliness
brought to pass.   Thou art the Christ, the Son of the living
God."

Or again, in other words, " Thou art the God who hast long
ages ago made thyself known to Abraham, and to all the
Patriarchs of our nation.   Thou hast made choice of thy
people Israel, and hast showed Thyself to them by the great
deliverance Thou didst work for them, giving them Thy laws
and commandments.   Thou hast made Thy coming known by
the prophets whom Thou hast sent to speak to Thy people,
and Thou hast everywhere spread through the nations the
expectation of Thy coming.   Now I confess that this great
MYSTERY, so long expected, which so many kings and
prophets have desired to see and yet did not see, is fulfilled
and is now before me—' Thou art the Christ, the Son of the
living God.' "

The reward on S. Peter's part of this outspoken confession,
of his full and hearty belief in this great " Mystery of Godliness," and of his unreserved adhesion to it, including all the
consequences flowing from it, was the blessing, " Blessed art
thou, Simon Bar Jona."

There must then be, we are entitled to conclude, something
very pleasing to God in the act of an open confession of a full
and unreserved belief in the truth of the " Great Mystery of
Godliness."   And this will fully warrant the affirmation " that
the devotion of the Holy Rosary " is to be justly pronounced,
in a pre-eminent way, pleasing and acceptable to God.   For
what in its simplest analysis is the act of those who meet
together to recite the Holy Rosary in common, but their
public and avowed act of homage to, and profession of faith in,
the truth of the great Mystery of Godliness, "God manifest
in the flesh?"   " What do you meet together for, good people?"
a stranger might ask, and the common answer of all will be,
" Good sir, our first thought in meeting together is to make an
honourable public profession, in common, of our faith in the
truth of the one great Mystery, ' God manifest in the flesh,'
and of the various subordinate mysteries of this one great
sovereign Mystery, which our devotion of the Holy Rosary
specially brings before our minds.   In a word, sir, our prayers
in the Rosary are built upon, and have for their foundation

1872.]   POPULAR THEOLOGY OF THE WORD "MYSTERY."   11

S. Peter's holy confession, 'Thou art the Christ, the Son
of the living God.' We intend to offer our prayers to God
in virtue of the public confession of our faith in this great
Mystery."

Thus we come to perceive the truth that the first lesson in
popular theology which is to be learnt in the school of the
Holy Rosary is to make the complete and unreserved adhesion of mind, heart, and of the whole intelligent soul, to the
truth of the Great Mystery of Godliness, "Thou art the
Christ, the Son of the living God." Now we are by our
creation such eminently social beings that what we do in
company with a great multitude we find we can do far more
vigorously, heartily, and with a better spirit than we can possibly do the same alone. "Woe to him," says the Scripture, "who
is alone; if he falls he has none to help him. Two shall be
warmed, for they have the advantage of each other's society;
but how shall one be warm?" (Eccles. iv.) From which it
comes to pass that when a great number recite the Holy
Rosary together, there arises a very strong sense in the mind
of each one of the united power and vigour of their joint act
of confession of the one Sovereign Mystery, "Thou art the
Christ, the Son of the Living God." Even the very voices
of a multitude saying the Rosary sound like the vigorous
combined tread of a company of soldiers who are marching on
with a purpose which they all know and understand, and which
they are determined to carry or to lose their lives in the attempt.

Who can return from having joined with a great multitude
in reciting the Rosary without experiencing a strengthening,
invigorating effect on the mind, which seems to say, how good
and joyful a thing it is to make a public and unreserved
confession, in company with others, of the truth of the Great
Mystery of Godliness; how it strengthens and invigorates
faith, and does good to all the intelligent powers and faculties
of the mind; how it fortifies and calms the spirits, and how it
freshens up the soul for renewed activity in the battle of life!

Now, all this becomes a matter of still greater moment
when we come to consider that the point where the path of
faith first breaks off from the way of unbelief is the confession
or acknowledgment of "mystery." This point passed, the
two ways of life become perfectly distinct, and the further the
respective travellers advance in their respective ways, the more
they increase their relative distance from each other. The
sacred text says to me, "Plurima ostensa sunt tibi super

sensum hominum" (Many things have been shown to thee
above the understanding of men, Eccles. iii. 25). If I
believe and give in my adhesion to this truth, by so doing I
become a learner in the school of "mystery." It is not
certain as yet in whose hands I may chance to fall, nor can it
be predicted what sort of doctrines I may, or may not, take up
with, according to the teachers to whom I may have the good
or the bad fortune to entrust myself; but if I do but believe
what the Scripture says, "that many things have been shown to
men above their natural understanding," and if I follow this up
with the sincere desire to learn and to understand, by so doing I
make my first entry into the path of faith. Where I shall end
in this path is another question, but at least I make my entry
into this path. If, however, I refuse to believe that anything
has been shown to men above their natural understanding,
then, like many, unfortunately, who live around us, I choose a
totally different path in which to walk, and in which, the more I
advance, the greater the distance I place between myself and
S. Peter's confession, " Thou art the Christ, the Son of the
living God."

The practical conclusion which all devout lovers of the Holy
Rosary may draw from this little chapter on the theology of
the word "MYSTERY" is, I will venture to say, twofold. The
first instinct of humanity is "self-preservation." Now, our
generation is full of the unbelievers who openly and audaciously
deny the Scripture assertion that "many things have been
shown to men above their natural understanding," and who
have, in consequence, advanced to very great lengths in the
way of unbelief, in which, except in the way of miraculous
conversion, they are never likely to retrace their steps. All
such men as these necessarily hate faith with a deadly hatred.
Animated by the same spirit which caused Lucifer to fall from
his high estate, they resemble fallen Lucifer in their hatred of
faith and in their desire to exterminate from the earth that
which they rightly understand to be so contrary to their own
minds. As these men openly glory in their disdain and contempt of mystery, the counterpart of their denial on the part
of the believers is their own joyful and generous confession of
their belief in and adhesion to mystery. And every time the
Rosary is recited in public the company of the believers unite
in this joyful and generous act of confession of their belief in
mystery. They become thus in the devotion of the Holy
Rosary a source of strength and protection to each other, and

the louder and more profane are the voices outside making a
mock of mystery, the louder and stronger is the union of hearts
and voices within making the united confession of their
adhesion to that which the unbelievers despise. The devotion
of the Holy Rosary is thus for Catholics self-preservation
against the lures of unbelief.

But it is also the voice of charity, calling the vast multitude
of those who, however they may be misguided and misled by
their uncommissioned teachers, are still honest disciples of
the sacred text, "Many things have been shown to thee above
the understanding of men," to the only true school of divine
mystery, the Catholic Church which is built on S. Peter's confession, "Thou art the Christ, the Son of the living God."
All devout lovers of the Holy Rosary can at all times say to
their neighbours, "Come and join with us in reciting the Holy
Rosary; it will do you good. Leave the unbelievers to their
own ways 'O, come and magnify the Lord with me; let us
praise His name together' (Ps. xxxiii. 4). 'Let every spirit
praise the Lord'" (Ps. cl. 5).   H. F.

THE LIFE AND TIMES OF B. ALAIN DE LA ROCHE IN THE
FIFTEENTH CENTURY.

RESTORER OF THE CONFRATERNITY OF THE MOST HOLY ROSARY.

CHAP. I.—THE VOCATION OF B. ALAIN.

THE same day which brought joy to the world and terror to
hell by the birth of the Blessed Virgin Mary was that on
which Alain de la Roche, one of the chosen children of the
Mother of Mercy, first opened his eyes to this lower world.
We know but little of the early years of his life, the circumstances of his family, the events which led him into the Order
of St. Dominic, or how he spent the first part of his religious
life. All that we can gather from his own writings is that
in later years he wept over the memory of these times as
days of unbelief and lukewarmness. Corneille Sneckis, his
contemporary, and Michel de l'Isle, his pupil at Cologne, tell
us no more than that he was born in Brittany; and their testimony is confirmed by the traditions of the Dominican monastery at Dinan, in Brittany, which glories in reckoning him
among its many illustrious children; and it is in this monas-

tery that the documents are extant which give an account of
the events of his life. From them we learn that, soon after
his ordination as priest, he left Dinan, for a monastery in Holland, to which he was attracted by the perfection with which
the rule was observed. Its Prior, John Excuria, received
him with joy, having a presentiment that the young religious
would one day become an honour to his house and to
the whole Order. He was not deceived, for Brother Alain
became before long, through his learning and capacity for
the work of teaching, one of the principal persons of the
Universities of Rostoc and of Cologne, at the same time
that he gained general reputation as a preacher. According
to the testimony of the celebrated Abbé Trithème, he was
as well versed in the knowledge of the Sacred Scriptures as
he was eloquent in preaching the Word of God to the people.
We are also assured by the same Abbé Trithème that his life
and conversation were consecrated to the service of God.
He ever evinced a most special love and devotion to the
Blessed Virgin, who appeared to be never absent from his mind.
He never began or ended any of his sermons or lectures
without saluting her through the "Hail Mary;" and we are
told by one of his historians that this prayer was constantly
on his lips while walking, speaking, or preaching.

This ardent devotion sprang at first from gratitude to the
Mother of God for a vision with which B. Alain was favoured,
and which was in a great measure the cause of his conversion
and rapid progress in virtue. Some say that it was at La
Roche, a little town in the Duchy of Luxemburg, others at
La Roche, in Brittany, that the Blessed Virgin appeared to
him and ordered him to cultivate the devotion of the Holy
Rosary as instituted by S. Dominic, and to preach it with
great zeal and fervour to every nation, and to people of every
condition of life in the Church. She assured him that the
practice of this devotion would be the starting-point of his
progress in virtue, a source of new life to others, and at the
same time a most powerful means of averting the chastise-
ments that were being prepared by Divine Justice for the
crimes of the whole world. She also warned him that terrible
trials were in store for him; that all hell would be up in arms
against his efforts; that the world, and even his own brethren,
would try to upset his plans; but that he would triumph over
all his enemies in spite of these obstacles, if he placed his
trust in God and in her.

This vision, as the event showed, brought forth abundant fruit in the well-prepared ground of Alain's heart. He began immediately to form himself to become a true disciple of the Rosary, and from that time he never let a day pass by without saying the fifteen mysteries, and often, not content with saying them once, repeated them many times over with great fervour. It is said that he united the exercise of mortification to that of prayer, and that the cries of his severely chastised body were often sent up to Mary's throne together with the Aves of his Rosary.

The Blessed Virgin was not satisfied to see him become merely the disciple of the Rosary; it was her will that he should also be its apostle and its restorer. This task greatly alarmed B. Alain, and it was no little time before he could make up his mind to undertake it. In S. Dominic's time, and during the first century of the Order, the Rosary had been an object of love and veneration to the Christian world; but these days were now gone by, and in all but a few provinces the Rosary was as nearly as possible forgotten. It had suffered from the same causes which had weakened faith and piety in so many lands, and which had brought ruin and desolation on so many holy institutions. B. Alain well knew how many difficulties would surround the work of its restoration, and felt sure that he could not preach the revival of a devotion that belonged to an earlier age without raising against himself storms of opposition. These thoughts and fears agitated Alain, and kept him irresolute; he himself prayed diligently to Mary through the use of his Rosary, but he did not yet dare to go forth to preach it to others. Again did the Blessed Virgin appear to him, and this time with threatening aspect and urgent words. He had been chosen, and he must fulfil his mission, under pain of enduring her displeasure and that of her Son; and if he resisted, he was warned that a speedy death would be the penalty of his disobedience. On the other hand, he was encouraged by no less than Our Blessed Lord himself, who condescended to show him the advantages to be gained by all through meditation upon the mysteries of His life and death, and who filled him with a great desire to be the preacher of this form of prayer. S. Dominic, his Father, and the inspired founder of this devotion, also united his own entreaties to the commands of Our Lord and His Blessed Mother, and was urgent with him to give proof of his zeal for the salvation of souls by the propagation of that prayer

which he had loved above all others while upon earth. B.
Alain relates these visions, and the threats and promises
which had accompanied them, as if they had happened to
a third person.

Not once, but many times, did he receive these commands
from Heaven; and at last, feeling that he could no longer
resist these manifest tokens of the Divine will, and the multiplied assurances of protection from on High overcoming all
his repugnance, he began preaching the Rosary with a zeal
which seemed to be all the more intense from the length of
time it had been fostered in the depth of his heart. He tra-
versed in turn Saxony, Lower Germany, the seventeen United
Provinces of Flanders, Picardy, L'Ile de France, and Brittany,
appearing everywhere as a messenger from the Queen of
Angels and an apostle of Our Lord. Through the Rosary,
as a sacred pledge of the love of Jesus and Mary to men, he
converted sinners, gave strength to the just, confounded infidels, supported the weak, healed the sick, comforted the
sorrowful, delivered captives, and brought back lost sheep to
their true Shepherd. He re-established the Confraternity of
the Holy Rosary, and enrolled in it thousands of people, both
men and women, of every class and condition, and before long
armies of these associates were to be seen saying this " Psalter
of Mary " with the greatest fervour and devotion. If we
may believe his contemporaries and disciples, more than a
hundred thousand persons were thus enrolled under the
banner of the Rosary, and all received from it more or less
wonderful graces.

(To be continued.)

No. I.—ON THE HUMILIATION
WHICH THE SOVEREIGN PONTIFF AND WITH HIM THE WHOLE BODY OF
THE CATHOLIC PEOPLE THROUGHOUT THE WORLD ARE NOW SUFFERING
AT THE HANDS OF A CATHOLIC SOVEREIGN AND A CATHOLIC PEOPLE.

NOTHING happens to the Church without the permission of God;
and without some supremely wise and good end for the advancement of the Kingdom of God, which is known indeed
to God, but cannot always be known immediately to us,
the events which now grieve the hearts of so many Catholic
people could not have come to pass. Thus our Lord Him-

self said to Peter, "What I do thou canst not know now, but thou shalt know hereafter." (John xiii. 7.) Doubtless it will be given to a later age, looking back upon the events that are now passing, to understand, far better than we in our lifetime can ever hope to know, why it has pleased God in His Wisdom to allow the head of the Church to become the victim of such a dreadful indignity at the hands of a reputed Catholic prince, as that a son should be publicly seen by all the nations of the world, in the open face of day, to lift up his heel against his father, and by force of arms to take away from him his little independent principality. He has himself declared this to be the very provision of Divine Providence itself, indispensable for securing to the Supreme Government of the Church the freedom and independence necessary to the discharge of its sacred trust in behalf of all the Christian people of the world; and notwithstanding, the reputed Catholic Sovereign treats his declaration as mere idle words.

In the old law God punished the sins of the former Israel by not only suffering them to undergo a most disastrous and humiliating defeat at the hands of their enemies and oppressors the Philistines, but by also permitting the very sacred Ark itself of His Covenant with Israel to become a captive in the hands of the Philistines and to be subjected to the indignity of being put on one side as lumber in the temple of the Philistine idol-god Dagon. But in this public humiliation of the former Israel there was at least the saving clause that it was endured by the people of God at the hands of an avowed enemy, and was the natural enough consequence of a defeat incurred in a fair stand-up fight against their enemy entered into with their eyes wide open and on equal terms. Whereas in the case of the present humiliation which God is pleased to suffer to fall upon His Vicar, and with him on the whole body of the Catholic nations, there is entirely wanting the act of the open enemy, as also the doubtful issue of the fair fight upon equal terms, terminating in, at least, honest defeat. It is a case to which the words of the Psalm apply quite literally :
"*Had it been an enemy that had cursed me, I could have borne it, and if he that openly hated me had spoken great things against me; but thou, O man of the same mind with me, my guide and my known friend, who hast partaken of sweet food together with me, and we have walked together in mutual agreement in the house of God.*" (Ps. liv. 13–15.)

We have now a Catholic prince who, in the face of day,

comes with his cannon and his soldiers, in time of peace; forces un entry into the city of the Sovereign Pontiff of his religion; who, treating his warnings with absolute contempt, abolishes the civil government of which he was the crowned head; substitutes a national government, of which he is himself for the time being the ostensible head, in its place; and who, even while acting thus, has the hardihood to profess to have merited well of his generation, and plumes himself upon being in full harmony in all that he does with the ideas of his century.

The whole Catholic world, in the meantime, finds itself reduced by this to play the extremely humble part of the distressed impotent spectator of the act of violence and sacrilege by which its supreme head loses his civil dignity and freedom of action. The king who acts in this manner incurs, indeed, the penalty of excommunication, together with all who are active participants in the consummation of his crime; but the particular expiation which Divine Justice will exact from the guilty Catholic prince and the adherents of his sacrilege remains hanging in suspense over his head, and we do not know what it will be: all that we are allowed to know is that the guilty sovereign himself and his adherents appear outwardly scarcely at all concerned for the future that awaits them, and quite resolved to brave it out to the end, let what may come come; making about as little account of the sentence of the Church against them as Esau did of having sold his birthright.

God, who does nothing in vain, and without whom, says our Lord, "Not even a sparrow falls to the ground" (Matt. x. 29), has beyond all doubt had His own designs in permitting what we have witnessed to come to pass; and, as we have said, aftertimes will know more of His designs than we are allowed to know. But we may reverently, and for edification's sake, seek to divine some small portion of what God may be understood to intend by what He thus permits.

Now let us all ask ourselves, "may not God, for one thing, by this signal humiliation of His Vicar intend to rebuke and put to shame the light and idle spirit of national self-complacency which makes the various Catholic nations and people so nationally pleased with themselves and so puffed up with their little small national vanity and conceit about themselves, that they have scarcely any eyes or discernment left whereby to see their own crying sins, and wherein they fall short of the real virtues which God expects from them; blinded by which vanity they also come to neglect the real service which it is in their

power to do for the building up the kingdom of God amongst
themselves?" "Touch the mountains," says the Psalmist, "and
they shall smoke." Let a Catholic population at the present
day be but ever so little touched in its national vanity, and its
people appear as if they were carried away by a spirit that
makes them ready to trample under foot the altar and all that
they have ever learned to revere as sacred. To rebuke this
empty, idle, and foolish spirit, what does God do in His love
and wisdom? He exhibits to the world His own Vicar, an aged
and venerable Pontiff, dear to the whole of Christendom for
his long-suffering patience, his apostolic courage, and his
unshaken fidelity to his sacred trust, as the victim of the national blindness and ambition of one particular Christian
nation, the Italian people. The whole of Christendom has to
suffer a deep, universal humiliation for no other reason except
that one particular nation is minded to seek its own false exaltation at the expense of the honour and well-being of the whole
kingdom of God.

"The holy archangel Michael," says S. Jude, "contended
with the devil for the possession of the body of Moses, and
prevailed over him, not by bringing a railing accusation against
him, but in the strength of the holy words, ' *Imperet tibi
Dominus—The Lord show His power over thee.*'" In the same
manner, the Christian people of the universal world will not
be able to prevail against the spirit that animates the Italian
people in any other strength than that which gave the
"victory" to S. Michael. They must not cease to cry aloud
and say against the Italian people, "The Lord show His power
over thee, humble thee, and take the city of Rome out of thy
hands, and abate thy false pride." But how can other Christian people call upon God, the Lord of all, to humble the
national pride and exaltation of Italy, and to take Rome out of
its hands, when, led away themselves by precisely the same
deceiving spirit, they may discover themselves to be equally
foolishly seeking the similar false exaltation of their own
particular national pride?

What if they also are seeking an exaltation entirely outside
their faith as Christians, entirely outside the exaltation of
the Holy Church, entirely outside the extension and spread
of the common Faith of the Catholic Church; not for the
glory of God, not for the honour of Jesus Christ, His Virgin
Mother, and the saints; not for the good of the souls of men,
but for precisely the same deceitful and illusory national vanity

and exaltation which, as they may perfectly well see, in the case of Italy, perverts the Christian Italian nation into an anti-Christian power ? The nation that seeks to take away the holy City of Rome from the Christian people of the whole world, to degrade it to its own purposes, may glory indeed in a victory, but their victory can never be anything else, as long as the world lasts, than the deep humiliation and degradation of the whole Catholic people throughout the entire world, and the laying up a store of the wrath of God against itself. But still how shall those who are being led away by precisely the same deceiving spirit ever cry to God effectually against the Italian nation on account of the humiliation which it is now inflicting upon them, together with all the other Christian nations ?

"It is good for me,": says the holy Psalmist, "that Thou hast humbled me that I might learn Thy justifications." (Ps. cxviii. 71.) As good Catholics, we can never do otherwise than well understand and know that the humiliation of the Sovereign Pontiff of Christendom in the sight of the nations of the world is also the humiliation of every good Catholic throughout the entire world. In the spirit of the Holy Psalmist, therefore, we must all learn at the sight of this great crime of the Italian people humbly to strike our breast and say, "Lord, we have all had our share in the grievous sins and offences which have provoked Thee to send this great humiliation upon us. Lord, remember us in Thy mercy, and enable us to take occasion from this humiliation to learn Thy justifications. Enable us to see the folly, misery, and ruin of being led away by national vanity and conceit into seeking any other exaltation except the exaltation of Thy kingdom, and any other good except the promotion of Thy glory and the good of souls. Queen of the Most Holy Rosary, come to our aid by thy merciful intercession, to teach us the holy lesson which we ought to learn from this exceeding great humiliation which God has sent upon us all, wherever we are found, throughout the entire world."

FAITH.

Faith is no weakly flower,
By heat, or chill, or blight, or stormy shower,
To perish in an hour;

But rich in hidden worth,
A plant of grace though striking root in earth,
It boasts a hardy birth;

Still from its native skies
Draws energy that common shocks defies,
And lives where nature dies!

E. CASWALL.

THE WIDOW PALMA THE ECSTATICA OF ORIA, IN THE SOUTH OF THE KINGDOM OF NAPLES.

A CORRESPONDENT of the "Semaine Religieuse" of Tournai gives the following account of one of the miraculous manifestations of supernatural gifts with which it pleases God in our present infidel times to check the downward progress of the mind of the century to its beloved dull materialism, that must always be the natural forerunner of the grossest and most degrading sensualism.

Somewhere about the year 1863 there appeared in the "Osservatore Romano" a short notice of a holy widow woman of the kingdom of Naples who had been favoured with supernatural gifts, such as the stigmata, or marks of the Five Sacred Wounds, and ecstasies. Her name was Palma, a person of blameless life, and an inhabitant of the little town of Oria, in the south of Italy.

Among other things above the common order, the "Roman Journal" mentioned a prophecy which Palma's spiritual director, by the desire of his penitent, had caused to be forwarded to the Holy See. The Neapolitan "Ecstatica" foretold bloody wars, particularly civil wars, the advent also of three republics in France, Spain, and Italy respectively, and a time of great oppression for the Church.

Certain recent events put me in mind of the prophecy of

Palma, and as the invasion of Rome of the 20th of September
had interrupted my regular employment, and even rendered a
temporary absence desirable, I resolved upon a tour in the
south of Italy.

I shall not stop to give you any account of the interior of
Palma's house, or indeed any particular description of her
stigmata and ecstasies; suffice it to say that she is now in her
47th year, and that tokens of her supernatural gifts are everywhere present in her abode, where everything breathes the
spirit of Christianity.

That which is her distinguishing mark among others similarly possessed of supernatural powers is the gift of prophecy
and bilocation.   Our Lord appears to be pleased to reveal the
future to this chosen soul, whom He honours in so marked a
manner, causing her to know whither the course of events is
leading us, and the way in which Divine Providence will
finally overrule them so as to bring about the eventual triumph
of the Church. Palma communicates the knowledge of all that
she receives to her director, that he may in turn convey it to
the Holy Father. " Pius IX. knows all," said the worthy Priest
to me.   " Mark all that she may say, and weigh well all her
words."

As far as I have been able to learn, these prophetic revelations announce a great triumph of the Church, of which
PIUS IX. will see the beginning, while for France are reserved afflictions greater and more terrible than those through
which the unhappy country has already passed.

But more remarkable still than her gift of prophecy is the
gift of bilocation with which this Ecstatica of Oria has been
favoured.   During her ecstasies her body frequently becomes
wholly immovable, and of a deathlike insensibility. At such
times her spirit appears to traverse space in a marvellous
manner, and to go and visit the most distant countries.

More than once she has visited in this way distant parts of
China, and on her return she gives the most minute and
detailed description of the places and things which she has
seen. Her director, who keeps note of everything, has sent for
different books descriptive of the Chinese Empire, by which
he has been able to certify himself as to the literal accuracy of
her descriptions. Amongst others he mentioned to me the
great Wall of China, as an instance in which her description
of it perfectly agreed with what trustworthy travellers have
said about it.

I have myself also been able to verify another circumstance of more special interest to you. From comparing letters written by the director of your Ecstatica of the Hainault with the journal kept by the worthy priest of Oria, it appears beyond all doubt that Palma was well acquainted with Louise Lateau before any human source of information could have made her acquainted with that young person, and with the signal favours which she has received. Palma describes herself as having gone to visit the village of Bois d'Haine during one of the ecstasies of Louise, and in fact she has given with reference to Louise, to her room, her parents and their dwelling, descriptions perfectly agreeing with details contained in the letters of different persons who have since written to Oria. What I may be allowed to remark is that, according to what has fallen from our Neapolitan Ecstatica, a great destiny is in store for her sister of Hainault.

Perhaps the annals of Mysticism can scarcely point to a single person favoured in so complete and remarkable way as the widow Palma. Besides the gifts of which I have been giving an account, she possesses others scarcely less wonderful. Amongst these the blood which falls from her stigmata frequently produces remarkable cures. For many years this holy woman's chief nourishment has been the Holy Eucharist, which she receives each morning, not uncommonly administered to her in a miraculous manner by our Lord Himself.

In the presence of such manifestations as these of the power of God, a good Christian can but bow his head and endeavour to draw from them the fruits of salvation and eternal life.

MISCELLANEOUS ANECDOTES.

AN ANECDOTE OF S. EPHREM THE SYRIAN.—There is an anecdote related of S. Ephrem the Syrian, in his Life, that having at one time a great desire to visit the chief city of the Edessenes, he prayed to God, saying, "O Lord Jesus Christ, grant to me that I may visit this city, and that on entering it there may meet me a man who will begin to speak with me out of the Holy Scripture." It happened that as he approached the city, and was in the act of passing through the gate, a certain woman met him, whose outward appearance caused him a feeling of such pain, that he said to himself as he looked at her, "O Lord Jesus Christ, thou hast surely made light of the prayer of Thy servant; however, shall such a creature as this

say anything to me out of the Scripture?" The woman, however, stood still, looking him full in the face, to whom the Saint
said, "Young woman, what makes you thus stand still, fixing
your eyes on me?" To whom she replied, "There is nothing to
be wondered at in the circumstance of a woman looking at you,
man though you be, since it was from man that woman was
taken. Rather, how is it that you who are a man do not take
more care how you fix your eyes on a woman, and not on the
earth from which, as being a man, you have been yourself
taken?" Hearing the which words, the servant of God,
Ephrem, looked up to heaven and glorified God for having
given her such wisdom as to be able to make to him an answer
of the like sort, by which he knew for certain that his prayer
had not been despised. And entering into the city he remained
in it some time.

THE FIG AND THE FIG TREE.—A Protestant minister taking his
walk one day on the outskirts of a French town on the coast
of the Mediterranean Sea, passed by a small farmer of his
acquaintance, who was busily engaged in the work of grafting
a fig tree. "Good day, Peter," said the minister, stopping to
speak to him; "were you at your church last Sunday?" "Yes,
sir." "Well, on what subject did the parish priest preach?"
"On the Blessed Virgin, sir. He told us all how much we
ought to love her, because she was both the mother of God
and ours, and because she was all-powerful with God."
"Great mistake that, my good man; you ought to know very
well that the Virgin is not the mother of God at all," and
thereupon he began to harangue against devotion to Mary,
finding great fault with the various acts of respect and homage
which Catholics are in the habit of paying to her. The farmer,
an honest Catholic, not at all relishing his long harangue, after
bearing with it for a time, at last sharply interrupting him,
burst in and said, "Sir, are you fond of figs?" "What do you
mean by such a rude interruption?" "I mean what I say, sir;
are you fond of figs?" "To be sure I am, and what of that?"
"Well, sir, a man like you who is fond of a fig should know
better than to speak ill of the fig tree that bears the fig."
Indeed, who can truly love the son who allows himself at any
time to speak with contempt and disdain of the mother? It
was in the above plain and straightforward way that the good
common sense of an honest labourer effectually silenced and
put to shame the stock-in-trade cavils of a Protestant minister.

RECORD OF EVENTS.

THE Sovereign Pontiff continues his Apostolic ministry of receiving the visits of the various Catholic deputations and others who come to him in his retirement in the Vatican to hear his words of warning and consolation. It was in the same manner that S. Paul, when he was a prisoner in the hands of the Roman Empire, received the Hebrew deputation who came to him. "And when they had appointed him a day, there came very many to his lodgings, to whom he testified of the kingdom of God, out of the law of Moses and the prophets, from the morning to the evening." (Acts xxviii. 23.) The result of what he said on that occasion was that the "Jews had much reasoning among themselves;" but the Evangelist S. Luke relates: "He continued two whole years in his own hired lodging, where he received all who came to him, preaching the kingdom of God, and teaching the things which concern the Lord Jesus Christ, with all confidence, no man forbidding him."

It is the same now with Pius IX. In his prison of the Vatican he receives all who come to him, preaching to them the kingdom of God, and teaching them the things which concern the Lord Jesus Christ. His words, like those of S. Paul, give occasion "to great reasoning" among many, but God has so provided that no one should as yet dare to think of forbidding him to speak.

On the 4th of June Pius IX. received the visit of a number of young men and women, members of the Society of S. Aloysius (S. Louis Gonzaga). After their addresses had been read, the Pope addressed them in words to the following effect :—

My dear Children,—I will give you my benediction after I have addressed you, according to my custom, with a few words of instruction. Under the protection of S. Louis Gonzaga you have undertaken to do good and holy works. I remember what I said to you on a former occasion, and of which you have reminded me in one of your addresses. I remember how, with true Christian generosity, you offered to God even the sacrifice of your lives, if it were necessary, for His glory and the triumph of the Church; and I said that I accepted the offer, but that I prized even more highly a life spent in works of virtue for the benefit of yourselves and your neighbours. I now add to what I then said to strengthen you in your good resolutions, the example of S. Louis Gonzaga to teach you what is to be done by good works, and by prayer, and by example, and by counsel, for the good of our neighbour; especially in these days, when it is so necessary to uphold virtue which is in peril, and to discourage vice which is triumphant. S. Louis Gonzaga was happy in his solitude in the company of Jesus, where he enjoyed peace of

conscience and tranquillity of soul as a saint can do in the house of the
Lord. But in his father's house events came to pass, as often happens in
the world—events that disturbed the peace of the family, and produced
discord between several princes. It was on that account that S. Louis
received orders from his superiors to leave the cloister for a while, and go
to his father's house, and put into his family that same peace which he
was enjoying in the house of God.

God could not but bless the work of the holy youth who was so dear to
Him. Thus, by the help of God and by his charity, his sweetness, and his
prudence, he succeeded in extinguishing all causes of dissension, and,
after having seen the minds of all disposed to harmony, he returned to
the cloister, where he died some short time after; for, as you know, he is
of the number of the saints who died in the first flower of their youth.
At the last hour of his life, when he was asked, "Brother Louis, how are
you going on ?" he replied, " *Laetantes imus*—we go rejoicing." He meant
that, after having done so many good works during his life, he was happy
in going to receive his eternal reward. This, then, is the wish I form for
you. May you all be able to say, at your last moment, " *Laetantes imus*
—we go rejoicing." May you be able to remember the good works in
which you shall have spent your life. May you remember the good
examples you shall have given; the good you shall have done to your
neighbour, whether in preventing the scandals that are so common in our
days, or in restoring peace wherever it is disturbed; and, lastly, in propa-
gating virtue according to your own abilities, and in avoiding vice, so
that you may be able to reply to those who shall ask you, " How are we
going ?" " *Laetantes imus*—we are rejoicing to receive our recompense
in the bosom of our God." That is my hope and my wish for all of you.
Take care, then, my children, to live so that you may do good to all, and
may deserve the blessing of God and man in this world and in the world
to come.

Meanwhile I bless you, and your families, and your spiritual directors.
May this blessing go along with you even to your last moment, so that
you may then be able to say, *Laetantes imus*.

On the 13th of June the Pope received a deputation of
Catholic ladies of the Roman Union, whose address was read
by the Marchesa Chiara Antici Mattei, to which Pius IX.
replied at length, uttering amongst others the following touching words:—

This is the point I wish to recall: You know how the elder brother
when he heard, on returning from the fields, the sounds of the music
which the father, in excess of joy, had ordered to be played to celebrate
the lost son's return, and when he heard from the servants how a magnificent feast was being prepared, he, the elder brother turned away in
a rage, and refused to go in. *Noluit intrare in domum suam.*

My dear daughters, this is the true representation of what is going
on in our day. We go into the churches, and they will not go in; we
take care to approach the Eucharistic table; they, not satisfied with ab-
senting themselves, even blaspheme the holiness of that august mystery.

They imagine—they and those like them—that all religions are alike
good to soothe the miseries of this life. I read this the other evening in

RECORD OF EVENTS.

one of the papers which call themselves "semi-cfficial"—truly I know not what they are. They imagine, I say, all religions to be good: and that, consequently, the blasphemies of Luther and Calvin, the pride and arrogance of Photius, and the degrading errors of Mahomet are sufficient to give peace to the soul. And yet, alas! these very men are the most restless and unhappy.

Let us pray for them : let us pray much, that they may desist from persecuting the Church of Christ—a course fatal to themselves.

MYSTERIOUS CROSSES IN BADEN (SOUTH GERMANY).—The people of the Grand Duchy of Baden have been for some weeks past alarmed by the preternatural appearances of the sign of the Cross on the windows of the houses. What is especially remarkable in the apparition of the Crosses is that they are to be seen from the outside by those in the street, when no trace of a Cross is visible to the spectators within the house. The alarm created by them has been such that persons are afraid to speak of them. The following is an interesting extract from the letter of a correspondent of the *Tablet* newspaper, dated Lucerne, July 8, 1872 :—

I asked two of the waiters about the crosses, on which one of them, with whom I had before been speaking in English, suddenly found himself unable to comprehend that language, and referred me to another. I asked another; he looked awkward, and stoutly declared he knew nothing about it at all. The next day I visited the cathedral and interrogated the old sacristan. He owned to the crosses at once, only not, he took care to say, in the cathedral, but on the house windows; and he said they were now no more to be seen. I asked how he explained it, at which he shrugged his shoulders, and said he did not know. On Saturday morning, having some purchases to make, I asked the shopkeeper about the crosses. He also told me they had been seen, but he said it was all from the state of the atmosphere, or the light. He told me they had been seen on a window next door to his. I asked him to show it to me, that I might at least see a pane of glass where they had been. He took me to the place, and there the crosses were, visibly before our eyes, both in the morning light and when I returned in the afternoon. The same shopkeeper took me at my request inside the room, but not a trace of the marks was visible to one looking *through* the glass. From the outside street they were plainly to be seen. The black lines on the glass were from one to two inches wide, but I was told the width of the lines varied in different windows, though in other respects they were always alike

The same evening I travelled on to Bale, and called on the venerable priest who, with the assistance of four vicars or curates, has charge of the 13,000 Catholics now in that city, for the number has been augmented by recent immigrations from Alsace. This worthy priest told me that one of his vicars had lately been visiting friends in Baden, and had made many experiments in regard to these marks upon the windows. Among other things he had had panes of glass on which they were seen removed from the windows, and other panes on which nothing could be seen substituted in their place, when, lo and behold! the mysterious crosses were visible on the newly inserted panes of glass as they had before been on those which were removed.   I asked the Bale priest if he himself believed the crosses to be miraculous.   "I believe they are," was his reply.

In the Second Book of Machabees (v. 2) mention occurs of remarkable apparitions of armed men and horses which were seen in the streets of Jerusalem, and which caused the people to pray that these prodigies might turn to good.   The " Sign of the Son of Man" is always believed to be a good token for those who have faith.

On June 16 Pope Pius IX. addressed a letter to his Cardinal Secretary of State, of which we are prevented by want of space from giving extracts ; they shall be given in our next number.

ACTS AND DECREES OF THE HOLY SEE, RELATING TO THE HOLY ROSARY.

INDULGENCES GRANTED TO THE RECITATION OF THE ROSARY.

(TITLE OF THE DECREE: SANCTISSIMUS D.N.)

OUR most holy Father Pope Benedict XIII., moved by his profound piety for the Rosary of the Most Blessed Virgin Mary, and desiring to increase and propagate more and more among the Christian people a devotion so useful to the Church and so agreeable to God, having duly advised with the Sacred Congregation of Indulgences and of Holy Relics, has granted an indulgence of one hundred days for each Pater and each Ave, to all the faithful of both sexes who shall piously recite the Rosary, or at least a third part of it.

He has moreover granted once in the year, on a day to be chosen by each one, a plenary indulgence applicable to the departed, to all who shall recite the Rosary or the third part of it during an entire year, provided that they confess and communicate, and pray for concord between Christian princes, the extirpation of heresies, and the exaltation of the Church.

His Holiness has also declared that in order to gain the above mentioned indulgences, it is necessary to use a Rosary blessed, according to custom, by a Friar Preacher.

Given at Rome the 13th of April, 1726.

L. CARD. PICUS, *Prefect.*

Raphael Come de Hieronymis, *Secret.*

Monthly Magazine of the Holy Rosary.

No. 2.]   SEPTEMBER.   [A.D. 1872.

S. JOSEPH,

PROTECTOR OF THE UNIVERSAL CHURCH.

" THE Lord, for the honour of His own Name, has destined
S. Joseph to be the chief and the special patron of the entire
empire of the Church militant. For this reason it will come
to pass that before the day of His judgment all the people of
the earth will learn to know, worship, and adore the Lord, and
to acknowledge the wonderful gifts that He has given to S.
Joseph—gifts the more wonderful from His having willed that
they should remain concealed for so long a time. The name
of S. Joseph will obtain the place of honour in the Calendar
of the Saints. He shall be no longer among the least, but
shall be placed at the head; for there shall be made expressly
for him a feast-day of the highest rank. The Vicar of Jesus
Christ upon earth, obeying an impulse from the Holy Ghost,
will order that the feast of the putative father of Jesus, the
spouse of the Queen of the World, a man most eminent for his
sanctity, is to be celebrated throughout the whole extent of the
Church militant."*

Thus spoke a pious and learned son of S. Dominic in the
sixteenth century, Isidore of Isolanis, in words that have
proved to be truly prophetic.†

On the 8th December, 1870, an Apostolic Decree (*Quemad-
modum Deus*) conferred upon S. Joseph the title of Patron of
the Universal Church, and raised his feast to the rank of a

---

* Isidorus de Isolanis, *Summa de Donis Sancti Joseph*, p. 3, c. viii.

† Isidore of Isolanis, of the order of Friars preacher, lived in the
beginning of the sixteenth century. Benedict XIV. cites him as among
he writers who had contributed most by their works to extend the
devotion to S. Joseph. His book, *Summa de Donis Sancti Joseph*, is a
monument of science and piety raised to the honour of S. Joseph.
Isidore, say the Bollandists, is the first who has professedly written a
treatise on this great subject.

double of the first class. This act of the Sovereign Pontiff, which adds an additional lustre to the aureole of S. Joseph, had been for a long time desired by the whole body of the Faithful. Each year had seen an increase of devotion to the glorious Patriarch who had been the spouse of Mary, the foster-father of Jesus Christ, and the head of the Holy Family. Holy souls would seem to have been guided in this by some supernatural impulse from the Holy Ghost, and the solemn act of the 8th of December in due time came to ratify and confirm their asperations.

Now nothing is permitted to happen in the kingdom of God by blind chance; and, let a light-minded and rash world judge as it will, the Church always proves herself to be in possession of the secret as to the proper time and occasion when to move. She never either speaks or acts at the wrong time. The particular title of honour decreed to S. Joseph is a new proof of this supernatural tact, and of the gift of discerning the right time, which never fails the Spouse of Christ when the need arises.

The Apostolical Decree to which we have already referred makes known the reasons which have induced the Sovereign Pontiff to place the Church under the special protection of S. Joseph.

"In the same manner that God had brought about the elevation of Joseph, the son of the Patriarch Jacob, over the whole of the land of Egypt, in order that he might lay up a timely store of corn for the use of the people, so when the fulness of time was drawing near for the sending upon earth His only Son, the Saviour of the World, He chose another Joseph, of whom the first Joseph had been the figure. He made him lord and steward over the possessions of His House, and chose him for the keeper of His chieftest treasures; for it has ever been the custom of the Church, after the blessed Mother of God, to load with honours her spouse, the blessed Joseph, whose intercession she has never failed to invoke in critical times." For the above reasons, says the illustrious Bishop of Poitiers, "our Holy Father Pope Pius IX., having regard to the prayers and demands of nearly all the Fathers of the Vatican Council, and moreover, moved by the deplorable condition of affairs at the present time to place himself and all the faithful of the Church under the most powerful patronage of the holy Patriarch Joseph, has solemnly decreed him to be the Protector of the Universal Church."

But, again, to use the words of the same illustrious Prelate, "the House of Christ, is this not eminently the fitting residence of His representatives here below? The earthly possessions of Christ! What are these if they are not the territory that is burdened with the duty of protecting the free exercise of the spiritual power of the Church, and of providing storeroom, so to speak, for all the principal treasures of truth and grace? Yet, at the very present hour, the Father of the great Christian family is dispossessed of his house, his sceptre of royalty is broken in his hands, his crown is torn from his brow. In this world, redeemed by Jesus Christ, there is no longer a square foot that belongs in royal guise to His Vicar, and it is not from the want of any disposition on the part of the revolutionary faction, if the Saviour of men is not once more crucified and laid in His tomb. In such an extremity the Church has recourse with full confidence to the protection of one, who, having been here below the spouse of Mary, the foster-father of Jesus, the temporal guardian of the holy household of Nazareth, is in a very high and real sense the Father of the whole nation of the elect, the head of the mystical body of Jesus Christ."

Very possibly the clever wits of the age may freely indulge themselves in smiling at seeing us set so high a price on the patronage of a simple carpenter of Galilee. And yet, matter-of-fact men as they may plume themselves upon being, there are not wanting certain repeated checks and humiliating disasters within their own experience that might make them a little less out of conceit with their wisdom, and not quite so confiding in the value of their human powers and alliances, so that they might possibly do well to leave us in peace in our own particular reliance upon the power and protection that comes from above.

The learned religious whom we have above quoted tells us that S. Joseph greatly rejoices over "the progress of the Church, for which he nurtured with the greatest care the Christ who is its Bread, its Chief, and its Sacrifice." He must, consequently, grieve for its present sufferings, and not fail to be ready to interpose his powerful influence to obtain the speedy triumph of the Christian society. Let us turn to him, therefore, with redoubled confidence, and, again to quote the words of Isidore, "You who are devout to the Holy Virgin, when you recite her Rosary, do not fail to add at the end of it a prayer in honour of the Holy Joseph, her husband.

Your petitions will be all the better heard.   Can Jesus, indeed,
refuse anything to Joseph, whom he has always loved with
all his strength?   What son, except he be ungrateful, can
forget the good deeds of his father?"—*From the French of
"La Couronne de Marie."*

THE LIFE AND TIMES OF B. ALAIN DE LA ROCHE IN THE FIFTEENTH CENTURY,

RESTORER OF THE CONFRATERNITY OF THE MOST HOLY ROSARY.

CHAP. II.—THE TRIALS OF B. ALAIN.

THE great successes in the ministry of B. Ablain, which have
been already related, were not long unaccompanied by terrible
trials.   It is generally the case that all great undertakings
meet with obstacles and opposition, increasing in proportion
to the importance of the work.   These obstacles came to
B. Alain from three quarters: from the devil, from men, and
from himself.

The many recent victories gained over heresy, and the
innumerable souls brought back to God through the Rosary,
made the restoration of this devotion most terrible to the
enemy of mankind, who therefore employed all his forces
against B. Alain, hoping to strike a deadly blow at the Rosary,
by attacking him who was labouring so earnestly to propagate
it.   It is one of the ordinary devices of the devil to try to
diminish the zeal of the apostles of divine truth, and of
preachers specially chosen by God to increase the faith and
devotion of the people, by raising up in their souls violent
conflicts.   He assails them with all kinds of temptations, and
attempts to destroy their peace of mind by every sort of
mental anguish.   The war which he wages against them is
continual, and sometimes becomes so fierce that these courageous warriors of Christ would despair of victory if they were
not upheld by special graces from God.   Such were, in the first
ages of Christianity, the temptations of S. Paul and S. Jerome,
memorable temptations, which have been suffered over and
over again by many servants of God, who have all been
encouraged by their example to make the same efforts, in the
hopes of gaining the same victory.   Such, also, were the
temptations of B. Alain.

I shall not attempt to describe either their intensity or their
extent; suffice it to say that they left him no peace either by

day or night, and that he would have preferred death a thousand times to the torments he daily endured. Assaulted by the same attacks as S. Paul, he made use of the same means of victory, namely, mortification and prayer. With S. Paul he could truly say, "I chastise my body and bring it into subjection;" for he did in truth discipline himself most severely, hoping to keep down the rising of his rebellious flesh under the cruel blows of pain. Again, with the apostle, he besought the Lord that it might depart from him; he prayed through Mary that God would deliver him from the tempest which was raging in his soul, and would enlighten it once more with the peaceful light of grace. But for some time Heaven remained closed against him, and it seemed as though his cries of sorrow and supplication were unheard by God.

When, however, the powers of darkness had used all their efforts against him, the gates of heaven began to open upon him again, and the Blessed Virgin, having pity upon her servant, banished from his mind all thoughts of despair, and filled his soul with that light whose rays had power to still the tempest and bring back brightness and peace after the darkness and turmoil of battle.

When B. Alain had, by the grace of God, overcome these attacks of the devil, he encountered other difficulties. It may often be noticed that the holiest and most useful institutions are most violently opposed in their infancy, and by those very persons whom we should imagine ought to give them most encouragement and support. Actions performed under the inspiration of God may sometimes appear strange to human eyes, and faith often urges men to undertake works which are condemned as rash by timid souls. Sometimes the opposition does not arise from ignorance or pusillanimity alone, but the violence of the reproaches and the severity of the censure must be attributed in some measure to hatred.

Whatever may have been the motives of the detractors of B. Alain, it is certain that he suffered from their persecutions. One historian tells us that certain men who sought their own interests more than those of God began murmuring against him, and trying to prevent the establishment of the Rosary Confraternity, while the man of God was preaching to the people the glories of Jesus and Mary, and was putting into their hands a practice most efficacious against ingratitude for the graces of redemption, and opening to them a new and powerful method for increasing in the love of God by meditat-

ing on the virtues of their Father and of their Mother. Those
who ought to have defended and helped him declared themselves his enemies, disapproved of his efforts, found fault with
his proceedings, condemned his devotion, and disputed his doctrines.   They strove to set the people against one whom they
called a fanatic, a visionary, an adventurer, and a dangerous
innovator.   They even went so far as to suggest doubts as to
the holiness of his life to those very persons who were the
daily witnesses of it.

This persecution must have been specially painful to this
apostle of Mary's favoured devotion.   Up to that time he had
been, in the eyes of all who knew him, a deep and learned
theologian, an eloquent preacher, a discerning director, and a
most fervent religious, and now he was suddenly attacked by
every kind of malicious insinuation.   But what affected him
much more than the calumnies against his good name was the
injury inflicted on the Rosary by the blows which were directed
against himself, and the dishonour to God caused by the hindrance of so much good to souls.   This thought was painful
beyond measure to his soul, and his only consolation was the
testimony of his conscience, and the inward knowledge that
he was fulfilling his duty; but at the same time he was filled
with sorrow at the diminution of the Confraternity of the
Holy Rosary.   He wrote a defence of the doctrine and the
glory of the Rosary, which he addressed to Mgr. Ferrie,
Bishop of Tournai, hoping, no doubt, to silence the opposition
which had arisen against the devotion, and then to begin
again to preach it with renewed fervour.   This pamphlet,
apparently, did not produce the desired result, for now it was
that B. Alain was troubled by his third great trial—discourage-
ment.

Some souls feel their courage renewed bp difficulties.   Con-
fident of success, they seem to take a pleasure in striving with
all the more eagerness after victory the more difficult its
attainment appears to be.   Others, on the contrary, more
diffident, if they do not actually shun the conflict, give way
when it becomes severe, and wait till happier circumstances
give them some hope of victory. If a man is dependent merely
on his own counsels, such conduct is often the most prudent;
but it is mere cowardice if he has the promises of God for his
encouragement.   Thus it was cowardice in B. Alain to allow
himself to be disheartened by the obstacles which were raised
against the accomplishment of his mission, and our Lord

Himself reproved him for it, as he tells us in his book on the Rosary.*

One day, while he was saying Mass, he saw our Blessed Lord hanging on the cross, and heard, him say these words : "Behold me nailed to the cross ; you it is who have crucified me anew." B. Alain answered : "How, Lord, could I be so miserable as to commit such a deed ? " Jesus said : "Your sins have crucified me; not your deeds, but your omissions ; for, having knowledge and power to preach, you are guilty of all the sins that would have been prevented by the preaching of My Rosary. The world is full of devouring wolves, and you, unfaithful dog, know not how to bark." B. Alain adds that at the same time there was shown to him the future reserved for unfaithful guardians of our Lord's flock, and these words were said to him : "If you remain any longer silent, there is your place. Go and preach my Psalter, fearing nothing. I will defend you against all who desire to attack you." The Queen of Angels also testified her displeasure at his silence. She reproved him severely for having, like a slothful labourer, forsaken his work, and showed him in spirit a large and beautiful city, like the Heavenly Jerusalem described by S. John in the Apocalypse, and promised to him and to all those who should faithfully practice the devotion of the Rosary such a dwelling for all eternity.

Fear and hope—two great means employed by God to move the heart of man—being thus excited in Alain's soul by these supernatural manifestations, all his former fervour was renewed. Unmindful of anything that might oppose him, he continued his exercises with great constancy, and now again was to be seen going round from village to village, from town to town, from province to province, carrying with him wherever he went, like another "vessel of election," the sacred names of Jesus and Mary. His fervour and labours were so pleasing to God that He showered upon him His graces and favours. As He had supported him in his trials, so did He reward his fidelity, thus fulfilling His promise to be faithful to those who are faithful to Him. From this time the life of B. Alain became an uninterrupted course of heavenly favours, of which a short account will be given in the next chapter, thus bringing to an end this short sketch of a life so pleasing to God and so useful to souls.

* De Dignitate Rosarii, cap. iii.

No. V.—THE SCIENCE OF THE HOLY ROSARY.

OUR readers, we think, will be pleased to find our chapter on the theological value of the word "*Joyful*," as characterizing one portion of the mysteries of the Holy Rosary, resolve itself into a beautiful and comforting Homily on the title of the Blessed Virgin in the Litany of Loretto, "*Cause of our Joy.*"

We have learned from the preceding chapter on the theology of the word "Mystery" that God has been as good as His Word. His coming had been pledged by many prophets to His people Israel, and even made known in such a way to the nations of the East, that they were able confidently to expect and look out for Him. He is come as He promised, and accordingly we confess in the Holy Rosary that *He* is come in the flesh of whom we say with S. Peter, "Thou art the Christ the Son of the living God." But the fact that He is come does not by itself alone contain the guarantee that we have good cause for rejoicing that He is come! In a word His coming is doubtless a Great "Mystery," and this the Holy Rosary already teaches us both to believe and to confess. But how do we come to know it to be a "Joyful Mystery?"

Now it is plainly by no means every coming of God that is of a nature to be a cause of joy; therefore there must be some special reason proper to the particular coming in question, which we confess, and which makes it to be to us a joyful coming. Unquestionably it is becoming that we should know what this reason is. God is expected to come again, and then His coming will be far from a cause of joy.

> Quid sum miser tunc dicturus,
> Quem patronum rogaturus,
> Quum vix justus sit securus.
>
> (Hymn *Dies Iræ.*)

"What shall I then say, wretched man that I am, whom shall I ask to speak a word for me, when even the just man is scarcely free from alarm?" Such is the language of Holy Church even in simple anticipation of this expected future coming of God, and what will be its dread reality? If, therefore, the future and expected coming of God is greeted by anticipation with such words as these, what is it that has

transformed the coming, which in the Holy Rosary we confess
as having now been accomplished, into a Joyful Mystery? Of
the effects of the future Coming the Church says:—

> Mors stupebit et natura
> Cum resurget creatura
> Judicanti responsura.

"Death and Nature shall stand aghast when Creation shall
rise to answer to the call of the God who comes to sit as
Judge." How then is it that all Creation can be called to
rejoice at that Coming of God which we acknowledge as
having actually come to pass. Of the one coming of God,
the prophet says, "all shall flee from before His face and
shall hide themselves in the clefts of the rocks and in the
holes of the mountains from before the fear of the Lord and
from the Glory of His Majesty" (Isaiah ii. 21), while of the
other coming of God the same prophet says, "Let the
Heavens above rejoice and the clouds rain down justice"
(xlv. 8). What is it that makes the wonderful difference
between the two comings? The answer is very obvious.
When God comes as Mary's Son, and shows Himself to His
people either in the arms of His Mother, or under her
jurisdiction and control, then all is joy and rejoicing at
His coming, "Let the mountains distil sweetness and the
hills joy" (Joel iii. 18). The Mystery of His Coming is none
the less a Mystery, but it is all purely joyful. The Son of
Mary, during the period of time that He gives Himself entirely
into the hands of His Mother Mary, foregoes all the attributes
of His Godhead which properly inspire terror and dread.
" I bring you," says the Angel to the shepherds, " good tidings
of great joy which shall be to all the people. For this day is
born to you a *Saviour* who is CHRIST THE LORD, in the
city of David" (Luke ii. 10). But when the same CHRIST
THE LORD having passed from under the direct control of
Mary His Mother, speaks, not indeed of His actually sitting
as judge, but only of the preliminaries to His coming as judge,
viz. of the Sign of the Son of Man appearing in the
Heavens, He says, "Then shall all the tribes of the earth
mourn" (Matth. xxiv. 30).

From this it becomes plain that it can be no other than
Mary who is the cause of our Joy. If God is merciful and
good to us sinners as we are, and if sinners as we are we
can rejoice in coming near to Him, it is solely because He

has condescended to make Himself to be Mary's Son. It is because He has condescended to give to Mary His Mother that very motherly power and control over Him which is our security for coming near to Him with joy. By condescending to become Mary's Son, and to own Mary's maternal control, God makes it possible for us to rejoice to come near to Him, the tidings of Jesus while He is with Mary and S. Joseph are good tidings of great joy to all the people. But removed from Mary and Joseph, at even the Sign of the Son of Man in the Heavens, all the tribes of the earth shall mourn.

Mary then is in a true sense the "cause of our Joy, not as the first fountain and source of our joy to the prejudice of the Godhead, but because God has by a wonderful mystery interposed her maternity as the shield to stand between us sinners and those awful attributes of the Godhead which, being inaleinable from the Godhead, must ever have prevented sinners having any joy in coming near to their God, had He not in mercy to them made Himself Mary's Son, in order that they might, being shielded by her maternity, be able to come near to Him with joy.

Perfectly agreeing with the above, we shall find that all the joyful Mysteries of the Holy Rosary present to us Jesus not by Himself alone, but in the care and custody of Mary and S. Joseph. So long as this care and custody lasts, all is pure Joy. The five Mysteries which present Jesus to us thus are all joyful Mysteries.

But in the next five Mysteries, Jesus appears all alone, Mary is absent from them, and then the Mysteries of the Rosary are all pure sorrow, as they before were pure joy. Towards the close, indeed, of the time of abandonment and sorrow, Mary comes to stand by the Cross, and with her appearance on the scene there is the first intimation of the approaching change to a new period of triumph and victory. Mary at the foot of the Cross is invested with the duty of maternal solicitude in the person of John in behalf of all the new multitude which Jesus is presently to acquire to Himself as the fruit of His most sacred Passion and death. Again, in the remaining Glorious Mysteries, when the fifteenth Mystery shows to us a vision of Jesus reunited to Mary, and never again to be separated from the Mother who is the "cause of our Joy"—then again there recurs an express note of joy conveyed in its title, which is now commonly received, viz. the Coronation of Mary in Heaven and the joy of all the Saints.

The Holy Rosary then, in common with the Litany of Loretto, proposes Mary to us as the " Cause of our Joy."

It will also be appropriate here to observe, with what *express* care the five Joyful Mysteries of the Holy Rosary present to our contemplation Jesus as Mary's Son, in her maternal keeping and custody, and after His birth conjointly in her custody with that of S. Joseph.

In the first Joyful Mystery there is but one solitary witness on earth that Jesus has become the Son of Mary, and this is the Blessed Mary herself.

In the second Joyful Mystery, two additional witnesses bear their testimony that Jesus has become Mary's Son, the holy Elizabeth, and her unborn babe, the future precursor of Jesus.

In the third Mystery, the shepherds of Bethlehem run together in haste to see " Christ the Lord," who has been born as Mary's Son, and they find him wrapped in swaddling clothes and laid in the manger in the care of Mary and Joseph.

In the fourth Mystery, the aged Simeon in the Temple receives Him from Mary's arms into his own, and says, as he looks at Mary's Son, " Mine eyes have seen Thy salvation."

But most wonderful of all is the witness that is given in the fifth Mystery, of Jesus being Mary's Son. For here we see Mary the Mother asserting her maternal right in her Son, by the disposition of Divine Providence, as it were over the right of the Eternal Father Himself, and recalling her Son from the Temple, where He had signified that he was rightly engaged on His Father's business, to come and be subject to herself and S. Joseph in the holy house of Nazareth; and we see the wondrous Mystery of Jesus acknowledging the call of His Mother Mary, in such a way as to forego at her call the business of the Eternal Father Himself.

The popular Theology, then, of the word " Joyful," as learnt in the School of the Holy Rosary, is that Jesus is of very truth the Son of Mary, and that the reason of our joy in Jesus is the maternity of Mary.

No. II.—THE PRESENT HUMILIATION OF THE SOVEREIGN PONTIFF:

A Homily, applicable to present Times, on the Text, " Lord wilt Thou at this Time restore the Kingdom to Israel?" (Acts 1. 6).

At so supreme a moment as that when the company of the Apostles understood that their Lord was about to make good his Words: " It is expedient that I go away from you, for if I go not away, the Paraclete will not come unto you," it is not to be supposed that they could have asked such a question as the one contained in our text out of the mere feeling by itself alone of wanting to know the future, which is common to all men. In justice to the Apostles as men, we are bound to believe that the question which at first sight looks like coming from curiosity, and as being the dictate of their national spirit as Jews, overcoming and getting the better of their sense of their functions as Apostles sent to teach all nations, was really founded on reasons that rendered it becoming and in place, even at such a moment.

What could these reasons be? First then, they knew their Master as One, to whose mother it had been promised that He should sit on the Throne of David His Father, and they had the quite recent memory of His having accepted His title of " King of the Jews" in connection with the public Death upon the Cross, to which He had humbled Himself in the sight of all the people. Now, therefore, that He had given proof of His power by rising again from the dead, there was a manifest fitness in their question, which, put in other words, might be taken as though spoken as follows: " Lord, wilt Thou at this time, seeing that Thou hast now shown to the Jews how thou who art their King couldst endure to have Thy royal Dignity exposed to public contempt and rejection by Thy death on the Cross, vindicate Thy power in the sight of Thy people and the whole World, by restoring the Royal Throne of David Thy Father, in the midst of Thy people?" To this question our Lord makes no direct answer, neither saying what He will or will not do; but simply saying to them, " It is not for you to know the times and the seasons which the Father hath put in His own power." " But you shall be witnesses to me in Jerusalem, in all Judea and Samaria, even to the ends of the world."

The same Lord who then suffered His own Royalty in

Judea to be rejected and trampled under foot on the cross without vindicating His power as King of the Jews by re-establishing, or so much as even giving any kind of distinct promise that He ever would restore the Throne of David in Israel, suffers at the present moment the Royalty over Rome and the States of the Church, hitherto the possession of His Vicar, to be subjected to something of the same kind of public contempt and rejection with which the Jews rejected and trampled under foot His inherited Royalty over themselves. There seem, however to be in existence prophetic announcements not unworthy of credit, which foretell a not very distant triumph for the Church, the beginning of which it is to be granted to the aged Pontiff who has been dispossessed of his Royalty over Rome to live to see.

Let us weigh the bright expectations to which the prophecies above mentioned, esteeming them to be really worthy of a certain credit, properly give rise, by the light of our Lord's answer to His Apostles, when they evinced to Him their latent desire that the kingdom might be restored to Israel, in their eager inquiry, "Lord, wilt Thou at this time restore the kingdom to Israel?"

What would have been the consequence had it pleased their Master to restore the "kingdom to Israel?" This, at the first outset, must necessarily have repeated on a vast œcumenical scale the Wars of Israel under Josue against the tribes then inhabitants of the land that was given to the Israelites; the Roman Empire must have been suppressed, and an Israelite Empire, subduing all nations by force of arms, erected in its stead; and as a consequence, the Apostles must have become military princes—in the vast International dominion that would have been subjected to the re-established Throne of David, in the restored kingdom of Israel.

Now the work of an Apostle, for which Jesus Christ had chosen and trained S. Peter and his colleagues, was to preach and to teach, to form the nations of the earth to obedience to the Commandments of God, and to the Worship of the Christian Altar, according to the new Christian Calendar, which provided a new order of the year. You are to be witnesses to Me, said our Lord, beginning from Jerusalem, and extending yourselves to the ends of the earth. It is not difficult to understand, even supposing that the Israelite Empire could have taken the place of the Roman Empire without bloodshed and the ravages of war, that the character and dignity of

great princes in the New Israelite Empire would have pre-
judiced more than it would have benefited the labours of the
Apostles in their work of forming and teaching other nations
to become Christians.   S. Paul, for example, says (Cor. iv. 9),
" For I think that God has exhibited us the Apostles as the
last of men, as if destined to death, for we have become a
spectacle to the world, to men and to angels."   God, then,
according to S. Paul, judged it better, for the success of the
Apostolic office and its labours, to exhibit his Apostles in the
manner described by S. Paul, in preference to giving them
the dignity and emoluments of princes of the restored kingdom
of Israel.   And Jesus Christ said, in answer to His Apostles'
inquiry after their hoped for restoration of the kingdom to
Israel, " It is not for you to know times and seasons, in matters of this kind.   You are to be My witnesses, beginning in
Jerusalem, &c.," as if He intimated, you will find quite enough
to occupy you in this capacity.   Leave the question of the
kingdom of Israel and its restoration alone—for it does not
concern you.

If we had at the present time the privilege of putting a
question to our Lord, such as the Apostles had on the occasion above referred to, it would naturally be something very
much of this kind : " Lord, wilt Thou at this time restore the
kingdom of the City of Rome and of the States of the Church
to Thy Vicar?" And why should not our Lord's answer to such
an inquiry as this be of a similar tenor to that which He
gave to His Apostles, " It is not for you to know the times
and the seasons which the Father has reserved in His own
power.   It is, doubtless, a very great humiliation for you, in
the sight of all the nations of the earth, that the glory and
dignity of the chief city of the whole world should be taken
away from you, and that your Sovereign Pontiff, the infallible
Judge and keeper of the Revelation in which you believe
and have your hope for the life to come, in the place of being
left in possession of his time-honoured, tranquil and honourable independence, as an equal with the prince of the earth,
should be the prisoner of one of his own children, spoiled by
him of the Dignities which it is My Will that he should
have; but then, have you not justly deserved that I should
bring this great humiliation upon you, and that I should
make you a spectacle to all the people of the Earth, by suffering it to be seen in the face of day by them, that all that you
can do and say, throughout all the nations in which you ar

scattered, is not to avail to undo the evil act of the one single
nation which, with its prince, brings this heavy humiliation
upon you. You may easily see that you have well deserved this
humiliation, through your sins. In consequence of your sins
it has come upon you, and until you learn to repent of your
sins, it will remain fastened upon you—beyond any power of
yours to remove it. All that you can do or say will not
avail one tittle to shake it off in any other path, than the one
only path of repentance for your sins."

In the Lenten pastoral letter of the Diocese of Tarbes (the
Diocese of our Lady of Lourdes) of last year, 1871, the Bishop
says: "When the '*Immaculate Conception*' (it was thus the
heavenly apparition named herself) manifested herself in our
beloved Pyrenees, the eyes of the Blessed Virgin appeared in
a single instant to take a survey over all the earth, and immediately afterwards to assume an appearance of the deepest
sorrow, as she turned them towards the young girl at her
feet. What is the matter? what must I do? murmured the
child. Pray for the sinners, said the mother of the whole
human race. Thereupon the heavenly apparition exclaimed,
three several times, 'Repent,' 'Repent,' 'Repent,'
('*Penitence*,' '*penitence*,' '*penitence*,') and the girl repeated
her cry three times, Repent, Repent, Repent, creeping on her
knees to the end of the grotto."

This is the warning, this is the lesson, which the echoes of
every age have not failed at all times to bring home to us;
and it is now as it were a last cry of alarm raised before the
grevious events through which we are now passing. We
might have escaped the terrible scourges which have fallen
upon us if we had but known in time how to understand its
meaning; and we shall not come safe out of them except upon
the one only condition of learning how to turn it to better
account.

What, then, may we conclude, will be the nature of the
triumph of the Church, which the voice of trustworthy prophecy appears to announce for the consolation of the faithful,
as so far near at hand that it will be given to PIUS IX. to
see its first beginnings? What else can the beginning of this
triumph be, but the first beginning of the day of repentance,
which is everywhere to be preached to the people of the
Catholic Church throughout the nations of the World. Between the children of pride, as long as they remain such, and
the call to repentance, there will always be a chasm no

bridged over by any practicable passage ; but the children of
the Church, however egregiously they may be frequently misled by their follies, vanities, and passions, are not so irredeemably
the children of pride as to hold out in stiffnecked supercillious-
ness and contempt against the call to humble themselves
and correct the evil of their ways, when this call is seriously
and repeatedly made to them by the fearless voices of those
to whom they are accustomed to look up for guidance and
direction.   The first fruits, therefore, of the real triumph of
the Church, which we devoutly hope it is the good pleasure
of the Lord of all that it should be given to PIUS IX. to see,
at least in its beginning, will be found in the multiplying of the
earnest calls to repentance and amendment that will need to be
made on all hands, and in the docile and generous spirit in
which these calls are listened to on the part of the good
Christians to whom they may be addressed.   "Cry aloud
and spare not," was said to the prophet of Israel of old; "show
to Israel their transgressions, and to my people their sins."

Let us hear the words of PIUS IX. himself, which were
addressed on the 3rd of July (1872) to the students of the
various national colleges who were on that day admitted to
an audience :—

"Hope on, then, dear children, and pray to God always.
Pray with humility, with constancy, with resignation, that He
may keep you firm and assured in faith, in hope, and in
charity.   Then you will see that the triumph will soon arrive.
We know that the earthly triumphs of the Church are not for
her to go up crowned to the Capitol.   No, the Church's
triumphs are the conversion of sinners, the spread of the
Catholic religion, the blessing of God, the holy lives of the
clergy, the good example of the laity.   And you, too, young
as you are, may become an example to all by your saintly
lives.

"These are the Church's triumphs, and they are brought
about by Almighty God through persecution.   By means of
persecution the good redouble their strength and courage.
That is why God takes in hand the wine that is to purify
His Church ; to purify even those within the Church, but who
are sick, to make her more beautiful, more stedfast, more
mighty for good.   See, then, dear children, what you have to
do ; and in order that you may be enabled to do it, I give you
my benediction.   May it give you strength and courage to
put in practice the short instructions that I have given you.

Also recommend the Pope to Almighty God; recommend to God your respective nations; recommend to Him Germany of which I spoke the other day, and about which I desire not to speak again, because it has disquieted some. Such disquietudes are, however needless, for I shall always say and say again the same things, without regard to the angry feelings I may rouse."

FEAST OF THE NATIVITY OF MARY.
(September 8.)
Song of the Angels on the Birthday of Mary.

Hail to the Flower of Grace divine !
Hail to the Heir of David's line !
Hail to the World's great Heroine !

Hail to the Virgin pre-elect !
Hail to the Work without defect
Of the Supernal Architect !

Hail to the Maid ordained of old,
Deep in eternities untold,
Ere the blue waves of ocean rolled !

Ere the perennial founts had sprung,
Ere in ether the globe was hung,
Ere the morning stars had sung.

Welcome the beatific morn
When the Mother of Life was born—
Only hope of a World forlorn !

What a thrill of ecstatic mirth
Danced along through Heaven and Earth
At the tidings of Mary's birth !

Happy, happy the Angel band
Chosen by Mary's side to stand,
As her defence on either hand !

Safe beneath our viewless wings,
Mother elect of the King of Kings,
Fear no harm from hurtful things.

What though Eden vanished be,
More than Eden we find in thee !
Thou, our joy and jubilee !

E CASWALL.

PERE MONSABRE,

A Preacher of National Penance in France.

THE great and urgent present spiritual need of the Christian society in our times in all the various nations in which Catholics are found is the spirit of national penance. We are all members of one and the same kingdom of God on earth, the Catholic Church, in which we are united together in a common faith and in a common enjoyment of the same Sacraments, the same Sacrifice of the Altar, and the same Divine Presence in our churches. But, as regards civil society, we are estranged by being divided into various nationalities, and nationalities are now all alike more or less steeped in the spirit of self-sufficiency, self-laudation, rebellion against the Christian yoke, contempt of the Divine Revelation and the insane belief that they will be able to uphold human society in a prosperous state, without being beholden to either the knowledge of God or to fear and respect for His laws. The salt of the earth must, therefore, necessarily be now largely sought for in the spirit of national penance.

That all nations are all alike equally guilty in the above respects is not for us to know. We are not to be admitted to the secrets of the Divine Tribunal. It must be sufficient for us to understand, each in our own sphere, that in the place of being puffed up and filled with the spirit of national pride and exaltation, we are, as good members of the Catholic Church everywhere, called to cultivate the contrary spirit of humiliation and penance for the sins of our particular nation ; and instead of forming part of the silly and deceived multitude, whom the Evil One deludes by making them believe that their particular nation is the one choice flower of the earth, far above all other people, we should most humbly and penitently pray God to pardon the many and grievous sins of our particular nation, and to avert from it the judgments which it has most justly deserved.

With these thoughts, what edification may we not draw from seeing an example of the courageous preaching of national penance in the neighbouring nation and people of France, which has just been visited by the chastening hand of God in a manner to make all other nations, and ourselves in particular, humble themselves in the sight of God, and pray that God in his mercy would make known to ourselves the particular evil of our ways, that by a timely return to more Christian counsels we may put away the evil of our doings, and avert the certain anger that is being laid up against us.

The Dominican preacher Pere Monsabrè has been vigorously preaching this very national penance to his countrymen in France in the pulpit of Notre Dame in Paris during the Lent of the current year, and his conferences have recently made their appearance in a volume which we hope will go far beyond the limits of his own countrymen, to whom it is, of course, more particularly addressed. All good Chritians will join in the prayer that the example of France confessing her national sins by the mouth of one of her accepted preachers, may induce other nations to do the same, and that preachers may rise up everywhere to confess their national sins in like manner, and everywhere preach that their people should diligently put them away, and return to the paths in which they may walk blamelessly before God, obeying his laws and teaching His doctrines to their children.

The Pere Monsabrè in his volume acts vigorously on the principle that the Christian doctrine is the one only salt of the whole earth, and that there must be no fear or backwardness on the part of the Christian prophet when there is a question of dealing with false and bad principles. Truth must be spoken, falsehood must be overthrown, the evils of modern society must be dealt with. The doctrines contained in the "Syllabus," must be brought out and acted upon. His volume touches on the great questions on which human society is built, such as "*The Duty of the Christian to Truth*," the "*Fidelity of the Christian to his Duty*," "*The Constitution of the Christian Family*," "*Christian Education, Civil Government, Society*."

The last discourse of the series is that which was preached on Good Friday. It is the "Miserere" of France, and is a vigorous, but somewhat impassioned and characteristic lament for the sins of France and for the judgments that have fallen on her people. It has, however, a most practical conclusion in the following confession of national sin made in behalf of the whole French people :—

"I believe—I proclaim it on high—it is possible that France may be the object of the great mercy of God; but for this France must acknowledge her sin—and she must acknowledge it publicly.

"Unfortunately, we allow the preoccupations of our lives to turn us

aside from the examination of conscience, whence we receive light, the
first principle of repentance. The fault is attributed by some to a fallen
dynasty, which they say has for twenty years corrupted the nation to such
a degree that she must inevitably fall under the blows of a vigorous
enemy. Others ascribe it to the criminal folly of those incapables who
have taken possession of supreme power, and have prolonged, for their
own ambitious purposes, a struggle the end of which could only be an
aggravation of shame and suffering. Each forgets his own part of the
responsibility in the sorrows of his country.

'Let this ridiculous and most dangerous war of recrimination, which
blinds instead of enlightening, vilifies instead of justifying us, come to
an end. If there be a great criminal in the case of our national misfortunes, it is the nation herself—the entire nation. She has of her own
free will enervated herself in a prosperity too greedily sought after. She
has exhausted her generous sap in pleasure and the shameful materialism
of her manners. She has dimished the number of her children, by
contradicting the providential law which provides that families should
increase. She has broken the glorious staff of her strength by setting
at nought the most elementary principles of discipline and social order.
She has abandoned herself to every kind of adventure, through her
servile adoration of success and fortune. Self-possession in the hour of
peril, concentration of effort—patriotic enthusiasm, the spirit of self-
sacrifice, were they possible in such a state of things? O France, see
thy sins, they are rising up against thee, thou must indeed acknowledge
them.

" *Quoniam iniquitatem meam ego cognosco et peccatum meum contra me
est semper.*

"But it is Thee, O God, whom we have offended, it is before Thee that
we have done this evil! To have sinned alone against Thee is too much
for our misery.

" *Tibi soli peccavi et malum coram Te feci.* Thy name, the name of
Thy dear Son, before which every knee should bow, we have dishonoured them by our blasphemy.

"Ignorance, and science falsely so called, have rivalled each other in
this crime, of which it has been justly said that it is the crime of the
damned. In word and in deed we have blasphemed, and as for the
blasphemers themselves, we have surrounded them with cowardly and
shameful fawning, we have honoured, crowned, and incensed them.
On the very eve of our disasters, official hands have raised a statue in
honour of the shameless writer who taught our present generation the
art of impious laughter and sacrilegious mockery.

"The glory of which Thou art so jealous, we have taken it from Thee,
O Lord!"—(P. 278.)

Here is a Christian Daniel confessing the sins of his
people :—"Lord, to us is confusion of face, to our kings, to our
princes, to our fathers, who have sinned. But to thee, O
Lord our God, is mercy and forgiveness, for we have departed from thee, and we have not heard the voice of the
Lord our God that we should walk in His law which He has
given to us by His servants the prophets, and all Israel hath

transgressed thy law, and have turned aside that they should not hear thy voice, and the malediction and the curse hath fallen upon us that was written in the book of Moses the servant of God because we have sinned against Him." (Dan. ix. 8.)

There cannot fail to be hope for the nations of the world, if the edifying example of the Pere Monsabre's preaching of penance to the French people can by the mercy of God find numerous other zealous and courageous imitators.

That there is rising up in France a holy and Christian spirit at least to confront and oppose the torrent of blasphemy and unbelief—God grant that it may overcome and tread it down under foot!—is manifest from the general desire to consecrate France to the Sacred Heart of Jesus, the advocacy of which is the theme of the concluding discourse in the volume. The following is proposed as the form of the vow of consecration:—

NATIONAL VOW OF FRANCE, &c.

"In presence of the misfortunes which are desolating France, and of those greater ones which may menace her yet—

"In presence of the sacrilegious outrages committed at Rome against the rights of the Church and of the Holy See, and against the sacred person of the Vicar of Jesus Christ—

"We humble ourselves before God, and uniting in our hearts the love of our Church with that of our country, we acknowledge that we have been guilty, and justly chastised.

"And in order to make due satisfaction for our sins, and to obtain from the infinite mercy of the Sacred Heart of our Lord Jesus Christ the pardon of our faults, as well as the extraordinary aid which alone can deliver the Sovereign Pontiff from his captivity, and cause the misfortunes of France to cease, we promise to contribute to the erection, in Paris, of a Sanctuary dedicated to the Sacred Heart of Jesus.

"The inscription over this Sanctuary will be: To Christ and to His Sacred Heart—France penitent and consecrated. *Christo ejusque sacratissimo Cordi Gallia penitens et devota.*"

May God bless and give the victory to these Christian efforts in France, and to us also the grace to profit by the light of an example of national penance by which on so many different grounds we urgently need to take pattern, before the hand of God smites our nation in a similar manner for its crying sins!

NOTICES OF BOOKS.

THE BOOK OF THE HOLY ROSARY. 4to. By the Rev. Henry
Formby, Tertiary Priest of the Dominican Order. Dedicated
to the members of the Confraternity of the Rosary.

This work, we cannot doubt, will be welcomed by all lovers
of the Rosary as being the first large and important work in
the English language professedly treating of the mysteries
of the Holy Rosary. The task of its revisal was among the
last works completed by Father Peter Mackey just before his
death, in pursuance of his being commissioned to do so by the
Provincial of the order. Our readers will be interested in
learning his report upon it, written not many days before his
last illness set in, which is as follows:—

"I willingly certify that it is in perfect accordance with sound doctrine
and morality. I have been exceedingly pleased and interested in the
manner in which the various parallels from the Old Testament have been
set forth, and I feel convinced that its publication will tend very much
to the increase of piety among the faithful. Members of the Confraternity
of the Rosary, especially, will find it a most fruitful mine of devout thoughts
for meditation whilst reciting the mysteries."—March 28th.

It is a distinctive feature in the work that it has gathered
together a rich and varied body of extracts translated from
the chief Fathers and Doctors of the Church, in order to give
the lovers of the Holy Rosary an opportunity of becoming
acquainted with the manner in which the great teachers of
Christendom speak and write of the mysteries of the Catholic
faith, the far largest part of which extracts have never before
been accessible to any Catholics, except to those acquainted
with the original languages and having access to the large
folio volumes from which they have been taken and translated.
This feature is one that cannot fail to recommend the book as
a really lasting and valuable household possession for every
Catholic family. We do not, indeed, know of the existence of
any other work by which a family will be able to make the
acquaintance, so to speak, of so many of the great teachers
and doctors of the Catholic people, and this in the especially
winning form of explanations of the Mysteries of the Rosary.

In addition to this, the young people of the family will
discover endless employment for themselves in turning over
the thirty-six pages of pictures in the book, which depict all

the fifteen Mysteries, and nearly forty scenes besides from the Old Testament, the typical reference of which to the various Mysteries will be found explained in the pages of the book. It appears under the joint sanction of the Archbishop of Westminster and the Provincial of the Order in England.

GRACES OBTAINED THROUGH THE PRAYER OF THE ROSARY.

AMONG the various records of graces obtained by the favour of Our Lady of the Holy Rosary we read the following in the August member of *La Couronne de Marie*, Lyons, in France:—

"*N.*—I have obtained by the intercession of Our Lady of the Holy Rosary, the preservation and happy return of my two sons. The one served in the Army of the East, and the other was at Metz. Both were frequently exposed to the greatest danger. During the six months of my anxiety for their safety, I found no greater consolation than in reciting the Rosary every day for them. I never missed this for a single day, and I owe to this perseverance the happy return of my two sons."

"*Parthenay.*—At the moment when many hearts were invoking the aid of our Lady of the Holy Rosary, whilst the enemies of our unhappy country were pressing in from all sides, I likewise, a humble child of the Rosary, cast a suppliant look to our good Mother, and begged of her to preserve to the affection of a family to whom he was very dear a member of it who for five months was surrounded with every kind of danger. My confidence was very great, and, also, it was not disappointed. So I beg of you, my Reverend Father, to assist me to fulfil my promise, in causing these few lines to be inserted in the *Couronne de Marie*, as a homage of filial gratitude to the Holy Virgin of the Rosary; for I have a firm conviction that it is she who has visibly protected the one for whom I have so oftened prayed."

"*Poiters.*—(June.)—Permit me to communicate to you the account of a remarkable grace obtained by the intercession of Our Lady of the Holy Rosary. I receive the news from a distant island on the African coast, M———. But to the Blessed Virgin all distances are alike. My good friend Mme. A. G. is chief of a division in that country, and I have been fortunate enough to make her acquainted with our beloved 'Perpetual Rosary;' and now, for some years, she has taken an active part in it, with a signal success that I did not dare to hope for.

"Still she suffered from a mental distress which quite upset her, as she told me, and of which she could never get the better by reasoning with herself. Peculiar circumstances at the time prevented the possibility of recourse to her director, so the only help she could obtain had to come direct from above.

"At this time, she happened to read in the *Couronne* that a soul in much the same condition of suffering with herself, had received interior peace from invoking Our Lady of the Holy Rosary, promising that if her prayer was heard, she would make it known through the pages of the *Couronne*. This was like a ray of light to Mme. G. She

immediately promised a mass at the Altar of the Rosary at Poitiers, a
gift to the altar, and an alms to some charity, also a few lines to the
Couronne in proof that no one ever invokes in vain the 'Help of Christians.
"From this moment her mind has never been troubled, all her former
anxieties have quite disappeared."

We may here say to our readers that we shall at all times
be happy to open the pages of our magazine to similar wells
attested records of graces granted to the invocation of our Lady
of the Holy Rosary, for there is no limit of space or country
to her power to benefit.—(Note of the Editor.)

RECORD OF EVENTS.

THE LETTER OF THE POPE TO CARDINAL ANTONELLI, JUNE 16.
—We hasten to redeem the promise given in our last number
of furnishing our readers with an account of the letter written
by the Sovereign Pontiff to his Cardinal Secretary of State.
Considering the persistent mendacity with which the enemies
never cease to assert that, under the present Italian occupation
of Rome, religion is not only respected but maintained secure
against all outrage, the whole body of the faithful owe a new
debt of gratitude to the Holy Father for the public testimony
which he gives in this letter, and also for the example of
unshaken fortitude with which he continues to resist and to
assert his rights. The letter is addressed to the Cardinal
James Antonelli, and bears the date of the Vatican, June 16th.
The Pope in it circumstantially recounts the crimes of the
Italian Government, both past and in prospect, against the
liberties of the Church, and set forth the reason why he refuses to enter into pact or treaty with them. After having
thus recounted what has been done, he says :—

"It is difficult to understand how any one can speak seriously about
reconciliation between the Roman Pontificate and the usurping Government. In fact, what reconciliation could there be in the existing state
of things? The matter in dispute is no mere question arising in the
political order or in the religious order, such as might admit of con-
cession on either side so as to bring about a fitting compromise. The
matter in dispute, on the contrary, is about a state of things produced
by acts of violence done to the Roman Pontiff, and which entirely
destroys that liberty and that independence which are indispensable to
the government of the Church. To lend himself, then, to any reconciliation of that kind would be, on the part of the Roman Pontiff, not only to
surrender all the rights of the Holy See which have been transmitted
o him as a deposit of his predecessors, but it would also be to resign

himself, by an act of his own free will, to the frequent encounter of obstacles to the exercise of his sacred ministry; it would be to leave disturbance and disquietude in the minds of the faithful, to shut the door to the free manifestation of the truth—in a word, it would be to resign himself of his own accord to abandon to the caprice of a Government that sublime mission which the Roman Pontiff has received directly from God, with the stringent obligation of guarding its independence against every human power.

"No; We cannot bend, either to assaults directed against the Church or to usurpation of her sacred rights, or to the illegal interference of the secular government in religious affairs. Unshaken in Our resolution to defend honourably, and by all the means still left Us, the interests of the flock committed to Our charge, We are ready to undergo still greater sacrifices, and, if necessary, even to shed Our blood, sooner than fail in any of the duties imposed upon Us by Our supreme Apostolate. Even more! With the Lord's help We shall never fail to set an example of strength and courage to the pastors of the Church and to the other consecrated ministers who, in these unhappy times, sustain so many conflicts for the cause of God, for the good of souls, for the defence of the holy deposit of the faith, and for the maintenance of the enternal principles of morality and justice.

"And now, my Lord Cardinal, what shall we say about those pretended guarantees which the usurping Government professes to be willing to give to the Head of the Church, with the plain intention of deceiving the simple and unreflecting, and of supplying a weapon to those political parties who have but little at heart the liberty and independence of the Roman Pontiff.

"To waive all other arguments, what is daily occurring at Rome, where the Government has a great interest in persuading Europe of the strength and efficiency of the much vaunted Law of the Guarantees, may suffice to demonstrate their futility and impotence. In fact, of what avail is it to proclaim the immunity of the person and residence of the Roman Pontiff, when the Government does not even possess the power to protect us from the insults to which our authority is daily exposed; and from the repeated offences offered in a thousand ways to Our very person; and when together with all honest men, we are compelled to be afflicted spectators of the manner in which, in certain cases, penal justice is administered? Of what avail is it not to keep locked the door of our abode, when it is impossible for Us to go out therefrom without witnessing impious and revolting scenes, or without exposing Ourself to outrages from persons that have crowded into Our Rome to foment immorality and disorder; or without running the risk of Our becoming the occasion of a deadly conflict among the citizens?

"What does it avail to promise personal guarantees for the high dignitaries of the Church, when they are even obliged to conceal in the streets the insignia of their dignity in order to avoid being exposed to ill treatment of all kinds; when the ministers of God and sacred things are an object of derision and of mockery to such a degree that it is for the most part necessary to discontinue the public celebration of the more august ceremonies of our holy religion; and when the holy pastors of the Catholic world who, from time to time, are obliged to come to Rome to render their account of the affairs of their churches, may find themselves exposed without any real guarantee to the same insults, and perhaps to the same dangers? It avails nothing to proclaim the liberty of Our pastoral ministry, when all legislation, even on the most important subjects, such as are the sacraments, is in open conflict with the fundamental principles and universal laws of the Church.

"It avails nothing to recognize by law the authority of the Supreme Pastor when the effect of the acts emanating from him are not recognized, when the Bishops whom We have appointed are not legally recognized, and, with unparalled injustice, are forbidden to enjoy the lawful patrimony of their churches, or even to enter their episcopal houses. Indeed they would be reduced to a state of complete destitution, unless the charity of the Catholic people, which supports even Ourself, furnished them, at least temporarily, with the means of sharing in the alms of the poor. In one word, what guarantee can the Government give for the observance of those promises, when the first of those fundamental laws of the State is not only trampled under foot with impunity by any citizen, but is rendered null and void by the Government itself, which continually, sometimes by new laws, and sometimes by decrees, just as it pleases, evades the respect and observance due to those fundamental laws."

INSECURITY OF RELIGIOUS PROPERTY IN ROME.—The following is a copy of a letter which has been received by Mr. Maguire, M.P., which shows that the British power does not neglect its duty in protecting its subjects against the agressions of the Italian Government:—

"Foreign Office, July 8th, 1872.

"Sir,—I am directed by Earl Granville to acknowledge the receipt of the letter from the Rev. John Pascal O'Hanlon, which you have lately communicated to his lordship, calling attention to the apprehension which is felt by those interested in the foreign conventual and other establishments in Rome, lest some measure tending to their suppression or confiscation by the Italian Government should be carried out, and appealing for the protection of Her Majesty's Government, especially with reference to the college of S. Isidore.

"I am now to inform you that, although Lord Granville has every reason to hope that the establishments in question are in no such danger as those parties immediately interested in them appear to apprehend, seeing the frequent assurance which he has received from the Italian Government on the subject, his lordship has nevertheless again called Sir Augustus Paget's attention to this subject, and has instructed him to take such steps as, upon inquiry, the necessities of the case might appear to require.—I am, Sir, your most obedient humble servant,

"John Francis Maguire, M.P.   "E. HAMMOND."

"The letter from the Rev. J. O'Hanlon (Guardian of S. Isidore), which accompanied your communication, is returned herewith."

IRRELIGIOUS POLICY OF THE ITALIAN GOVERNMENT.—The policy of the Italian Government continues its evil career, and their determination to injure or suppress if they can the religious orders is more pronounced than ever.

The *Tablet* correspondent of the 29th July writes:—

"The *Capitale* (the name of a daily newspaper) is every day inventing the most vile accusations against the Religious. The *Liberta* is giving long letters from apostate priests and monks, and the *Fanfulla* informs the public that all the celebrated works of art are being spirited away by the Religious Orders and privately sold to England and France. No means are spared for carrying out the policy of Cavour, namely, vilifying and degrading the Religious Orders in the eyes of the public, in order to oblige the Ministry to suppress them."

CATHOLIC PUBLIC MEETING IN LONDON.—On Tuesday, July 16th, a public meeting was held in Willis's Rooms, St. James's, London, at which the Duke of Norfolk presided, to protest against the recent legislation of the German Empire against the Jesuits and other teaching orders. Various resolutions were passed, and, towards the conclusion of the meeting, the Archbishop was present, and passed a warm eulogium on the fathers of the Society, and on the fidelity of the distinguished laity of England to the cause of religion.

SUDDEN DEATH OF THE REV. FATHER A. DENT.—Died suddenly by apoplexy, on Wednesday, July 24th, in his sixty-first year, at Stoke-upon-Trent, the Rev. Aloysius Dent, O.P. He was born July 17th, 1812, was professed November 9th, 1845, and ordained Priest on Holy Saturday, 1850. He was buried in a vault in the conventual church at Stoke on the following Saturday. The Bishop of Birmingham, who preached at his funeral, from the text, "The Lord gave, and the Lord hath taken away," said—

"In removing from amongst us the Rev. Fr. Dent, whose remains are reposing under that funeral pall, Almighty God has taken away one whom he had given us for our edification. You, my brethren of the Dominican Order, have lost in him a loved and venerated brother; you, my sisters, in whose church and convent he laboured, have to lament the loss of one who was for many years to you a true father and director. You, my brethren of the Secular Priesthood, have to regret the departure from among you of one whom you had learnt to admire and esteem. You, faithful laity, have to sorrow for a devoted and beloved pastor, while I have to grieve over a son, to whom I never communicated how great was the affection I felt for him." In addition to these affecting words, his Lordship proceeded to detail several instances and traits of character which could not fail to arrest the devout attention of all present. He related, for instance, how unflagging he was in the work of the parish. For example, last Good Friday, after all the hard work and long services, he went off immediately, and without breaking his fast, in obedience to a sick call. And this is only one instance out of many. He was very assiduous in his attention to his sick, visiting them several times a day, so that many who saw how anxious he was for their spiritual good have often expressed a desire that they might be attended by him on their death-bed. The homliness and simplicity of his instructions (especially of those he gave the children whom he was preparing for the Sacraments) were much remarked by devout people, and made the late Mother Margaret often say : " His simple instructions remind me of the Curé d'Ars." As a further illustration of his solicitude in the performance of his pastoral duties the Bishop likewise mentioned that he made a little agreement with his sister, a Carmelite Nun at Darlington, that every Sunday, about half-past 11 (the time when he supposed he should be preaching to his people), she should go before the Blessed Sacrament to beg grace for him to speak in a befitting manner to his flock. May he rest in peace.

A Sudden Miraculous Cure.—In the month of June of the present year Isabella, the youngest and sole surviving daughter of a family of six children, was suddenly by miracle restored from the point of death to her parents in perfect health. Her mother, Lady M. Murray, was taking her by easy stages to Lourdes, and the miraculous cure took place at Agen, ones of the stages on the route from Bordeaux to Lourdes. We have received, as we are going to press, too late for admission, a copy of the letter written by the mother, Lady M. Murray, addressed to Monsieur Deville, secretary of the Confraternity of our Lady of the Angels, of No. 16, Grande Rue Nazareth, Toulouse, giving a detailed account of the wonderful circumstances connected with the cure; but we hope to give our readers the interesting particulars of the miracle in our next number.

THE

Monthly Magazine of the Holy Rosary.

NEW SERIES.

| No. 3.] | OCTOBER. | [A.D. 1872. |

No. I.—THE SOCIAL DEVOTION OF THE HOLY ROSARY.

A School of Christian Improvement for all the Catholic People, Both the Rich and the Poor.

S. Paul says, "*I am a debtor to the Greeks and to the barba-rians*" (Rom i. 14); in other words, the religion of which I am the preacher is equally for the civilized people and for the rude and the barbarous people. For the civilized people, its function is to teach them to distinguish the good from the bad in their civilization : that is, to show them the evil which they are called to reject and abandon, and to point out the good which they should not only retain but seek to improve and ameliorate. For the barbarous people, it has to begin with them at the very beginning, and to show them not only how to abandon their barbarous way of life but how to improve their social condition, by learning to acquire all the useful and excellent arts of life, at the same time that they all, both Greeks and barbarians, learn to conform their morals to the standard of the Gospel and to become worshippers of the true God before the altars of the Church.

Many centuries have come and have gone upon the earth, and the religion of Holy Church has had experience of very many different tribes and nations of people since she received her first charter to become a debtor to the "civilized" and to the "barbarians" in the words "*Go ye into all nations and teach them*," and at the present hour she possesses amongst her scholars and people over the earth a great variety of nations and people speaking a great many different languages. These many different people are actually at the present moment found living in every sort of personal and social condition, ranging from the very next door to the most abject and extreme state of barbarism, rudeness, ignorance, dirt, rags and poverty, up to the contrary extreme of profuse wealth, luxury, idleness, refinement and pleasure-seeking; and, agreeably with S. Paul's words, the Holy Church con-

tinues, and always to the end of time will continue, to be a
debtor not only to both extremes of the social scale, the
Greeks and the barbarians, but also to all the immense
multitude of those who occupy varying conditions ranging
between the two extremes, and who are neither, on the one
hand, what may be properly called barbarous, or, on the
other, remarkable for any excess of refinement or luxurious
display. It is for the most part within the happy medium
bounded by these two social extremes that the Church finds
the greatest number of promising scholars for her school of
improvement. Still we cannot shut our eyes to the social
phenomenon of the marked tendency shown in our nineteenth
century by the occupants of what may be called the "medium
territory" to be continually moving in opposite directions, the
one towards the extreme of barbarism, and the other to the
extreme of refinement and luxury. Repeated transgressions
against the divine law, the degrading vices of lying and
drunkenness, of impurity, blasphemy, and foul speaking, beget
a chronic dulness of mind, a deadness to all honest desire to
rise up and improve, on which charitable reproofs and ad-
monitions fall in vain and fail to produce any fruit, and thus
one large section is continually drifting away to dirt and
misery, rags, poverty and barbarism. On the other hand,
the vast number of lucrative employments, and the great
opportunities for making money by traffic, which the commerce
and enterprize of our times afford, put others in the way of
rising quickly to opulence and refinement, when they throw
themselves into these paths with the requisite industry and
capacities. If the consequences to the falling class are
disastrous, they are scarcely less so to the rising and prosperous.
Their sudden rise tends to beget a condition sadly verifying
the sacred proverb, "the prosperity of fools is their ruin."
A self-conceited and vain state of mind is produced, which
makes them above being spoken to, and to which the words
of the Apocalypse, perhaps, best apply : "For thou sayest, I
am rich and increased in goods, and have need of nothing,
and Thou knowest not that thou art wretched and miserable,
poor, blind, and naked." (Apoc. iii. 17.)

One of the necessary and unavoidable evils of the two
different movements towards the above described opposite
social extremes, is the mutual estrangement that naturally
follows upon the downward movement of the one class to
dirt, drunkenness, sin, rags and misery, and the upward

movement of the other to opulence and social advancement. The falling and miserable people naturally keep aloof from contact with their more prosperous brethren, from the feeling of being ashamed of themselves, and from a certain misgiving that if it were not for their own very great fault they might also have been likewise raising themselves, and in a similar way of bettering their condition. And to the rising and prosperous people, these numerous sinking miserable people are a great abomination. They owe them a grudge for the fact that, by being known to be Catholics, their social equals who are not Catholics do not fail to point a finger of scorn at them, and to say, " Serves them right; if they will be Papists and believe such silly and degrading superstitions, where is the wonder that they should be the ' objects ' that they are ? It is just exactly what you might expect." Thus the social misery of the miserable brings a bad name on the Catholic Religion, and the bad name makes the thriving and prosperous people disposed to be secretly, not a little ashamed of their religion ; and one signal further evil consequence is that the common proverb "Extremes meet," comes to be dreadfully verified in both. And the point in which the two extremes meet is the very great and deplorable ignorance of the Catholic Religion that, from different and opposite causes, comes to be characteristic of both the extremes.

To the sinking and falling class, knowledge of their religion, instead of being a source of happiness, is a burdensome thing and a weariness. It calls for effort and painstaking to acquire it; and this would be " *improvement*," whereas, what they want is not improvement, but to be let alone; to sink down and indolently perish away off the earth in their dirt and their wretchedness. What can there be in common between them and the knowledge of their religion, which would be only a troublesome monitor to them, continually reproving them for the very condition into which they want to settle themselves down, and in which they wish to die ? And, as regards the thriving and prosperous class, what again, speaking generally, do they want with acquiring greater knowledge of a religion which, in their secret hearts, they look upon as a thing quite outside the pale of anything like knowledge at all, thinking it quite a sufficient, if not a most ample, conformity that they remain outwardly on good terms with its requirements, and keep clear of giving any cause of complaint.

With two such social phenomena as these, each in its
way continuing to make progress in a direction diametrically
opposed to the other, and in view of the manifest evils
certain to flow from the increased mutual estrangement that
cannot fail, in consequence, to grow up and become more
visible between those who nevertheless at times when they
reflect know themselves to be united in the bonds of a common
faith in a common salvation, it is a thought of no little comfort
to be able to perceive that the society of the faithful is not left
without its remedies to oppose to the progress of the evil, the
social mischief of which is by no means a thing to be under-
rated. However, thanks be to the mercy of God, the physician
is not without the power of applying a remedy. We are not
to flatter ourselves with illusory hopes of any sudden and
immediate cure; the disease is one the seat of which is very
deep in human nature; its roots are very old, and have spread
themselves in many and divers directions; they are wonderfully matted and intertwined from long continuous growth.
We are not then likely to see them rooted out, or to have the
ground cleared of them all at once. What we may do, however, is, we may put into the ground a plant possessed of a
strong, vigorous power of growth of its own; we may see that
it has, in the first outset, sufficient room and space to spread
its roots, and having provided it with all it needs for the
putting forth its own powers of life, and for holding its own,
we have then but to leave it to contest the possession of the
ground in which the tangled growths already alluded to have
obtained their hold. This plant to which we refer is the
assembling of people together for the recitation of the Rosary
in common. We are not here speaking of any particular kind
of social organisation, such as the "Confraternity of the Holy
Rosary," any particular summoning together of Circles of the
"Living Rosary," or, indeed, of any particular attempts which
may be made to unite people together under any form of
obligation to recite the Rosary in common, but simply alluding
to what is within the competence of every missionary priest
in charge of a congregation, should he think well to open his
church for the recitation of the Rosary in common by his
flock; or, again, what is permissible to every householder,
viz., to open his house, if he be so disposed, for the assembling
of a few friends and neighbours for the same purpose of
reciting the Rosary in common.

The Apostle's rule is "not forsaking the assembling of our-

selves together " (Heb. x. 25), words which necessarily, in the
Apostle's meaning, can directly inculcate only the higher duty
of frequenting the offering of the Holy Sacrifice of the Mass,
on days when this is a duty of religion, and apply only
relatively to the pious practices which are to be advocated
as things in their nature voluntary.   Cornelius a Lapide
has the following remarks on the passage : " The apostle,"
he says, " understands by the word ' collectionem ' the
assemblies of the Church and the gatherings together of the
faithful for the Holy Sacrifice, for hearing the Word of God
preached, and for public prayers.   The apostle desires that
these assemblies should be diligently·frequented by the Christians ; both that they may publicly profess their faith and
worship God, and render Him their public tribute of praise
and thanksgiving, and also that they may excite and provoke
each other to good works, and particularly to constancy in the
faith at the approach of persecution."

(To be continued.)

THE LIFE AND TIMES OF B. ALAIN DE LA ROCHE IN THE FIFTEENTH CENTURY,

RESTORER OF THE CONFRATERNITY OF THE MOST HOLY ROSARY.

CHAP. III.—THE FAVOURS GRANTED TO B. ALAIN.

IN speaking of the favours which it pleased God to bestow
upon B. Alain, we will chiefly dwell upon those which were
the means of his sanctification.   We have seen how he 'was
consoled by heavenly aid in his troubles and discouragements.
Nor was this a solitary instance.   More than once did the
Blessed Virgin appear to him full of majesty to raise his
sinking heart.   She often said to him, " Know, my son, that
no one can pass through this world without suffering ; neither
my Divine Son nor myself nor any of the Saints were exempt
from this law.   Prepare yourself like a good soldier enrolled
under the banner of faith and patience to suffer much.   This
is the end for which I have destined you, and not that you
should live in luxury and idleness.   Be not surprised at the
evil desires of your soul, but receive them as sufferings
deserved by your sins, as useful exercises for advancing in
virtue, and as a sure means of obtaining your own salvation,
and of benefiting the living and the dead."   At other times
she dispersed by her presence the darkness which filled his
soul, comforted him in sickness, strengthened him in weak-

ness, encouraged him in tepidity, and delivered him in
temptations.   All his life long she was his protectress, and
as it was through her that God first called him to a holy
life, so it was through her intercession that he was enabled to
persevere to the end.   Without speaking of all these graces,
we will only consider those which specially helped B. Alain
in his mission.   If he was in truth raised up by God to revive
the devotion of the Rosary, and through it to renew the
spirit of Christianity in the world, it was of course necessary
that his words should be followed up by his actions, and
that the sanctity of his life should prove the truth of his
mission.   Thus the greatest grace and the one most calculated to
convince his hearers, which could have been bestowed upon
Alain was the revival in his soul of all the virtues of his
holy Father, S. Dominic, for he used to say that as long as
the Rosary was practised and venerated according to the
instructions of S. Dominic so long did the flower of perfection flourish in the Order.   This perfection of life was
found in a very high degree in B. Alain.   The thought
that as a Religious and priest he was consecrated to God, and
devoted to His service, and therefore bound to make Him
known, loved, and honoured in the world, filled him, says
his historian, with such a holy joy, that it caused him to
trample under his feet all that the world holds most dear,
and to give himself no rest till he had acquired all virtues
necessary to a true disciple of Jesus Christ.   Through the
whole of his life he practised with the utmost perfection
all those virtues which form the life, the glory, and the ornament
of the religious life : obedience, poverty, chastity, fidelity to the
rule, recollection of mind, prayer, mortification, silence, and
study.   A large portion of his time was devoted to meditation
on the mysteries of God, and on the life and death of Our
Lord Jesus Christ.   Like his father, S. Dominic, it was of or
with God that he spoke, souls that he loved, and heaven that
he called upon in his necessities.   He took special delight in
calling to mind the benefits of the religious state, in which
falls are more rare, progress more easy, resistance more
energetic, combats more glorious, and the reward obtained
more blessed.   He said mass every day with such devotion
and recollection that it seemed as if he saw with his eyes that
which to others is revealed by faith, and was several times
transported out of himself and wrapped in an ecstacy of contemplation.   For a short time, actuated no doubt by reverent

fear, he interrupted his daily mass, but soon recommenced it, finding by experience that holy confidence is of greater profit to the soul than too great timidity.

Such a high degree of sanctity can only be attained through the special blessing and grace of God, and the truth of this is confirmed by the history of B. Alain, who relates as having happened to a third person many of the heavenly favours which were granted him; and in reading of them we are led to realise more fully his great perfection. These are his words : " This disciple of the Blessed Virgin had received, among other graces, the gift of tears of repentance, which flowed from his eyes in such abundance that he could not check their course, while at the same time he felt at the bottom of his heart such a sorrow for his sins that he had a firm conviction that they were forgiven; and he then was divided between sorrow and joy, though his mind was not troubled but filled with a calm hope full of comfort. The Holy Spirit had taken full possession of his heart through the gifts which He gives to all in a state of grace, and finding him perfectly obedient to His inspirations, He penetrated him entirely with His unction, and taught him to distinguish between the impulses of grace and nature, and always to follow the inward voice of the Good Shepherd. This soul was one of those faithful sheep of whom Our Lord speaks, who know the voice of the shepherd and distinguish it from that of strangers, 'My sheep hear my voice.' 'Mine know me,' that is those who love Him and are loved by Him, and who, far from desiring to leave His fold, assemble joyfully around Him. But," continues B. Alain, " besides this hearing and recognizing the voice of God, teaching and urging the soul to do the Will of God and keep His laws, this disciple of Mary was gifted with an infused knowledge which extended the horizon of his soul. That which few only attain after hard and incessant study, he saw at once by the power of a light from God in a far clearer way than he could have done by years of laborious work. His knowledge was not a dry and confused science like that acquired in secular schools, but a science full of unction and life, which instead of leading away from God conducts the soul to His love. Therefore, learned as he was before receiving these illuminations, when once their brightness had shone upon him his former knowledge appeared all darkness and weakness, and he counted that he had known nothing till the happy day on which the eternal Sun had enlightened his eyes." Since that time, whether preaching or teaching, his words touched his hearers and disciples to the bottom of their hearts, while they set before them the truths of religion in a way which shut out all evasion and admitted of no reply. They felt that the Spirit of God was speaking by his mouth, and it is evident that this was also his own feeling, for he never entered the pulpit or began teaching without first spending some time in fervent prayer. It is not difficult to imagine what rapid progress in sanctity was made by B. Alain under this heavenly direction, and how his soul became a treasury of spiritual graces and gifts of the Holy Ghost, and a source of edification for the whole Church. Being thus formed by the Hand of God Himself, he reproduced in his life the actions of our great Example, and appeared before men a faithful representation of our Blessed Lord. That such was his life cannot be better shown than by saying that having been raised up by God to teach men to meditate on the life, death and glory of Jesus Christ, he practised the virtues he taught, and imaged forth the glory he promised. After having spent fifteen years in preaching the Rosary and enrolling in its Confraternity innumerable souls in many different lands; having suffered, as we have seen, from the devil, from men, and from his own weakness, and having sanctified himself by the exercises of a most mortified life, he went to receive the crown which his labours, sufferings, and virtues had merited. It has been remarked that the Blessed Virgin often grants to her faithful servants the grace of dying on one of her feasts, as if she wished to show how pleasing to her their devotion has been, and to prove to them that she remembers their services at the hour of their death. This privilege was not denied by Mary to the restorer of her Rosary, and it was on one of her festivals that he entered upon his reward. He was taken ill on the feast of the Assumption, and gave up his soul to God on the Nativity of the Blessed Virgin, 1475, at Zoulle, a town in Flanders. The Abbé Tritheme, Anthony Posssevin, Michoviensis, Sixtus of Sienna, and all our chroniclers mention this great man. Our chronicles give him the title of Blessed, on account of his great reputation for sanctity during his life and after his death, and one of the Chapters of the Congregation of Holland ordered the publication of his works.

No. VI.—THE SCIENCE OF THE HOLY ROSARY.

THE POPULAR THEOLOGY OF THE WORD "SORROWFUL."

OUR explanation of the popular theology of the word "*Sorrowful*," as our readers will find, resolves itself into a homily on the words of our Lord in the Gospel of St. Luke, "O ye fools and slow of heart to believe in all things which the prophets have spoken, ought not Christ to have suffered these things, and so to enter into his glory." (Luke xxiv. 25.)

We may take it for incontestably certain that if our Lord could say, *ought* not Christ to have suffered these things, there must be good reason in the nature of things to explain why He ought to have suffered them; and it will consequently belong to the popular theology of the word "sorrowful" to make it known what these reasons are. It will not suffice to say that the sufferings of Christ were prophesied in the Books of Moses and in the Prophets, and that Christ ought to fulfil what was prophesied, for this would only throw back the inquiry and oblige us to raise the question, How then could such things come to be prophesied of Christ?

There must evidently, therefore, be some very great reason for these sufferings of Christ, because they are well known to prove a most serious stumbling-block to great numbers. "To the Jews," as S. Paul says, "they are a stone of stumbling and to the Gentiles foolishness," and yet he himself glories in them, and says in the most open manner possible, "God forbid that I should glory, save in the Cross of Jesus Christ." (Gal. vi. 14.) The very thing that is the stumbling-block to the great bulk of the Hebrew people, and which has caused their fall, and which also, to this very day and hour, provokes the derision and contempt of the unbelievers, the same as it has always done, is the especial joy and glory of the Apostle. He speaks exultingly of the Cross, as the foolishness of God which is wiser than the wisdom of men, and as the weakness of God, which is stronger than the strength of men. (1 Cor. i. 25.)

There must, consequently, be some exceedingly strong reason in the nature of things, which, if we could only know what it is, will explain to us how our Lord has come to say, "*ought* not Christ to have suffered these things, and so to enter into His glory."

First, then, we must bear in mind the principal lesson

that the first five Mysteries of the Rosary have fixed in our minds, viz., that Jesus has become the Son of Mary. By becoming the Son of Mary, He becomes of the house and lineage of David, and He is the inheritor of the throne of David.

Further, when the time comes He is to be called by a voice from Heaven, saying, "This is my beloved Son; Hear ye Him," to the public office of a prophet of God and a teacher of the people.

Further, He is a Priest, not after the order of Aaron instituted by Moses, but after the order of Melchisedec, and He must in due time abolish the order of Priesthood which was instituted by Moses, and substitute in the place of it the new Priesthood after His own order.

Again, He must provide a Sacrifice to be continually offered by the New Priesthood, which he will create and put in the place of the Aaronic Priesthood that he will abolish, and in this sacrifice He will Himself be the Victim, as in the words of an old ecclesiastical hymn :—

> He who once to die a Victim
> On the Cross did not refuse,
> Day by day upon our Altar
> That same Sacrifice renews,
> Through His Holy Priesthood's hands,
> Faithful to His last commands.
> (Hymn *Hoste dum victo triumphans*, Caswall's version).

And, last of all, He comes into the world to lay down His life, which had never been forfeited, as a ransom to Divine Justice for the transgressors, and by His death to purchase new conditions of reconciliation with God for all people; that in His blood the kingdom of Heaven may henceforward be opened to all who believe.

Let us see in what way we have now a clear and certain prospect of the future of suffering that awaits the Christ who has thus come into the world as the Son of Mary.

As the Son of David, and as an inheritor of David's Throne, He will unquestionably be an object of hatred to the foreign usurper Herod, whom the Romans have made king over his people, who will certainly seek to murder him even as an infant.

As the Son of Mary nd the reputed Son of Joseph, who are in humble life, he will be despised by his people, who will say, "Is not this the carpenter's son, and whence hath this man these things?" or, as Joseph's brethren said to him, "What, shalt thou be our king?"

As a prophet he is certain to be hated and feared by all

whose vices he must denounce, while they harden their hearts, as He Himself says, "Which of the prophets have your fathers not stoned?"

As a Priest about to abolish the victims of the Mosaic law, and to substitute both a New Priesthood and a more acceptable Sacrifice, He will have all the narrow minded national spirit of His people, jealous of their national privileges, up in arms against Him.

Lastly, as the Divine Victim, who is to purchase new conditions of peace and reconciliation with the justice of God, for all the people of the earth, He has to lay down His life, intending, indeed, to take it again, afterwards. For this end He will choose a form of death in which He will be a spectacle to all the people, not only of His own city and nation, but also to spectators out of all the nations of the earth, who will see Him die on the Cross, the most ignominious indeed of all deaths, but also one which ensures the greatest possible number of witnesses bearing testimony to the truth and verity of His death. He who came to redeem the forfeit of all men by His death will choose a mode of death to the truth of which He would be certain to have the largest possible amount of witnesses; so that it should never be possible afterwards to deny or conceal the fact of His death.

How, therefore, can the Christ, who is sent into the world, as the Son of Mary, to sit on the throne of His Father David as King, who is to preach the kingdom of God and His justice as the Prophet of God to sinners, who is to abolish a national priesthood and local sacrifices, in order to establish as Priest, a New Priesthood and a New Sacrifice for all people, and who is to suffer an ignominious death at the hands of others as a ransom for sinners, in such a way as that He may have the utmost possible number of witnesses of the truth of His death, possibly escape suffering? How is this Christ, thus sent, being the Son of Mary, not to suffer?

Thus the word "sorrowful" in the Holy Rosary proves to be a homily on the text, "O ye fools and slow of heart to believe in all things which the prophets have spoken, *ought* not Christ to have suffered these things, and so to enter into His glory?" We cannot, consequently, as Christians have redemption upon any other terms than the sufferings of the "Christ" who has been sent to redeem us.

Christ the son of Mary *must* suffer, as the Inheritor of the fallen throne of David.

He *must* suffer, as the Prophet of God, who teaches the way of God in truth, and rebukes the sins of men.

He *must* suffer as the Priest, who institutes a new and higher priesthood for all the people of the earth, with its new and clean oblation.

He *must* suffer as the Divine Victim, whose death on the Cross in the sight of all people is the price of our reconciliation with the justice of God, and of the purchase of the terms on which we are to be received into a new Covenant with God. Christ's sorrow is, therefore, the necessary price of our Redemption, and there must be "sorrowful mysteries" in the religion which He teaches us. Blessed for ever be Jesus the Christ, who has thus suffered.

Such is then the popular "Theology" of the word "*Sorrowful*" in the Holy Rosary. If our space permitted, it would be full of instruction to trace the fitness of the special sufferings of Christ, as these are set forth in the five sorrowful mysteries which respectively commemorate, (I.) His Agony and prayer in the Garden of Gethsemane; (II.) His scourging at the pillar; (III.) His being crowned with thorns; (IV.) His carriage of His Cross; and lastly (V.) the manner of His Death on the Cross. But this would lead us outside our proposed limits, which is to put into the minds of our circle of readers the desire to understand how great is the mine of knowledge contained in the Holy Rosary, which lies ready for them to work diligently for themselves to their own great profit, and to inspire them with the sincere purpose both to do this for themselves and also to use all their influence with others to engage them to do the same likewise, remembering that the Christian who continues in wilful ignorance is on the way to displease God and to forfeit the grace of faith.

As long as there are souls in the world to be saved there will always be a huge harvest to be reaped through the sufferings of Christ; and who can doubt but that the Devotion of the Holy Rosary is called to perform a wonderful work for the saving of these souls. To contribute, therefore, in any degree whatsoever, however small, to its extension by the propagation of the Devotion of the Holy Rosary, in company with the mine of saving knowledge connected with it, is a work which we may be quite certain will in no wise lose its reward. In our next number we shall have to treat briefly of the popular theology of the word "Glorious."

THE UNFADING CROWN.

(A Poem for Rosary Sunday.)

WOULDST thou twine a wreath for Mary
  Of flowers that never die,
Of fragrant blossoms wafting
  Their perfumes to the sky?

Say thou, with deep devotion,
  In joy, in grief, and care,
The angels' heaven-born "Ave,"
  The saint's and sinner's prayer.

Go with the Maiden-Mother
  From Nazareth's calm retreat,
O'er bleak Judea's mountains,
  Elizabeth to greet.

Then to the lowly stable,
  With Bethlehem's shepherds, bring
Gifts for the new-born Saviour,
  Thy Infant God and King.

Hear Simeon's song of rapture—
  Behold the ransomed child.
Earth now to Heaven has offer'd
  One victim undefiled.

With Mary seek for Jesus,
  And live those hidden years;
Share all her joys and sorrows;
  Pay tribute of thy tears.

Stand by when Calv'ry's shadows
  Close round her broken heart;
Thy sins, too, were His burden;
  Take thou a mourner's part.

Weep by His tomb, and comfort
  The sorrow-stricken Queen,
Until her eyes "The Risen
  And Glorified have seen."

And when the closing heavens
  Have hid Him from her gaze,
Stay with the childless mother
  Thro' life's remaining days.

Lift up thine eyes, when Jesus
  Lays on His mother's brow
The crown of fadeless splendour
  She wears beside Him now.

Then lay thy lowly chaplet
  Before her throne, nor fear
The beauteous Queen of Angels
  Thy whisper'd words will hear.

And sweeter far than music
  Of earth her voice shall be,
Imploring love and mercy
  From Jesus' heart for thee   E. M. D.

THE VENERABLE ANNA MARIA TAIGI.

OF late years many curious prophecies, all of which claim
more or less fulfilment in recent events and calamities, have
been in circulation amongst Catholics.   People have thought
very differently about them. By some they have been received
with a kind of delight, by others with almost angry disbelief.
The greater number, perhaps, while suspending anything like
actual belief, have regarded them with a good deal of respectful interest, and this feeling exists in a more special manner
with regard to the revelations of the Venerable Anna Maria
Taigi, for many even date the dawn of their devotion to the
Holy Father to one of her remarkable predictions about Pius
the Ninth, realized in his elevation to the Chair of S. Peter
some years after her death, which took place in 1838.
    Quite lately, too, a prophecy that the present Pope would
reign 27 years, and another that three days' darkness, accompanied by pestilence, would reign over the world, have been
attributed to her on what appears to be good authority.   But
we must observe that great caution and reserve have been
used about the publication of her revelations, and that though
they are most carefully attested and preserved at the Vatican,
they will probably not be divulged in any authentic manner
until the final steps are taken for the canonization of this
venerable servant of God.   Perhaps the prayers of those who
may be interested in the following details of her life will hasten
this happy end.
    Anna Maria was born at Sienna, on the 29th of May, 1769,

and baptised in the church of S. John Baptist, in the same
town.   Her parents were then in easy circumstances; but
a few years afterwards her father was ruined by his own fault,
and they were obliged to leave Sienna.   So great was the
poverty to which they were reduced, that little Anna Maria,
then only six years of age, had to walk the whole way from
Sienna to Rome with her father and mother.   Thus early
began the suffering which was to mark nearly the whole of
her life.

If there were neither School Boards nor Educational
Committees at that time, there were, at least, abundant means
in Rome by which the most poverty-stricken child could
obtain a good Christian education, and learn an honest trade.
Anna Maria was placed at the school of a religious community,
called the *Maestre Pie*.   Here her intelligence and amiability
endeared her to the nuns, and she acquired a perfect knowledge of the different kinds of work they taught.   She was
confirmed at the age of eleven, and made her first communion
at thirteen.   After remaining six years with this community
she left them to rejoin her mother, and she was then able to
support herself by her own labour.

She appears to have been very lively and pleasing in
character, and her extreme love of pleasure was at this time a
source of great danger to her.   The grace of God, however,
preserved her from what might easily have proved a fatal
snare.   She seems at all times to have had real love of virtue
joined to good sense, and her biographer* praises her prudence
in determining at this period to enter into matrimony, and to
choose a husband solely for his virtue, and without aspiring
to a higher rank than that to which her family were now
reduced.   He also commends her, rather amusingly, for deciding, moreover, to marry some one " whom she not only *did not
dislike*, but who would be actually likely to gain her affection !"

These good qualities were found in the person of Domenico
Taigi, a Milanese, and one of the under-servants of the house
of Chigi.   After a very few days' acquaintance the marriage
took place on the 7th of January, 1789, in the church of
S. Marcellus, in Rome.   He was a man of good moral
character, but his exacting and difficult temper was a great
source of merit to his wife in after-life.   His humble position
also accorded with the designs of Providence in her regard,

---

* Monseigneur Buquet, Bishop of Heschon.

for she was destined to sanctify herself in a life of practical poverty, always verging upon actual want.

The early part of Anna Maria's married life was certainly far from being saint-like. Without transgressing her duties as a wife in any flagrant manner, she gave herself up with all the ardour of her character to the amusements which are so passionately sought after by the Italians, and especially by the people of Rome. She loved dress, theatres, and entertainments, and shut her eyes to the evil of forgetting God for the world. She had no criminal intentions, it is true, in her excessive love of personal adornment; but vanity, and that instinctive desire of pleasing and shining in the world, which made her lend a willing ear to its flatteries, exposed her to all the dangers of a thoroughly worldly life.

By degrees, however, Anna Maria began to experience that sadness and weariness of heart which are, as it were, the first touch of the grace of God in recalling a soul to himself. She found—what all find sooner or later—that a life of pleasure and dissipation, even if unstained by great crimes, can never give true happiness or satisfy the human heart. Conscience also told her that she had strayed from the path of salvation, and that she could find peace in God alone; but she shut her ears to its voice, and tried to drown remorse in fresh amusements and diversions.

Notwithstanding her infidelity, the mercy of God pursued her in a remarkable manner. One day she entered S. Peter's, decked out as usual, and full of that worldly gaiety which covers so much bitterness of heart. A holy Religious, who was a complete stranger to her, saw her approach, and at the same time heard, as he afterwards attested, the voice of our Lord, saying to him, "Thou seest this woman; one day thou wilt have the care of her soul; thou wilt be the means of her conversion, and she will become a saint." This Religious, who belonged to the Order of the Servites of Mary, was greatly impressed by this extraordinary circumstance. In imitation of the Blessed Virgin, he "kept these words, and considered them in his heart."

The struggle between nature and grace continued in the heart of Anna-Maria. One day, when she was more than usually agitated, she formed a resolution of changing her life and reconciling herself with God. She went into a church, and entered one of the confessionals, where she found a Religious who was hearing confessions.

"Father," she said, "you see at your feet a great sinner!" These were her first and last words.

The priest repulsed her rudely, exclaiming, "Go away; you are not one of my penitents."

Frightened and discouraged, the poor woman departed, and her repentance was delayed.

(To be continued.)

No. III.—THE PRESENT HUMILIATION OF THE SOVEREIGN PONTIFF.

A Homily on the Text:

"As fish are caught with a hook, and as birds are taken in a net so men are caught, in an evil day, when it suddenly comes upon them."— Eccles. ix. 12.

The inspired moralist is here reflecting on the fact that no man knows what his end will be; indeed it is no slight mark of his possessing the gift of wisdom that comes by the grace of God if he knows that his end must come, so far as never to neglect to keep himself prepared for it. "Blessed is he that waketh and keepeth his garments," says the Book of the Apocalypse. The guard which performed garrison-duty during the night on the walls of the Temple were under orders, if they found, on going their night rounds, any sentinel asleep at his post, to set fire to his dress, and to leave him to put the fire out as best he could. Happy, therefore, was the sentinel on the walls of the Temple who kept his garments, and who was never found sleeping at his post.

Such, then, is the model S. John proposes to the Christian, viz., the watchman on the Temple walls, of whom it could be said with truth, "Blessed is he that waketh and keepeth his garments." It will not indeed be given to the Christian to know what his end will be, or how or when it will come, only when it does come it will find him persevering in his habitual practice of "watching and keeping his garments," and in being blessed for so doing.

But the inspired moralist goes on to say, "As fish are caught with a hook and as birds are taken in a net" so men too are caught in an evil time when it suddenly comes upon them. They have failed to understand the need for being thus habitually watchful; so when the evil time comes upon them, it takes them by surprise, and they are caught,—and

the manner in which they get caught is the same, he says, as
that in which the fish are caught with a hook or the bird is
entangled in the net.

But the way in which a fish comes to be caught with a
hook is because it is the art of the fisherman to float before
the eyes of the fish that which the fisherman knows from
his acquaintance with its ways and habits to be proper to
move the appetite of the fish, and to cause it to rise up from
the depth below to seize hold of the object which is thus
floated before his eyes with a purpose. If the fish did but
know of the hook which is prepared for him, do we suppose
he would then rise up from the depth to rush blindly on a
thing cunningly devised for the express end of capturing him
to his ruin, and making a prey of him ? Certainly not; and for
this reason; the art of the fisherman is exclusively directed, in
the first place, to the study of the best way of tempting the fish
to rise up from the deep; and in the next how best to hide from
his sight the hook and line by which he is to be caught and to
become the prey of the spoiler. The fish thinks he sees a
something floating down the stream, which he has only to
seize upon, on the principle of not letting a good thing pass by
him which he will never see again, if he once lets the stream
carry it out of his grasp, and of doing the same as he sees
all the other fish doing; but in that which seemed to him to
be the thing that he sets a value upon, to his surprise, there is
found what he failed to suspect. A line is sharply drawn
tight against him. The unseen hook strikes him; and from
this moment there is a check on his freedom of moving about
that, let him do what he will, sticks to him. In vain he
swims to the right; in vain he swims to the left; the hook
remains, and the hold of the line upon him is not relaxed.
In anger at feeling a sudden unknown restraint, he leaps up out
the water; time after time he tries to shake himself free, but
the strain follows, without mercy, all his movements, and he
finds himself held tight wherever he goes. In despair, he
plunges down to the depth of the stream, but still the same
strain pursues him down to the depth. It does not indeed
seem strong enough to over-master him there and then, nor
does he appear to be conscious that his freedom is gone for
ever; but somehow he finds that he is held tight, and that it
is not an easy matter to break loose. Tired of being held in
check, he comes again to the surface, again he plunges, again
and again he struggles for his freedom against the line that

holds him, but in vain; the line yields indeed to all his convulsive movements, but likewise invariably follows him where-
ever he goes. Again he goes down to the deep, but his
strength is not now what it was at first, and somehow, the
line which at first seemed not to threaten total loss of liberty
tightens and pulls harder upon him than before. He would
gladly now if he could remain in deep water, but, against his
will, he finds himself forced by the strain to come up to
the surface. Again a convulsive struggle to break loose, but
again in vain : the line tightens upon him still more. He
would be glad to return to his accustomed haunts, but he can
no longer do so. His head is held in an element in which he
cannot breathe, and losing more and more of his strength in
each successive struggle, at last he surrenders himself up to his
captor, who drags him to the shore and makes him his prey.
It is the same with the bird that is caught in the net.
The wise moralist already quoted observes, "In vain
is the net spread in the sight of those that have wings."
If the bird could but see the net, where would be the hope
of the fowler? All his hope of prey is centred, not only in
his net, but in his ability to keep his net out of the sight of
his intended prey. The net being kept in the back-ground,
out of sight, there is nothing, then, that the fowler will omit
that is proper to lure on and bring the bird within his reach;
hence the proverbial saying of antiquity—

"Fistula dulce canit volucrem dum decipit auceps."

"The fowler's pipe never plays so sweet a tune as when he
is deceiving the bird." When the old serpent came into
Paradise to catch Eve in his net, it would never have
answered his purpose to have let her into his secret, and to
have said to her, "Now, what I want with you and what I
am come here for is to persuade you to fall into my net, in
order to have you bound fast in the meshes of a sin that will
cling to you and to all that will, at any time, be born from
you, for ever. From this sin nothing that you or Adam can
ever do for yourselves will be able to set you free. You must
both of you be my prey, and I must have you both safe in my
net." The old serpent knew well that he had to keep his net
out of sight; and when he said to his prey, "You shall be as
Gods, knowing good and evil," he omitted to say what would
be the consequence of their attempting to become as Gods.
In vain, then, would the net have been spread in sight of the
bird; "but as fish are caught with a hook, and birds are

caught with a net, so men are caught in an evil day;" and as this could come to pass even in Paradise, as Eve and all born of her have reason to know to their cost, in the very abundance of peace and prosperity, much more may the same happen, as the wise moralist says, "in the evil day, when it suddenly comes upon them," and finds them not all at once prepared to understand how evil the day really is, and how deadly is the snare that is set for them. The only difference will, perhaps, be, that the fish as a victim is the more honest of the two. The fish is usually seen to be conscious that it is caught, and it accordingly honestly surrenders itself as prey to its captor; while, when men are caught, they are seldom equally honest, and commonly try their utmost to deceive themselves either by imagining that they are still in possession of their liberty, or by formally concluding that their servitude is the preferable condition. There is, however, one power in the world which, however evil the day may be, and however artfully the hook may be concealed, and how skillfully soever the net may be kept out of sight, can never be either caught with the hook or involved in the meshes of the net. This is the See of Rome, with its occupant, the sacred person of the Sovereign Pontiff of the Universal Church and the Vicar of Jesus Christ. Here is a power that the Devil can never deceive. He can, indeed, as he has often done, take advantage of the occasion furnished to him by the sins of men to raise storms against the Vicar of Jesus Christ, by means of which he has more than once driven him into exile from his own city, or even he may, at times, be able to hand him over to the prisons, or even to the scaffold of persecutors, who, before now, have put many among the Vicars of Jesus Christ to death with their swords. All such deeds as these he has done, and may do again; but one thing he can never do, and that is, he cannot deceive him.

The times latterly have been for the Sovereign Pontiff what in the words of the wise moralist may, indeed, be called "the evil day," and the evil day has supervened suddenly enough. The unprincipled invader has come, disguising the hook and concealing the net, and has said, "We are good Catholics; we have the deepest respect for your august dignity, and your most sacred person; here are the treasures which we bring you for the supply of your needs." The Vicar of Christ leaves them to take their treasures back by the way by which they brought them. They next make a

parade of legislating publicly to provide, as they would have
him believe, guarantees for the security of his sacred person and
authority; and the Vicar of Jesus Christ replies, "You may
make guarantees, and you may unmake them. What you cannot do is to deceive me by them." Counsellors who believe
themselves to be good Catholics, gifted with the spirit of
wisdom, come to him, and entreat him, for the peace of the
whole body of the faithful, to reconcile himself with the
power which has so violently invaded his rights, and they
go away as they came, to learn, indeed, if they have enough
humility, that the Vicar of Jesus Christ is not left to depend
upon the stray counsel and advice that comes to him by the
wayside.

Thus, although the day is evil enough, and has supervened
suddenly enough, still, for the edification of the faithful, and
for their guidance by the light of an example which is set,
so to speak, on a height from whence it can be seen and contemplated by the whole world, the Vicar of Jesus shows
us how to act towards the various tempting deceptions that
are sure to lie the thicker and the more frequent in our path
the more evil the day is, and the more suddenly it supervenes.
The Vicar of Jesus Christ plainly shows us by his example
that he will not trust the gifts and subsidies of the Italian
Civil Government, knowing very well the hook that is concealed in them, with which "men are caught as fish are
caught with the hook," knowing very well the presence of
the net into the meshes of which these gifts are intended to
be the lure and the decoy. Such is the gift of wisdom that
is given directly from above to the Vicar of Jesus Christ;
while, as regards the remainder of the body of the faithful,
the gift of wisdom is given to them through the light of his
example. We may know very well, if we will take the least
time to reflect, that in almost all the various existing civil
governments there reigns in our time one and the same spirit
of anti-Catholic unbelief, against which the Catholics in their
respective countries have precisely similar reasons for being
on their guard, as the Pope has for distrusting and being on
his guard against the Italian Government. They have precisely the same reasons as the Pope for doing all that is requisite for their social well-being by temporal means, not obtained on conditions in which the hook is concealed, and
behind which lies hid the net, from either of which the
chances of escape are, to say the least, extremely precarious.

But this is precisely the nature of the caution contained in the words of the inspired wisdom. It is when "the day is evil, and when it supervenes suddenly," that then men are caught as fishes are caught with a hook, and as birds are taken in the net. May God in his mercy grant to us the grace to profit by the example of wisdom which we see shining forth for our guidance in the acts of the Holy See; and inasmuch as fish sometimes escape from the hook and birds from the net, may He grant us, if there be need, also the courage and the strength to burst through whatever bonds wherewith we may have unwittingly suffered ourselves to have been bound, to the hindrance of the work which God expects from us.

ON THE VARIOUS INDULGENCES GRANTED TO THE DEVOTION OF THE HOLY ROSARY.

THE indulgences granted at various times by the Holy See to the Devotion of the Holy Rosary may be conveniently classed under four heads.

I.—The first are those attached to the simple recitation of the Rosary by any one of the great body of the faithful, of whatever nation, age, sex, or condition, throughout the entire world, on the mere twofold condition—First, of using a suitable chaplet or string of Rosary beads which have been blessed by a priest of the Dominican Order, or by another who has received the requisite faculties either from the Dominican General or from the Pope; and, secondly, of meditating upon each of the fifteen mysteries successively, as the prayers are recited upon the beads of the chaplet. The Pope who gave these indulgences was Benedict XIII., and the date of the Bull is 13th of April, 1726. As most ordinary prayer-books contain the requisite particulars as to the nature and extent of these indulgences, they need not be specified here.

II.—The favours above referred to are granted independently of any condition of forming part of an association in which the members procure their names to be entered on a register binding themselves to the rules and duties of the association; but, from the first beginning of the devotion, the Holy Rosary has not failed to be a power in the Church, associating the vast multitudes of the faithful of different countries and races into the "Confraternity of the Rosary," which confraternity dates from the time of S. Dominic himself, and in membership with which the faithful alone obtain the full and perfect measure of tho favours of the Church that have been granted to the devotion of the Rosary.

III.—Next to the favours granted to the Confraternity of the Rosary, are those granted to the Association of the Perpetual Rosary by the reigning Sovereign Pontiff Pius IX., in a Brief dated the 12th April, 1867, the text of which we hope to give in full in a succeeding number.

IV.—Fourthly, and lastly, are the indulgences granted by the predecessor of Pius IX., Gregory XVI., to the associations which bear the name of the "Living Rosary."

As very many of our readers belong to these Circles of the Living Rosary, it will be interesting to them to know in what terms the Holy See approves of their association, and encourages them to persevere in the zeal and fervour of their pious undertaking. In our next number, therefore, we may promise them a translation of the Bull "Benedicentes," in which Gregory XVI. formally approves of the living Rosary (Jan. 27, 1832).

A BRIEF HISTORICAL NOTICE OF THE ARCH CONFRATERNITY OF OUR LADY QUEEN OF THE ANGELS,

FIRST ESTABLISHED IN THE PARISH OF POURVOURVILLE, NEAR TOULOUSE, IN FRANCE, BY FR. DE BRAY, S.J., AND OF THE SUBSEQUENT SPREAD OF THE DEVOTION INTO MANY DIFFERENT COUNTRIES.

OUR readers will be deeply interested in the ensuing brief account of a religious work which has been recently founded in France by a Father of the Society of Jesus, and which is rapidly spreading itself over the whole world, giving the encouraging hope of its being found to possess a most remarkable degree of power in opposing a barrier to the progress of impiety and unbelief, and in reanimating the drooping courage of the faithful.

The circumstances under which the august Queen of the Angels first made known her will, shortly related, are as follows :—

About sixteen years ago, on the night intervening between the 21st and 22nd of July, 1856, at the moment when the clock of the Castle of Belleve, in the district of Toulouse (south of France), was striking midnight, a man in the prime of life, by name Mary Frederic de Bray, lay at the point of death in one of the rooms of that beautiful building, and nothing was looked for but his breathing his last breath.

For thirty years he had been a sufferer from a complaint which had latterly become further complicated by three other diseases equally fatal. Every means, ordinary and extraordinary, had been tried. The most celebrated physicians of Paris, Montpellier, Turin, and Florence had been consulted. Medical skill had avowed itself at fault, and God Himself appeared to turn a deaf ear to every prayer. But just as he seemed about to die, he said to the august Queen of the Angels, who stood by him assisting him in his last moments,

"I MAKE MY VOW."

This vow had been demanded by the Holy Virgin as the condition of his cure, and by the terms of it the sick man bound himself to go on a pilgrimage to "Our Lady of the Angels" at Assisi, in the States of the Church. Hardly had he made the vow when, to the great amazement of his mother and other distressed relatives, he rose up perfectly cured. The family physician, who had been in constant attendance, could but exclaim

"IT IS A VERITABLE MIRACLE."

Some days afterwards, when summoned by his grace, Mgr. Mioland, the Archbishop of Toulouse, who sought to know the details of his cure, he replied to the inquiries of the illustrious prelate, saying, "My Lord, I am ready to attest my statement, and even, if called upon, to sign it with my blood."

The intelligence of the miraculous cure being made known to Pope Pius IX. by one of the prelates of the Roman Court, he was pleased to grant to the parish of Pouvourville the favour of the indulgence of the "Portiuncula," which was joyfully celebrated the same year in the church of the parish, the whole surrounding neighbourhood taking part in it with the greatest fervour.

The details of the subsequent entry of Mary Frederic de Bray into the Society of Jesus are for the present not made public, but we find the subject of the miraculous cure of the 22nd of July, 1856, appearing in the year 1864 as a professed Father of the Society, animated with the desire to found a congregation which should give especial honour to our Lady Queen of the Angels, and be capable of being extended over

every part of the world, thereby opening to all an easy access
to the graces which the Queen of Heaven has been used to
bestow with so great abundance upon those who have already
placed their confidence in her and have implored her succour.

The object of this association was to be, to honour in an
especial manner the most Blessed Virgin as Queen of the
Angels, and to obtain through her intercession, (I.) The
triumph of the Church throughout all the world ; (II.) the
conversion of sinners.   In other words, to spread and extend
the kingdom of Jesus Christ, to procure an abundance of
spiritual succour, not only to the associates themselves, but
to all besides who might be recommended to them to render
thanks to God and His only Son, Jesus Christ, for all blessings received, and this through the intercession of our Lady
Queen of the Angels.   Such was the plan of the person to
whom God had inspired this holy desire in question, and
great as it was, and destined to encounter difficulties neither
few in number nor small, yet through trust in the protection
of Mary it has been crowned in the event with the most
complete success.

His Grace the Archbishop of Toulouse no sooner heard of
it than he gave it his approbation in a public letter dated
June, 1864, and again on the 8th of December in the same
year he gave a formal written approbation to the statutes of
the congregation.   On the 8th of December, 1866, and again
on the 21st of February, 1867, His Holiness the Pope deigned
to approve of the congregation, verbally expressing, at the
same time, the desire for its extension throughout the entire
world.

At length, on the 3rd of March, 1871, His Holiness
Pius IX., in his love for the Holy Trinity and for souls, erected
the Confraternity of Our Lady of the Angels of Pouvourville
into an Arch-Confraternity.   Thus (glory be given to Mary,
Queen of the Angels !) the pious desires of its founder, the
Rev. Fr. de Bray, and those of the associates of the congregation, received their fulfilment.

Wonderful, certainly, are the ways of the Providence of
God !

[Limited by space, we regret to be obliged to reserve to
our succeeding number further details with reference to the
Statutes and to the Indulgences granted to this remarkable
Arch-Confraternity.]

ANECDOTES.

A Court Physician not ashamed of his Rosary.—The Count Malet, an old soldier of the first Napoleon, who afterwards became a priest, was confined to his room by sickness. Dr. Masse came, together with his father, to pay him a visit in his sick-room. As they were engaged in conversation upon indifferent subjects, the door was opened, and a servant announced the arrival of the physician in attendance, Dr. Recamier, whose name, at that time, was celebrated all over France. After courteously saluting all who were in the room, the physician approached the bed of his patient, and, after having made all the customary inquiries, he proscribed some change of medicine, and was preparing to take his departure, when, with the action of a person who appeared suddenly to have recalled something of importance to his mind, he laid down his hat and cane on a chair, and, rumaging in his pocket, he exclaimed, " What is the matter with my head ? I was just about to forget an important thing." " What can it be ?" " My dear sir, I have had an accident." " Nonsense ; you must be joking." " No, not at all ; a real accident, which you are just the man to set right when you get better." " Let us hear." " Well, then, there has been a fracture—something for you to mend, which you can do in five minutes when you get better." And as he was speaking thus, the celebrated professor of medicine, the physician of the Court and of all the nobility of France, the author of so many learned treatises, pulled out of his pocket, and showed with an air of triumph—guess what!—a string of Rosary beads. The learned theologian Masse, who relates the anecdote, adds, " I must confess I stood mute with surprise. But the celebrated physician recalled me from my amazement, by turning towards us, and saying with a smile, ' Why, of course, I say my beads, and when a patient's case perplexes me, and I am at my wits' end to know what to prescribe, I have recourse to her who is called '' Salus infirmorum,'' and she always aids me. It is not always an easy thing for me to say the whole chaplet all through, but I do what I can. I get into my carriage, lay hold of my Rosary, and when I come to my patient, I leave it to take it up again afterwards.' My father and myself," adds Dr. Masse, " approved highly of his practice, which rather put us to the blush. The Count took the string of beads in his

hands, which he promised to repair and give them back in
good condition, and Dr. Recamier went away, leaving us full
of admiration at his faith." The Holy Rosary, then, like the
wisdom from above, is good for all, and fit for all emergencies.
It is for this reason that it has been not only the favourite
devotion of saints but equally of men of the world distinguished by their merit and social position. To cite only a
single instance, we will mention Joseph Haydn, one of the
greatest musicians known in Europe in the last century. He
was very devout to the Rosary, and used to recite it on his
journeys, never allowing himself to be hindered by the ridi-
cule of the profane or the accidents of his journey.

RECORD OF EVENTS.

Copy of a Letter addressed to Monsieur Deville, Secretary of
the Arch-Confraternity of Our Lady of the Angels, by
Lady M. Murray, Directress of the Association at Cal-
cutta, relating to the miraculous cure of her daughter
Isabella, at the point of death :—

"Toulouse, June 14, 1872.

"Monsieur,—I have called to-day (Friday) at the residence of the
Jesuit Fathers, about eleven o'clock in the morning. The Rev. Father
De Bray not being in, I asked the brother porter where I could find him.
He replied, 'Go to M. Deville, Grande Rue Nazareth, No. 16; perhaps you
will find him there.' I rang there several times at the first landing
(rez de chaussée), but no one came; so I returned to the hotel for breakfast. About one o'clock I came again, and this time, before ringing at
the door, I asked a woman who was passing if it was true you lived
here. 'No, no,' she answered, 'he does not live here at all.' At loss what
to do, I went again to the Fathers, where I was told that Father De Bray
was come back, but that he was so tired that it was impossible to see
him. I then decided to return to the hotel in order to write to you, for
we were to take the train the same day for the Pyrenees.

"The following is the reason of my writing to you. I have had six
children, and I have lost five, who I hope already enjoy the vision of
God. The only child who remains is a young girl of nineteen years of
age, good and pure as an angel, suffering now for two years from the
same complaint which has carried off all her brothers and sisters. She was
all but at the point of breathing her last on Wednesday, 12th instant,
when we were at Agen, coming from Bourdeaux, on our way to Lourdes
by easy stages, and while we were reciting the prayers for the dying (I
have omitted to say that my daughter had just then received the last
Sacraments), in the midst of the tears and sobbing of my mother, my
sister, and my husband, we saw the door of the room open, and a priest
came in, who said to us, 'My children, what are you weeping for?'

"'What for?' I replied in a paroxysm of grief; 'do you not see that
my daughter is dying, if indeed she is not already dead?'

" ' No, no; do not weep; but have confidence.'

" Whereupon, taking the hand of my daughter, who had ceased to give any sign of life, he raised his eyes upwards, and, after some moments of prayer, said to her, ' My daughter, in the Name of the Lord Jesus, and in the Name of the Immaculate Queen of the Angels, rise up and walk.'

" At the same instant my daughter opened her eyes, sat up upon her seat, and threw herself into my arms.

" Describe my joy I cannot. As regards the priest, he had disappeared. No one in the house had seen him either come in or go away. When I had gone to make inquiries, and had come back to my daughter and family full of joy and saying, ' I have asked all the people of the house, and no one has either seen him come in or go out,' Isabella exclaimed, ' How would you have any one see him, mamma? He is Father De Bray.'

" ' But then he must be in Agen,' said my husband.

" ' No, papa; he is at Toulouse.'

" ' But how, child, would you have him to be both at Toulouse and Agen at one and the same time.'

" ' Ah, papa, that is the secret of God.'

" Thereupon my husband went out to make inquiries by the telegraph at Toulouse if Father De Bray was really there. Towards evening the answer was brought back that Father De Bray had never quitted Toulouse for several months.

" ' But,' said my husband to Isabella during dinner, ' how came you to know it was Father De Bray?'

" ' I learnt it the moment I was about to breathe my last. The Blessed Virgin appeared to me, and said, " My child, have confidence. I shall send you the Director of my Arch-Confraternity of our Lady of the Angels; he will call you back to life." Immediately I returned to life, and when I opened my eyes I saw the Father, and the only words which I heard from him were these, " I am the messenger of our Lady of the Angels, her ambassador on earth. I am Father De Bray." '

" The above is the reason why I so much wished to see you, not having been able to see Father De Bray, and if I have not sent this letter to him, the reason is because I have been told that no direct correspondence with him was permitted.

" Be pleased to present to Father De Bray my respects and the homage of my most profound gratitude, and to accept the assurance of the distinguished sentiments with which I remain your obedient servant,
                                                              " M. MURRAY."*

We have received some most interesting particulars of the remarkable life and beautiful death of Br. Mary Aloysius Wragg, a Tertiary of the Dominican Order, who died at an early age on the 3rd of August, at Nottingham. We hope to be able to give the account in full in our November number.

---

* The above letter has come into our hands from a source which perfectly guarantees its genuineness and authenticity.

THE

𝔐onthly 𝔐agazine of the 𝔥oly 𝔥osary.

NEW SERIES.

| No. 4.] | NOVEMBER. | [A.D. 1872. |

No. VII.—THE SCIENCE OF THE HOLY ROSARY.

The Popular Theology of the Word "Glorious."

As there is a whole system of Theology in the word "JOY-FUL," recalling to the mind the entire of the sad history of the transgression of Adam and Eve in Paradise, and the long night of sorrow to which at length succeeded the joy of the Redemption accomplished through Mary, the Ark of the New Covenant; and as there is a whole system of Theology in the word "SORROWFUL," declaratory of the causes which made the work of our Redemption by Jesus Christ a work to Him of Sorrow and Death, voluntarily submitted to by One who, for the Joy that was set before Him, endured the Cross, despising the Shame,—again so there is a whole body of popular Theology in the Word "GLORIOUS," and it appertains indispensably to the right understanding of the "Rosary," to be possessed of a competent knowledge of the doctrine that is contained in it.

Now, if we briefly run through the five Mysteries which bear the name of Glorious, we find that, in a certain sense, they are all "joyful."

Of the first, which is the Resurrection from the Dead, the Church sings, "In Thy Resurrection, O Lord, let the Heavens and the Earth rejoice." Of the second, the Ascension into Heaven, Our Lord says, "If ye loved Me ye would 're-joice,' because I said I go away from you." In the third Mystery we learn of the coming and abiding presence of One who fills the hearts of the faithful with "joy and gladness." In the fourth, we are invited to rejoice with the Angels, because Mary, their Queen, is assumed into Heaven; and thé fifth and last Mystery proclaims the "Coronation" of Mary and the joy of all the Saints. And yet, notwithstanding the unanimous voice of all lands and all times, does not give the name of Joyful to these Mysteries, but the Name of "GLORIOUS." There must plainly then be a doctrine contained in the name Glorious which would not be adequately expressed by the name of Joyful, but which demands the Name of GLORIOUS, and cannot be expressed by any other. What is this doctrine?

When the Angels of God were for the first time admitted to see the Work of Creation, the Book of Job says "the morning stars praised Him, and all the Sons of God made a joyful melody (Job, xxxviii. 7). This universal jubilee had been preceded by no previous suffering or affliction, and it is thought that on this occasion they sang the following Psalm:

> Praise the Lord of Heaven, praise Him in the Highest.
> Praise Him all ye Angels, praise Him all ye Hosts of His.
> He spoke the Word and all was made;
> He gave command and they were created.

Next in degree to the pure joy of intelligent creation on beholding the wonders of the Works of God, and on seeing the good gifts with which their Creator has surrounded their life, will come the Joy of Redemption, or the delight with which fallen creatures hail the approach of a Deliverer, and welcome His coming.

It is this latter joy of which the Five Joyful Mysteries of the Rosary contain the expression. And so great is this joy, that even the very Angels in Heaven came down to testify their delight at seeing the Infant Deliverer of men in the Arms of His Virgin Mother Mary, singing in chorus, "Glory to God in the Highest, and on Earth peace to men of good will."

The Joy of the Glorious Mysteries, however, is not the same with either of the foregoing. There is an element in them which is entirely peculiar to themselves. It is neither joy for the wonders of creation nor simply the joy of the liberated captive on seeing himself unexpectedly liberated. There is more in it than either of these; there is the exultation in it over a deadly enemy who is laid low; there is the glory and triumph of those who are on the side of the Conqueror, over their fierce and merciless adversary, who is confounded for ever. Such is the Christian Joy of the "Glorious Mysteries." And we may see this exemplified in the way of figure in many striking events of the old law. Thus, to take a single instance; in the case of the delivery of Israel out of the hands of the Egyptians by the closing in of the waters of the Red Sea over the Egyptian host; the song of triumph which Moses sang on the shores of the sea brings out in the strongest relief this feeling of a conqueror's exultation over the fallen foe; and the triumph and jubilee of the victory over the defeated pride of the adversary:

"The enemy said, I will pursue after and overtake; I will divide the spoils, and my soul shall have its fill.

"I will draw my sword, and my hand shall stay them.

"Thy breath went forth, and the sea covered them. They sank like lead in the mighty waters.

"Lord, who is like unto Thee among the strong; who is like unto Thee glorious in Holiness, doing wondrous things." (Exodus, xv. 9.)

If space permitted, we might also quote the similar songs of triumph of Debbora and Judith.

Again, the prophet Isaias, under the figure of the fallen Empire of Babylon, describes a kind of forlorn jubilee of exultation, extending even to the lost themselves, who take up their parable to rejoice over the fall of the prince of pride that sought to exalt himself above God:

"How art thou fallen from Heaven, O Lucifer; thou Son of the Morning, how art thou fallen to the earth that didst wound the nations.

"And thou saidest in thy heart, I will ascend into heaven; I will exalt my throne above the stars of God; I will sit in the mountain of the covenant.

"I will ascend above the height of the clouds, I will be like unto the Most High.

"Is this then He that troubled the earth, that shook kingdoms, that made the world a wilderness, and destroyed the cities? How art thou fallen!" (Isaias, xiv.)

But if the fall of defeated pride is a just cause of such a forlorn kind of congratulation as at the best that must be which can be supposed possible to those who themselves are sharers in the fall, with how much more of truth and justice is the same fall of the adversary not a cause of joy and triumph to those who were marked out to be the very victims of his pride and malice, and who are now delivered from the cruel gripe that sought to seize them. "He boasted," sings Judith, "that he would set my borders on fire and kill my young men with the sword; that he would make my infants a prey and lead my virgins captive, but the Almighty hath slain him, and hath delivered him into the hand of a woman."

The Devil, who boasted that he would lead the whole race of Adam captive, has been overthrown by Jesus through the Cross of Calvary, and the Almighty has delivered his spoils into the hand of a woman, the Blessed Virgin Mother of God, whom Jesus, her Son, has assumed into Heaven, and whom

He has crowned Queen over the whole Blessed company of Angels and Saints. As Heirs of Redemption, then, in the Glorious Mysteries, we glory over the fall of our great adversary, we take up the parable of the partners of his condemnation, and we re-echo their cry:

"O Lucifer, thou Son of the Morning, how art thou fallen, thou that said I will be like unto the Most High; how art thou fallen to the depths of Hell."

As Redeemed by the Blood of Jesus, so we say to our Lord and Deliverer, "How hast Thou humbled Thyself for us, and hast become obedient to death, even the death of the Cross; and how hath God highly exalted Thee, and given Thee a Name which is above every name, that at the name of Jesus every knee should bow of things on earth and things under the earth." (Phil. ii. 8.) Children of Mary, by the deed of gift spoken from the Cross in the gracious words, "Lady, behold Thy Son," we say to our Mother, in these Glorious Mysteries, "How hath God had respect unto the lowliness of His handmaiden, and hath exalted thee above Angels and Archangels, above thrones and dominions, and above all the host of heaven, and hath set upon Thy head the royal diadem" as Queen of all Creation.

Such is the Christian Joy of the GLORIOUS MYSTERIES. It is the joy of the great Christian victory which obtains for its fruit our Redemption and the restoration to us of our forfeited inheritance. The Glorious Mysteries celebrate the triumph of the leader and Captain of our Salvation in the glory and benefits of whose victory we are admitted to participate; and they proclaim the glory and exaltation of the lady whom we honour as the "cause of our joy" in the Joyful Mysteries, as an earnest of the reward which is promised to us if we remain faithful in the discharge of our obligations, and continue to conduct ourselves as becomes fellow citizens of the Saints, and co-heirs of the Kingdom of God and His Christ.

(To be continued.)

THE VENERABLE ANNA MARIA TAIGI.

AFTER the cruel rebuff Anna Maria had received, several months passed away before she had courage to make a second attempt to approach the Sacrament of Penance. It happened, at length, that she felt one day irresistibly drawn to enter the Church of S. Marcellus, and there make her peace with God. Not knowing what confessor to choose, she entered, as before, the first confessional in which she saw a priest. It was the same Religious who had met her at S. Peter's. "So you have come at last," were his first words, and we may imagine the feelings of wonder, contrition, and ardent love which filled her soul when he made known to her the interior revelation he had received from God in her regard. Under the guidance of this holy and charitable director, she made a general confession, and began the entire reform of her past life. With the consent of her husband, she renounced all vanity in dress, and wore nothing but poor and mean clothes, and her exercises of penitential atonement for her sins were performed with a fervour which only required to be kept within due bounds. These good dispositions were extraordinarily increased in the following manner. She was one day listening to her mother, who, in reading aloud a book of devotions, came to a passage which treated of the Last Judgment; at this, the soul of Anna Maria became, as it were, pierced through with the love of God and contrition; her heart seemed to her to be opened, her eyes became fountains of tears, and she was inundated with the ineffable delights of the love of God, joined to the desire of penance; while she heard the voice of her Spouse saying to her, "Behold, O daughter, O beloved spouse, the Father who has never ceased to seek thee, and who hast chosen thee for sanctity from thy mother's womb. Thou must never love anyone but me, and I will be thy guide. This is why I have never abandoned thee in the midst of the vanities of the world, and have preserved thee from so many dangers, and death; for I love thee tenderly, and one day thou shalt know who it is that now speaks to thee."

From this time her soul was consumed with divine love. Her penances were redoubled; torrents of tears gushed from her eyes, and in her horror for having offended God, and hatred for her sins, she would strike her face against the ground with such violence that blood would flow from her mouth, according to the testimony of one of her confessors, until she was prevented, after a time, from so doing.

The conversion of Anna Maria is a most consoling proof of what sometimes appears the startling doctrine of theologians, that God not only forgives, but is ready to unite himself at once to the repentant soul, so that it may aspire to any height of sanctity; and that when He does forgive He is the God of the perfect, and that soul is as though it had never sinned. "When a sinner," says Taulerus, "rising from his sins and turning himself entirely away from them, resolves to serve God perpetually, and to live in Him alone; then that Eternal and Infinite Goodness shows Himself as loving to him as if he had never fallen into sin. For He perfectly forgives him all his sins, though they should be as many as those of all mankind, provided he repents from the heart, principally because he knows they displease God. . . . In fine, whatever familiarity and whatsoever revelation of His secrets God ever imparted to anyone, He is now able to impart to such a converted sinner. For God is the God of the present; and such as He finds anyone to be, such He takes him up and assumes to Himself."

These words seem literally verified in Anna Maria. After years of thorough worldliness and sinful negligence, she no sooner responded with her whole heart to the first graces of her conversion, than she was favoured with those extraordinary and permanent supernatural gifts, the full scope and extent of which the Church will one day be called upon to decide.

Equally wonderful is the reflection that these raptures, ecstacies, and prophetic inspirations were vouchsafed not to a cloistered nun, nor even to a holy virgin or widow, living in peaceful seclusion from the world, but to an active, hard-working wife and mother, continually struggling with poverty and the cares of bringing up a large family. We shall see, later on, that her domestic virtues fitted her to be a perfect model for all daughters, wives, and mothers; it would appear indeed that Divine Providence destined her life to be, as it were, a visible and palpable realization of the great truth that perfect sanctity is to be found in the fulfilment of the ordinary duties of family life, performed in union with the will of God. And we cannot resist the feeling that our dear Lord intended to manifest how precious in His sight are the most trivial actions done in this spirit, where we see that it was precisely at the moments when this pious woman was occupied with the most lowly and commonplace cares of her household, that her celestial Spouse was wont to appear to her, and that she heard the sweetness of His divine voice. Vainly did she carry on an incessant but useless struggle to continue her domestic occupations without falling into constant ecstacies of divine love. " Beautiful was it to see," says one who knew intimately the secrets of this great soul, "how, after a time, she could no longer resist the heavenly attraction, but would remain up-right, motionless as a statue, and entirely ravished out of her-self. Sometimes these transports obliged her to sit down suddenly, or to lean against the wall, to prevent herself from falling to the ground; there she would stay, deprived of the use of her senses, and entirely absorbed in God."

Sometimes, also, when at table, taking her meals, she would become motionless as if struck by lightning, without so much as moving her eyelids. It may easily be believed that this state of things was far from being understood by her family. From her husband, indeed, as well as from her children, her wonderful graces and favours were, by the inscrutable designs of Providence, always hidden. At such times, indeed, her husband would sometimes become uneasy when she did not answer his rough calls, and think that she was struck by apo-plexy; and when she had come to herself with her sweet joyous look, as if just awakened from a peaceful slumber, he would scold her and ask what she meant by sleeping at meals. Her eldest daughter, who had more intelligence, used to sus-pect that she was praying at these times, but the youngest would weep and exclaim, " Mamma is dead ! Mamma is dead !" She said, indeed, that when they tried to move her she gave no sign of life.

The same thing also happened very often in the evening, when the family were assembled round the domestic altar to recite the Rosary, and were obliged to wait until she came to herself. Her husband would then angrily reproach her, and tell her it was a shame for her to go to sleep even at her prayers, when she had the whole night to repose.

These states of rapture and excesses of spiritual consolation lasted during many years, and were so often repeated that she would lovingly complain to her Divine Spouse, and entreat Him, with holy simplicity, to remember that she was the mother of a family, with duties to perform, and to withdraw the delights of His presence. But it was always in vain. She even tried outward distractions without effect. For she said

the most simple objects of creation so filled her with proofs of
the Divine wisdom and goodness, that all nature spoke to her
that language so well known by those who love God alone.
Consequently the efforts she made to divert her mind only
increased her union with God, and riveted the chains of
heavenly love which entranced her soul. For this reason she
did not dare trust herself to walk, even in the streets, without
a friend to lean upon; the song of a bird, the scent of a
flower, even the lightest breeze of air was more than sufficient to ravish her soul in God,

When these ecstacies happened in public places they were a
source of great suffering to this servant of God. When she
received Holy Communion, for instance, her transports became
so irrepressible, that it seemed as if her soul were on the
point of leaving the body, and the persons around her were
filled with astonishment. Some admired her fervour, and
would stay to recommend themselves to her prayers, while
others would consider her either obsessed by the devil, or a
hypocrite. She saw how displeasing these rash judgments
were to God, and both charity and humility caused her deep
distress. She would watch for an opportunity of leaving the
church unobserved, and then hasted home full of timidity and
confusion. At one time she tried to avoid notice by making
her Communions in different places; for this she was reproached
by her Divine Spouse, who commanded her not to heed the
vain words of men, and assured her she was not responsible
for their sins against charity. She returned, therefore, in
obedience, to her accustomed Church of the Madonna della
Pietà, in the Piazza Colonna. Our Lord permitted her patience
to be exercised, not only by criticism but by grave insults.
The Communion cloth was snatched from her to oblige her
to leave the church, and a Priest one day even passed by her,
when about to receive, without giving her Communion. On
another occasion an unconsecrated host was given to her, of
which she was instantly conscious.

One of her confessors, who has given authentic testimony
on many facts of her life, declares that he himself witnessed
what he has related concerning her states of ecstacy and the
suspension of her bodily powers and senses after giving her
Holy Communion, and at other times. He relates an instance
which occurred while they were making the pilgrimage of
the Seven Churches with Cardinal Pedicini, and he saw her
become motionless and in a state of transport. "I mentally

commanded her," he says, "to resume the journey, and she
immediately, under the force of obedience, rose out of her
ecstacy, and broke off her heavenly intercourse in which the
most hidden secrets of the Church, and of those for whom
she prayed, were ordinarily imparted to her."

The effect of these sensible graces was to fill Anna Maria
with humility, fear of illusion, and an ardent desire to participate in the sufferings of her crucified Lord. We shall see
that her longing for the Cross was soon to be abundantly
gratified.

(To be continued.)

ALL SOULS' DAY.

(Prayers for the dead.)

O vos fideles animæ.

Ye souls of the faithful who sleep in the Lord
    But as yet are shut out from your final reward;
Oh, would I could lend you assistance to fly
    From your prison below to your palace on high.

O Father of mercies, Thine anger withold,
    These works of Thy hands in Thy mercy behold:
Too oft from Thy path they have wandered aside,
    But Thee, their Creator, they never denied.

O tender Redeemer, their misery see,
    Deliver the souls that were ransom'd by Thee;
Behold how they love Thee despite of their pain,
    Restore them, restore them to favour again.

O Spirit of Grace, O consoler divine,
    See how for Thy Presence they longingly pine!
Ah, then, to enliven their sadness descend,
    And fill them with peace and joy to the end.

O Mother of Mercy, dear soother of grief,
    Send thou to their torments a balmy relief;
Attemper the rigour of Justice severe,
    And soften their pains with a pitying tear.

Ye Patrons who watched o'er their safety below,
    Oh think how they need your fidelity now;
And stir all the Angels and saints of the sky
    To plead for the souls that upon you rely.

All ye too who honour the Saints and their Head,
   Remember, remember to pray for the dead ;
And they in return from their misery free'd,
   To you will be friends in the hour of your need.
      (Printed by permission of the Author.)   F. CASWALL.

THE MONTH OF NOVEMBER SACRED TO THE PIOUS PRACTICE OF PRAYERS FOR THE DEAD.

A HOMILY ON THE TEXT:

" It is therefore a holy and salutary thought to pray for the dead that they may be loosed from their sins."—2 *Machabees*, xii. 46.

THE month of November is by a holy and excellent custom of the faithful in an especial manner sacred to the pious exercise of prayers for the dead, and the custom, of course, reposes first on the general truth conveyed in the words of the sacred Scripture above quoted : " It is a holy and salutary thought to pray for the dead that they may be loosed from their sins;" and secondly, on the circumstance that on the second day of November, viz., on the day after the solemn celebration of the Feast of all Saints, the whole Church keeps a day of solemn commemoration of the Souls of all the Faithful departed, from whence the piety of the faithful has gradually built up the excellent practice of treating the whole month of November as in an especial manner sacred to the pious and holy exercise of prayer for the repose of the souls of the departed.

There is always a great and precious value in a good custom, and we can seldom do anything better than seek to introduce a good custom where it either does not exist or has fallen through, or endeavour to strengthen and invigorate by all means in our power what is already in existence. As returning November, then, brings round its annual memory of the departed, we cannot do better than seek to reinvigorate and refresh our minds with considering anew some of the principal reasons which render it a "holy and a salutary thought to pray for the dead, that they may be loosed from their sins."

This thought we must consider is holy and salutary in two different respects ; first, for the reason that it is by the mercy of God that it comes to be granted to these prayers greatly to benefit the dead, by their effect in loosing them from their sins ; and secondly, because the charity of offering such prayers is very greatly blessed to ourselves.

What the particular sufferings are which those of the de-

parted suffer who are in the condition to be benefited by our
prayers, it is not granted to us to know. It is sufficient for
us to know that the suffering is real, and that it is caused by
their sins, for the sacred text is particular in specifying the
effect of the prayer that is to be piously and charitably hoped
for on behalf of the departed, namely, that they may be loosed
from their sins. What the precise happy effect to the departed of being loosed from their sins may be, is not a thing
placed within our ken or knowledge. These things are the
secrets of the unseen world, which we are not allowed to
know; but taking the world which we do see and know as
a mirror of the world which is veiled from our sight, we
ought to be able, without difficulty, to come at least to such
an understanding of the benefit that must accrue to the departed from being loosed from their sins, as should be quite
sufficient to awaken and keep alive our charity in their behalf.   The sins which are taken notice of and which are
attended with penalties and suffering in our world, are not by
any means either fully commensurate or precisely identical
with the sins that carry with them penalties and sufferings in
the world that is out of our sight.   We must guard ourselves
from falling into any such error as this ; but notwithstanding
in a general way the parallel is such that there is very much
to be learned from it.

Sin in our world, then, is known to bring two kinds of
penalties with it.   Direct penal suffering such as is visited upon
proved offences against human law, of which kind are
imprisonments, hard labour, floggings, and the like ; and
secondly, disqualification from eligible social promotion, and
exclusion from desirable society with others.   To be loosed,
then, from sin in our world, has the effect which we can quite
understand, of opening the prison doors for restoration to
personal liberty and freedom, and the removal of the social
bars and disqualifications which cause the exclusion of the
sufferer from much that is pleasant and eligible in this world.
And in this manner we may very sufficiently understand what
a great gain it cannot fail to be to the departed, if the being
loosed from their sins has the analogous effect in the world
where they now are, of putting an end to the positive suffering
that they may be enduring, as also of removing the bar and
disqualification under which they lie of being admitted to
the heavenly society, the joy of which they so greatly long to
share.

If, therefore, God in His great mercy has been pleased to grant to the prayers of those who are still on earth the gracious efficacy that they avail to loose the dead from their sins, it needs no further insisting to make it plain, at least as regards the departed, how holy and salutary a thought it is "to pray for the dead that they may be loosed from their sins."

But the benefit of such prayers is by no means restricted to the departed. If they bring, as we are taught to believe, a great relief and advantage to the dead for whom they are offered, they bring also at least equal blessings and benefits of another kind to the living who have the faith and charity to offer them ; and the thought to pray for the dead is not holy and salutary solely with respect to the dead, but also equally holy and salutary in its way for the living.

In the first place, prayer for the dead is pre-eminently an exercise of the virtue of faith. Many other good deeds, such as visiting the sick, and relieving the pressing necessities of the poor, bring with them a present reward of their own, in our being able to see with our eyes the happy results of our charitable efforts; and there is a certain reward also in the gratitude and thankfulness which we may frequently receive in return for our assistance. But in the case of prayer for the dead, we can receive nothing whatever of this kind that we can appreciate by sight, for all rests purely on faith. It is simply from faith in the assurances of the Church that we know that our prayers occasion any relief to the sufferers, and we can as little see the sufferings themselves which are relieved as we can either see the relief which our prayers have been the means of bringing, or receive any manifestations of gratitude from those to whose relief we have been instrumental. And yet such prayer is far from being without its reward in its own kind, namely, in the way of greatly strengthening the very faith which has prompted and sustained the prayer. "Lord strengthen our faith," was a prayer of our Lord's Apostles to Him. And nothing tends more solidly to strengthen and confirm faith than the pious practice of praying for the dead that they may be loosed from their sins.

Again, praying for the dead is holy and salutary for the living, because it puts them in mind of what is impending over themselves, in a way that cannot fail to make a salutary impression. "Remember thy latter end," says the sacred text, "and thou wilt never sin." The charity of praying for the dead is rewarded by the fixing in our minds the salutary thought that we must die ourselves. And this thought is one that is fruitful in the best results. It is not only one of the best preservatives from sin, but it is also one of the most powerful stimulants to industry and the good employment of time. As the wise man says, "Whatsoever thy hand findeth to do, do it with all thy might, for there is neither knowledge, nor wisdom, nor understanding, in the grave whither thou hastenest."

And again, the object for which we pray in behalf of the dead is "that they may be loosed from their sins," and in doing this we confess that that which occasions suffering and distress to them in the world where they are is their sin. It cannot, therefore, but strike every one's mind how very contradictory it must be to have the charity for the dead to pray on their behalf, that they may be loosed from their sins, and to be without charity to ourselves, to beware how we may be binding ourselves in our own world with the chains of sinful practices in which we wrongly indulge ourselves, not attending to the truth that the sinner is equally bound by his sin as well in our visible world as in the world which we cannot see. If, therefore, we were to pray for the dead that they may be loosed from their sins, at the same time that we are binding ourselves with sins of our own, we should be having charity which we confess to be for suffering brought upon others by their sins, and no concern for the sufferings which we could not but equally know that we are bringing on ourselves by our own sins. And this seems too palpable a contradiction to be possible, except through almost inconceivable blindness and perversity. It is, therefore, a most holy and salutary thought, as far as we are ourselves concerned, to pray for the dead that they may be loosed from their sins, for in so doing we procure for ourselves the best possible admonition to keep out of the way of sins ourselves, and the charity which we show to the dead, by prayers for them, comes back to ourselves in the form of the best possible charity for ourselves, which dictates the most scrupulous abstinence from the ways of sin, and the most watchful vigilance against contact with anything that may be an occasion of temptation to sin.

And these considerations must now suffice to commend and encourage, to the utmost of our power, the pious and holy custom of making the month of November especially sacred to the charitable practice of praying and causing masses to be offered for the dead that they may be loosed from their sins.

HOLY LIFE AND DEATH OF A DOMINICAN TERTIARY.

Br. Mary Aloysius Wragg, the subject of our narrative, died at Nottingham, August 3, at 7 p.m., being the First Vespers of the Feast of S. Dominic. He had previously received, at the hands of Father Baron, of the Cathedral, all the last rites and Sacraments of the Church. He was a convert, having been received into the Church on All Saints' Day, 1868, by the Rev. Father Augustine, a Monk of Mount S. Bernard's Abbey. From the very first he appeared to receive a special grace, a high appreciation of the things of faith, and a desire for perfection. He wished much to become a monk, and though he lived at that time at Sheepshed, a village more than three miles from the Monastery of Mount S. Bernard, and his health was very feeble, still he contrived tolerably often to make a pilgrimage thither. All the difficulties of the hilly road were as nothing to him through the eagerness of his desire. When he was too weak to walk the whole way, he was carried part of the way in the arms of some one else.

His love and adoration for our Lord in the Blessed Sacrament was intense. It happened once that his mother being sick, the Blessed Sacrament was brought to her at her house by the Priest. The boy remained in the room when his mother was communicated, and when the Priest was gone he walked about the room with his little hands joined together in great delight, sometimes going to the table on which the Holy Sacrament had been temporarily placed, kissing it with great devotion. At last, unable longer to control his emotions, he cried out, "O mother! O mother! you'll never leave this house. This house is a church now." Ever afterwards he used to like to say his prayers in that room, which had been sanctified by the reception of so great a guest.

When himself approaching to receive Holy Communion, he used to perceive a most delicious fragrance coming from the Sacred Host. He spoke of it to his mother, not as revealing something unusual, but supposing that she herself perceived the same. "Isn't it a beautiful odour," he said, "that comes from the Body of our Lord when we go up to Communion?" He was quite surprised that she did not at once understand what he meant. When she questioned him about it, he said it was not like any flowers that he had ever smelt, but much sweeter. It was the "beautifullest" odour; unlike anything else, in short, that he could not describe it, it was so grand. Once his brother being in a dangerous sickness, the Holy Viaticum was brought to the house. The moment the Priest entered the house he perceived the glorious fragrance from the Body of our Lord. The Priest had to pass through the room in which he lay, and he said that for half an hour after he was gone the wonderful odour remained in the house. When he was well enough to go to church, he used to communicate once or twice every week, but when sick less frequently. It was the greatest pleasure he had. He received his First Communion on Christmas Day, 1868, about two months after his reception into the Church.

He had long desired the habit of S. Dominic, which was given him by Father Augustine, who was his director, on August 30, 1871, this Father having faculties for this purpose from the Provincial of the Friars Preachers. This made him as near a Religious as he could be, still living in the world. His exclamation on receiving the Tertiary Scapular, with which he was clothed, was, "Oh, how I have longed for this. Now I am a little monk." This indeed he was in spirit and intention. On account of his illness becoming more critical, he was several months later admitted to profession. He then, of his own suggestion, desired to make a vow of perpetual chastity likewise. Being allowed to do this, he cried out with joy, "Now I am the spouse of our Lord." This profession took place in 1872, he being then twelve years old.

His love of chastity and modesty was such that he was very careful of being touched unnecessarily by any one. A most painful abscess broke out in his back. When the doctor required to examine this, he would have all leave the room whilst he did so. He had a most beautiful face, which, heightened by a sort of spiritual light, looked often like Beato Angelico's Angels. On account of his comely appearance, strangers would sometimes stoop down to kiss him, but learning this by experience, he got one of his little hands ready as a shield and turned his face away. Sometimes the rebuff appeared to them rather rude, but his mother excused him, saying, "You must not be offended. It is more than two years since he has let his mother kiss him, and if she may not, can you expect to be allowed to do so?"

A kind friend made him a present of some white mice, thinking it might beguile some of his time to watch them, but he soon desired to have them taken away out of his room, as being a distraction to him. He gave them away later to the doctor who attended him, and who, on leaving Nottingham, asked him for something as a remembrance, he had taken such a fancy to him. As his illness increased, Fridays became in a marked manner his worst days. The pain he then suffered left him quite worn out the whole of the next day, and he could perceive it coming on as the night of Thursday advanced. As his moments of life ebbed away he seemed the more anxious about his relatives, begging of them to be regular at the Sacraments. Almost the last words he uttered were an earnest pleading with his grandmother, a Protestant, to give her heart to God and become a Catholic. He could not obtain so clear a promise as could set him at rest. The last two days of his life were spent in his death agony, during which he gave no outward sign of consciousness. On the 3rd of August, at seven in the evening, he quietly passed away, going to keep the Feast of his patron S. Dominic in heaven. It was his joy that he was born on a Feast of our Lady, the Visitation of the Blessed Virgin. He had a good day therefore for his entrance into this world, and for his departure from it. His body was carried to Sheepshed, by his own desire, to be buried. His hands after death became glisteningly white, a thing noticed by many. He held between them his book of Tertiary Rules. The burial took place on the Feast of the Transfiguration, the same Father who received him into the Church laying him in the grave. He had on his coffin his Tertiary name, Br. Mary Aloysius Wragg.

A TRANSLATION OF THE BULL "BENEDICENTES."

Gregory XVI. Jan. 27, 1832. Approving of the Devotion of the Living Rosary.

RENDERING due thanks to the Lord of all Consolation, we have received the information which has been laid before us by our beloved son, Lucius Cardinal Lambruschini, Presbyter of the Holy Roman Church, concerning a certain pious exercise which the sedulous and active piety of certain persons has now for some time planned and carried into effect, under the title of the "Living Rosary" (Rosarii Viventis). With the help of God, we confidently trust that the result will be very beneficial, not solely because we hope that the mode of prayer, which is well suited to cultivate piety at every time and in every place, may, through the facilities now procured, daily extend itself more and more; but because it cannot fail to come before God with a certain increase of power, from the consent of so many uniting together, for God is ever wont to be moved to mercy and to incline His ear to the prayer of a multitude when they join together in making it. We have, therefore, resolved with a willing mind to approve of this method, extending to it the favour of the Pontifical authority and the grant of Indulgences; for we do not fail gladly to bear in mind the great advantages which accrued to the Catholic cause when the faithful first began to obtain the aid and protection of the Blessed Virgin through the use of chaplets devised for her honour.

Wherefore, in order to the glory of Almighty God, and to the honour of the Most Holy Virgin Mary, Mother of God, being, moreover, rightly certified of the fact, we, by the plenitude of our authority, grant to all the faithful of both sexes who are enrolled among the votaries (cultores) of the Holy Virgin for the practice of the particular pious devotion which bears the name of the "Living Rosary" a Plenary Indulgence, which may be applied to the departed, on the festival that occurs next after the day on which they have undertaken this pious work, provided that, being duly penitent, they have approached the Sacraments of Penance and the Holy Eucharist. Moreover, in addition to the Indulgences which the Roman Pontiffs, our predecessors, have granted to the recitation of the Rosary, we grant an Indulgence of One Hundred Days as often as the portion of the Rosary prescribed by the rule of the pious institute shall be duly recited on the ferial days ; and we grant an Indulgence of Seven Years, with the same number of quarantines, whenever the above-mentioned pious work is performed on Sundays and other feast days, including those from which the precept of hearing Mass has been taken away, likewise also through the Octaves of Christmas, Easter, Corpus Christi, Pentecost, the Assumption, Nativity, and Conception of the Blessed Virgin. We also grant, for the more solemn feasts of Christmas, Epiphany, Circumcision, Easter, Ascension, Corpus Christi; also on the Sunday of Pentecost, and the Feast of the Most August Trinity ; likewise for all the Feasts of the Blessed Virgin, including those of lesser rank; also for the Festival of the Holy Apostles Peter and Paul, and of All Saints ; likewise also for the third Sunday in every month, a PLENARY INDUL-GENCE, which may be applied to the dead, provided that the prescribed daily recitations have been duly kept up at least

during an entire month, exceptions being allowed in the case of
legitimate hindrances, and provided also that the Sacraments
of Penance and the Holy Eucharist have been frequented, and
the usual pious prayers have been offered in some church.
As regards the Indulgences above mentioned, we declare that
those persons may gain them who, through bodily infirmity,
or any other sufficient cause, are unable to come to the church,
provided that they substitute some other pious work approved
by their confessor. But while we are thus solicitous that the
minds of all may be inflamed with a great increase of veneration, love, and devotion towards the Virgin Mary, and while
we strive, by the extremely rich offer of Indulgences, to
stimulate even those who are already running, we also do
not fail to urge with all earnestness that by diligent attention to all the other duties of religion, charity, and virtue,
and the careful conforming of their lives to the pattern of
Christian discipline, all should endeavour to endear themselves still more to their Most Holy Mother, who promises
that they who labour thus to order their lives shall gain
eternal life. In this way our desires and purposes will obtain
a happy result, and we shall rejoice that this work may prove
to be healthful and beneficial to the faithful people; decreeing
that these present letters shall always remain valid, and that
they ought to obtain, and shall always have their full and
entire effect; and that they are to have their effect for all
future times, anything whatever to the contrary notwithstanding.

Given at Rome, at S. Peter's, on the 27th of January, 1832.
(*Bullarium Rom. Contin.* Vol. xix., p. 84.)

THE ARCH-CONFRATERNITY OF OUR LADY OF THE ANGELS.

Our readers will be pleased to know that a little book has just
been published in the English language,* containing a much
more extended account of the rise and growth of the Arch-

* "The Devotion of Our Lady of the Angels, established at Pouvourville, near Toulouse." Translated from the French. Dublin: J. Elwood
and Son, 2, Capel Street. 1872. Price 6d. We are requested to notice
an omission at page 24, where it is stated that whole parishes may be
enrolled; but this is only done preparatory to individual enrolments.

Confraternity than the brief compendium which we gave in
our last number. In it are related many marvellous instances
of the especial favour with which our dear Lady Queen of
Angels regards this devotion. So rapid has been its progress,
that more than five million names have already been entered on
its Registers. Twelve Cardinals, one Patriarch, eighteen Arch-
bishops, ninety-one Bishops, two mitred Abbots, and innumerable Priests in all parts of the world, have given it the sanction
of their approval. Father de Bray, in a letter which he has
recently addressed to a lady in Scotland, says that he is receiving from all parts of Europe information of a very crowd
of miracles, with the most touching details of both spiritual
and corporal graces.

We gave in our number for October an account of one of
these miracles, and as opportunity may offer, shall be glad in
our future numbers to insert others, as, from time to time, we
may receive authentic narratives of them, for which, however,
we shall carefully forbear to claim any further credence than
can be prudently given to narratives that have not been
taken down before a properly constituted tribunal of the
Church.

In this great work, therefore, now stamped with such
exalted sanctions, we may piously hope that the Catholics of
the United Kingdom will be favourably disposed, fervently
and perseveringly, to join. Of it the Holy Father himself is
credibly related to have said, "The finger of God is there.
I regard it as established for the saving of France, and for
the benefit of the whole Catholic world."

The only conditions required for admission are:—1st, to
make open profession of the Catholic Faith; 2nd, to bear a
good character; 3rd, to be inscribed on the Register of the
Arch-Confraternity.*

The Associates are invited:—1st, to recite daily three "Ave
Marias," with the invocation: "Queen of Angels, pray for
us" (40 days' Indulgence to all who recite this invocation);
2nd, to communicate once a month.

N.B.—These duties do not bind under pain of sin: they
are merely counselled, and they should be fulfilled for the
honour and love of Our Lady of the Angels.

* Names for enrolment may be sent to the Honble. Lady Sausse,
Beaufort Castle, Beauly, N.B.

·

RECORD OF EVENTS.

On the 20th of September, the day on which the Italian
national party made a point of busying themselves in demonstrations of rejoicing for the success of their sacrilegious
seizure of the city of Rome, a select number, comprising
persons of·the best character, birth, and position in Rome,
assembled in the Vatican to condole with Pius IX. on the
recent death of his elder brother, the Count Gaetano Mastai
Ferretti, and to record their protest against the sacrilege of
the invaders.   The *Sala del Trono* and a part of the Raphael
loggias were filled with company.   There were present nearly
the whole of the Cardinals resident in Rome, the Roman
noblesse, the leading men of the city, as also large numbers of
the *employés* of the Pontifical Government who have remained
faithful to their lawful sovereign.   On the appearance of the
Pope, acclamations of welcome and loyalty were uttered by
the entire assemblage.   The address was presented by the
Confederation of Pius IX., and was read by the Cavaliere
Mencacci, who represented the Marquis Girolamo Cavalletti,
its President.   The Holy Father replied to the following
effect :—

Acts of injustice are committed by the permission of Providence; let
us not be too much moved at them.   When they shall have reached their
height, then comes the day of victory.   The salutes of cannon which I
heard this morning went to my heart.   There are demonstrations that
might well be omitted; they are ill-befitting conquerors who possess the
slightest feelings of generosity.   But the men who ordered those salutes
to be fired are devoid of such feelings, and therefore it is that they act
as they do.

Let not that, however, prevent us from praying for all, even for the
persecutors of the Church.   Let us pray that God would be pleased to
enlighten their minds and make them see that in their blindness they
are but labouring for their own ruin, and for the ruin of that new order
of things without God, and in opposition to the Church, the imperishable
spouse of Christ.   Pray, then, my children, and receive my benediction,
which I extend to all present, and to all those absent who go in heart
along with your devout sentiments; to you, your families and friends,
and to all the societies of associated Catholics.   *Benedictio Dei,* &c.

The Pope then seated himself on the throne and the Marquis
Serlupi advanced towards him and read an address representing the wishes of the assemblage generally, and praying

for the benediction of His Holiness. The Holy Father, then raising his eyes to heaven, replied to the following purport :—

From my heart do I bless all the good men here present, and those too who are not here to-day but who are animated by the same feelings as you are and who practise the same good works. Let us ever remember that we live in a world full of sorrow and tribulation. What can we do to escape from it ! The clergy recite in the office of to-day the interesting history of Tobias, which tells of the virtues of the father and of the son, and of the recompenses which they obtained of God for their good deeds. During the afflictions and slavery of his people, Tobias visited their families and relieved their sufferings, encouraged them to obey the law of God, and reclaimed those who had gone astray from it.

In these days of sadness, you are like a nosegay of choice flowers which God has ordained to shed the sweet odour of piety. He it is that has brought you here to listen to the words of His unworthy Vicar. Now hear what the Vicar of Jesus Christ says to you : Do all that in you lies to preserve any of your friends from wandering from the path of justice in the midst of so many scandals, disorders, and incitements to do evil. Endeavour that not one of those around you may be forgetful of his Christian character or of the duties incumbent on him. Let fathers and mothers of families be very careful to keep from their homes all sin ; and let them prevail on their relatives, friends, and acquaintances, to follow their example, so that sin and corruption may find no entrance into their dwellings. Such is the memorial I leave with you ; and, that my words may have their due effect, I charge you to convey this my benediction to all who belong to you. *Benedictio Dei*, &c.

The anniversary of the *"plébiscite"* or day (October 5th) when the votes were taken which were supposed to declare the desire of the inhabitants of Rome to be united to the rest of Italy, was made the occasion of presenting two addresses to the Pope, which drew forth from him two precious replies, of which we much lament to be unable to give our readers more than the following extracts.

Signor Tollé read the first address, to which the Pope replied as follows :—

I am consoled at the words that have been addressed to me in the name of the whole Roman youth ; at all events, of the large number who share your sentiments ; and I thank my good God that they come so often to me to support my feebleness by the expressions of their devotion. By so acting, they increase the fervour not only of themselves and of those who listen to them, but also of me, who ought to be the first in the thick of this great conflict.

Well, you have rightly characterized the act of which to-day is the anniversary ; and yet, truth to tell, I must own that it was a less noisy event, and by so much the less painful to me, than the act of the 20th of September, simply because it was not accompanied by the same outward acts. The engines of war at least were silent, and that allowed us to pass the day without having our feelings so much harrowed.

However, I have been reading a paper in which a certain man—I will not name him—invites all his colleagues, nay, all the Romans—"to celebrate the regeneration of this city."

I own that I am unable to understand in what sense the city or the people of Rome can be said to be regenerated. Can it be that they have been relieved from "enormous taxation," which they had to pay prior to the 20th of September, 1870? I think not. Can it be that the "monstrous immorality" by which Rome was disgraced prior to that date has been purged away? Again I think not. Can it be that the "liberty of action" previously withheld has been restored? On the contrary, that very liberty is now withheld—which to the good man is most precious of all—the liberty to do good. The insults and outrages daily heaped upon the clergy; even blows and public contumely given to persons consecrated to God—are not such things a violation of liberty? In what, then, does this boasted regeneration consist?

But, as our Lord Jesus Christ said to the first, *hypocritæ tristes*, so also may the same be said of these later followers of the sect of Caiphas, who are recalling the saying of the impious Sanhedrim, *Expedit ut unus moriatur pro populo.* They say among themselves: *Expedit ut multi moriantur pro populo:* nay, *pro populo barbaro, pro populo indigno, pro populo peccatore.* Thanks, however, be to God, I see that the peoples are opening their eyes to their position. I see the Catholic peoples throughout the world meeting the spirit of impious unbelief that threatens to flood the earth, meeting it with a holy and humble reaction.

I see in one place pilgrimages made to the famous sanctuaries; in another the churches resounding with the prayers of good Catholics. All this gives us courage, and makes us hope that God will vouchsafe the hour of His mercy sooner perhaps than we think for.

Let us then thank the Lord for this spirit which exists amongst Catholics, and of which you who are here present have given so eloquent an example.

Courage then; let us then walk along the paths of this desert; We have hope and charity to guide us. We have the pillar of the cloud to lead us through the day; that pillar is the memorial of the old institutions that still flourish in this city. And we hope that like the Hebrews who arrived safe and sound at their journey's end, we shall be permitted, after wonderfully traversing this period of persecution, to sing the song of Moses: *Cantemus Domino, gloriose enim magnificatus est; equum et ascensorem projecit in mare.*

Here the Holy Father appeared to tremble with emotion; he pronounced the words last quoted like one inspired. The Holy Father then bestowed his benediction in the accustomed manner.

Both on entering and on leaving the Hall of the Consistory the Pope was cheered with the enthusiastic acclamations of the numerous assemblage.

On the same day, a deputation of the Roman *noblesse* had audience of the Pope in the Sala della Contessa Matilda, when the following address was read by the Duca Don Pio Grazioli. The Holy Father replied as follows :—

I thank you with all my heart. Your words prove that if the *plebiscite* was a lie on the day on which it was made, it is even more so now. All honest men, all good Christians, all right thinkers, are deploring what has come to pass, and are praying to the God of all goodness that such a state of things may soon end, and that virtue, justice, and order may be restored. We trust that our prayers, united to yours and to the whole Catholic world, may move the Almighty to mercy, and that He may be mindful of us. He will strengthen us for the conflict, and grant us soon the consolation of seeing all things again in their normal state. Yes, the change, the triumph, will surely come. I know not if it will be in my lifetime—in the lifetime of this poor Vicar of Christ—but I know that it must come. The resurrection will take place, and we shall see an end to all these impious atrocities. I bless you; may my benediction strengthen and encourage you; may it be an encouragement to your families; may it purify those members who need to be purified; may it bring parents to watch over the education of their children and restore wanderers to the right path. In a word, may it preserve in families peace and concord, piety and faith: that faith which they are endeavouring to tear from our children's hearts by impious schoolmasters, by corrupt example, and abominable books. This Faith is our precious treasure. I enjoin you to guard it faithfully in your hearts. I recommend you to the Sacred Heart of Jesus, and I bless you with all the affection of a father.

The New German Empire has consummated the first of its premeditated acts against the liberties of its subjects. The Fathers of the Society of Jesus have been selected for the first victims. They have been virtually banished from the Empire by a decree interdicting the performance of any acts of their ministry. But whether the New Empire will be even the immediate gainer by this act of tyranny may be doubted. Nothing in the experience of the Catholic Church draws the bond of sympathy and attachment closer to any body of men than to see them become for conscience sake the victims of unjust oppression and tyranny. The Archbishop of Cologne has addressed the following letter to the Father Provincial of the German Province :—

From the communications which have reached me from your Reverence and other sources as well as from the public prints, I have learnt with great sorrow that the law against the Society of Jesus is being carried out with a severity far beyond what is justified by the letter of the same law. Having just returned from a long visitation journey I hasten to express to your Reverence the painful and sincere sympathy I feel for you all in this heavy affliction which, according to God's inscrutable, though no doubt wise and loving, counsels, has fallen upon the Society in our German fatherland. I cannot but express my conviction of the

falseness and groundlessness of the reproaches and accusations brought
against the Society, as also of the great injustice which has been inflicted
on its members.   At the same time I take the opportunity of thanking
the Society for the great and numerous benefits which the labours of the
Fathers have conferred upon us during the last 20 years—since my predecessor called them to labour in the diocese.   I cannot without pain
and anxiety think of the loss and injury which the departure of so many
able and zealous members of the regular clergy will inflict upon my people
—a loss which, through the want of clergy to take their place, is irreparable;
especially as the Fathers have always devoted themselves, and that without hope of reward, not only to the ordinary but even to the extraordinary
work of the diocese; and have contributed not only to the salvation of
the people but also to that of the clergy.   My efforts to avoid such an
evil have hitherto proved ineffectual; I do not, however, give up the hope
that the united efforts of the Episcopate and of all true Catholics will at
last succeed in getting the worth of your Society recognized and valued,
and that at no very distant time; while it is a comfort to recognize the
fact that the present circumstances render you a remarkable likeness of
our Divine Exemplar, inasmuch as in all times and in all places you are
chosen by the unbelieving world as the special object of its persecution.
Meanwhile, I will never cease, as far as the limits of the law and my own
feeble powers point, to work towards this end.   I conclude with the expression of my heartfelt esteem and love; I commend both your Reverence and all your brethren to the merciful providence of the all-good
God, and myself and the Archdiocese to your pious prayers, giving you
at the same time my pastoral benediction.

✠ PAUL, Archbishop of Cologne.

We have had a similar public testimony of sympathy from
the Chapter of Westminster, addressed to the Provincial of
the Society of England, to which Father Whitty has replied
in a letter that want of space alone prevents us from giving
at length.   Now we have in the "Catholic World" for October
a testimony from the New World beyond the Atlantic, showing how deep and unanimous is the sympathy which is felt
for the Fathers of the Society, who are singled out by the
German tyrant to be the first victims to suffer the penalty
of expatriation in the name of Liberty.

What are we to do? says this leading organ of Catholic
opinion in the United States,—We have power and we must
use it.   We have the genius of our own constitution on our
side.   We must speak out plainly and boldly as Catholic
Americans.   We must do what has already been done in
London at the meeting in St. James's Hall, presided over by
the Duke of Norfolk; where peer and ploughman, gentle and
simple, priest and layman, were one in protesting against
this slavish policy of Prince Bismarck.   Let us do the like.
Let our eminent men, and they are not few, call us together

here in New York, in every city throughout the nation—in behalf not only of our suffering brethren, but of those rights which are inalienable to every man that is born into this world—in protestation against a principle and a policy which, if they found favour here, would sap the life of our nation, and throw us back into the old slavery that we drowned in our best blood.   Our standpoint is this : as there are rights which the State does not and cannot give us, those rights are inviolable, and the State cannot touch them.   To God alone we owe them ; to God alone we give them back, and are answerable for them.   The State is not supreme in all things, and never shall be.   These are the principles we defend, and are happy in being their persecuted champions.

It is not merely a question of creed; Bismarck does not attack a creed.   It is a broad question of right and wrong, of justice and injustice, of *absolutism* and freedom.   Power was never given into the hands of the German Chancellor to be abused at the very outset, to oppress his subjects, Catholic and Protestant.   It is not and it must not be supreme ; and we very much mistake the genius of the great German people if they long allow it to continue so.   It is not for him to deprive 14,000,000 of his people of their natural rights ; the right to educate their children as they think proper, *and as the law allowed them;* the right to consider marriage a sacrament sanctified by God, and not a civil contract, to be loosed or unloosed at will by a magistrate ; the right of listening to their most·eminent teachers : the right of holding the seminaries and churches, built by their own money, for the use of their own Priests ; the right, above all, of believing that there is a God beyond all governments, from whom all government, which people make for themselves, springs ; that God has set a law in the conscience which they must obey, even though princes and kings rage against it, and that it is not in the nature of things for this first and final law of conscience to clash with any other unless that other be wrong.   When Prince Bismark succeeds in eradicating these inborn notions from the minds of the German people, he will then have attained his supremacy ; but that then is—never.

MEMORANDUM OF THE GERMAN BISHOPS.—The Catholic Bishops of Germany have quite recently held a meeting in Fulda, at the tomb of S. Boniface, from whence they have promulgated a memorandum, addressed to the citizens of the

Empire, regarding the present position of the Catholic
Church in the German Empire. We hope in our next to give
extracts from this important document.

DEATH OF THE VERY REV. F. AYLWARD, O.S.D.—We have
to record with much regret the death of the Very Rev. Fr.
James Dominic Aylward, D.D., of the Order of S. Dominic.
He was well known in England for his rare accomplishments
both as a scholar and a theologian, and for his deep and practical acquaintance with ascetical theology. He was born at
Leeds in 1813, received the habit of S. Dominic at Hinckley
in 1833, in his 20th year; and was ordained Priest by Bishop
Walsh in 1838. He twice occupied the important position
of Provincial of the English Dominicans. Hidden as his
youth had always been, buried in books, and ever shunning
popularity, he won the affections of all who were privileged
to share his acquaintance. His public lectures, both upon
subjects of literature and art, and in defence of religion, were
always brilliant and captivating. His sermons were full of
unction and of power ; and his spiritual Retreats have left
lasting impressions in the memories of all who heard them.
Fr. Aylward was one who tried to see God in everything, and
all that was beautiful in art, science, and nature, as lit up in
the beauty of eternal truth. His universal gentleness and
tenderness of heart secretly attracted the affections of all.
None knew him without loving him. For the last two years
the uncertainty of his health kept him ever watchful, and it
was only a few days ago that he finished a Retreat, which he
made as an immediate preparation for death. He said Mass
last Saturday; and during the evening made three visits to
the Altar of Our Lady, to gain the Plenary Indulgence of
Rosary Sunday, His last illness lasted but two hours, during
which time he repeated many beautiful acts of faith, submission, and love. It was an hour before midnight, and the
prayers following Extreme Unction were being brought to a
close, and having exclaimed, " I renounce the devil and all his
works," in a few brief moments he calmly gave his soul to God.
His body was brought to the Priory church at Woodchester
on Tuesday evening; some of the community watched around
it all night reciting the Psalter, according to ancient custom,
and on Wednesday morning he was buried in the quadrangle
of the monastery, amongst his brethren. We commend him
to the prayers of the faithful, and especially to the members
of the Confraternity of the Rosary.

ANECDOTES.

S. Dominic's Devotion to the Holy Angels.—The following interesting account of S. Dominic's devotion to the holy angels, and of their ministering to him, occurs in the valuable little work on devotion to the holy angels translated by E. H. Thompson.* S. Dominic was one of the most fervent lovers of Jesus and Mary who ever lived, and he was also the well-beloved of the angels. He received at their hands all kinds of help during those long watches of the night which he spent prostrate at the foot of the holy altar, pouring forth the affections and longings of his heart without restraint in the presence of his Good Master in the Most Holy Sacrament, and invoking with tears the protection of the Blessed Virgin. However wearied he might be while he was journeying on the road, he was never tired of watching whole nights in prayer, and used his utmost endeavours that it should be before the Adorable Eucharist. The angels, enraptured with this indefatigable love, associated themselves with him. These spirits of Heaven took pleasure in accompanying this heavenly man. They were seen to bring lights, and take them to the room into which he had retired, open first the doors of the house, and then of the church whither they conducted him; and afterwards, when the time was come, they escorted him back in the same manner. The servants of a Bishop with whom he lodged, having observed this marvel, mentioned it to the prelate, who watched the holy man about the time when the prodigy used to occur, and had the consolation of witnessing it, beholding with admiration the goodness of the heavenly spirits to men." (Page 49.)

The Curé of Ars twice obtains Miraculous Help through Devotion to the Rosary.—It is related of the Curé of Ars, by a Priest of the diocese of Belley, that he bought a large quantity of wheat from a farmer in Ars for the House of Refuge, where he received and educated a number of poor girls. Not having at command the whole of the required sum, he asked for delay, giving at the same time a promissory note, which was accepted without difficulty. On the day on which his bill ar-

* " Devotion to the Nine Choirs of Holy Angels." Translated from the French of Boudon by E. H. Thompson, M.A. P. 49. London: Burns and Oates.

rived at maturity the good Curé found himself without a
penny of ready money, and did not know to whom to apply.
Notwithstanding this, in place of being discouraged, he redoubled his confidence in God and in His holy Mother, and
calling for his walking-stick, he went out into the fields, to
enjoy greater freedom for his meditations. As he was busy
reciting his Rosary with great devotion, a lady came up to
him and said, "Are you not the Curé of Ars?"   "Yes,
madam."   "Then, here is the sum that I have been commissioned to place in your hands."   "Do you mean, perhaps,
for masses to be celebrated?"   "No, sir, the donors only recommend themselves to your prayers."   This said, the lady
walked away, and the Curé, full of gratitude, went and handed
over the money to the farmer who had sold him the wheat.
The same servant of God also was once in a similar distress
for want of money.   He had undertaken some repairs in the
parish church of Ars, and when the day came for paying the
workmen he was without money.   As was his custom whenever he found himself in great distress, he went out into the
fields to recite his Rosary.   He scarcely found himself fairly
clear of the village when a stranger on horseback accosted
him, and inquired after his health.   He replied that as regarded health he was very well, but that he was in great
distress of mind, as the time was come for paying his workmen for what they were engaged in doing at the church, and
he had no money.   Hearing this, the stranger reflected for a
moment, and taking from his pocket 20 louis d'or (pieces of
16s.), he gave them to the Curé, saying, "Here is what you want
for paying your workmen.   Adieu; pray for me."—*Gastaldi.
Historical Essays on the Life of the Curé of Ars.*

THE

𝕸𝖔𝖓𝖙𝖍𝖑𝖞 𝕸𝖆𝖌𝖆𝖟𝖎𝖓𝖊 𝖔𝖋 𝖙𝖍𝖊 𝕳𝖔𝖑𝖞 𝕽𝖔𝖘𝖆𝖗𝖞.

NEW SERIES.

| No. 5.] | DECEMBER. | [A.D. 1872. |

No. VIII.—THE SCIENCE OF THE HOLY ROSARY.

ON THE PRIVILEGE OF TEACHING THE KNOWLEDGE OF THE MYSTERIES OF
THE HOLY ROSARY TO OTHERS; OR, SUGGESTIONS ADDRESSED TO ALL
IN GENERAL, BUT SPECIALLY TO MEMBERS OF THE CONFRATERNITY OF
THE HOLY ROSARY.

(Conclusion.)

THE readers of the foregoing series of papers will not fail to
have observed that there are two in particular of the seven
gifts of the Holy Ghost which the Devotion of the Holy
Rosary appears to be in an especial manner intended to cultivate among the people of the Church. These are, the spirit
of piety or of prayer, and the spirit of knowledge.

The language of the Holy Church, at the season of Pentecost, on behalf of all her people, is that God would give to
them the "*sacrum septenarium*," the outpouring of the whole
of the seven gifts of the Holy Ghost. But St. Augustine
says, God has not sought us without requiring a corresponding act on our part to seek Him in return, "*nos non sine
nobis.*" The gifts of the Holy Ghost consequently only come to
obtain their effect where there is a suitable effort made on our
part to cultivate the gift which we receive. Where such
efforts are not duly and gratefully made on our part, the gift
fails of its effect.

The Holy Spirit of learning (*disciplinæ*), says the Book of
Wisdom, will withdraw Himself from thoughts that are without understanding, and He will not stay when iniquity
cometh in (Wisd. i. 4). And the prayer of the holy David
is, "Take not Thy Holy Spirit from me." The reason, therefore, why the faithful fail to exhibit the fruits of the gifts of
the Holy Ghost, in all such cases where the failure is too dis-
cernible to escape notice, is not because God is not willing to
give His gifts, and not because He is not ever, as it were,
watching and waiting to find those to whom they may be
given, but because, through some unhappy fault of ours, we
fail to do our own part which God requires from us to prepare

ourselves to be the receivers of His gifts, and without which
labour and diligence of ours, His gifts are not suffered to take
their effect.

In this respect we may all very properly remember that
we are constituted by the grace of our Christian calling
"members of one another," and no man, as the Apostle says,
lives or dies to himself.   And certainly there is nothing so
fitted to prepare the Christian people, more particularly Christian youth, to receive and turn to good account the gifts of the
spirit of piety and of the spirit of knowledge, than kindly,
patient, and charitable instruction given by those who are
qualified to give it by reason of their superior knowledge.
Without then in any way attempting to lay down the doctrine
that membership in the Confraternity of the Holy Rosary
necessarily carries with it, in any sense, the burden and duty
of labouring to teach others, we ought not to omit to point
out what a field of charitable labour for the good of others
lies open to the zeal and to the goodwill of those amongst its
members who may be conscious of possessing the capacity to
teach others, if only the opportunities for its exercise were to
present themselves. Let all such be assured that opportunities
cannot fail to be found by those who will humbly and patiently
persevere in seeking for them.

Let it be fairly considered what a very mean and selfish
appreciation of the privilege of membership with the Confraternity it could not fail to be, to look upon it only in the light
of an association having for its sole end to combine together
to obtain, by the force of united prayer, a number of gifts and
miraculous manifestations of Divine power for the advantage
of the members, such as they could not otherwise have hoped
to succeed in obtaining.   Undoubtedly, by the mercy and
goodness of God, numerous such proofs of the Divine bounty
are given to the members of the Confraternity through the
power of their united prayers in great abundance; and there
is no reason why such graces should not be given to them in
far greater abundance still; for God has not set Himself any
limits in the extent of His bounty, and His power to give will
always remain in excess of and superior to our power and will-
ingness to combine together to ask.   But to act towards God
as if His power and riches were nothing but a bank of supply
for our wants, and the devotion of the Rosary were nothing
else than a ready form, so to speak, of drawing cheques upon
His bank of supply, would be, to say the very least, an exceedingly unworthy and narrow-minded way of acting.

Membership with the Confraternity of the Rosary, then, besides being regarded as a title to claim the benefit of the united power of the prayers of the members in behalf of intentions which the applicants desire to be granted solely for reasons known to themselves—(this it certainly is)—ought also to be looked upon, not indeed as imposing a duty, but certainly as conferring the privilege of a title to be a teacher to others of the knowledge of the mysteries of the Holy Rosary.   There will, we apprehend, be little difficulty in finding numbers of people who stand in the condition of crying need of the charitable help of a teacher, if only teachers can be found who have the charity to offer their services. All the members of the Confraternity of the Rosary, then, who rightly understand the full extent of the dignity and privileges conferred upon them in their membership in the Confraternity, will see that they do not merely gain the somewhat selfish advantage of being able to enlist the combined power of prayer of their fellow-members in behalf of their own particular wants and petitions, but that they also acquire the unselfish honour and dignity of being entitled to labour charitably to make themselves apostles of the Rosary to others.

Now let us ask the question—What does being an apostle of the Rosary to others mean, and what does it imply? It implies, in the first place, the grace of attaining some degree of a resemblance to the Divine Model of all Christians, Jesus Christ, so as to be able to say with Him, " Misereor super turbam "—I have a compassion on the multitude.   I see a great multitude of the people around me, who are in a most woful state of ignorance, and would to God that I could do something to enable them to rise out of their deplorable and degrading condition.   The office of an apostle must always be founded on Divine charity, and must be sustained with the sincere and persevering desire to benefit others by what we are able and willing to teach them.   Yet charity alone does not itself convey that title to teach which the apostle's work, nevertheless, needs.   This is, doubtless, true, but the membership in the Confraternity of the Rosary does, in a certain limited sense, confer this title, not, indeed, to be an apostle or preacher in the broad sense of the word, but in the limited and restricted sense of becoming a teacher of the Mysteries of the Rosary.   For this end the Confraternity of the Rosary is covered with the mantle of the great order of the Friars

Preachers, and as the vocation of the Friar Preacher is to carry the knowledge of the Gospel and to do the works of an apostle in all and each of the four quarters of the globe, among all the people of the whole earth, so the members of the Confraternity of the Rosary possess, in their membership in the Confraternity, a title to give themselves charitably and of their own free will up to the work of patiently teaching to others all that they have learned or are able to learn respecting the Mysteries of the Rosary ; and, in so doing, they will always be able to appeal to their membership in the Confraternity as an incontestable proof that they are labouring in a vocation to which they have a rightful claim and which all good people will cheerfully recognise.

So much, then, for the title to become a teacher of the Mysteries of the Rosary ; the next point to consider will be, What is needed to become an efficient teacher of the same ?

In order to be in reality a teacher or an apostle of anything, the knowledge and understanding that is requisite for teaching is indispensable, and, of course, not simply knowledge in general, however advantageous this must be.   If we are to become teachers, there must be special knowledge—that is, knowledge of the thing in question, and of all that directly appertains to it.

Hence the zealous members of the Confraternity of the Rosary will never be willing to rest satisfied, or to think that they have acted up in any way to a just and generous sense of their privilege, if all that they do to extend the Rosary is limited to occasionally giving away a string of Rosary beads to a child or poor person.   There is far greater, far more honourable scope for their exertion than this.

The first work, however, to be done will be with themselves.   All that has been written in the preceding Numbers goes to show that the "Rosary" is founded on a system of Christian doctrine, and that its fifteen Mysteries contain a large body of Christian knowledge most fitting to be possessed by all the Christian people.   Moses said to the people of Israel, "Let not these words go out of thine heart all the days of thy life.   Thou shalt teach them to thy sons and to thy grandsons" (Deut. iv. 9).   With how much more of force may not the same be said of the fifteen Mysteries of the Rosary.   "Let not these words go out of thine heart all the days of thy life."   A member of the Confraternity of the Rosary, to whom God gives the desire to labour to teach others, should, therefore, consider it to be a true part of his or her vocation to take the necessary pains to fit themselves as opportunity may offer for being able to speak familiarly as becomes a teacher, on each one of the Mysterie of the Rosary, as also on the general body of Christian doctrine which, as has been explained, is contained in the four words, *Mystery, Joyful, Sorrowful,* and *Glorious.*

The Devotion of the Rosary, we must always remember cannot exist in its true nature separate from its appropriate knowledge ; and it must never be suffered to pass out of the mind that the Holy Rosary is a body of Christian knowledge and doctrine, as well as a form and method of prayer. Members of the Rosary Confraternity must consequently not be ashamed to acknowledge their want of knowledge where they may be conscious of the want, but must much rather set themselves courageously to the work of remedying their deficiency and of acquiring the knowledge which they may lack. Knowledge thus acquired, not for selfish purposes of personal vainglory, but for the charitable purpose of being able to teach others, will be sure to bring with it a rich reward of Divine blessing. It will be labour doubly blest, both to the person who acquires the knowledge, and to those to whom he or she may be afterwards instrumental in communicating the knowledge.   And it is a truth confirmed by no little experience, that no knowledge is acquired so easily and so pleasantly, and at the same time so firmly and solidly to the persons themselves, as that which is acquired for the purpose of being communicated to others.   S. Ignatius Loyola became so convinced of the deficiency of his attainments, that when, at an advanced age, he felt his vocation within him strongly impelling him to become instrumental in teaching others, he was not ashamed to go and sit in a school, in company with schoolboys, and learn the necessary rudiments of the knowledge which he perceived to be indispensable to the success of the work to which he desired to devote himself. The same kind of spirit should in its measure animate the members of the Confraternity of the Rosary ; and for the sake of fitting themselves to be better teachers and propagandists of the Devotion, they cannot love too much to be devout students of its Mysteries themselves and to bestow their constant care, " not to let its mysteries go out of their hearts," but to seek for every opportunity to acquire such knowledge as may fit them to become teachers of the Mysteries to others.* God has formed his Church on the plan that we should all study how to be useful to others, and should find our own happiness and enjoyment in being the instruments of bringing good to others, for "no one lives and no one dies for himself," says the Apostle; and if we can spread to others the knowledge and devout use of the Holy Rosary, we may know, from the experience of many centuries and nations, that "*the hand of God is in this thing.*"

H. F.

No. III.—THE VENERABLE ANNA MARIA TAIGI

THE ineffable consolations which Anna Maria received during the early years of her conversion, prepared her soul for that share in the Cross of her heavenly Spouse for which she so ardently longed, and which was to overshadow the remainder of her life. During the last thirty years of her existence her bodily sufferings alone were a continual martyrdom. Her health had been excellent in youth, but by degrees it declined, and although she suffered apparently from physical ailments, still the increase of her pains, when she had any special favour to obtain for souls, sufficiently showed that there was something supernatural in her state of continual bodily torment. She had constant headache, which became much worse on Fridays, and terrible pains in her eyes and ears; her hands and legs, also, were at times grievously afflicted with gout, so that she seemed to suffer in every part of her body. The sensible graces with which her soul had been inundated were withdrawn, and she entered the dark valley of spiritual desolation and abandonment. It is impossible to do more than glance at a state so utterly unknown to all but highly favoured and interior souls, and so far surpassing the most acute material torments. It is true that she was never deprived of the heavenly lights and communications with which she had been favoured from the beginning; but in the sterility of her soul, and her inability to feel any longer the expansions of Divine love, these celestial communications only increased her agony.

---

* Members of the Confraternity may be referred to the list of works advertised on the cover, for more than one publication that they will find useful to them in prosecuting their studies on the Rosary.

She touchingly compared them to the rays of light which
enter a prison, and cause the unhappy captive fresh torture
by showing him his chains and revealing the horrors of his
dungeon, which had been concealed by the darkness of the
night.   Our Lord, indeed, from time to time, gave her the
sensible support, without which she could not have endured
this state of torment; nevertheless, this martyrdom continued,
and even increased, till the time of her death, as she herself
declared.   When we add that she experienced violent temptations to hatred of God, and against faith, besides many other
exterior and interior torments on the part of hell, it must be
owned that the measure of her inward sufferings was complete.

Not the least wonderful fact in her life is, that this constant
pressure of bodily and mental affliction never prevented her
from attending to the duties and labours of her state of life.
Of her it may truly be said, that she " prayed as if everything
depended on prayer, and worked as if everything depended
on work."   She was the perfect model of a wife and mother,
providing with the most tender, watchful, and minute super-
vision for the wants' of her family, and giving them a constant
example of industry and cheerful confidence in God, through
their life-long trials of poverty and privation.   From the time
of her conversion, she was perfect in all the duties of a daughter,
wife, and mother, and she spared no pains which might contribute to the welfare of her children, as long as they were
consistent with the ordinary resources of her position in life.
But she would never make use of her spiritual gifts to procure
for them temporal advantages, nor even to provide for their
actual necessities.   When in extreme want, she cheerfully received the alms of the wealthy like other poor persons, but
rejected with firmness and indignation whatever went beyond
this.

In this manner she always refused pecuniary aid from those
who had received special favours through her prayers.   " I do
not serve God out of interest," was her constant reply.   " Go
and thank our Lord, or the Madonna, or such and such a
Saint."   It was the same with the many personages of exalted
rank who, being attracted by her sanctity, sought her counsel
and assistance, and were eager in their offers of temporal aid.
One of these was Maria Louisa of Bourbon, Duchess of Lucca,
and Queen of Etruria, who loved her as a friend and revered
her as a mother.   " More than once," says her intimate friend,
" the Duchess complained that this pious woman had never

asked her for anything. She opened a desk full of gold, and
said to her, '*Prendi, prendi, Nanna mia, quel che vuoi.*' *
And Anna Maria, smiling, answered with the same simplicity,
'*Ma quanto siete pazzarella.* † I serve a Master who is much
richer than you. I trust to Him, and I have the firm hope
that He will provide for me.' "

This disinterestedness and confidence in God was the constant lesson she gave her family in the midst of the most
severe privations. She frequently exhorted them when in
distress, especially in temporal matters, to invoke the help of
Our Lady and the Saints,. especially that of S. Philomena, to
whom she had a great devotion, and whom she appointed at
her death the guardian and patroness of her family.

This perfect resignation to the Divine Will, in the heart of
such a tenderly loving mother as Anna Maria, was in the
highest degree meritorious in the sight of God. Our Lord
Himself consoled her and assured her that He would protect
her children during this life and the world to come. " I will
save them," He said to her, "because they are of thy blood;
because they are poor, and because I love the poor. I will
save them although they have many faults."

For her greater perfection in this abandonment to Providence, it seemed to please God that she should live from day
to day like the birds of the air. She laboured with her
whole strength, and in the sweat of her brow, to earn daily
bread, and when this failed, accepted the alms of benefactors
with as much gratitude and humility as she had shown dignity
in refusing them on other occasions.

Her family being numerous, and her husband's salary very
small, the strictest economy and much exertion on the part
of the mother of the family were necessary at all times; but
during the extreme misery to which the Roman people were
reduced during the ephemeral Republic of 1798, her husband
no longer received anything from the princely house which he
served; and though Anna Maria laboured during the night
as well as the day to provide food for her family, the time
came when every resource failed, and starvation became imminent. Anna Maria then resolved to seek the public relief
distributed in the streets to an immense number of applicants.

* " Take, take, dear Nanny, whatever thou wilt."
† "Oh, how silly you are!" It is impossible to give the exact meaning of
the word *pazzarella.*

She would then stand for long hours, jostled by the crowd, till her turn came; and though overwhelmed with fatigue, and about to become a mother, she continued this humiliating application until the famine had ceased.

Although her family were never again reduced to similar extremity of want, there were many times in which they were sorely tried by poverty. When all human means failed, she resorted to fervent prayer, which never failed to procure her help. Often were the hearts of persons who had known her moved to send her succour, even when they were far away. This was several times the case with Cardinal Pedicini and others. But such was her trust in God that whenever they supplied her with more than was necessary for immediate pressing wants, she distributed the surplus to other poor families.

In her family relations Anna Maria had to bear those constant trials, so inglorious in appearance, so sanctifying in reality, which fall to the lot of so many in her condition of life. She had much to suffer from her parents, especially from her father; he was a man of bitter and violent temper, who showed her constant harshness and injustice, and even at times ill-treated her. It is possible that her patience and filial piety in early life may have drawn down upon her the wonderful graces which she afterwards received. After her perfect consecration to God, these virtues attained the most sublime degree, especially during the old age of her parents. Her father, at the end of his life, was attacked by a hideous disease of the skin, during which she nursed and attended to him entirely, with the utmost devotion.

Her husband, as we have said, was in the main an honest, well-meaning man, but of a nature totally opposed and uncongenial to her own. His rough manners, rude conduct, and uneducated mind, joined to a total want of consideration for his wife, clashed incessantly with her elevation of soul, and her extraordinary delicacy and refinement of mind and character. He was a constant trial of patience, and it is no small praise that, during nearly fifty years of married life, this angelic woman contrived to avoid everything which might disturb their domestic harmony. She took the utmost care of her children from their earliest infancy; spared no pains to educate them, and continued to help them even after they were settled in the world. But they did not all turn out according to her wishes, and she had to bear the Cross which

afflicts so many Christian mothers.   She had many other
domestic trials from her daughter-in-law and son-in-law, as
also from another person who lived in her house.   Thus she
continually practised the divine lesson taught her by our
Lord Himself.   " The evil spirit is one of contradiction," He
said to her in one of those delicious revelations with which
she was favoured.   " My spirit, on the contrary, is the spirit
of love and peace, condescending to everything which is not
sin.   To be able to condescend to the weakness of others, for
the sake of peace, in families, is a particular grace which I do
not grant to all."

This gift of peace, in the midst of contradictions and crosses,
was the veil under which the extraordinary sanctity of this
holy life was, in part, concealed.

(*To be continued.*)

A CHRISTMAS VISION.

(A passage from an unfinished poem, by the late Father Aylward.*)

WHILE thus the little maiden knelt, and long'd to see again
        The Angel guide, her eyes descried
                Reclining on the plain,
        Keeping their watch amid their flocks,
                A group of shepherd men.

* The above fragment is taken from an unfinished poem found among
the papers of the late Father Aylward.   The plan of the poem supposes
a child, of seven years of age, to have received the promise of being
taken to midnight Mass, for the first time, on Christmas night.   Looking
forward with joy to the coming of the festival, she falls into a trance,
in which she imagines herself carried by an angel to Bethlehem, where
she sees in a vision what the poem proceeds to describe.   The following
lines introduce us to the child herself :—
        " But of all the Church's festive times, the one she loved the most
                        Was Christmas morn,
                        When Christ was born
                To save the souls that were lost.
        And oft she would sit her down and think how sweet it were to see
        Our gracious Lord, in His baby robes, seated on Mary's knee.
        To see Him draw the stream of life so sweetly from her breast,
        And then to slumber peacefully like a bird within its nest.
        Thus ever turned the child's fond heart to the thought of our
                Saviour's birth,
        So deep was the natural piety of this innocent child of earth

Some were entranc'd in quiet prayer, and some, with look
    serene,
Seem'd drinking in the loveliness of that still and beauteous
    scene ;
And some did lift their heads on high, with earnest, searching
    eyes,
As if to spell the mystic things deep printed on the skies,
Which God's own hand had written there in characters of
    flame—
A witness unto all mankind of the glories of His Name.

Whilst her heart thus grew to these shepherd men, and she
    could not look away,
A form shot down from the starry skies to the ground whereon
    they lay,
Brilliant and swift as the lightning dart, or beam of the new
    spring day.
'Tis her angel guide—she knows him well, by the glory that
    he brings,
And by his waving locks of gold, and by his sounding wings ;
He stands before those shepherd men, in beaming robes
    arrayed,¹
But the sudden glory troubles them, and their hearts are sore
    dismayed ;
They hide their faces in their hands for fear and dread sur-
    prise,
          The glittering light
          Of his raiment bright
      So blinds their dazzled eyes.

But soon from forth his gracious lips rich sounds of music
    broke
(The common language of the blest) ; and whilst the seraph
    spoke,
His voice o'er all that silent plain the slumbering echoes woke.

        " I come, ye gentle shepherd swains,
           The herald of great joy,
        For you and all the tribes that dwell
           Beneath the circling sky.

        " Fear not, ye gentle shepherd swains,
           For on this happy morn
        To you, in yonder royal town,
           A Saviour Christ is born.

"And this shall be a sign to you—
The Infant ye shall find
All wrapped in swaddling-clothes, and in
A manger crib reclined."

*   *   *   *

Straightway the herald Angel flew, his glorious tidings told,
And plunged amid those waves of light that wide around him
rolled,
E'en as a flaming gem might melt in a sea of molten gold.
And busy swarms
Of Angel forms
Were flying to and fro,
With golden crowns upon their heads, and robes of glorious
hue;
The vista lengthening into heaven—far as the eye could view.

Ten thousand radiant spirits of light, all swift upon the wing;
Ten thousand minstrels sang the song which they alone could
sing;
Ten thousand harpers of the sky struck loud the golden
string.

"Now glory be to God on High,
And peace henceforth be given
To every man of blameless will,
That dwelleth under heaven."

Thus underneath that sounding vault pealed out that happy
song,
From heaven to earth, from earth to heaven, in echoes clear
and long.

THE HOLY SEE AND THE NATIONS OF THE WORLD.

A Homily on the Text, "Set a Legislator over them, O Lord, that the nations
may know themselves to be but men." (Ps. xi. 21.)

THE LIV. error proscribed in the Syllabus runs thus:
"Kings and princes are not only exempted from the jurisdiction
of the Church, but are superior to the Church in the decision of
all questions relating to jurisdiction;" and the LXII. error runs
thus: "The principle of what is called NON-INTERVENTION is to be
proclaimed and observed."—Let us see how these two errors
come to be connected together.

The providence of God has judged it to be good for the world of men that there should no longer be any one universal Empire as there was in the days of the old imperial sovereign ty of Rome under which Jesus Christ was crucified, and which served in a wonderful manner to promote the work of the Apostles in the first beginnings of the Church. The Roman power, which held all the then known world together under one uniform system of jurisprudence and government, has long since been broken up, and in tho place of the one great power there have been permitted to riso up a large variety of smaller sovereignties, who perform tho functions of civil government more or less well for those who are subject to them, and who endeavour to keep such peace with each other as their continual rivalries, quarrels, and jealousies will permit.

.Our Lord predicted "that nation should rise up against nation, and kingdom against kingdom," and He said, ."Be not afraid when you hear of wars and rumours of wars." This condition, therefore, of the world, where there are so very many masters in it, is thus manifestly not as favourable to peace as if all the world were under one gigantic sovereignty against which nothing could rise up to attempt to make war with it. But though peace is a very great blessing, and though the Christian people are diligently taught to pray for the blessing of peace being granted to the world, through the concord of Christian and other princes, God has not judged it to be good for the estate of the world to permit hitherto the growth of any one power to be such as that it should be able to swallow up the independence of other powers. It appears to be His Divine Will that there should be a variety of sovereignties each independent of the other, dividing the earth amongst them, and each claiming its portion. And the reason of this further appears to be for the sake of His Church and the preservation of His Revelation made to men. If there were one universal Empire, the head of it would have to be a man, and a man would then hold in his hands the power of legislating against the Kingdom of God for tho whole earth; he would be able to institute measures for the suppression of the Holy Sacrifice of the Mass, the abolition of the Church Calendar and Festivals, the prohibition of all instruction of the people in their Catechism, and to inflict penalties upon all open practice of the Worship of the Catholic Church. It would, in short, rest with him to say whether the Kingdom of God on earth should have an honourable place in it, or should be proscribed and reduced to the condition of a secret society, everywhere compelled to conceal its existence, and to hold all its meetings by stealth and under the cover of darkness. Such a power would be in a condition to contest supremacy over the earth with God Himself, and until such time as it pleases God to permit the sovereignty of Antichrist to hold for a season an absolute dominion of this kind over the earth, for the just punishment of the sins of His own people, we may expect to see the existing state of things continue. The people of the Catholic Church will have to live as they are now doing under the various lesser or greater civil sovereignties which are permitted to divide the earth among themselves, each claiming its own particular territory and the power to legislate supremely free from all intervention on the part of others, within its own limits.

Now that which would be comparatively easy for the one great Antichristian empire of the whole world to attempt whenever the time may come, when God will permit such a power to rise up, namely, to set itself completely above the Kingdom of God, is just what the smaller local powers have at all times been, and are still at the present hour tempted to try their hands at effecting each within its own territory. And to baffle the pride which impels their statesmen to these profane attempts, God has so ordered that such attempts should never be able to be anything more than the fable of the frog trying to swell itself out to the size of the bull. We cannot say what terrible times those will be when it is given to one really Universal Antichristian power to be supreme for its season over all the people of the earth; but when the local statesmen of the various smaller existing sovereignties try to set themselves above the Kingdom of God, their mutual jealousies against being interfered with, and their secret distrust of each other and of their respective designs, prevent all possibility of their acting in concert; and thus it always happens that, after they have served the purposes of God as scourges, with which He may think fit to punish the sins of His people, such statesmen invariably come to some contemptible end or other, or, in the words of Holy Scripture, "they go to their own place," leaving only a bad name and an ill savour behind them in the world, out of which they have perished never to be seen or heard in it again.

If they were not, by the instincts of their state-craft, above
all things jealous of intervention, and did not openly proclaim
and cry out that the principle of "*non-intervention*" was to be
observed, they might perchance be better able to combine
together and conspire against God and His Christ.   Thus
herein may be seen the Wisdom of God providing in a remarkable manner for the continuance of the safety of His Church
against the evils that statesmen otherwise might have far
greater power of inflicting.

A certain local danger to the wellbeing of the people of the
Church, however, must always arise from the various local
statesmen who, claiming the supreme mastership over all
within the limits of their own jurisdiction, fall into the snare
of the Devil, and, forgetting that they are but men, arrogate to
themselves the prerogatives of God.   They claim for their
State an irresponsible power, and to be above being judged,
which is only possible by arrogating to themselves the
attributes of the Godhead and investing their State with the
powers of Divinity.   Such a State is, of course, liable to the
danger of being destroyed by an uprising from below in the
form of popular revolution and entire social convulsion; but
apart from this possibility, which it takes measures to neu-
tralise as far as may be, it sets itself up as the one Supreme
Power, than which nothing higher or greater is to be known
within its sphere.   Its throne or its parliament is to be the
one Supreme Voice within its own limits, and there is to be
nothing higher known or to be tolerated under its sway.   But
this can only be brought about on one condition—viz., that
those who attempt it must forget themselves to be men.
They must, perforce, shut their eyes to the truth which God
speaks in His Scriptures, saying, "All flesh is grass," and must
fall, "and all flesh shall come before Thee" (Ps. lxiv. 3.)

To prevent the numberless evils that must flow to human
life from the false pride and undue elevation of the statesmen
of the various States into which the people of the earth
are divided, God has heard the inspired prayer of the Psalmist,
and has set up the person of one Legislator over all the nations
of the earth, to teach the nations to know themselves to be
but men.   This one Legislator is the Roman Pontiff, the
successor of S. Peter and the Vicar of Jesus Christ.   When
he declares the Faith of the Church, his words go over all
the earth and pass with ease over all the frontiers which are
closed against the decrees of any one else.   When he legislates

he legislates for all the nations alike. When he constitutes and confirms prelates, he takes no account of the particular civil jurisdiction where the act of his authority is to take effect, otherwise than in courtesy and prudence he judges to be becoming and opportune. As regards the statesmen of the earth, to all of their acts, however otherwise they may wish to arrogate absolute supremacy for them, there always adheres the incurable limitation to certain narrow boundaries of territory beyond which they are null and void of all effect, and may be ridiculed and criticized with perfect impunity by whoever likes. When these statesmen therefore see the acts of a power to which there are no limits of territory assigned, which invades their own ground equally with that of others, and passes with ease through any barriers which they can raise up against them, then, if they do not know themselves to be only men, by studying the contrast between its acts and theirs, it is only because they are so blinded by their own pride that they cannot see what the simplest of mortals can see with the greatest ease who is not equally blinded by sharing in their pride.

Thus the glory of the Catholic Church, as all Catholics should be careful to know and understand, is its Supreme See. Here sits the Legislator whom God has raised up over the nations of the earth, to abate their pride and cause them to know that they are but men. All Catholics should be cautioned to know that all attempts, from the Tower of Babel downwards to the end of time, that men may make by themselves to construct a dominion that arrogates the prerogatives of God and "reaches up to heaven," must end in discomfiture and humiliation. Whatever, then, God may permit, for holy and wise reasons known to Himself, to come upon the Holy See in the way of distress and humiliation that is to last for a time, we may have a perfect reliance that He will never fail to maintain and uphold the Legislator whom He has set up to teach the nations to know themselves to be but men, and that none of the gates of Hell will ever be able to prevail against the Church which He has built on the Rock of Peter.

A WARNING TO BLASPHEMERS.

The following narrative is the statement of Mr. Zacariah Mills, of Bradley, near Bilston, in the county of Staffordshire, a gentleman of independent means. He has no other motive in giving publicity to it but the hope that it may prove a timely warning to any blasphemers to whose knowledge it may come. It was given verbatim by Mr. Mills, September 21st, 1872, to Mr. William Davies, also of Bradley, near Bilston, and taken down in writing by him at the time :—

"About the year 1846 one of my workmen (Benjamin Hughes) told me that he had been playing the flute* on the previous night for a party of Socialists, at their usual place of meeting in Bilston, and gave me the following narrative :—

"One of the party, the usual and principal speaker, a Mr. ———, after holding forth for some time, stepped from the platform and walked down the room, exclaiming, '*Here goes a better man than ever Jesus Christ was.*' He (B. H.) said, ' I was so horrified, that I immediately left the room, and on my way home could hardly help believing but that some diabolical agency was pursuing me.' He (B. H.) said that on that very night a small blister appeared on the end of the speaker's tongue, and continued to increase for some days. It then became putrid, and was ejected from his mouth by expectoration, until the tongue had disappeared even to the root in the depth of his throat.

"The foregoing is what I, Zacariah Mills, heard from the mouth of the above-mentioned Benjamin Hughes. The following is what my own eyes were witness of :—

"After this I was repeatedly told of the frightful condition in which this unfortunate man was lying, and at last I determined to find him out. I made my way to Bilston, and by accident met with an acquaintance who knew the man and all the circumstances connected with the case. I invited him to accompany me to the residence of the person of whom I was in quest, but he excused himself by saying that it would be said that he was making the matter public. He, however, took me to the house, and there left me.

* It may be mentioned that Mr. Mills afterwards bought this flute from his workman, and threw it into the fire.

"After knocking at the door, a young married woman came, and appeared very timid and suspicious. I learnt that she was the daughter of the person I was seeking for. After I had made a few inquiries respecting the health of her father, she invited me inside. I then asked permission to see her father. She hesitated, saying he was in such a prostrate condition that I should not like the sight. I reassured her on that point, and was shown into the room where he was. He lay reclining upon a sofa, with his face downwards. The daughter said, 'Father, here is a gentleman come to see you.' Of course, speech was gone; he could only reply by some nasal sounds or movement of the head or hands. I said: '*Mr.* ———, *you are very ill,*' and from the signs he gave he appeared to agree with me. I then said: 'Do you think you shall die?' and he appeared to be of that opinion. I then said: 'I think you will, and very soon too; and don't you think there is another world after this?' He muttered, as well as he could, 'Pooh, pooh.' 'Well,' I said, 'I am come to tell you that there is another world, and that you will be judged there—aye, and by that same *Jesus Christ* and the Scriptures against whom you have uttered such horrid blasphemy; think better, and make your peace with God whilst you can.'

"His appearance at these words was something awful. His fingers clenched, his eyes stood glaring out of their hollow sockets, his lips kept attempting to say 'Pooh, pooh,' and his whole body lay writhing in contortions terrible to behold. It was a scene I shall never forget.

"I then left him. His daughter thanked me for coming, and apologised for the coolness with which she at first received me, and explained that she feared it was one of his old companions. He died the next day."

THE BULL OF PIUS IX. GRANTING INDULGENCES TO THE MEMBERS OF THE ASSOCIATION OF THE PERPETUAL ROSARY.

Pius IX.—Ad perpetuam rei memoriam.

After that, at the call and summons of God, S. Dominic, the founder of the Order of Friars Preachers, had implored the help of the Immaculate Mother of God, to whom alone it appertains to destroy all heresies in the world, in order to overcome the errors of the Albigenses, and had begun to preach the Rosary as a defence of marvellous power against heresies and vices. The above mentioned devotion of the Rosary was spread in a wonderful way among the ranks of the faithful. And, moreover, in these latter times, many of the faithful, and especially the brethren of the Order of Friars Preachers treading in the footsteps of their holy founder and patriarch, have studied to cultivate the devotion of the Rosary, from which they have known so many blessings and advantages to flow forth upon the society of the faithful, as also to cause it to become more acceptable to the Mother of God. Hence, as has been made known to us, the association of the faithful called by the name of the "Perpetual Rosary," was begun at Bologna, in the outset of the 17th century, through the zeal of a brother of the Order of the Friars Preachers, the members undertaking in succession to recite the Rosary at every hour of the day and the night, in order that a perpetual honour should be paid to the Mother of God.

Moreover, in these latter times, through the zeal of our venerable brothers, the Bishops of France, as also of the brethren of the Order of Friars Preachers, the above mentioned association, which, by reason of the most deplorable convulsions that befell the country of France at the end of the last century, had become well-nigh extinct, has been again recalled to life and more firmly established with new rules.

This society, where it is duly erected, exists under the direction of a President (*moderatore*) and Council, composed of brethren of the Order of Friars Preachers, and receives as members persons of both sexes from the general body of the faithful. It is divided into two classes, one section of which is called the "section of the days" (*sectio dierum*), and the other the "division of the months," and each has a Prefect chosen from their own society, who takes his name from his respective class. The *Prefect of the division* chooses thirty and one associates, according to the days of the month, and assigns to each of them a specified day of the month in question. Each of these thirty and one persons is called a *Prefect of a section*, and it becomes his function to enlist twenty-four associates, and to appoint to each of them an hour of either the day or night. From the above accurate division of days, months, and persons, it comes to pass that, at each hour of the day and night there are found faithful of both sexes who are enrolled in this

society, and who recite the Rosary in such a way that they
keep up a perpetual service of devotion to the Mother of God.
And, to our exceeding great consolation, we have learned that
some hundred thousands of the faithful have caused their
names to be enrolled in this association.

But recently our venerable brother the Archbishop of
Lyons, in his own and in the name of our other venerable
brothers the Bishops of France, to whom were added others
of the faithful, especially our beloved sons of the Order of
Friars Preachers, has caused earnest and humble prayers to
be laid before us that we would deign from our apostolic
goodness to enrich the above mentioned society with the
heavenly treasures of Indulgences.   We, therefore, who after
God have placed our whole trust in the Most Blessed Virgin
Mary, and are comforted with the hope, that the frequent
recitation of the Rosary, being everywhere carried into effect
among the faithful, she may at length, as in former times, destroy the monstrous errors which are now in circulation, and
avert and overthrow the impious attempts of wicked men,
have willingly thought well to accede to the requests that have
been made to us.

Wherefore, trusting in the mercy of Almighty God, and in
the authority of His Apostles Peter and Paul, we mercifully
grant in the Lord to each of the faithful who may be chosen
to the office of Prefect, whether of a *Division* or a *Section*
of the association bearing the name of the " Perpetual Rosary,"
in whatever diocese it has been or may hereafter be canonic-
ally erected, a Plenary Indulgence and remission of all their
sins on the day on which each one shall first discharge the
duties of his office, provided that, being duly penitent and
having approached the Sacraments of Penance and Communion, they have visited some public church, and have there
prayed to God for the concord of Christian princes, the extirpation of heresies, and the exaltation of Holy Mother Church;
also, a like Plenary Indulgence and remission of their sins to
all of the faithful of both sexes who shall have duly performed
the work undertaken by them at the day and hour within the
month appointed to them, to be gained by them provided that,
having duly Confessed and having received Holy Communion,
they shall, on the said day, have visited some public church,
and have there prayed in the manner above specified.

Also, we grant to each of the Prefects, whether of a Division or of a Section, as often as in fraternal charity, which is

patient and kind, they shall prevail upon any of the faithful to enroll themselves in this society, or shall take any part in stirring up the members of the association at their meetings to increased fervour and perseverance in the recitation of the Rosary or shall have performed in the Lord, any other pious work according to the institution of the society, an Indulgence of Three Hundred Days of the penance either enjoined or incurred in any other way, in the accustomed form of the Church, provided that, before commencing the work in question, they shall at least with a contrite heart have devoutly recited once the hymn "Veni Creator Spiritus," and the Angelical Salutation three times.

All and each of which Indulgences, remission of sins, and relaxation of penances, we permit to be applied, by the way of suffrage, to the souls of the faithful who have departed this life joined to God in charity.

[The remainder of the brief prescribes the formalities which must be complied with in order to its obtaining its effect, the certificate being appended, signed by "Phillippus Can. Cossa," that all has been rightly done.]

Given at Rome, at St. Peter's, under the ring of the Fisherman, 12th of April, 1868, the 21st year of our Pontificate.

(*N. Card. Paracciani Clarelli.*)

THE BLESSED NICOLAS VON DER FLÜE IN SWITZERLAND.

A SAINT OF THE FIFTEENTH CENTURY, THE CAUSE OF WHOSE CANONIZATION IS NOW BEFORE THE HOLY SEE.

MOST of our numerous *summer* tourists in Switzerland are now returned home for the winter, with pleasant remembrances of the beautiful route that leads from Lucerne to Brienz, on the lake of the same name, over the pass of the Brünig. The steamer conveys us over the famous Lucerne lake through the little lake of Alpnach to the Alpnach Gestad, or landing-stage for the pretty village of Alpnach, distant about a mile. From thence, by an excellent road up the pleasant valley of the river Aa, we reach the town of Sarnen, the capital of the Canton of Unterwalden, about three miles distant from Alpnach. The river Aa here flows out of the lake of Sarnen, and the town is situated on the banks of the river, just as it emerges from the lake.   To the south-east of Sarnen lies the romantic Swiss valley called Melchthal, or Valley of the Melch, down which a mountain-stream winds its course to become a tributary to the Aa, just below the town of Sarnen.

It was in this valley of the Melchthal that the subject of our narrative was born and died, and where his name continues to be held in such benediction among the people, that there is scarcely a house in the whole Canton of Underwalden, and even of those adjoining, which does not possess a statue or a picture of " Bruder Klaus."

What is peculiar in his history is, that as a child he had a love of solitude next to that of a hermit, yet at the call of duty he became a soldier, was afterwards a married man, a judge, and finally died in the odour of sanctity, a hermit.

At the beginning of the fifteenth century, in one of the most beautiful Cantons of Switzerland, the Canton of Unterwalden, there dwelt, not far from Sarnen, the chief town of the great Valley of Melchthal, in the little village of Flühli, a brave, God-fearing man, Henri von der Flüe, and Hermenna Robert, his virtuous wife.   Leading the independent pastoral life of the country, holding the first place in the respect and affections of their neighbours, as their ancestors had done for four hundred years before them, possessed of ample means, the fruits of their labour, these worthy people divided their days between work, prayer, and acts of Christian charity.

On the 21st of March, 1417, their union was blessed by the birth of their first child, Nicolas von der Flüe, but known as Blessed Brother Nicolas.

The child shadowed forth the man ; and the actions of the little Nicolas were early characterised by that seriousness, order, and piety that earned for him amongst the neighbours the name of *Der Knabenspiegel*, or Childhood's Mirror.

He delighted to be alone ; and deep in the woods, or far up the [mountains, tending the flocks, would spend the day in prayer : the flocks safely housed, before ever he went to the evening meal, he would first visit the little church of Flühli, where he often spent hours together in prayer.   When night closed in and the church was shut, the child would seek out some lone spot, and make that his oratory ; and many a rough piece of rock is still carefully cherished by the simple peasants because it was the *prie-Dieu* of the child Nicolas.

To his unwearied prayer the boy added long and rigorous fasts. The days of fasting appointed by the Church did not satisfy his longing for penance: four out of the seven days of the week were made Lenten days with him. His parents feared the effect of such severities on the delicate frame of a child; but Nicolas soon showed them he could bear fatigue and give evidence of strength greater than could any one of his young companions.

But his piety was not all severity: it had its gentle side as well, and this shone out in his tender love of Mary. He looked forward to her Feast Days, and then, rising with the sun, would seek on all sides, in the valleys or the mountains, the brightest, rarest flowers, and coming, offered them, all sparkling with dew, to his Mother.

Neither must it be supposed, because he was naturally of a grave, solitary nature, that he was gloomy and silent with his companions. No; with them he indulged in gentle gaiety, whilst his manner to all was kindly and affable.

About his sixteenth year he first began to visit and frequent the Ranft, a wild, rugged, savage glen, the stillness of which was broken only by the sullen roar of the Melch as it dashed along, bearing everything before it in its headlong course. Here he first formed the resolution of embracing the solitary life, and of giving himself up to the contemplation of divine things.

But a rude blow awaited him. When the Austrians invaded his country, Nicolas was called to arms. He must go: there can be no resistance; the voice of his superiors is, to him, the voice of God. It is a bitter trial, but it must be borne.

Like all strong natures, the young hermit could do nothing by halves. It was God's will that he should fight for his country, so, grasping his sword in one hand and his rosary in the other, he goes to battle, and fights with the same ardour and zeal with which he had hitherto prayed.

We see him distinguished for his valour in the long campaigns against Zurich; then, in 1446, we find him fighting at the battle of Ragatz, where the Swiss put to flight 3,000 Austrians; again, in 1460, we see him at Dissenhofen, now as ensign, now at the head of a company; and finally, for his bravery, raised, at the invasion of Thurgau, to the rank of captain.

Distinguished for his bravery, he was no less distinguished

for his merciful, compassionate disposition and warm heart. We have an instance of this in the last named engagement. A division of Austrians had taken refuge in the Convent of the Val de Sainte Catherine.   The Swiss, burning for re- venge, were about to reduce the whole place to ashes.   Nicolas at once sought the chiefs of the army, and pleaded with such force and eloquence on behalf of the community, and urged so strongly the impossibility of the enemy's holding out much longer, that the place was spared.   This is only one out of the many instances of the beneficent influence he exerted over those fiery soldiers.

They were wild times, and, to realise his power, we must remember who were the men he repeatedly withheld from dread acts of violence and crime, from sacking monasteries, burning hospitals, robbing the widow and orphan, seducing the innocent.   They were the bold men who could face and put to flight Charles of Burgundy and his fierce followers— men who had suffered wrong, and had tasted blood, and were victors.   But they were men who looked up to valour, and when they saw their grave companion-in-arms—who, whilst they were resting from the heat and strife of battle, would pass the hours allotted to repose in prayer and gentle works of mercy, who was kindly and just towards friend and foe— excel them all in deeds of bravery in fighting for their common cause, they submitted to his sway, and learned to say with him "It is a shameful thing for a soldier who has conquered the enemy to turn coward and yield himself to vice."

The war ended, Nicolas returned to Flühli, and laid down the sword he had wielded so bravely.   Not so the rosary he had clung to so faithfully: whatever path in life he walked, that should never leave him; and in each great event of his life the chronicles specially draw our attention to the rosary always grasped in his hand or hanging at his side.

He did not choose his first career in life, neither was he to choose the second.   The strong will that subdued so many, learned first to bend his own; and now, once more putting aside his own desire, and respecting the advice and earnest entreaties of his parents, he resolved on marriage, and sought and gained the affections of Dorothée Wissling, a virtuous maiden of one of the first families of Saxeln.

A numerous family was the fruit of this union; the children grew to bless the love and careful attention bestowed upon them by their parents, and did honour to the country that proudly claimed them for its own. The eldest son, during the father's lifetime, was created Landsmann, and, some years later, was succeeded in the same office of dignity and trust by his second brother. Nicolas, the youngest, having completed his studies at the Universities of Bâle and Paris, was graduated Doctor in Philosophy and Theology, " *Suprema philosophorum studiorum laurea donatus est,*" says Pierre Hugo, and died Curé of Saxeln, after a long, laborious, and useful life.

The chronicles of the time also make mention of the eldest daughter, the mother of the celebrated Conrad Scheuber, and of her sister Barbara, who married André Meyer, member of the Great Council of Lucerne.

(To be continued.)

MISCELLANEOUS ANECDOTES.

A MIRACULOUS CURE RECENTLY OBTAINED BY THE PRAYER OF THE ROSARY.—In the village of Marmagne, near Mont Cenis, in the diocese of Autun, a young girl had her brother laid up with a disease pronounced incurable by the physician, who, in consequence, had given him up and had ceased his visits. All the family and friends were in despair, and the signs of approaching death were beginning to show themselves, when his sister remembered that he belonged to the guard of honour of Mary—that is to say, that he was an associate of the Perpetual Rosary. Taking her Rosary beads, she threw herself at the et of an image of the Most Holy Virgin, and prayed to her in the most earnest manner to give a proof of the power of the Rosary. As she was fervently praying, with her eyes constantly fixed on the features of the image, it seemed to her as if the Holy Mother was looking favourably upon her. A sudden inspiration came to reanimate her drooping courage. She made a vow to recite her Rosary at midnight during eight days, and if the Holy Mother would but deign to cure her beloved brother, to make the cure publicly known. Scarcely had she made the vow when the young sufferer began to open his eyes, and from that time forward he kept continually improving, and at the present moment is completely recovered, "thanks to Mary, the powerful comforter of the

afflicted, health of the sick, and remedy of all our sufferings.''
Such were the words of the sister, Maria Soclier.—(*From
the French of the "Couronne de Marie,"* September, 1866.)

A GRACE OF OUR LADY OF THE PERPETUAL ROSARY, IN
BALLINRODE, IRELAND.—We are pleased to have to record a
grace granted by Our Lady of the Perpetual Rosary to an in-
mate of the workhouse, at Ballinrobe, in Ireland.   The
Superioress of the Sisters of Mercy, in that town, writes
(October 15th, 1872):—A grace was given to one of our
Children of Mary, in the workhouse, during her hour of
guard.   Her hour being 6 a.m., it was rather dark—early in
November, 1871—when she was saying her Perpetual Rosary.
She says the Blessed Virgin—"like as a large statue in the
chapel, but she had a blue sash on," came to the foot of her
bed, and, bowing to her, said, "Bridget, your sister Mary is
no more—pray for her," and then disappeared.   Bridget had
a sister Mary in America, and last January she got a letter
telling her that she was two months dead.   What attests the
truth of her story is, that Bridget at the time told a great
number of people in the house that she knew her sister was
dead, but they told her she was dreaming.   To this she always
replied by positively asserting that she knew she was perfectly
awake, saying her Perpetual Rosary, and could not possibly
have been deceived.

RECORD OF EVENTS.

THE Holy Father continues his apostolic work of preaching
to the whole world, taking the occasion of the visits that are
paid to him in his prison at the Vatican to utter words to
those who come to him which will be repeated in numbers of
languages and be carried over the whole world.

The "Trasteverini," that is those who live on the other
side of the Tiber, in other words, those who live on the same
side of the Tiber as that on which the Vatican palace stands,
sent a deputation to the Pope on S. Edward the Confessor's
Day with an address expressive of their loyalty.   The Pope
made a lengthy reply, of which the following words form
part:—

"I know—for the facts may be read in the public papers—I know
that every day some cashier runs off with the cash, or some tax

gatherer with the taxes, or some forger forges with his pen, or some official of the post-office absconds with notes which he has abstracted from the letters. In a word, there is scarcely a day but the newspapers tell us of some fact of this sort.

"Now, to whom will these men give an account? Very few of them are arrested. They are swift and successful in their flight. When, then, will come th e *Redde rationem*? Ah! it will come; it will come on that terrible day when Jesus Christ shall say to each of them : *Redde rationem*. But I say also: Wherefore so much corruption? Wherefore such greediness after pelf? Wherefore such forgetfulness of God, of the faith, of religion? It is because men have no faith and no religion.

"In all ages, doubtless, there were unfaithful administrators ; but never were there so many as in our day ; certainly not in any one kingdom of Italy.

"So it is that when men have neither faith nor religion, when there is no fear of God's justice, and it is possible to escape from the justice of man, then it is that men rob without risk, and ruin everything.

"I recollect a person of distinction, now deceased, who resided some years at Rome and was known to you all. This man was not an infidel ; he was one of those who call themselves ' Liberals.' He once said to me : 'I hear Mass on Sundays, and I go to Communion at Easter.' That is all very well; but I know not what put it into his mind to question the Pope about the eternity of hell—about the fire, and the torments,

"'I am persuaded,' he said, ' that no torments exist; and that there is nothing in hell'—(he believed in hell and in eternity)—' nothing but gloom and melancholy.'

"I told him in reply that the words of Jesus Christ were not about gloom or melancholy, but about fire. He did not say, *In moestitiam aeternam*, but He said and He will say, *Discedite à me maledicti in ignem aeternum.*

"If a man of the *juste milieu* principles, as this man was, believed in a hell with so few terrors, what would those say who are smitten with total unbelief—that unbelief which is taught in Rome itself?

"It has come to pass in Rome that a teacher asked a boy, ' Where is God?' and the child answered : ' God is in heaven, on earth, and everywhere ;' and the master replied: ' I do not see Him; He is not under my desk.'

"This is how they turn faith into mockery, because God has given them over to a perverted mind.

"Oh! let us guard, let us jealously guard in our hearts the precious treasure of the faith ; and let us be assured that there is an eternity to come, and that it will be blissful for the good and miserable for the wicked stewards, for the sinners and for the ungodly."

On Monday, October 28th, the Holy Father received a deputation from the inhabitants of the Monti quarter of the city, whose address, testifying their loyalty, was read by Prince Aldobrandini. The Pope again made a long reply, of which the following are the concluding words :—

" Look at what is going on in the Catholic world ; at the pilgrimages hat are being organized to beg of Almighty God His protection on behalf of the Church; at the prayers that are going up from all parts to the throne of the Most High;—at the institutions that are being founded to get people to lead a good life and to provide for the pressing needs of the time.

"See how the Bishops are defending the rights of religion.

"We can wait : the day of the Lord will come. But, you will tell me —at this moment we are *sicut super flumina Babylonis.* Yes : but do not cease to trust in God. He can reward our constancy and our firmness under suffering. He will remember His mercy towards us. Let us ask of God the courage to be able to withstand the wickedness all around us.

"O my God! sustain Thy Vicar, and give us courage. Bless this people that surround me, and may Thy blessing descend on the whole of the Catholic world.

"May Almighty God bless you. May He grant you strength and courage to finish your lives with his blessing upon you. May God the Father bless you ; may He vouchsafe you the gift of strength ; may God the Son bless you ; may He vouchsafe you the gift of perseverance; may God the HolyGhost bless you : may He vouchsafe you the gift of His light, until you reach the life everlasting.—*Benedictio Dei, &c.*"

The Church sings in the office of Good Friday "*For thy sake I scourged Egypt.*" The unbelievers of Egypt at the time doubtless saw no connection between the hail that destroyed their crops and the murrain that carried off their cattle, and the oppression of a handful of people who demanded their liberty to go to offer sacrifice to the Lord their God. The unbelievers of Europe, in the same way, doubtless, see little connection between the floods that have devastated whole districts of Italy and the North of Germany, and the sacrilege that has been perpetrated against the rights of the Vicar of Jesus Christ.

The Italian State was plotting to sequestrate the houses and property of the religious orders in Rome, but for the moment it has to turn its attention to providing shelter for the multitudes of its people whom the floods (the cataracts of the heavens) have rendered homeless. "Propter te flagellavi Egyptum."

THE ARCH CONFRATERNITY OF OUR LADY QUEEN OF THE ANGELS.-- We have received an interesting letter from Fr. Rooke, O. P., late Prior of Haverstock Hill, relating the incidents of a personal interview which he has had with Fr. de Bray, S.J., the founder and director of the Arch Confraternity of Our Lady Queen of the Angels, at Pouvourville. We are reluctantly compelled by want of space to hold over extracts from it until our next number.

THE

Monthly Magazine of the Holy Rosary.

NEW SERIES.

| No. 6.] | JANUARY. | [A.D. 1873. |

A TWELFTH-NIGHT ADDRESS OF THE EDITORS TO THEIR READERS.

DEAR FRIENDS,—

In the beginning of a fresh year it is an excellent old custom for friends to greet one another and mutually to wish each other the good wish of a happy new year, with many prosperous returns of the same. The custom is excellent, because such mutual good wishes do a great deal to strengthen and cement friendship. To honour, therefore, so good and excellent a custom with due honour, we here enter on the new year with the most cordial good wishes to all our readers, that it may bring to them, from the goodness of God, the prosperous issue of all their undertakings which they either have already commenced or may be about to enter upon for the honour of God, and that it may be blessed to them in every way that a Christian can lawfully desire. And, having thus complied with the good and time-honoured custom that belongs to the entering upon the new civil year, we hasten to turn our eyes to the new year as it is ushered in to us by the Calendar of the Church. The whole course of the year, as we hope to be able to make it our business to show as we proceed with our work, is, so to speak, lighted up as it advances by the Calendar of the Church; and during each part of its course the light that it receives is exactly of the kind that shines in the manner best suited to the holy season, and its needs.

The first day, then, of the new year, according to the Church Calendar, we keep as a feast in honour of the day on which the new-born Christ enters, by circumcision, into the covenant which God made with Abraham and his children, and learns His first early lesson for hereafter becoming the man of sorrow, who is to be afflicted and acquainted with grief, therein teaching us that the cup of mingled joy and sorrow is pretty much what we have to look forward to as our lot in the present life. To this Feast of the Circumcision

there soon succeeds a day kept holy in honour of an event in
the early infancy of the Saviour of Men, which must always
remain to the end of time a day of solemn observance and a
feast of the greatest joy to all the people and the nations of
the whole earth.   This is the Epiphany or "Twelfth-Night,"
so called from its commencing on the twelfth night after
Christmas, when the nations of the world first made the acquaintance of their Redeemer.

The Holy Child, as promised to Mary by the Archangel,
was to sit on the Throne of His father David, and to reign in
the house of Jacob for ever.   He belonged, consequently, by
His human parentage to the family of David, and by His
nationality to the house of Jacob; and the seal is further set
to this exclusive family and national character by His being
still more cut off from all participation with the nations of the
world through His admission by circumcision into the covenant which God made with the family and children of Abraham, which was always on both sides understood to be the
establishment of an impassable wall of separation, cutting off
the Jew from all except common, ordinary, and indifferent
intercourse with the other nations of the world.

The future Saviour of all the tribes and nations of men
being then actually come into the world, thus separated from
the nations by His birth as a Jew and His incorporation in
the covenant made with Abraham, there is notwithstanding a
stirring of the depths among the nations of the world, in consequence of His coming.   Though it is true that He is born a
Jew, and that He has submitted to be incorporated in a
covenant hitherto known to cut off all who have entered it
from sympathy with everything that is outside itself, still He
is expected by all the nations, and His coming is looked for
by them as the coming of One in whom they do not fail also
to have their claim.

So strong is this expectation that there are those in the
remote East who understand a star which they see in the
heavens to be the sign of His having been born into the world,
and, after conferring with each other, their knowledge is able
to descend so far into detail that they come to the conclusion
to go and look for him among the Jews.   "The wise men,"
says the Church in her Office, " upon seeing the star, said one
to another : ' This is the sign of the great King; let us go and
inquire for him, and take him our offerings of gold, myrrh,
and incense.' "

On arriving in Jerusalem they seem to have no doubt but that every one in the city will know quite well all about the birth of their King, and they accordingly appear to have asked the first persons they met, saying: " Where is He who is born King of the Jews, for we have seen His star in the East and we are come to adore him ? "

Their inquiry soon comes to the ears of Herod, and a certain panic throughout the court and city is the consequence, which ends in the doctors of the Temple being consulted by Herod.   They bring forward a prophecy which foretels that " the Ruler of Israel is to come forth from Bethlehem."

Upon this Herod calls the travellers from the East to a private interview, when he instructs them to go to Bethlehem, and pursue their search there.   They accordingly set out for Bethlehem, and, to their joy, the star which they had seen reappears, and conducts them to the very house where the young child is in search of whom they had undertaken their journey.

The house, however, turns out to be a simple private dwelling, and men of such rank and station as our travellers know better than to break rudely into private dwellings, without respecting the rights of their inmates.   Arrived, therefore, at the house, under the guidance of the star, nothing is possible except the respectful inquiry as to who is within, and whether the Child who is born King of the Jews is really there.

There is only one who is able to answer the question, and this is the mother of the Child.   It is she alone who has heard the promise of the Angel, that " He shall sit on the Throne of David His Father;" and, consequently, she alone can assure them that her Infant is born " the King of the Jews."   The mere fact of His lineage from the family of David has, by the experience of many preceding generations, long ceased to convey any appreciable claim to a kingdom.   It is, therefore, Mary only who can give the travellers the testimony necessary to satisfy them that they have really found the object of their search. The star has, it is true, directed their steps to the house where they may know that the child is to be found; but who He is, this none can say but the mother alone.

Then, again, the house is a private dwelling, and they are strangers.   What is their title to claim admission into it ? They can but ask for an audience from the mother, and, appealing to the star which has conducted them thither, pointing

also to the gifts they have come to offer, thereupon entreat to
be admitted into the house to see the Child, in order to adore
Him, and to be permitted to offer their gifts; and it will, of
course, rest with Mary to judge whether their request shall be
granted or denied.

Thus, the first acquaintance which the nations of the earth
make with the Salvation that God has sent to them is to find
it committed to a custody before which they must present
themselves, and be approved by it, preparatory to being permitted to approach. And, what is still more to be observed,
they find the Infant, whom on being admitted into His presence they willingly adore, in a state of helplessness that renders the custody indispensably needed. The fact of helplessness is obviously no hindrance to their adoration, for it was a
child of whom from the beginning of their journey they were
in search, and the helplessness of the state of infancy was, of
course, not unknown to them.

That, then, which, above all things, would not fail to be
impressed on the minds of the travellers from the East would
be the combination of the infiniteness of the treasure which
they had been permitted to behold, with its helplessness in the
custody and care of the natural guardian—the mother; and we
may well picture to ourselves the memory which they would
carry away to their distant homes of the sweet demeanour
'and graceful courtesy of the mother, in showing her Infant to
them, and in permitting them to draw near for their adoration
and for the offering of their gifts.

That which was the first experience of the nations of the
world in the persons of their first representatives, who came to
see and adore, continues, in a vast variety of ways, to be their
same experience still. The Salvation of the World, which the
princes of the East found in a state of helplessness in the
arms and keeping of Mary, continues to retain, in numberless
respects, its helplessness and its need of courtesy and a service
similar to that of Mary, in order to its becoming known to
those for whom it has been given.

Now, it is not solely for edification in general that we are
here calling the attention of our readers to this particular
lesson of the Feast of the Epiphany. We wish it to serve as
the occasion of a special word between our readers and well
wishers, and ourselves, at our mutual entry upon a new year.
Our little magazine of the Holy Rosary we intend, with the
help of God and His Holy Mother, to be entirely given up to

the proper work of the Friar Preacher, which is to preach the self-same truth that, being entrusted to the custody of Mary, was, with admirable courtesy and condescension, shown and manifested by her to the nations who had come in search of it. But, our particular work is by its nature also quite helpless to make itself known and extended, and its very condition of being is that it stands in continual need, on the part of its readers, of a service and a nursing care, formed on the pattern of hers who, overflowing with courtesy and good will, so cheerfully and willingly brought her Infant forward to show Him to the nations of the world.   In proportion, then, as our readers find by experience that our magazine brings a benefit and a pleasure to them, we may ask them to take pattern by the courtesy and good will of Mary, in diligently exerting themselves to show it to others, persuading them, if they can, to become readers of it also.   Ours is a reading age, and though it is unhappily not every reader who, like the wise men, is purposely in search of Christ, still less one who is likely to find Him in every chance leaf that may come into his hands, nevertheless the prophet says of Christ, for the encouragement of our friends: "I have been found by those that looked not for Me." This is the burden of our Twelfth-Night Address to our readers—namely, that we shall continue to look hopefully to their courtesy and good-will for a service of which our work stands in continual need by the terms of its being; and we shall trust that they will not omit to keep patiently showing it to others, endeavouring, if possible, to prevail with them to take it in and become its readers.   We are well known to be preachers by vocation, and as our magazine is for the time become our pulpit, nothing so strengthens and rejoices the heart of the preacher as the knowledge that a great multitude are waiting to hear him preach, and nothing is more common than for friends of the preacher to invite others to join with them in going to his sermon—so, if our good friends will only try to see the matter in this practical and sensible light, we may hope through their persevering and friendly co-operation to be able, as time goes on, greatly to add to the numbers of our auditory: a success which, it may be charitably hoped, will also not be without its good effect in giving us an accession of courage for the better prosecution of our work.

No. I.—HALF-HOURS WITH THE SAINTS.

THE DEATH OF ST. THOMAS BECKET, AS RELATED BY ROGER OF PONTIGNY.

OUR extract from the narrative of Roger of Pontigny intro-
duces us to the scene in the private room of the Archbishop in
his palace in Canterbury, where the four murderers, Raynald,
or Reginald Fitz Urse, William of Tracy, Hugh of Moreville,
and Richard Brito, had presented themselves at the palace,
and had been admitted to the Archbishop's private sitting-
room.

After remaining for some time in the room, saying scarcely
a word, but looking intently at each other (Reginald is said in
contempt to have let fall the expression, "God help thee!"),
Reginald, with angry gestures, first broke silence, saying,
"The King sends thee a message by us from his dominions
beyond the sea; say whether you prefer to receive it in private, or in the hearing of all that are present." The Archbishop said, "Just as you wish, gentlemen." "No," said
Reginald; "let it be according to your wish." Then, at a sign
from the Archbishop, all his clerics retired to another chamber, and no one of the Archbishop's suite remained except his
doorkeeper. Reginald then began to lay before him certain of
the requirements of the King; but the man of God. at once perceiving what he was coming to and what he was about to say,
said, "These are words not to be spoken in secret; open the
door, and call all who have gone out back again; I must not
be separated from those who are to be my advisers." It appeared afterwards, from their own confession, that they
thought to have taken advantage there and then of his being
alone to have murdered him, deliberating whether they could
not strike him down with his crozier, as they had come in
without arms. When the clerics had come back again into
the room, Reginald recommenced: "My Lord the King sends
word to you that he made peace with you in perfect sincerity,
but that you have not kept your part of the agreement; for he
has heard that you have been passing through his towns with
a large number of armed followers; and, besides this, you
have excommunicated the Archbishop of York, with the other
Bishops who complied with his wishes in the coronation of his
son, and that you have turned a large number of his people out
of their churches. All these things have a very ugly look; or,
rather, they make it next to certain that you aim at taking the
crown away from his son, and that you intend to put yourself

in an attitude of antagonism to him. Our Lord the King,
therefore, wishes to know whether you are willing to put in an
appearance in his Court, to stand your trial on these charges ?''
The Archbishop: "Have you anything more to say ? If you
have, speak."   "First," said Reginald, "we will hear your
answer."

The Archbishop replied, to the effect that it was with the
King's licence that he had returned to the kingdom and to his
see; that he had no designs whatever against the King's
son; that the people who came out to greet him had none
other than the most peaceable and friendly intentions; that
the Bishops had been excommunicated by an act of the Pope;
and that, as to being judged, he was always quite ready to
answer for himself.   Reginald retorted: "Nay, but the
Bishops have been excommunicated by you, and it is the
King's will and command that you absolve them without loss
of time."   "I do not deny," said the Archbishop, "that it has
been brought about by me; but the act is that of the Pope,
and, therefore, except they first present themselves before the
Pope with the requisite humility and promise of satisfaction,
they cannot be absolved by me."   "Then," replied Reginald,
"the King commands you to depart out of his kingdom at once,
with all your foreign-born clerics and everybody belonging to
you, and you had better look to yourself as best you may."
"Never," said the Archbishop, "shall there be the sea again
between me and my Church of Canterbury, except I am
dragged from it by force. I did not come here to turn fugi-
tive; and, as for you, you have no right to bring me any such
messages from the King. I know his prudence and reserve
far too well to suppose that he ever commissioned you to say
anything of the kind."   They all answered with one voice,
asserting that such were the King's words. "And I, in like
manner," said the Archbishop, "have reason to complain of
the King's men, who are chargeable with many insults and
grievances against me since my return. Amongst other
things, they have been guilty of assault and battery against
my servants; they have cut the tail off from one of my mules,
in contempt. They have seized by main force some casks of
wine which the King gave me, and which were being conveyed here at his cost." To this, Hugh of Moreville replied :
"If the King's men have done anything wrong to you, why
was a report of this not sent to the King, and how came you
to take the law into your own hands, and excommunicate

them?" To this the Archbishop replied: "How high you carry your head, Hugh! If anyone infringes the rights of the Church in any matter, and refuses to make satisfaction, I wait for no man's licence to take proceedings against him." Reginald said, contemptuously: "These are high and mighty threats." Whereupon all the knights, rising up with menacing gestures, stood in front of the Archbishop; when Reginald said: "In the name of the King, I outlaw thee." The rest also cried out in the same manner. The Saint replied to them: "I know that you are come to murder me; but I take God for my shield;" and, pointing with his hand several times to his head, he said, "Here you shall find me." The knights then left the room, ferociously threatening the Archbishop, and charging everyone, in the name of the King, that the Archbishop should be watched, and not allowed to escape; and they threatened all the servants, saying to them that everyone who remained with the Archbishop would be counted as an enemy of the King and to have forfeited his life. The Saint, hearing their threats, rose up and followed them to the door of the chamber; and to one of the knights, as he was uttering his threats, he said: "What you have to say, say it out." They, however, went away, paying no attention to him. The Saint, then returning to the members of his houshold, sat down upon his sofa. John of Salisbury said to him: "This has always been your way, that you say and do just what you alone think to be right." The Saint answered: "What is it you want, Master John?" "You ought," said John, "to have called together your advisers, knowing for a certainty, as you ought to do, that these men-at-arms are looking out for nothing less than an occasion against you to put you to death." The Saint answered: "We have all to die, and we ought not to be turned aside from the path of justice by the fear of death. I am more ready to suffer death for God and justice, and the liberty of the Church, than they are to inflict it." "Yes, but we," rejoined John, "are sinful men, and are not yet prepared to die." I see no one but yourself who is in so great a hurry to die. The Archbishop replied: "The will of God be done."

Some interval elapsed while the knights went out to collect together their followers and to decide what measures they were to take, for it does not appear that they had deliberately premeditated what they were to do in the event of the Archbishop failing to surrender to their threats. It was not long, however, before they returned, prepared for any act of violence the occasion might be deemed to require, murder included, if necessary. In the meantime, the palace doors were barred; and when they found it impossible to force them open, one Randolph de Broc, who was well acquainted with the house, brought them by a private way through the orchard, and they found an entrance through a portion of the building which was undergoing repairs. During this delay, the monks had, partly by force and partly by entreaties, conveyed the Archbishop towards his place in the choir, barring the entrance, after they had passed through, into the church. The knights, having forced their way into the cloister, had now come to the last remaining barrier, and were endeavouring to force it open, when the Archbishop exclaimed (we now proceed with Roger of Pontigny's narrative) :—

" By holy obedience I command you to open the doors without delay; we must not make a castle of the House of God." Again the monks crowded round the Archbishop, pressing him forward to his place in the choir, to whom he said, " Let me alone, and do you retire; you have nothing to do here; let God Almighty dispose of my affairs as He thinks best." Whilst this was passing, the knights had entered the church, uttering terrible threats,vociferating, and cryingout, "Where is Thomas, the traitor to the king?" To this the man of God said not a word. Again they cried out, and said, " Where is the Archbishop? " Then the saint said, " I am a priest and the Archbishop; if you seek me, you have found me." Saying this, he went to meet them down the steps of the choir, which he had ascended, and turning aside to the northern part of the church, he stood close to the wall, near the altar of S. Benedict. The four knights above mentioned, and a certain cleric whom they had brought with them, one Hugh Mauclerc (literally, *evil clerk*), came to him, and said, " Straightway absolve the king's bishops whom you have excommunicated." To which he replied, " I will do nothing except what I have said and done." Then they began to threaten him with death; to which he answered, " I do not fear your threats, for I am ready to die in the cause of God; but I charge you to let all my people go, and to do no harm to them." Then they all laid hands upon him, endeavouring to pull him away, and to lift him on to the shoulders of William, that they might carry him out of the church: but the Saint stood firm on the step, and could not be moved from his place; for Master Edward Grim, the only one of his attendants who had remained with him, stoutly resisted them.

As Reginald Fitz Urse, the first who laid hands upon him, was dragging him with all his might, the Archbishop shook him off, with such determination that he almost fell on the floor of the church, saying, at the same time, " Get thee hence; thou art my man, and hast no right to touch me." Reginald replied, " I owe thee neither homage nor service against my duty to the King." Reginald, seeing that he could not be moved from his place, and fearing lest he should be rescued out of their hands by the people who were beginning to come into the church to hear vespers, drew his sword and came near. The Saint, seeing his martyrdom to be imminent and his murderer close at hand, he covered his eyes with both hands joined, and, inclining his head, offered it to the mur- derer, saying, " I commend myself to God, to S. Benet, and S. Elphege." As these words were uttered, Reginald drew near and struck him with his sword obliquely, cutting off the crown of his head, and causing his cap to fall on the floor. The sword fell on the left shoulder, and cut through all his wearing apparel down to the flesh. Master Edward, who stood close by and saw the blow aimed, interposed his arm as with the intention of shielding the blow and had it all but cut off. Then William of Tracy came near, and dealt him a heavy blow on the head; from which, however, he did not fall. The same William then struck him a second time with still greater force, and at this blow the Saint fell at full length on the floor of the church. Richard Brito then struck a blow at him as he lay on the floor, and broke his sword in the middle as it struck against the pavement. Whilst these things were being done Hugh of Moreville was employed in keeping the people back who were pressing forward, and in this way it happened that he never struck a blow. Hugh Mauclerc, however, the greatest reprobate of all men, coming to the dead body as it lay on the ground, placed his foot on the neck, and scattered the brain on the floor, crying out, " The traitor is dead enough now; let us go." Having then done their work, the knights went out of the church by the same way by which they came in, with their swords drawn in their hands, and cry- ing out, " We are the king's men, the king's men."

The sequel of the history we must abridge. The monks as hastily as possible closed the church, and proceeded to lay the body out for burial; and, to the joy and surprise of all, they found that the Archbishop wore a hair shirt, and drawers of the same material, which caused him continual suffering.

"Behold," they exclaimed, "a veritable monk and hermit! Behold a true martyr, a man who not only suffered torment in death, but also in his life." They buried him in the crypt of the church, and the fame of the miracles which were worked at his tomb soon filled the length and breadth of the land. He was martyred on the 29th of December, in the year of grace 1171.

No. IV.—THE VENERABLE ANNA MARIA TAIGI.

THE whole life of Anna Maria, from the time of her conversion till her death, may be said to have been one continual act of the love of God. Our Lord had repeatedly told her that He desired to take up His abode in her soul, and to make it His resting-place. We have seen how wonderful were the effects of this Divine union during the first years of consolation, and the incomparably more sanctifying time of her desolation and interior crucifixion, when she became indifferent and dead to all things save the pure love of God.

But this holy detachment was far from causing anything like apathy or carelessness about the welfare of others. On the contrary, Divine love produced in her soul that indefatigable and universal charity to her neighbour, which was one of the chief features of her life. When we recall her poverty, her laborious home duties, and her constant ill-health, it is marvellous to find how much time she was able to devote to active works of charity. When she could not otherwise help the poor, she sought alms for them from the rich, and was assiduous in nursing them in sickness. Her constant work was attending the hospitals, especially that of S. James, for incurable women, to which she often took her daughters, that they might practise works of charity. Above all, her spiritual works of mercy were incessant. Her zeal for the glory of God, her love of souls and hatred of sin gave her an irresistible force and energy of character, which made her the life and soul of all with whom she came in contact. She had an extraordinary power of consoling others, and of imparting to them her own spirit of faith, and her peace of soul—that grand peace, which was never shaken through years of agonising dereliction. It is not surprising that the long mar-

tyrdom she voluntarily endured procured for her graces of
the highest order both for herself and others. Many were the
miraculous conversions obtained by her prayers and penances.
On one occasion, a priest desired her to pray after Communion
for three malefactors who were about to be executed that very
day. After praying, it was shown that one of them, a woman,
was reprieved, and that the two others were about to die im-
penitent, not so much on account of the crimes for which they
were condemned as for their unworthy behaviour towards
their parents. Anna Maria suffered most cruel torments the
whole day, which increased up to the time of the execution.
Our Lord assured her in the evening, that they had received
the grace of conversion and been saved, on account of the love
He bore to her, but that He had inflicted upon her the satisfaction due to the Divine Justice.

The wonderful graces which Anna Maria thus obtained for
others are far too numerous to be recorded in this slight
sketch. It may be supposed, however, that her counsel and
assistance were eagerly sought for by persons of every condition. And we cannot but admire the spirit of faith and
justice, which made her give the same attention to all, without
regarding their rank or class. To her there could be nothing
little or trivial where an act of charity had to be performed,
or a sorrow to be consoled. While she never allowed a word
against charity to be uttered, she had extraordinary tact in
allowing others to ease their hearts by pouring forth their
sorrows to her, and then, by her prudent advice, restoring
peace and healing family differences. In her eyes, a poor
woman reduced to misery in her hovel was as great an object
of interest and sympathy as a nobleman in disgrace, or a
sovereign driven from his dominions. Thus the Queen of
Etruria, who so often sought her prayers and advice, was no
more to her than the lowest servant whose trouble she could
relieve.

"It was admirable," says her intimate friend, "to hear her
one day consoling a poor woman who was in the depths of
grief because her hens no longer laid the proper number of
eggs, and giving her sage advice how to remedy the evil, with
the utmost good nature and kindness; and to listen to her,
soon after, treating of affairs of the highest importance, which
required most skilful and cautious management—deciding,
and giving suitable advice, with the same ease and simplicity
with which she had attended to the miseries of the poor
woman."

We are reluctantly compelled to omit many interesting details of Anna Maria's private life, and of her many heroic virtues, her penances and practices of devotions. We cannot, however, wholly pass over her extraordinary mortification in eating and drinking. She was naturally inclined to like delicate viands and agreeable drinks, but her fasting and self-denial on this point were carried so far that at length she lost all taste for food. Her abstinence from drinking any liquor whatever, which she sometimes practised for a whole week at a time, was the more painful, as she was tormented with almost continual thirst, in the extreme summer heats of Rome. It is notable that Our Lord frequently encouraged her in this mortification, and signified to her how agreeable it was in His sight. Her fasts were very frequent. She fasted on all Wednesdays, Fridays, and Saturdays, and sometimes for forty days together, when she had any particular favour to ask for others. At other times, the food she took was barely sufficient to sustain life.

We must now turn to the remarkable influence exercised by Anna Maria over the political events then happening in Rome, in which we are strongly reminded of that of S. Catherine of Sienna, under similar circumstances. Anna Maria, in the clear light vouchsafed to her, saw all the secret manœuvres and hidden assemblies of the revolutionary sects, and heard all their wicked designs. Her ardent charity caused her to intercede with her Divine Spouse, and to offer herself as a victim to avert these evils. "Her prayer," says the authentic record of her life, "was so assiduous and fervent, as much for this end as to implore the conversion of these ungrateful sons of humanity, that from the first years she obtained from God a special promise in favour of Rome. She obtained that the most impious of the sectaries should not prevail in her time; that God would leave them an open field to labour in their designs, but at the moment of execution all the threads should be broken at one blow; that for this motive, she should prepare herself to satisfy the Divine justice in return for so considerable a favour. In effect, each time that these plots were frustrated, the servant of God found herself assailed by mortal maladies or persecutions; by miseries, calumnies, and the most cruel interior desolations. Then, when she laid her pains lovingly in the heart of Our Lord, this good Master made known to her that the cause of her sufferings was the reciprocal promise made between Himself and the humble woman.

"The servant of God, then, was never discouraged; on the contrary, when she saw fresh plots being formed, and that great effusion of blood, particularly that of priests and the higher ecclesiastics, was threatened, she again reminded her Beloved of the promise she had received from Him, and renewed her prayer, with the result we have described. And this continued during the whole time that she lived.

"What prayers she offered for the Sovereign Pontiff, and for the most elevated ecclesiastical dignitaries! How much is the Church indebted to the prayers and penances of this servant of God! How much does not Rome owe to her in particular!"

The remarkable knowledge of future or distant events possessed by Anna Maria was not confined to what concerned Rome.   We give the following incident from an unimpeachable witness of the event: "She saw equally," he says, "occurrences which were remote as well as those which were near at hand.   She knew the death of the Emperor of Russia, Alexander; and she saw the soul of this Prince in a place of salvation, because he had shown mercy to his neighbour—because he had respected the Sovereign Pontiff, the Vicar of Jesus Christ, and had protected the Catholic Church; she saw, that for these reasons, God had granted him grace and lights for his salvation."

(*To be continued.*)

THE LEGEND OF THE CHERRY-TREE;
OR, AN INSTANCE HOW MARY WAS HONOURED IN ENGLAND IN THE CATHOLIC TIMES.

THE ancient city of Coventry was famous for its mystery plays which used to be acted by the several trades of the town on the Corpus Christi Festival.   Concerning the scenery, machinery, dresses, and decorations, and the stage management of those times but little is at present known.   It would seem, however, at least frequently, that they were acted on stages which were made movable upon four wheels, and could, consequently, form part of a great pageant.   The following passage occurs in Ormerod's History of Cheshire, relating to similar Chester mysteries, which were acted for the last time in the year 1574.   "They began first at the Abay Gates, and when the pagiante was played it was wheeled to the High

Cross before the Mayor and so to every streete." There were besides, says the same MS., " scaffolds and stages made in the streetes in those places wheare they had determined to playe their pagiantes."

In the VIII. Mystery (in the Cotton MS., preserved in the British Museum, Pageant XV.) the play commences by Joseph acquainting Mary with the necessity of his going to " Bedleem," and Mary says she will go with him.   As they are travelling, Mary espies a tree and inquires of Joseph—

Mary.—A my swete husband wolde ye telle to me,
   What tre is yon standing upon yon hylle.

Joseph.—For sooth, Mary, it is yclepyd a chery tree,
    In tyme of yer ye myght feede you thereon your
    fylle.

Mary.—Turn again, husbond, and beholde yon tree,
   How that it blomyght now so swetely.

Joseph.—Cum on, Mary, that we were at yon Cyte,
    Oellys we may be blamyd, I telle you lythly.

Mary.—Now, my spouse, I pray you to behold,
   How the cheryes growyn upon yon tree;
   For to have them of ryght ffayn I wolde,
   And it plesyd you to labor so mec'h for me.

Joseph.—Yo desyr to ffulfyle I schall assay sekyrly,
    Ow to pluck you of those cherys it is a werk
    wydle.

Mary.—Now, good Lord, I pray Thee grant me this boon,
   To have of these cheryes an it be yo' wylle;
   Now I thank it God, yis tree bowyth to me down,
   I may now gader enowe and etyn my fylle.

Joseph had made a disrespectful speech to Mary, which we have not quoted, and he perceives by the bowing down of the tree, that on speaking thus reproachfully to the Holy Virgin he had offended " God i trinyte," and he humbles himself.

The same legend of the sudden blooming of the cherry-tree, and of its bowing down to Mary on Joseph's refusal to gather the cherries, forms the subject of a Christmas Carol that is still occasionally found in circulation in London and in some of the Counties of England.   The text of it runs as follows :—

As Joseph and Mary
  Walk'd through the garden gay,
Where the cherries they grew
  Upon every tree,

O, then bespoke Mary,
  With words both meek and mild,
Gather me some cherries, Joseph,
  They run so in my mind ;
Gather me some cherries,
  For I am with child.

O, then bespoke Joseph,
  With words most unkind,
Let Him gather thee cherries
  From whom thou art with child.

O, then bespoke Jesus,
  All in his mother's womb,
Go to the tree, Mary,
  And it shall bow down.

Go to the tree, Mary,
  And it shall bow to thee,
And the highest branch of all,
  Shall bow to Mary's knee.

And she shall gather cherries,
  By one, by two, by three ;
Now you may see, Joseph,
  These cherries were for me.

O, eat your cherries. Mary,
  O, eat your cherries now ;
O, eat your cherries, Mary,
  That grow on the bough.

" All generations shall call me blessed," a prophecy of the
Holy Bible, which the misguided bulk of the English people,
sad to think, do their best to deprive of its due fulfilment. Let
us patiently try to teach them better things, and pray that
they may return to walk in the good ways of those who have
gone before them.

THE BLESSED NICOLAS VON DER FLUE IN SWITZERLAND.

A SAINT OF THE FIFTEENTH CENTURY,' THE CAUSE OF WHOSE CANONIZATION IS NOW BEFORE THE HOLY SEE.

So powerful an influence as that of the model household of Flühlin was felt even by "the pious Unterwaldens," and looked up to and consulted on all occasions of importance. Nicolas could not escape the office of Judge and Councillor, to which he was elected by the universal suffrage of his fellow-townsmen.   As a father more than as a judge, he for nineteen years discharged the duties of this twofold office; and we are quite carried back to patriarchal times when we read of the magistrate, a quarrel arising, summoning the disputants, and, seating himself under a linden-tree—which is still shown at Obwalden—with one on his right hand and the other on his left, there holding his Court and pronouncing judgment.   Many a time was the defeated one consoled for the loss of his case by the offering of some rare fruit from the garden of his judge.

Towards the end of his career as magistrate, Nicolas wrote to an ecclesiastical friend : " God be praised, I have pronounced many sentences during my lifetime, and there is not one of which I repent.   I have always hearkened to the voice of God speaking in my conscience; and before ascending the judgment-seat, it has ever been my practice to implore the light of the Holy Spirit.   Neither the address of the accuser nor of the accused has ever influenced me.   Blessed be the Lord."

That the people really loved him is shown by their frequent and urgent entreaties that he would accept the charge of Landamann ; but Nicolas always resisted them.   He was wearied of these honours he had never sought, and by degrees withdrew himself more and more from the public life he had ever shunned.   The old yearning for solitude had come back upon him with irresistible force.   Renouncing the almost passionate longing of his youth, he had striven as a soldier, a husband, a father, a magistrate; his had been a busy life; and now he must say good-bye to the world.   But there was a hard struggle to be fought before this could be accomplished ; and the man of strong mind and clear judgment, who had been the friend, counsellor, and support of so many, is now divided and torn between conflicting emotions.   The imperative call to contemplation and prayer drew him to the desert, the bonds of family affection held him to his home.   Must he leave them

the grant of powers to extend itself to all countries, and in connection with which miracles are worked that are too notorious to be denied, possesses at least two signal marks of credibility, either of which is a sufficient warranty to enable all reasonable persons who feel themselves attracted to it to put their faith in it.   But to these we have to add one which not uncommonly accompanies all works in proportion to their importance—namely, contradiction.

The founder of the Catholic Church, although a Divine Person, was truly and really Man (perfectus homo, Athanasian Creed), and God employs men as His instruments for all works, little and great, in His Church.   It is not given to the angels, but to men, to be chosen as instruments for beginning and directing the various works needed for the Church.   And when men are chosen as instruments for any particular work, in proportion to its greatness, contradiction, after the pattern of the work of Jesus Christ, is nearly always the distinctive accompaniment of their call.   Our Lord Himself, the Founder-in-Chief of the Church, as we all know, was a sign or mark for contradiction, and His own brethren also did not believe in Him.

With these few words of preface, we lay before our readers such extracts as we can find room for from the notes which Father Rooke, O.P., late Prior of Haverstock Hill, London, has sent us (dated 7th November), relating two interviews which he has been privileged to have with Father de Bray, founder and director of the Arch-Confraternity of Our Lady Queen of the Angels.*

"Father de Bray belongs to a noble and ancient family; in stature he is of full ordinary height, with no external signs of asceticism, but quiet, gentle, and humble in his manner. There is a subdued look of suffering in his face, and at times an unearthly expression in his eyes.   His age is about 56.   He has always led a holy life, and it is very generally known that he has never lost his baptismal innocence; but from a child he had continual ill-health, and such was the terrible nervous disease under which he suffered that if any one touched him on the back it threw him into convulsions.   From all of these sufferings he was perfectly cured at the time of his vow.   His

---

* Father Rooke, it should be said, went to Pouvourville as the companion of another Dominican Father, who went to visit the Shrine of Our Lady at Pouvourville, hoping to receive the favour of a cure from a malady from which he suffers.

visions have been numerous and are still of frequent occurrence, and he has worked several miracles; but Our Lord says, 'A prophet is not without honour save in his own country and in his own house.' On the first day he invited us upstairs to his private room, offering my companion his arm to help him up the stairs. There he insisted on lighting the fire on our account, and though evidently he was suffering from great weakness, he knelt down and lighted it himself. His sweetness and childlike simplicity of manner quite set us at ease, and gave us confidence to ask him anything we desired.

" We elicited an account of the work which has been revealed to him, and he gave us a description of the great church or basilica which is to be built at Pouvourville to Our Lady Queen of the Angels. The curé of the village, I may add, next morning after mass, showed us, from an upper window in his house, the spot where it is to be built—a magnificent site, on high ground, looking down on the River Garonne, with an immense stretch of flat country beyond, so that it will be seen on all sides for miles. Father de Bray said it will be more beautiful than the Temple of Solomon. In its plan it is cruciform, the four arms of the cross being nearly equal in dimensions. In the centre, at the intersection of the cross, is to be the high altar of Our Lady Queen of the Angels, raised high up under a magnificent dome. In the arm of the cross behind will be placed the altar of S. Michael; in the two transepts the altars of S. Gabriel and S. Raphael. An Order is to be formed in connection with it; but as yet he does not know full particulars, except that it is to have the rule of S. Augustine, with some special constitutions, and that a body of two hundred religious will keep up the chant in the church *perpetually*. When Our Lady told him all this, he said to Her, 'But how am I to support all these people?' and She replied: ' Fear not; I will provide for that.' He asked Her what kind of people he was to receive into the Order, and from what class of society, and whether if deformed people applied they might be admitted ? She replied that it mattered not from what class of society they came, nor even if they were cripples, but all depended on the truth of their vocation. The ground plan, which the Father drew out at Our Lady's dictation, though he understands nothing about plans and drawing, is in the possession of M. Deville, who very kindly showed it to us when we called upon him next day. The Father is undergoing very great trials and interior sufferings at the present time, and in all simplicity he told us of the great persecutions he is subjected to by many who look upon him as demented. . . . . .

"Some members of his family, though they love him, yet do not believe in his work. As I had been told that great blessings had been promised to the Society on account of his work, I asked him whether that was true. He replied, emphatically, '*Immense.*' He told us of a vision he had had at an earlier period of his life, betokening favours to him, and then a shower of little crosses fell upon him and surrounded him; and, after saying that he knew he was to be overwhelmed with crosses and sufferings, he said, in childlike simplicity and in accents of confidence, 'But Our Lady says she will never abandon me.' He told us of a vision he had on the previous day week, while celebrating mass in his private chapel. After the Consecration, when he broke the Sacred Host, it appeared to him red as fire, and a voice spoke to him from it, telling him he would have to suffer the greatest humiliation and trials in every way; and though feeling overwhelmed at the announcement, he interiorly said 'I accept them.' He also described a vision he had one day, when feeling very cast down, of Our Lord as the 'Ecce Homo,' with His flesh torn and hanging down in flakes, and His face dripping with blood, bruised, and crowned with thorns: at the sight of which, he exclaimed 'Who are you?—like a worm of the earth; you cannot be my God!' He answered that He was the veritable Jesus Christ, and that His sufferings far surpassed those of the Father. By this vision he was encouraged to endure his own heavy trials; but the tears would rise to his eyes as he spoke of them, especially when he said that he knew all would turn against him and disbelieve him. I had myself hard work to choke my own tears, so much did I feel compassion for him. But when his trials should be at their height, then would come the triumph, he added. But on saying these things, he looked distressed, and remarked that he feared he gave scandal by thus talking of himself; but he assured us that he did not do it from any motive of self-love, but for the greater glory of the Holy Virgin, and he felt compelled to relate them; which brought the words of the Apostle to my mind, who declared that they could not but speak of the things which they had heard and seen."

(*To be continued.*)

RECORD OF EVENTS.

In the Canton of Geneva in Switzerland the Catholics have for some months past been subjected to persecution from the civil authorities. The religious teachers of the schools have been forced to retire, and of the various civil disabilities which persecuting powers inflict on their Catholic citizens, some have been enforced and others have been threatened.

The Catholic clergy of the Canton, under the leadership of their eloquent Bishop Mermillod, sent an address to the Holy Father, to which Pius IX. has graciously replied. The Pope laments the bad faith of the rulers of the Canton, who have undone the work of their predecessors, and broken their international treaties. He encourages the priests and people to persevere, saying, "We do not doubt but that for your constancy you will be called 'seditious,' for it is no unusual occurrence for those to be calumniated whom it is intended to oppress. Persevere, then," concludes the Pope, "with undaunted courage in your present course, and continue, in union with your Catholic people, to avail yourselves of all lawful means whereby you may defend the cause of justice."

The Princeess Torlonia, with a most commendable charity and munificence, maintains a refuge for poor but deserving girls, where they receive a gratuitous maintenance and education under the care of Sisters of Charity. On the 5th of December the pupils of this institution, known as the Conservatorio Torlonia, were presented to the Pope at the Vatican to the number of 200. One little girl read an address, and another recited a piece of poetry in Italian, written for the occasion, and others presented a small sum of money, which they offered as Peter's Pence. The Holy Father, who appeared much pleased, is reported in the *Voce della Verita* to have replied as follows:—

"My dear little girls, I give you my blessing with all the affection of my heart. I have heard with real pleasure all that these two good little girls have said, because they have said it well, and have said it with modesty and with a little timidity. That is a praiseworthy and good thing; and it is a beautiful sign of the Christian and delicate education which they have received; for the boldness and forwardness one sees in children who have been educated in the modern schools does not well become young people of your age.

"I was reading but an hour ago, indeed I had not quite finished it, an article in a paper, the *Unita Cattolica*: the first part is not for you, but the second part may very well be applied to you. In the first part it said that one member of the Parliament—there is a Parliament in these days—

speaking to the other members and discussing their affairs, became quite
confused, and said, ' How are things going on ?   What will be the end of
it ?   Where are we going to ?   Where in the world are we already ?'   And
no one was able to reply to him.   But I also read what the Catholic paper
replies to him : it says—' You are walking in the road to the precipice ; in
the way to the abyss, in the path of destruction.   You know it not'—the
writer adds—'you know not whereabouts you are.   But we Catholics know
quite well whereabouts we are walking, and where we are : we are upon
the right road ; we are safe in this world, and are expecting to be saved in
the next.'
' " You, also, my dear little girls, can say you know whereabouts you are.
You are in a Conservatorio, where you are being taught to practise goodness, and to work, so that you may be able to earn an honest livlihood.   So
that you may say—' We are in a place of safety—in a place where we are
learning to love and fear God ; and He strengthens us with His grace and
gives us all His blessings ; we are in a place where we are learning our
duties ; where we have not to fear those evils that in our days are causing
such ruin of souls in the world.'   Then, thank God you are able to know
whereabouts you are, and try always to get more and more good from the
good instructions that are given you.   Be obedient, be fervent, frequent the
Sacraments, and labour diligently that you may escape idleness, the
greatest and most dangerous enemy to virtue.   I now give you my Apostolic
Benediction, that you may live well in the Conservatorio, and also in the
world, whenever the Lord shall call you there.   *Benedictio Dei, &c.*"

On the 8th of December a number of distinguished persons
were received to an audience by the Holy Father in the
Vatican, when, among other offerings which were presented,
was an album, richly bound, containing many thousand signatures to an address which was written on the first pages.
The Marchesa Serlupi read the address, which runs as follows :—

" Most Holy Father,—The Feast which we celebrate to-day, and which
records one of the most glorious events of your Pontificate, that of having
raised to a dogma of faith the Immaculate Conception of the Mother of
God, will, by the desire of this committee, be celebrated in many parts of
the world with the sole intention of hastening, as far as in our power, the
much wished-for day of your triumph.

"When Peter was in prison, by order of Herod Agrippa, we read in the
Acts of the Apostles, that the whole Church interceded for him, and Our
Lord heard the prayers that were offered up for him, and sent an angel
from heaven to deliver him.

"Now, the Successor of Peter is also in prison, and we, Holy Father,
your most devoted children, have sought to imitate the example of the first
Christians by inviting the whole Church, on this day and during the preceding Novena, to invoke the Almighty, through the Immaculate Virgin
Mary, with fervent prayer and redoubled earnestness, to listen to our ardent
demand, and grant the deliverance of your Holiness, and thus give peace
and tranquillity to the Catholic world.

"And to continue imitating the first examples offered us by the Church, to come in aid of the honourable poverty of the Vicar of Jesus Christ, we place at your feet this small offering, gathered from the faithful of both the Old and New World; while we implore your Apostolical Benediction upon ourselves, and upon all those who are united with us in this demonstration of filial love and of constant and unalterable devotion.

The Marchesa Serlupi, President, then presented to the Pope the offering which had been collected, to the amount of 70,000 francs, and which had been put into a white satin bag, tied with gold cord and tassels, and the whole enclosed in an elegant glass case, with gilt borders. The Holy Father was touched at so much devotion to the Holy See, and of such respectful affection for his sacred person. He thus briefly answered the above address:

" I rejoice indeed in listening to such beautiful sentiments, and accept with pleasure the magnificent gift you offer me. It makes me feel more and more that our position is like unto water; the more it is pressed down on one side, the higher it rises on the other. So is the Church of Jesus Christ in time of persecution. The more it is oppressed the more does it rise, and difficulties, instead of depressing it, serve only to show how great is the life of the Church, by enlivening and increasing fervour in every nation. ' Laudate Dominum omnes gentes, laudates eum omnes populi.' And now I will give you a blessing that will extend to every part of the world, to all those whose names are written in that volume, to all those who have taken part with you in praying for the Vicar of Jesus Christ. An especial blessing to you, pious souls here present, who have organized this work of devotion. *Benedictio Dei, &c.*" His Holiness then went to look at the album, which he much admired, and remained some time observing the binding, painting, and the names that were written in the book, showing how much he had felt and had been pleased at this demonstration of sympathy and affection which so many from all parts of the world had shown to him.

MISCELLANEOUS ANECDOTES.

THE CONVERSION OF ENGLAND.—Vague rumours of a prophecy concerning the conversion of England to the Catholic faith have been current among Catholics for some years back, and we think that an account of its origin will be pleasing and consoling to our readers. In an appendix to a pamphlet published some years ago, Mr. A. P. de Lisle states the following fact : " I was travelling, twenty years ago, into Wales, and passing the night in a town on the road, I inquired in the morning whether there was a chapel where I could hear mass ; on ascertaining that there was, I went, heard mass, and after mass, the priest having shown me his chapel, and all that he

had that was curious and interesting, our conversation turned
on the chances whether England would ever again be Catholic.
The good priest said with much earnestness that he believed
it would.   And he added a most remarkable history that tended
to confirm his opinion.   About a hundred and fifty years before that time, there was a saintly Catholic gardener in that
very town, who was a man of extraordinary virtue and prayer
—indeed, his life was one continued prayer—and next
to h's own sanctification no object occupied so prominent a place in his multiplied petitions to the throne of
grace, as the return of his own dear country, England, to the
unity of the Catholic Church.   One morning, three years before his happy death, he had received the holy communion,
and all at once he was wrapt in spirit, and Jesus, whom in the
sacrament of His love he had just received, manifested Himself to His humble servant, and with a sweet and gracious
aspect said to him, 'My son, I have heard your prayer so
often poured out before Me; I will have mercy upon England.'
At these words, the poor gardener, overwhelmed with gratitude, exclaimed: 'When, Lord, oh! when?'   'Not now,' replied our Saviour; 'but when England shall build as many
churches as she destroyed at the change of religion, and when
she shall restore and beautify the remainder.'"   This history
was related to me by this pious priest in 1837, and he added,
"Do we not see the first part of this prophecy in a fair way
towards accomplishment?"   Castiglio, in his " History of the
Order of S. Dominic," says, that S. Dominic, when on a visit
to the Court of France, found Queen Blanche the wife of King
Louis the Eighth in much distress on account of being without children.   Hearing this S. Dominic advised her to use
the Rosary.   The Queen not only followed his advice, but also
gave Rosaries to her attendants and people, so that they all
might join in prayer with her for a son and heir to the throne.
Our Blessed Lady heard their prayers, and the son who was
born was none other than the great St. Louis, whom Gibbon
even has called "a king, a hero, a man," and whom the Catholic Church calls "a Saint."

THE

Monthly Magazine of the Holy Rosary.

NEW SERIES.

No. 7.]   FEBRUARY.   ·   [A.D. 1873.

No. II.—THE SOCIAL DEVOTION OF THE ROSARY.
A School of Christian Improvement for all the Catholic People both Rich and Poor.

WE terminated our subject of the Social Devotion of the
Rosary in October of last year with quoting the words of
Cornelius à Lapide, commenting upon the Apostle's admonition not to forsake the public assemblies of the Church.   The
same commentator continues his commentary by further insisting on the reason—viz., "that these public assemblies
wonderfully nourish and keep alive faith and charity, which
are apt to grow feeble and languid if separation and isolation
is too long continued." S. Ignatius, the follower and disciple
of S. Paul, urges the same thing upon the people of Ephesus
and Smyrna—that they should be diligent in frequenting
these assemblies of the Church, adding, also, at the same time,
the reason, "*because they will greatly strengthen you:*" and he
warns them that if they once fairly get into the habit of staying
away from them, it will come to pass "*that they will fall away
from the faith altogether.*"

These words, beyond all doubt, are extremely well suited in
the way of opportune admonition in the midst of the state of
things which we have described, and with which we have to
deal—viz., the process of separation and estrangement which
is continually going on in consequence of the falling away of
great numbers of our people into a condition of deplorable
social degradation, mainly through their own fault, and the
contrary sudden rise of others through their intelligence and
industry, aided, also, by various favourable circumstances.

To continue our subject.   The Sunday or other day of
obligation comes round, and the law of the Church then lays
all under the common duty of assembling themselves to be
present at the celebration of the Holy Sacrifice of the Mass. The
decency, not to say splendour, of dress in which the prosperous
portion of the people of the Mission make a point of being
present at it, has been found, from the now uniform experience
of many years, to frighten away very large numbers of the

class who are falling into the sinking condition already described. The answer of this class to any charitable remonstrance that may be made to them has long been cast into the unchanging, stereotyped form, " I have got no clothes." In vain all expostulations, in vain all rebukes, in vain all denunciations of future penalties to be incurred by the neglect; the answer, " I have no clothes," is given with the conviction that not only is there no appeal from it, but that in it is amply contained whatever dispensation may be supposed to be needed for the non-fulfilment of an admitted duty.

The breach being thus fairly made, in the non-fulfilment of the one great primary duty of the Catholic religion—the obligation to be present at Mass—on the part of a large and numerous class, who seem, unhappily, to have little or no salutary sense of culpability on their own part as to the courses which have brought them into the condition of "having no clothes," it is needless to say what is the inevitable natural consequence. The experience of too many missionary priests can only too sadly tell tales of Catholic families who have been swallowed up in the ignorance, vice, and unbelief of their neighbours in the midst of whom they live.   The beginning of the evil has been, in such cases, the gradual ceasing to comply with the Apostle's rule of "not forsaking the assembling of ourselves," under the invincible conviction of being dispensed from the duty "by want of clothes."

Downward progress is often rapid, and the smoother the mountain-side we are climbing up, the more dangerous it is to slip and fall down.   Many a mountain climber has owed his life, after having fallen, to some providential obstacle which lay in the way.   A projecting stone or ledge of a rock, a root or a stump of a tree, has saved him from falling over the precipice, or has interposed to prevent him from sliding down into the torrent below, either of which would have been certain death.   Now, as to the falling class, whose case we are considering, when once they have come to the point of breaking off from the fulfilment of their duty of coming to Mass, on the plea of "having no clothes," they may be reasonably said to have fairly fallen down on the smooth side of the mountain, and to be sliding downwards, more or less rapidly, on the way to fall over the precipice, and lose their lives.   It is quite uncertain when they will so far retrieve themselves as to "obtain clothes," and again, it is quite uncertain whether the habit of staying away from the fulfilment of a known duty will not continue, even after the particular plea put in for its justification has ceased to exist, for bad habits grow upon us.

The Church, therefore, in her wisdom and care for the souls of her people, is invariably solicitous that, besides the necessary opportunities for assembling together for the supreme act of the Christian worship of God, the offering of the Holy Sacrifice of the Mass, other opportunities should be also provided, the coming to which should stand no longer on the terms of a command, but on the footing of an invitation freely thrown open to all, without implying any other obligation than that which is common to all invitations, which it is customary to accept out of love and respect for the person who gives the invitation, so long, that is, as no grave obstacle stands in the way.

We may thus very opportunely plead the cause of the Rosary as a public social devotion, on the ground of its holding out a pre-eminently charitable hand to arrest the downward progress of this falling class in the direction of the precipice, once fairly to fall over which is, of course, fraught with a peril frightful to contemplate. In many cases, next in degree after Mass, the Rosary to this class is the earliest and most familiar tradition of the Catholic faith. It has either been the well known family prayer of their early years, or they have in their minds numberless remembrances stored up of grandmothers and aunts and other relatives who always carried their Rosary beads about with them; and consequently an invitation to come to join with others in publicly reciting the Rosary is a kind of music to the ear, recalling good and pious memories of other days, and often likely to prove an attraction when many others fail to exert any charm.

Besides, the terror of having " no clothes" is very much tempered down in the case of the Rosary. It is, by custom, for the most part an evening devotion, and, therefore, safe against the full blaze of midday light, consequently much more secure from the dreaded contrast in the matter of the "clothes." And being, moreover, not of obligation, it is much more likely that those who will be there will be of the soberer and the more devout sort, who come exclusively for the sake of the prayer, and who will take little or no notice of the manner in which others who may come are dressed. The public recital of the Rosary may thus become to this numerous class the providential bush or ledge of rock which arrests their downward progress, and keeps alive in them the good habit of still frequenting the public assemblies of the faithful, notwithstanding that, under the idea of being dispensed by their destitute condition, they absent themselves from Mass.

As far as possible it must be charitably hoped that the plea " of having no clothes " really does stand between those who make it and the guilt of the open non-fulfilment of an acknowledged duty; and though there is no voluntary assembling for prayer that can be put in the place of the duty of being present at Mass, still, where it can be charitably hoped that there exist circumstances which for a time keep the duty in abeyance, charity will certainly rejoice to think that the good habit of frequenting the assemblies of the Church does not suffer in consequence an entire interruption. Here, then, we have a clear ground for pleading the cause of the Rosary as a school of improvement for a numerous class of our people. Let them only be brought to make due progress in this school, and the plea of "having no clothes," it may be hoped, will soon disappear as a reason for remaining absent from Mass.

(*To be continued.*)

No. V.—THE VENERABLE ANNA MARIA TAIGI.
(*Conclusion.*)

ANNA MARIA, amongst her other gifts, was eminently favoured with supernatural lights as to the souls of others. When those who were perfect strangers applied to her for counsel and help, she would at once declare to them the most hidden thoughts and actions of their past lives, and announce to them future events which never failed to be realised. She was thus enabled to give the most valuable advice on matters concerning the Church and public affairs.

"She possessed, in effect," says the authentic witness before cited, ' wonderful knowledge, not only of the natural order, but still more of that of grace. When consulted on any point of dogma—for example, on the manner of reconciling predestination with the goodness of God, or of explaining how in God the humanity united to the Divinity was capable of suffering—she gave such precise and true answers that every one was astonished; and she was able to treat of the highest mysteries. It was, therefore, a great consolation to hear her speak on the Incarnation of the Word, and on the maternity and virginity of Mary. By the aid of the same gift she could explain in a moment any point whatever of sacred or profane history.

"If she fixed her attention to contemplate, for instance, the poor house of Nazareth, she saw it," says the same witness; "she described it with all its details, and the different articles of furniture, and remarked the simplicity of the objects belonging to the Holy Family."

The different Pontiffs who reigned in her time were frequently the subjects of this supernatural gift. She predicted the death of Leo XII., the election and short pontificate of Pius VIII., the election of Gregory XVI., and the political events of his pontificate. At the desire of the venerable Pontiff Pius VII., she wrote to him the most minute details of his childhood; to which the holy Pope, smiling, answered that it was all perfectly true.

Anna Maria was also supernaturally acquainted with the revolutions in France and Spain, the events in Russia—a country for which she often prayed—and the terrible scenes passing in Poland, which she described with perfect accuracy. She also saw the disasters which occurred at that time in China and other remote countries.

From her numerous predictions to individuals, we select the following. One day she met Cardinal Marazzani, who was proceeding to S. Peter's with great pomp on being elevated to his dignity. On being asked what she thought of it, she replied: "All this pomp to-day; in a month the grave!" And so it happened. When the French invaded Spain, under Napoleon, she announced one day to her confessor that the General of the Trinitarian Order, of which she was herself a Tertiary, was dead, although no human agency could have caused the news to have reached Rome. She indicated to him that the General had been travelling with one of his religious; that they had both been attacked and massacred by the French, and that they had suffered and died with such patience and faith that they no longer stood in need of prayers. All the facts relating to their death were afterwards exactly verified.

On another occasion, the Queen of Etruria was very uneasy about the fate of her brother, the King of Spain, whom she feared had fallen into the hands of his enemies. Anna Maria desired her to be told that she need fear nothing, as the King was free. She described the place in which he was, the persons of his Court who surrounded him, and many other minute details, which all proved to be true.

The son of a great farmer near Rome was dangerously ill. He was recommended to Anna Maria's prayers, and she assured his family that he would recover from that illness; but she warned them that, five years later, he would be thrown from his horse and carried senseless to his house. "Then," she said, "prayers must be offered to God; he will recover consciousness, but for a very short time; let him receive the Last Sacraments immediately, for he will die." She indicated even the exact interior injury which would prove fatal. All this was verified to the letter.

Anna Maria had frequently the clear vision of the state of departed souls. The sight of those dying in mortal sin caused her the most bitter agony. She saw distinctly their judgment and condemnation, and the reasons for which they were precipitated into hell.

On the other hand, she was often consoled by the apparition of the souls in purgatory, delivered by her prayers, who came to thank her for her efficacious charity.

She had besides frequent consoling apparitions of Our Lady, her Angel guardian, and the Saints. (We must not omit to mention that devotion to the Blessed Trinity had been specially inculcated to her by her Divine Spouse. She constantly increased this devotion by the devotional exercises of the Third Order of Trinitarians, to which she belonged.)

Anna Maria's sufferings increased so much towards the end of her life that she was obliged to take to her bed, from which she never again rose, on the 24th October, 1836. Notwithstanding her intense agonies of body and soul, she always preserved her interior peace and tranquillity. She continued to direct her house, and encouraged every one around her by her heroic patience, and by the gaiety and charm of her conversation. When the time of her death drew near, she arranged her affairs, so that nothing might distract her in her last preparation. After receiving Holy Communion the Sunday before her death, she fell into a state of such languor and mortal agony, that she appeared at the point of death. She recovered, however, and, with a face shining with ineffable joy, announced to a priest who was in her confidence the precise moment of her death. Soon after, she called her husband, and thanked him for all the care he had taken of her; then she had her family assembled, and confided them to the care of her eldest daughter, who was a widow; she made them a fervent exhortation, and desired them, above all, to be faithful to the law of God and devout to the Blessed Virgin; she placed them under the special patronage of S. Philomena, for whom

she had particular devotion; then, having blessed her children,
and taken a last leave of her husband, she gave herself up to
recollection and prayer.

On the following Thursday evening she received Extreme
Unction, and became speechless. Her family retired, shedding
abundant tears, and every precaution was taken that she
should be assisted to the end, as was customary with a dying
person. But it was the will of Our Lord that she should have
a share in His three hours' desolation on the Cross. The
priests who assisted her thought she had still some time to
live, and retired for a while; only two servants remained, who
were talking in a corner of the room. A friend who was in
her confidence felt suddenly impelled to hurry to the chamber
in which she lay, and found her at the last extremity. One of
the priests was summoned in haste, and the last prayers were
hardly finished, when she gave up her blessed soul to God,
about one o'clock on the morning of Friday, the 9th of June,
1837, the very moment which she had herself predicted.
"Twenty years before," said the friend who had thus found
her dying alone, "the servant of God told me that at her death
she would be abandoned by all. At other times she told me I
should be with her. I could never reconcile these two state-
ments, but after her death I knew their explanation."

Almighty God permitted His servant to appear to many
persons after her death, to give them spiritual advice, and to
inform them of different events.

Numbers of persons flocked to her tomb, and she was
venerated as a saint. The documents connected with her life
and revelations were collected by command of the Cardinal
Vicar, and duly signed and authenticated, so as to serve as
materials for the future process of her canonization, should
such enter into the designs of Providence.

We have reserved for the close of this memoir her prophetic
declarations concerning the present Pontiff, Pius the Ninth,
many of which have been so wonderfully fulfilled in our own
times. They were published and attested during the beginning of his pontificate by the venerable priest who had
received them from her own lips:

"Anna Maria spoke one day to this same priest of the persecution which
the Church was about to suffer. She made known to him what the impious
were about to effect in Rome, as unhappily we have seen realised; she
indicated to him what the Conductor of the Bark of Peter would then
have to suffer. Desiring to know who this Pontiff would be, the priest

asked her if he were among the Cardinals? She answered that he was not, that he was a simple priest, then not in the State, but in a far distant country. [The Abate Mastai was at that time, in effect, a simple priest attached to the Nunciature of Chili.] Anna Maria described the future Pontiff. She said that he would be elected in an extraordinary manner; that he would make reforms; that if men were grateful for them, Our Lord would fill them with benedictions: but that if they should abuse them, His all-powerful arm would be heavy to chastise them. She said that this Pontiff, chosen according to the heart of God, would be assisted by Him with very special favours; that his name should be divulged throughout the whole world, and applauded by the nations; that the Turk himself should venerate him, and send to compliment him. She said that he was the Holy Pontiff destined to endure the tempest let loose against the Bark of Peter; that the arm of God would sustain and defend him against the impious, who would be humbled and confounded; *that he would have, at the end, the gift of miracles;* that the Church, after grievous vicissitudes, would obtain so glorious a triumph that the nations would be stupefied with astonishment."

Those who can look back to the reigns of former Popes will remember how little was personally known about them by the great majority of Catholics. The prediction that "his name shall be divulged throughout the whole world, and applauded by the nations," is truly fulfilled in a singular manner in the person of Pius the Ninth. It seems below the truth to say that no other man ever had the interest of the whole world riveted upon him as he has. Prisoner as he is—despoiled of his earthly kingdom and possessions—he is owned by his worst enemies to be the "keystone of European politics." Millions and tens of millions of his faithful children look up to him with most intimate personal love as to a real father, as well as intense veneration as to a saintly head. They hang upon his utterances—those simple, wonderful words, which flash to the remotest ends of the earth, which fill the hearts of mighty monarchs with anger and dismay, and the faithful with ever-increasing hope and confidence. His beloved lineaments are alike familiar to the Connemara peasant and a fresh home-tie to the settler in the New World. The very prolongation of his years is a sign of God's mercy and patience with men. When they cease, such a dirge as was never known will sweep throughout the earth. Those who come after us will call us happy who have seen his day.

Can we help sharing his confidence that the triumph of the Church is about to dawn?

"CANDLEMAS DAY."

A HOMILY FOR THE PRESENT TIME ON THE TEXT

"Lumen ad revelationem Gentium"—"A Light for the teaching of
the Nations"—(S. Luke ii. 32).

THE beginning of the work of creation was light. "The
earth was void and without form." And God said, "Let
there be light," and "light was made." And God approved
of His work. "He saw that the light was good, and He
divided the light from the darkness." "Hail, holy light,"
sings a great English poet—

> "Offspring of heaven first-born,
> Or of the eternal coeternal beam,
> May I express thee unblamed? since God is light,
> And never but in unapproached light
> Dwelt from eternity, dwelt then in thee,
> Bright effluence of bright essence increate."

Then, as the poet suffered the affliction of having lost his
sight, he goes on to lament over his own exclusion from
the light—

> "Thus with the year
> Seasons return, but not to me returns
> Day, or the sweet approach of even or morn,
> But cloud instead, and ever-during dark
> Surrounds me, from the cheerful ways of men
> Cut off."

God, then, who Himself is the absolute Life, dwelling in the
inaccessible light, on His being pleased to give being and
existence to creatures other than Himself, first creates light,
that, as creation is to share with Himself, by His gift, the
privilege of having life and being, so it may likewise enjoy
the good gift of a created light in which to dwell. "Darkness," says the Scripture, "was upon the face of the deep;"
but, for the sake of the creation that was about to be made,
God said, "Let there be light," and "Light was made."

The first work, then, of creation is light,

> "Bright effluence of bright essence increate."

But the first work of Redemption, at least as regards the
nations of the world, is also Light. The holy Simeon came by
the Spirit into the Temple, and taking the Holy Child into
his arms, said, "*A Light for the teaching of the Nations.*"

How did it come to pass that, at least as regards the
nations, the first beginning of Redemption must be the creation

of a Light specially intended for them? For the chosen
people of Israel the Christ comes, not as light taking the
place of darkness, but as the "Glory of His people Israel."
With the nations of the world it is not thus. With them He
begins from the beginning, and this beginning to them is
"light." So, when S. Matthew relates that Jesus, after His
baptism, went to dwell in the confines of Zabulon and Nep-
thalim, this was done, he says, that it might be fulfilled
which was spoken by the prophet: "The land of Zabulon and
the land of Nepthali, the way of the sea, beyond Jordan,
Galilee of the Gentiles; the people that sat in darkness hath
seen a great light, and to them that sit in the region of the
shadow of death, a great light is arisen"—(Matt. iv. 15).

Christ went to dwell in Capharnaum, a city of the Galilee
of the Gentiles, and not only did the people that sat in darkness there at once see a great light, but no sooner had Christ
begun to preach there than to all other people similarly sitting
in the region of the shadow of death "a great light arose,"
the shining of which has from that time forward never ceased.

Hear ye, then, all ye tribes and peoples of the world, who
glory in the memories of your race,* what the Feast of Candlemas teaches you year by year, as you assemble yourselves,
with the blessed light of the Sanctuary in your hands, in the
presence of the Altars of the Church. Hear ye this. To you
Christ is the light which frees you out of the darkness of your
natural state. What would you have been if you had never
been enlightened by this Light? You would have continued

---

* "Ridendo dicere verum, quid vetat," says the Roman poet—"What for-
bids telling the truth in a jocose way?" The following lines from a well-
known poet rather agree, in their way, with the more sober truth contained
in our homily as playfully exposing the follies of national vainglorying:—

There is not a nation in Europe but labours
To toady itself and to humbug its neighbours.
Earth has no such folks—no folks such a city,
So great or so grand, or so fine and so pretty,
        Said Louis Quatorze,
        As this Paris of ours.

*   *   *   *   *
*   *   *   *   *

Mr. Bull will inform you that Neptune—a lad he
With more of affection than rev'rence styles, Daddy—
        Did not scruple to say
        To Freedom one day,
That if ever he changed his aquatics for dry land,
His home should be Mr. B.'s Tight Little Island—

to be what your forefathers were—savages. Savages are known by various names, according to the tribe or people from which they come.   Years ago there were savages called Angles, Saxons, Celts, Britons, Scots, with a great variety of others, each of whom had their own barbarous names; and though there were then, as there are still in the world, varieties of the savage, as there were then and still are varieties in the birds who continue to live in our trees and hedges, there was extremely little to choose between one savage people and another. At the most you might be able to say of the leader of one particular savage people that he was a noble savage, and of another that he was a deceitful, blood-thirsty savage, and that the tribes took pattern by their respective leaders. Truth, however, as weighed in the balance of the Sanctuary, would, notwithstanding, be obliged to pronounce that both one and the other tribe equally sat in the region of the shadow of death, and equally stood in want of the Divine Light to arise which was to dispel the natural darkness of their condition, and equally needed the Divine Leader who would put into their hands the key to open to them the way both to the knowledge of God and to the liberal arts of life.

"Blessed is the man," says the Psalmist "whom Thou dost teach, O Lord."   Let us hear what the Prophet says to the Israelite people, as to their condition before God made choice of them, and condescended to enter into a covenant with them: "No eye took pity on thee in mercy to do any of these things for thee, but thou wast cast forth on the face of the earth in the abjection of thy soul on the day in which thou wast born" —(Ezech. xvi. 5).

He adds, too, that he,
    The said Mr. B.,
Of all possible Frenchmen can fight any three;
That with no greater odds he knows how to treat them,
To meet them, defeat them, and beat them, and eat them.
In Italy, too, 'tis the same to the letter;
        There each lazzarone
        Will cry to his crony,
"See Naples, then die"—and the sooner the better.
The Portuguese say, as a well understood thing,
Who has not seen Lisbon has not seen a good thing.
While an old Spanish proverb runs glibly as under,
        Quien no ha visto Sevilla
        No ha visto maravilla.
("He who ne'er has view'd Seville has not seen a wonder.")

                                    Ingoldsby Legends.

From this state of natural abjection the people of Israel were, through their covenant with the Lord their God, raised to the greatest glory and dignity, insomuch that the Queen of the East, when she came on her visit to King Solomon in Jerusalem, was forced to exclaim, " Greater is thy wisdom and greater are thy works than the fame that I have heard.   Blessed are thy people, and blessed are thy servants that always stand before thee and hear thy wisdom."

The people of Israel did not only obtain the knowledge of the future life from their Covenant with God, but they obtained, also, the blessings of the present life.   As long as they remained faithful to their Covenant, their Temple was held in honour among distant nations ; silver was as abundant as the stones in the streets of Jerusalem ; they were in general repute amongst others for being a wise and understanding people ; they enjoyed peace, and every Israelite lived secure under his own vine and his own fig-tree.

When Christ, then, came to them, it was not as a light to those that sat in the region of the shadow of death.   He came as the glory of His people Israel ; and had blindness not, as S. Paul says, in part happened to Israel, they never would have crucified the Lord of Glory ; but their fall, says the same Apostle, has proved the riches of the nations.

But in what condition did the " Light which was sent for the teaching of the nations " find them ?   It has found them, for the most part, exactly as the light, the first work of God, found the material world, "And darkness was on the face of the deep."   "But God said, let there be light, and light was made ; and he separated the light from the darkness."   The Virgin Mother brings the Divine Infant into the Temple, and a holy prophet of God exclaimed, " Behold the Light for the teaching of the nations."   But these nations were then all sitting in the region of the shadow of death ; they were in the same condition in which the people of Israel were before God made choice of them, and condescended to make His Holy Covenant with them, and to exalt them to great honour and dignity among the other people of the world.   Of every one of them it might be said, equally with the Hebrew, that before they came into the riches of the Covenant of Jesus Christ, and before the Light for the teaching of the nations arose to them, " No eye took pity on thee in mercy, to do any of these things for thee ; but thou wast cast forth on the face

of the earth in the abjection of thy soul in the day in which
thou wast born."

What has " the Light for the teaching of the nations " done
for those people to whom, as they sat in the region of the
shadow of death, it arose and caused them to rejoice like the
wise men when they saw the star, and to accept the gracious
offer of entering into the New Covenant with God, in the blood
of Jesus Christ?

What the Covenant of God, under the law of Moses, did for
the Hebrew people, so long as they were faithful to it, is only
a shadow of the better things which the Covenant of God in
Christ Jesus has done for vast numbers of the tribes and
nations of the earth. It has taken them out of their darkness
into the light.   What is creation without the light ?   What
is the life of nations and people without the Covenant with
God in Christ Jesus, the Light to give light to the nations ?

Listen, then, O ye people, to what the Feast of Candlemas
teaches you.   The Devil is particularly busy with you at the
present time, exhibiting himself to you and desiring you to
believe that he is " the light for the teaching of the nations."
He is making it his business to undo and destroy all that
the true Light for the teaching of the nations has done for
them.   In order that you may fall off in your gratitude to the
true Light for the teaching of the nations, he does not discourse to you of the region of the shadow of death in which
sat your barbarian forefathers, and out of which the true Light
of the world, having had pity upon you, has delivered you, but
he fills your mind with what he calls the glories of your race.
By all means, if there are attached to our people glorious
memories of great and good deeds done under the Christian
Covenant, let us never fail to glory in these, and to give to
God all praise and thanksgiving for them; but the Devil hates
nothing worse than these very glories, and these are the holy
memories which he would have us despise.   The Devil, as is
natural to him, goes to the region of the shadow of death to
find, in the memory of the times before Christ, the glories with
which he would like the minds of all the tribes of the earth to
be filled.

Then, again, the Devil is now trying to undo the great
work on their behalf of the Light of the nations, by which,
under His covenant of grace, He takes the natural contract of
marriage, and raises it to the dignity of a Holy Sacrament of
His Church.   The Devil says to the nations, "Away with the

Holy Sacrament.   Hasten back, ye people, to the condition of
the region of the shadow of death.   No more matrimony a
Sacrament ; rejoice in the natural contract, which you can be
at liberty to make and unmake as you like."

O, foolish and unwise people, said Moses to Israel, are these
things the return thou makest to the Lord thy God ?   Now,
with the memory of the blest lights of Candlemas fresh in our
minds, and asking the aid of the gracious Mother who presented in the Temple "the Light to teach the nations," let
us resolve ever to cultivate a special hatred and abhorrence of
these two current deceptions of the Devil ; let us say to Satan,
" Satan, I renounce thee and all thy works, all thy pomps,
and especially all thy deceits."

THE ARCH CONFRATERNITY OF OUR LADY QUEEN OF THE ANGELS.

(Continuation of the Letter of Fr. Rooke.)

THE circumstances of the miraculous cure of the Abbé de
Bray, the founder of the Arch Confraternity of our Lady
Queen of the Angels, are related in the letter of Fr. Rooke,
already partially quoted in our last number, and our present
extract gives an account of his personal interview with the
Abbé on the second morning of their visit to the Chateau
de Belleville.

"One day during his illness (he was then about forty
years old) our blessed Lady appeared to him in that room
(Fr. de Bray had taken his visitors into the room in question),
and told him that the doctors could not cure him, but that
he should be cured if he would make a vow to go to the
sanctuary of our Lady of the Angels at Assisi. He thereupon
asked his confessor, the next time he came to see him, to
approve of his making the vow, but the confessor for some
reason demurred. He grew weaker and weaker, and the Last
Sacraments were administered.   His pulse having ceased to
beat, and no sign of life appearing, he was left for dead in his
room amidst the sobs and tears of his family and the domestics,
and the passing-bell of the village was rung for him.

" He does not know *how*, but, after all had left the room for
the night, he found himself all of a sudden on his knees before

a small image of our Lady, saying with full consciousness that he made the vow (not at the time in any way adverting to the circumstance of his confessor having expressed himself adversely to it), and our Lady appeared to him and told him he was cured, and that he was to go at once to Assisi. After this he returned to bed, and slept soundly all the night, not having been able to sleep for many days before. In the morning he awoke, got up, and dressed himself, and feeling ravenously hungry, went into the corridor, but, finding none of the servants as yet come to their work, he went to his mother's room, who with an attendant was still bewailing her son's death. Going up to her to embrace her, she cried out that he was a spirit—a fiend come to mock her grief; that he could not be her son Frederic, for he died last night, and was a corpse in his chamber. The attendant touched him with her finger, to try if he really was a being of flesh and blood, and then ran off to call his father, who came, and, equally disbelieving, also touched him with his hand, to try if there was any tangible substance about him. M. de Bray kept on asserting his identity, and at the same time asked for something to eat, and ravenously devoured some refreshment that happened to be in the room. When they brought him a loaf of bread, some meat, and a bottle of wine, 'I finished it all,' he said, laughing at the remembrance of it. The doctor, who came during the morning, would not believe what they told him, and kept saying it was impossible, until his former patient came in from a walk he had been taking round the park; and then he said it could not possibly be anything more than some marvellous effort of expiring life, and that his patient would be certain to die before the day was over, or, if not, it was a most astounding miracle. To the words of the physician M. de Bray replied, that he might possibly be right, but that for his part he did not feel any symptoms of being about to die. His confessor delayed his going to Assisi for three months, and then instructed him to return to France immediately.

" At Assisi he had another vision of our Lady, who told him to go to Rome to join the Society of Jesus, and to become a priest, for she had a great work for him to do, and he was to prepare himself for it during thirteen years in the Society, and that he was to become the father of a great people, and that thousands of souls would be saved by the work that would be given to him. This put him into a state of doubt, and he related his vision to the Superior of the Franciscans at Assisi, consulting him as to whether he should return to France as his confessor had directed him, or obey the voice which he had heard. The Superior said that he would ask his brethren to join with him in prayer, that the will of God in the matter might be made known, and on the morrow, after Mass, he would give him his answer. Accordingly, after Mass the Superior called him, and told him to go to Rome. On two occasions, about this time, he fell into an ecstasy, one of which lasted for four hours."

His admission (to abridge Fr. Rooke's narrative) to the Society of Jesus was not devoid of miraculous incidents, by which the reluctance of the fathers to receive an unknown postulant, so far advanced in life, and totally ignorant of both Latin and Greek, was at length overcome. He was by a miracle made acquainted with both Latin and Greek, and, having passed his examination creditably, was in due time ordained priest by Monseigneur Pie, Bishop of Poitiers. After his ordination he returned to France.

Having heard (continues Fr. Rooke) that the Devil visited him at times, and beat and ill-used him, I ventured to ask if it was true, and he said it was, sometimes under the appearance of a secular priest, sometimes of a religious, sometimes in his own room, sometimes in the corridor. When he sees him he knows him to be the Evil Spirit by his commencing to use horrible filthy language, and then the Devil gnashes at him, and tells Fr. de Bray that he hates him and despises him; but by the use of a drop of holy water, or of an aspiration, he can drive him away; but, he added, if he has any fault on his conscience he has not the same power over the Evil Spirit, and our Lady permits the Devil to punish him. As to physically beating him, it is also true that the Evil One comes as a fierce, powerful man, and who stands over him and beats him with some instrument.

"On our taking our leave he again, with a distressed look, said he begged our pardon for having detained us with such a long account, but he felt compelled to do it, not by his own choice. His only desire was to proclaim the glory of our blessed Lady, and to manifest her power to whom he had entirely devoted himself.

"Such is the man who is by some accused of working miracles through Satan; but he is not the first who has been persecuted in a similar way, for we have an instance of a

canonized saint who was misunderstood and rejected; and One
greater than he, whose servant he is, was accused of driving
out devils, by Beelzebub, the prince of the devils.

"In conclusion, I may be allowed to state my impression.
It is that I have had the privilege of conversing with a living
saint, and one highly favoured by our Blessed Mother the
Queen of the Angels, and that truth is stamped on all he says
and does. My interview has, moreover, helped me to understand, more than I have ever done before, the great dignity
and power and glory of God's blessed Mother whom He has
made the august Queen of Heaven, and of her activity in
behalf of the Church of her Divine Son, and of her love for
the souls that have been redeemed; and also of the angelic
ministries under her direction. It has left on my soul a
sweetness and a confidence in this Queen of the Angels which
I am unable to express by words.—Your affectionate brother
in J. M. D.,

"FR. A. M. ROOKE."

CANDLEMAS DAY.

THE FEAST OF THE PURIFICATION AND OF THE PRESENTATION OF THE
HOLY CHILD JESUS IN THE TEMPLE.

ANGELS have sung their song,
　Shepherds have come to pray,
Kings with their royal gifts
　To Bethlehem wend their way.
Joseph has looked on God.
　Mary has clasped her child,
Earth now to Heaven may make
　One offering undefiled.

The morning breaks at last,
　Light spreads across the skies;
O sinful, thoughtless world,
　Messias comes, arise!
Open, ye Temple gates,
　Admit the Babe Divine,
The Holy spotless One,
　Replacing type and sign.

From Mary, Simeon takes
  The child of Juda's race ;
He folds him in his arms,
  And gazes on his face.
The day so long desired
  Has dawned; let him depart ;
He sees the Saviour Christ,
  Joy floods his aged heart.

But, mother, why thy grief ?
  He is thine own again ;
See, Simeon gives Him back ;
  Why throbs thy heart with pain ?
" Thy soul a sword shall pierce,"
  And it has entered now;
The thorns entwine thy heart
  Ere yet they wreathe His brow.

Joseph stands silent by,
  And Anna, raptured, prays ;
Angels, unseen, in crowds
  On child and mother gaze.
Saints who in limbo wait
  Have longed to greet this day,
But those to whom He comes
  Pass heedless on their way.

O bear Him far away
  O'er deserts bleak and wild ;
O guard Him, Joseph, safe ;
  Sweet mother hide thy child.
Let not the tyrant yet
  The sacred life-blood shed ;
Too soon, too soon 'twill flow
  From hands, and feet, and head.

The scourge, the thorns, the cross,
  Keep, mother, far away ;
Let nought but love and joy
  Thrill through our hearts to day.
The Temple's courts have seen
  The first pure offering given,
This morn, by sinful earth
  To purchase peace from Heav'n.
                    E. MD.

THE BLESSED NICOLAS VON DER FLUE IN SWITZERLAND.

A SAINT OF THE FIFTEENTH CENTURY, THE CAUSE OF WHOSE
CANONIZATION IS NOW BEFORE THE HOLY SEE.

(*Conclusion.*)

IT looks very stormy.   Charles the Bold is forming ambitious
projects for extending the boundaries of his newly inherited
kingdóm, and once more the liberty of Switzerland is threatened.   Under the auspices of the astute Louis XI., an alliance
is formed between the Swiss, the Archduke Sigismund, and
the *Basse Ligue*, against the Burgundian Duke.   The immediate
result of the alliance was the uprising of all the Alsatian towns
against the dominion of the Duke; and the tyrant Hagenbach
was seized, judged, and executed with the co-operation of some
of the allied Swiss and the *Basse Ligue*.

On learning the death of his faithful adherent, the anger of
Charles knew no bounds; and Diesbach, thinking it best to
anticipate his resentment, supported by a few councillors, took
it upon himself to declare war against Charles, Duke of Burgundy, in the name of the State of Berne, and of the whole
Confederation.   ·

Long, bloody battles followed : driven at last from the field,
Charles fled, leaving the Swiss victors of Grandson and
masters of the untold wealth of his camp.   He fled, however,
only to bring into the field a greater force; and on the 27th
day of May, 1476, he stood before Morat with a far more
splendid army than the one destroyed.   At the sight of the
new danger that threatened Switzerland all the curés of the
neighbouring districts of Morat flew to arms, the curé of
Neuech specially distinguishing himself by the length of his
lance of 6 metres, which, say the chroniclers, he wielded with
admirable effect.

The Duke gave battle on the 22nd June : that same night
he was without an army.   But this time Switzerland victorious
was Switzerland ruined.   What Charles and his army could
not do his wealth did; and for five weary years the unhappy
land was divided by quarrelling, and angry, sharp dispute
over the immense booty taken at Grandson and Morat.   To
add to the confusion, Fribourg and Soleure, who had been so
forward in the fight when their help was sought, now claimed,
and were refused, admittance to the Confederation, then
numbering only eight States.

At last the Diet of Stanz was convened, as a final effort to bring about a peaceful settlement of the long vexed questions touching the conflicting claims. But it was useless. After three days spent in fierce invective on either side, hope waxes dim. They are coming to blows; Switzerland is on the eve of civil war!

Dawn had scarce lifted the veil of night that shrouded the snow-clad glens and ice-chilled gorges of the Valley of the Ranft, on the Feast of S. Thomas, 1481, when the hermit of Unterwald was suddenly aroused from his deep prayer and meditation by the unexpected, agitated, travel-worn appearance of his old friend, M. Gruno, the patriot Curé of Stanz. His errand is soon told. "My brother, Switzerland is at this moment in great peril. Unless God comes to our aid, blood will be shed; and it is no longer the sword of Charles the Bold that will make it flow, but the hands of the Confederates themselves. Met together at Stanz, they are about to break up the Assembly, and to-morrow, perhaps, to fly to arms. I have prayed to God to turn away this scourge from our unhappy country, and God has not hearkened to my prayer. But He inspired me with a good thought—to seek you and implore you to have pity on poor Switzerland. Be quick, my brother; time presses. Come and speak to the Confederates. Something in my heart tells me that they will listen to your beloved voice."

"I come," said the man of God. "Brother, go tell the Confederates that Nicolas wishes to say a few words of friendship to them."

Back again across the mountains hastened the good Curé. Arrived at Stanz, everything betokened a hurried departure. The mules were saddled, bells were ringing, the stirrup-cup was being handed round. Not a moment was to be lost: unhesitatingly he sprang up the stairs into the great room of the first hostel reached; startled the parting Confederates with the abrupt, imperative command, "Brother Nicolas wishes to speak to you!" and was gone, e'er a question could be thought of, to the second hostel; and to the third he sped, repeating always the same brief charge. At the name of Brother Nicolas drinking-cups clanged upon the table; the deputies rose, and with one accord hastened to the Council-chamber. In an instant the hall was filled, not a Confederate was missing.

Meanwhile, the hermit was approaching as rapidly as age would allow him. Heads uncover, knees bend, as the venerable

1873.]   NICOLAS VON DER FLUE.   189

old man of lofty stature, bare-headed and bare-footed, his long white beard glistening with hoar-frost, leaning on his staff, and holding fast his rosary, with downcast eyes and lips moving in prayer, passed along the great street of Stanz.

Supported by two peasants, he with difficulty ascended the steps of the Council-chamber. What a wonderful sight it was, that Council-chamber! Men held their breath; stormy passions were stilled in presence of such great holiness; fierce warriors rose, uncovered, and bending lowly, the proud, fiery soldiers did homage to the poor, humble Solitary of the Mountains.

He stands before them like some prophet of old. His eye gleams with a supernatural light; and there is something of sternness mingled with his gentleness and humility that suits these untamed spirits, as with raised head and clear, ringing voice, he addresses them. "My dear Confederates, God be with you! I come here, led by the spirit of charity, with which I would inspire you. It is an old man, a feeble old man, who comes at the voice of a friend to speak to you of your country. I am a stranger to art and science. I can give you only that which I hold from God. I thought there was nothing for me to do but to pray in solitude for our dearly loved country; but here my brother, the worthy Pastor of Stanz, comes to me, with tears in his eyes, to implore me to bring you words of peace and concord. My good friends, I find you divided amongst yourselves, and at what a moment! Just when God has enabled you to triumph in three glorious battles. Have you then forgotten the Great Hand that gave you the victory? If God had not been with you at Grandson, at Morat, at Nancy, do you think that you would have vanquished the Burgundians? You have been made strong by the power of your united arms; and now you are going to disunite them for the sake of some paltry booty! Do not let the noise of this shame spread to the neighbouring countries. Be what you were at Grandson, at Morat, at Nancy—one soul, one body.

"Fribourg and Soleure want to enter the Confederation, and you repel them; but you did not repel them when, in the moment of danger, they came to give you their faithful and loyal support! You are not too strong, and the day will come when you will again have need of them. They did not stop to bargain when there was question of shedding their blood for you, and you dispute with them when there is question of a share in the booty! All must share alike, my good friends. Have but one heart and one hand, and God will bless you! You, men of the towns, renounce the rights that distress your allies; you, men of the country, think of the valour Soleure and Fribourg have shown in fighting for you! Receive them frankly into the League. Do not seek to extend your territories too far; do not meddle with the quarrels of foreigners; be good neighbours, and show yourselves formidable only to those who would oppress you. Above all, avoid dissension; love one another. Confederates, I will not leave Stanz until I have seen you, like good Swiss, grasp the hand of reconciliation! May God Almighty bless you! May He protect your towns and your fields! May He, as He has to this day, ever show Himself propitious to you!"

As he spoke, the hermit bent his penetrating gaze upon the assembled confederates, now almost commanding them, now entreating, as, with outstretched hand, he seemed like one begging an alms. Before he concluded they had all risen, grasped one another's hands, and in the kiss of peace wiped out all memory of their bitter enmities; then, in voices almost choked with emotion, they cried out: "Long live Brother Nicolas!"

His mission was finished; and whilst all, rejoicing, were singing his praises, and marvelling at the mighty power of their gentle saint, Nicolas glided unperceived from amongst them, and that same night regained his cell.

Rich presents and warm expressions of gratitude from all the States of the Confederation quickly followed him: the first he devoted to God's service; the latter he acknowledged in words burning with the triple love of God, his country, and his people.

Time passed on, and Nicolas felt that his powers were failing. Forewarned that his seventieth birthday would be his last day in this world, he sent for his old friend M. Gruno, and after eight days of intense suffering, knowing that death was near, he begged to receive the Holy Viaticum. Hastening to obtain one last blessing, the pious Dorothée and her children knelt around as the dying saint received his Lord. With outstretched arms he prayed, then, leaning back, gazed upwards, and gently died,

S. Benedict's Day, 1487, was a sad day for Switzerland: the people had lost their liberator—their father. Grief weighed them down, and, forgetting for the moment that their faith would have rejoiced for him, they could only sorrow for themselves.

In the Church of Saxeln they buried him, and told on his tomb how he had left his dear wife and children, to serve God in solitude for twenty years without tasting food. The hermitage now desolate, they brought the sick—the sick in body as well as mind—to the hermit's tomb, and so many and so great were the miracles there wrought that, in 1558, Paul IV. was petitioned for the beatification of Nicolas von der Flue. Later on, the petition was renewed to Pius V.; and again, 1572, to Gregory XIII. Then Urban VII. instituted an inquiry in Switzerland concerning the life and miracles of their saint; this inquiry was resumed in 1618. Ferdinand III., Emperor of Austria, and the kings of France and Spain, joined their voices to those of the Swiss people, and implored the Sovereign Pontiff to grant the oft-repeated petition; but it was not till 1669 that Clement IX., in a special Bull to the Prince Bishop of Constance, decreed to Nicolas von der Flue all the honours that it is the custom of the Church to pay to those whom she reverences with the glory of beatification. And now in the Collects of the Mass the humble solitary of Unterwald is supplicated under the title of Blessed Nicolas the Hermit.

RECORD OF EVENTS.

WE have to record the death of two Fathers of the Dominican Order, whose offices and functions have made their names of world-wide celebrity—Fr. Marianus Spada, appointed Master of the Sacred Palace, A.D. 1867, by the reigning Pope, to which dignity many important functions are annexed, specially the censorship of all books published within the precincts of the city, who died on the 15th of November, 1872; and the Right Rev. Fr. Jandel, Master General of the Order, who peacefully expired in his cell, in the Convent of the Minerva, on the 11th of December, 1872.

Up to Sunday 8th, the Feast of the Immaculate Conception, writes the Very Rev. F. Ligiez, hopes were entertained of his recovery, but on Tuesday Fr. Jandel himself, perceiving death to be approaching, made a formal request for the Last Sacraments, which request, however, he had to repeat before those in attendance could be persuaded to comply. After having received them, he remained passing his time in prayer till he breathed his last on Wednesday evening, in the presence of the Community of the Convent of the Minerva, who sang the Salve Regina, according to the traditional custom of the Order.

At the funeral, the Franciscan Fathers, according to ancient usage, sang the Mass, but, owing to the Italian occupation of Rome and its regulations, the interment took place in the cemetery of the Agro Verano. We hope in an early number to be able to give our readers a brief biographical sketch of the eventful career of the illustrious deceased.

THE PROGRESS OF THE GERMAN PERSECUTION.—The following abridgment of the project of a law for the German Empire against the free exercise of ecclesiastical discipline deserves a place in our brief record on account of the remarkable proof it affords that the spirit of the world is always the same. In St. Thomas Becket's time this spirit produced the Constitutions of Clarendon, which were so many attempts on the part of the then reigning King, Henry II., to fetter the action of ecclesiastical discipline.

Ecclesiastical discipline is the lion described by the Prophet: "The land and the fulness thereof was distressed by the voice of his roaring. And the nations gathered themselves together everywhere from their provinces, and they spread their net over him, and he was taken captive in the midst of their wounds" (Ezech. xix. 7).

Civil governments, to their own ruin, continually seek to fetter the action of the Catholic Church, and what follows is a nineteenth century sample of a very old practice :—

LAW AGAINST THE EXERCISE OF ECCLESIASTICAL DISCIPLINE.

"We, William, by the grace of God, King of Prussia, &c., do order, with the consent of both Houses of the Diet of this Monarchy, for the whole of the said Monarchy as follows :--

"§ 1. No minister of religion is authorised to threaten any citizen with disciplinary or corrective measures, or to proclaim him subject to the same, unless the said measures either belong to the purely religious domain, or merely concern the withdrawal of a right granted within the Church or the religious society of a citizen, or his exclusion from the same.

"§ 2. No minister of religion is authorised to threaten a citizen with even legally admissible disciplinary or corrective measures, or to proclaim him subject to the same, if the said penalties are incurred in consequence of an action . . . . . . ordered . . . . . . or necessitated . . . . . . by the laws of the State, or the commands of the civil authorities within their province. He is also equally forbidden to use the said disciplinary . . . .

measures for the purpose of preventing the committal of such an action (*i.e.*, one ordered by any civil authority).

"§ 3. No minister of religion is allowed to use . . . . . the said . . . . . measures, because citizens have exercised their rights as electors in a certain way, or have not exercised those rights in other ways. He is equally forbidden to use . . . . . the said . . . . . measures, in order thereby to bring about any special ways of exercising or not exercising the aforesaid electoral or municipal rights.

"§ 4. * No minister of religion is allowed to make public . . . . . any of the said . . . . . measures, if therein any citizen is designated by name.

"§ 5. Anyone acting in contradiction to the regulations contained in §§ 1 to 4 will be punished by a fine not exceeding 1,000 thalers, or with a maximum of two years' imprisonment. This penalty can be accompanied by loss of all rights to the holding of public offices, including ecclesiastical offices, this last penalty to last from one to five years. An attempt even to act in a manner contrary to the said regulations is punishable by law.

"§ 6. All persons are considered as ministers of religion in the sense of this law, who are acting as religious representatives, or ecclesiastical officers or officials, or as priests, in either the Evangelical or the Roman Catholic Church, or in any other religious body."

In one of the constitutions of Clarendon it was provided:

"VII. No one who holds directly under the King nor any of his attendants of his household, shall be excommunicated, nor their lands placed under an interdict, without first having had recourse to the King, or, in the case of his absence, to one of his justices."

The other provisions were all in the same manner intended, to use the Prophet's language, to involve the lion fast in the meshes of the net, and to make him a captive.

THE PAPAL ALLOCUTION OF THE 23RD OF DECEMBER, 1872.— On the 23rd of December last the Pope addressed an allocution to the Cardinals assembled in the Vatican, of which we give the following summary that has been published in the Catholic papers. The text of the allocution itself exceeds our space—

"The Church continues to be sorely persecuted. This persecution has for its object the destruction of the Catholic Church. This is manifested by the acts of the Italian Government, which summons the clergy to serve in the army, deprives the Bishops of the faculty of teaching, and heavily taxes the property of the Church. Above all it is manifested by the law presented to Parliament on the subject of religious corporations, a law that deeply wounds the rights of possession of the Universal Church and violates the right of Our Apostolic Mission." The Pope added : "In face of the presentation of this law, We raise our voice before you and the entire Church, and condemn every law which restricts or suppresses the religious communities in Rome or the neighbouring provinces. We consequently declare every acquisition of their property made under any title whatsoever to be null and void." His Holiness recalled to the minds of the promoters of this law the censures directed against those who encroached on the rights of the Church. He said: "But the grief We feel at the injuries inflicted on the Church in Italy is much aggravated by the cruel persecutions to which the Church is subjected in the German Empire, where not only by stratagem but even by open violence it is sought to destroy her. In that country, men who not only do not profess our holy religion, but who even do not know it, arrogate to themselves the power of defining the teachings and the rights of the Catholic Church. These men, adding calumny and mockery to the other means they employ, do not blush to inflict persecution on Catholics, by bringing against the Bishops, the clergy, and laity, the accusation that they refuse to place the laws and the will of the State before the sacred commands of the Church. The men who are at the head of public affairs have cause to know that none of their subjects better than the Catholics render to Cæsar the things which are Cæsar's, and for that very reason they render to God the things which are God's." The Pope added that some cantons of Switzerland appear to be pursuing the same path as Germany, and he recalled to recollection the events that have occurred at Geneva. His Holiness further spoke of Spain, declaring that the Clergy Dotation Law was opposed to the Concordats and to justice, and he protested against that law. The Holy Father spoke of schism among the Armenians of Constantinople, who persist in their rebellion, and who by a ruse have deprived the Catholics of their immunities. The Pope rejoiced at the constancy and the activity displayed by the episcopate and clergy of all countries, where, jointly with the faithful people, they defend the rights of the Church. His Holiness enjoined the Metropolitans to assemble their suffragans for consultation, in order to battle against iniquity, and concluded by invoking the Almighty to come to the aid of the Church.

INCREASED DEVOTION TO ST. BONIFACE, MONK OF NETLEY ABBEY AND APOSTLE OF GERMANY.—The Archbishop of Cologne has addressed a letter, in the name of his brethren the Bishops of Germany, to the Archbishop of Westminster, expressive of their gratitude for the sympathy manifested towards them in the letter of the English Episcopate. He suggests that a supplication be conjointly addressed to the Pope, that he would be pleased to extend the Feast of S. Boniface as a double, to the entire Church, in the hope that Germany may the sooner obtain aid in her affliction, through the intercession of S. Boniface. The Archbishop of Westminster has complied with the suggestion, and has addressed to the Holy See a petition to the above effect.

PRESENTATION OF THE OFFICERS OF THE LATE PONTIFICAL ARMY TO THE POPE.—On the 28th of December, the Feast of St. John, the Patron Saint of the Holy Father, the officers of the late Pontifical army, to the number of 300, were presented to him by General Kanzler. The following is a brief abstract of the reply of the Pope to their address:—

He said that it was an eloquent proof of the badness of the times when his late brave defenders could only appear before him without their arms. The Holy Father added that there is now no call from Heaven to fight; nothing indicates that it is the will of God that we should have recourse, at the present time, to arms. "I, therefore, His Vicar, must obey His will, and imitate His silence; I dare not authorize an appeal to war. As the Vice-gerent of the God of peace, who came on earth to bring peace to us, it is my duty to maintain peace. And yet the enemy is there; he surrounds us on all sides. The Revolution threatens us, and we must combat it, and vanquish it; but how? I am persuaded that the Revolution will fall of itself, it will perish by suicide; it will die by its own hands, by weapons of its own forging. When it does fall, may God grant it be buried for ever." The Holy Father went on to cite from Holy Scripture, as typical, the his-tories of David and Goliath, and of Judith and Holofernes. In both in-stances the warriors who had defied God were beheaded with their own swords, and by most unlikely instruments: the one by a stripling, the other by a woman. "The Revolution must perish, and it is by the sword of our enemies themselves that we shall be delivered from it. It will die by its own want of principles, by its own abuse of brute force, by its own injus-tice, and its own policy; by the breach at the Porta Pia and by the host of its other crimes, too long for me now to enumerate, but as well known to you as to myself. We must pray without ceasing, earnestly, as Judith did, and the downfall of the Revolution will come when we least expect it. For myself, I have not long to live; but I pray for the Church, for you, and for so many millions of souls spread over the earth, who have faith, hope, and charity, and who are united to me in these wishes, which they firmly believe they will see realized."

On the 29th of December, the Feast of St Thomas of Canterbury, the Pope received to audience a large assembly of the nobility of Rome. In reply to their address, which expressed their regret and sorrow at witnessing the iniquitous acts that were being attempted against the religious orders and discipline of the Church, the Pope said:—

"I remember in my youth, in this same Rome, conversing with a Roman Prince, who was then advanced in age, and who has passed for many years into eternity. He was a man of elevated sentiment and of truly Catholic principles; and he said that there were two supports to the Throne—the Clergy and the Nobility. These, said the good old man, are two pillars that ought to uphold the Monarchy. I perceive from your presence here to-day what your desire on this head is—the same as it has always been in times past. You are resolved to support the Throne, and if your support has been unable to uphold it—if for the moment it has fallen—the fault is not yours, as all the world will bear impartial testimony. I have a firm hope that God in His mercy has not forsaken us.

"Truly, Jesus Christ himself also loved the aristocracy; and, if I am not mistaken I once before expressed this same idea to you. He also chose to be born noble,—of the house and lineage of David; and the Gospels give us His genealogy, down to Joseph and Mary, *de quâ natus est Jesus.* Nobility is one of God's gifts; preserve it carefully, employ it worthily. You do so by practising the works of Christian charity and benevolence, to which you constantly devote your lives, to the great edification of your neighbour and to the great benefit of your own souls.

"I have said that the aristocracy and the clergy are two supports of the Throne. I go back to the subject in order to remark that thrones supported by the populace—thrones, that is, supported by those who entertain very generally infidel opinions, and many of whom entertain feelings of hatred against God and His Church—Oh God! those thrones resting on such supports, are weak, are hollow; and if other thrones, better supported on justice, have not resisted the attacks made upon them, how shall those resist which are founded on injustice, on violence, on robbery, and on calumny? Can it be possible that such thrones as these shall stand?

"The future is in the hand of God; but the history of the past has its lessons . . . . I remember when I was a little boy, like those that stand near me now, I played with one who was the son of a Jacobin—people who are now called 'Liberals' were then called 'Jacobins'—and who was growing up in the same notions as his father held. Here in Rome everyone knew him, and I myself saw him several times in 1848. He is now dead, and we are still alive. His father's example was fatal to him; but your example will be salutary and beneficial to these boys, and I begin with blessing these your little sons, that they may profit by the example of their good fathers and mothers who are giving them a holy education. Next I bless you fathers and your families: and I specially bless those who are in any affliction that they may have strength to bear the troubles which the Lord sends them but to purify them, and to enrich them with Christian virtues."

MISCELLANEOUS ANECDOTE.

A LONDON OMNIBUS-DRIVER A ROSARIAN.—A Correspondent writes to inform us that quite recently on an occasion when he was seated on the box-seat of an omnibus, in one of the crowded thoroughfares of London, he noticed the driver frequently busy with one hand under the apron; and presently, detecting that the man had a string of beads in his hand and was saying his Rosary between the stages of his journey to the Bank, he spoke to him, and learned from him that the good Christian generally managed to get through his five decades between the Bank and the place in the West End from which his omnibus started, thereby proving that the Rosary is a devotion for all persons and all times and places and ways of life, for the crowded and busy thoroughfare equally with the retirement of the cloister.

THE

𝕸𝖔𝖓𝖙𝖍𝖑𝖞 𝕸𝖆𝖌𝖆𝖟𝖎𝖓𝖊 𝖔𝖋 𝖙𝖍𝖊 𝕳𝖔𝖑𝖞 𝕽𝖔𝖘𝖆𝖗𝖞.

NEW SERIES.

No. 8.]   MARCH.   [A.D. 1873

S. JOSEPH, THE SPOUSE OF THE BLESSED VIRGIN, AND PATRON OF THE UNIVERSAL CHURCH:

A Homily on S. Joseph as a Pattern of Character, to be most carefully studied and imitated, in the present Age of cavilling against Faith.

Beloved of God and men, whose name is in benediction.—Ecclus. xlv. 1.

THE higher the degree of honour and exaltation which comes to be given to any Saint in the Church, the stronger becomes the call for the faithful to study the Saint's character, as the same appears in his life and actions. The call is to carry home to ourselves the more carefully, so to speak, the nature of the example which he leaves behind him, with a view to take pattern by it, and to be full of solicitude to regulate our own words, thoughts, and actions by the light of the example which is thus set before us in a more prominent manner.

We must, however, not forget the truth that every Saint belongs in the first instance, not to us, but to the Church triumphant, and it is only by a special grace that we who are on the earth are allowed the benefit of a tribunal which determines the scale of rank and honour that is to be paid to those in particular of the holy Saints, respecting whom the Providence of God appears to judge it to be good for us, that we should know and honour them in a special manner. The special honour which the Church Militant pays to certain of the Saints, and which may be greatly increased in particular instances as time goes on, has always in view some special benefits which are to flow from such honour being paid, either to the entire body of the Church or to the people of particular provinces and localities. Now one of the great benefits always arising from the special honour paid to any Saint is, as we have said, the special call, that arises out of the honour thus paid, to study the more carefully to know the Saint's example, and to set this example in a more decided way before ourselves for imitation.

We are, of course, very far from affirming that the Church

has no other reason for the public honours decreed to particular Saints, than to enhance the value of their example for the purpose of inciting the faithful to greater diligence in setting it before themselves for imitation. What we say is, that when an increase of public honour is decreed to any one of the Saints, there immediately arises out of the increased honour thus decreed, an increased call to all the faithful to stir themselves up to learn more of the example which he has given, and to be more diligent than ever in setting this example before themselves to take pattern by it.

S. Joseph is a case in point. He has quite recently received a wonderful increase of the honour which the Church pays here below to the Saints, by being raised to the dignity of becoming the patron of the Universal Church. Agreeably, therefore, to our doctrine, we at once proceed to a closer study of his character.

Our first introduction to S. Joseph, then, brings him before us at the particular juncture when he has become acquainted with the condition of his betrothed spouse which is no longer capable of being concealed, that is to say, with her prospect of an approaching maternity, of the source of which he is in complete ignorance. The Church expresses his trouble of mind thus :—

> " Almo cum tumidam germine conjugem
>   Admirans, dubio tangeris anxius."

> " Thee when amazed concern for thy betrothed
>   Had filled thy righteous spirit with dismay."—CASWALL'S *version*.

and S. Matthew relates what came to pass as follows :—
" When as His Mother Mary was espoused to Joseph before they came together, she was found with child by the Holy Ghost. Whereupon Joseph, her husband, being a just man and not willing publicly to expose her (by bringing her before a court), was minded to put her away privately. But while he thought on these things," &c.—(Matt. i. 18). Joseph, then, is clearly to be understood to have been in a distressed and doubtful state of mind, not knowing what course to choose, and anxiously revolving within himself on what his choice should eventually rest.

Here, as nothing in the study of an example is more important than to have the circumstances of the case fully before us, we must take the pains necessary to understand, how that which was under consideration in S. Joseph's mind would affect the conscience of one of whom it is said that he was a "just man," that is to say, a Jew who was a just and upright observer of the Law of Moses, holding himself bound in conscience to strict obedience to it.

The Blessed Virgin, as appears from her near relationship to Elizabeth, who was the wife of a priest, was, if not herself a priest's daughter, still of sacerdotal kindred, and it was an enactment of the Mosaic Law (Lev. xxi. 9), "that if a priest's daughter disgraced herself, she should be burnt alive, while the women of the other tribes similarly transgressing were to be stoned." S. Joseph's conscience of his obligations under the Mosaic Law distressed him with the thought that it was his duty to bring the case of his affianced wife before a judge, that she might be dealt with according to the Law of Moses, and made a public example; but to his merciful and gentle nature this proceeding was most repugnant, and he revolved in his mind if he could not rather put her away privately. S. Matthew relates, "that as he thought on these things, behold an angel of the Lord appeared to him in his sleep, saying, 'Joseph, son of David, fear not to take unto thee Mary, thy wife, for that which is conceived in her is of the Holy Ghost. And she shall bring forth a son, and thou shalt call his name JESUS, for He shall save His people from their sins.'"

To appreciate with any degree of proper understanding the example which S. Joseph here sets us of one who as it were annihilates or completely sinks himself in the presence of a manifestation of the will of God, and has no other thought than to conform himself to it in the most unreserved way possible, we must consider two things.

First, that the particular mode of communication by which it pleased God to make known His will to S. Joseph, though not without precedent in the history of Divine communications (see Job xxxiii. 15) is nevertheless the least direct of the means which God has been known to employ, and consequently the most open to demur and doubt on the part of the receiver, if the Divine intimation conveyed by it meets with any internal reluctance or indisposition to obey. There takes place no conference or dialogue between S. Joseph and the holy Angel similar to that which had passed between the Blessed Virgin and S. Gabriel, which would at least have had the effect of fixing in his mind an unmistakable certainty as to what it was that God required from him. S. Joseph awakes in the morning with only the impression on his mind which the waking man has from that which has happened to him in his sleep.   But then for a true servant of God, to obey whom is the only perfect freedom, the least clear intimation of the Divine will proves to be sufficient. And Joseph rising " up from sleep," says S. Matthew, " did at once as the Angel of the Lord had commanded him, and took unto him his wife." Here is certainly an example of compliance with the will of God on the part of a man not only as complete as any example on record in respect of the total merging of all the conflicting thoughts with which his own mind was at the time distracted, but in respect of the promptitude of the compliance founded on the least distinct of all the ways by which God speaks to men.

Compare in this respect S. Joseph's instant surrender of himself on a comparatively indistinct intimation of the Divine will with the reiterated struggle that Moses made in the presence of the Lord God Himself speaking from the midst of the bush that burnt with fire and yet was not consumed, to assert his own will against the commands of God.   Yet Moses, who only ended by submission, became the friend of God, and was, as S. Paul says, " a servant faithful in all his house."

Secondly, we must duly understand the extent of S. Joseph's surrender of his whole mind, in a word, his whole intelligent being, to the Divine communication. We Christians, to whom it has been clearly revealed that God is One God, but exists in three Divine Persons, readily submit ourselves, influenced by the example of innumerable generations of Christian people who have equally submitted themselves, to the mystery which the Church teaches, namely, that the maternity of the Blessed Virgin was the work of God the Holy Ghost ; but S. Joseph was very differently circumstanced to us.   Though of the royal house of David, he was still living in humble life in the village of Nazareth, and nothing more would be known to him than the ordinary doctrine respecting the Lord God of Israel which was learned by humble persons from the popular teaching which was current in the Israelite synagogues. Whatever, therefore, may have been known to the learned doctors of the synagogue in the way of a mysterious foreshadowing contained in their scriptures of the doctrine of the three Divine Persons of the Godhead, it is not easily to be supposed that S. Joseph, a man of the people, could be ac-

quainted with the secret doctrines of the schools of Jewish
Theology. When, therefore, he had before him the words of
the Angel, " For that which is conceived in her is of the Holy
Ghost," what action could his mind take upon words which
went entirely beyond his knowledge, except the action best
befitting the true servant of God, namely, complete submission? As formerly, the high priest Heli, to whom the
child Samuel repeated all the judgments that God said He
would bring on his house, only remarked, " It is the Lord, let
Him do what is good in His sight," so S. Joseph appears to
have said within himself, " These are the words of the Lord,
let Him reveal to me what is good in His sight, I bow myself
down and believe; let Him command me as He thinks fit, I
bow myself down and obey."*

What a pattern for the study of the generation of self wise
and opinionated people, who object to believe and conform to
the doctrines and laws which an Ecumenical Council, gathered
together in the Holy Ghost, under the headship of the legitimate successor of S. Peter, accredits to them as the true
revelation and the true will of God. Which is the more distinct and unmistakable of the two, as expressing the voice of
God, a communication made in sleep, by the channel of a
dream, or the united decree of the princes of the whole
Church, assembled in council under their legitimate head?

The same characteristic excellence in S. Joseph of the
prompt compliance with the will of God on the least clear
intimation, equally appears on three other occasions. In the
case of the flight into Egypt, S. Joseph and the Blessed
Virgin have quitted Nazareth and are now domiciled in Bethlehem, David's city, and are there taking care of the bringing

* We may, perhaps, here appropriately make an effort to correct a certain misapprehension into which some of our readers seem to have fallen,
to whom the beautiful legend relating the homage which inanimate nature
paid to the mother of God on her way to Bethlehem, given in our Number
of January, appeared to fail in the respect due to S. Joseph. The scene
quoted from the Pageant in question, represents S. Joseph travelling from
Nazareth on his way to "Bedleem" with Mary, having in vain attempted
to persuade her not to undertake the journey in consequence of her state
of approaching maternity, respecting which his mind had now been completely set at rest by the words of the holy Angel as being the work of
God the Holy Ghost. When asked to gather the cherries from the tree
that suddenly blooms in the winter, as they are passing by, he is represented
as replying with the most affectionate respect, and desire to oblige " Yo'

up of the child, to whom it has been promised that He shall sit on the throne of His father David. They have received the visit of the wise men from the East, and are consequently confirmed in their expectations if they need such confirmation. But now occurs an incident that appears singularly at variance with all their glowing expectations. A command comes to S. Joseph by the same comparatively little distinct way of a vision in sleep, saying, "Arise, take the Child and his Mother, and fly into Egypt, and remain there until I shall tell thee; for it will come to pass that Herod will seek the young child to destroy Him."

What, apparently, can be more in contradiction with their expectations than the very fact itself of a necessity for this sudden flight? And of all places to the land of Egypt; a country to which it was specially forbidden by the Law of Moses to any Israelite to return after the delivery of their fathers from their bondage in it (Deut. xvii. 16). What room is there not here for disputing and resisting the intimation received? If flight were necessary, would it be likely that God would have overlooked the prohibition of the Law of Moses to Israelites against being again led into Egypt? S. Matthew, however, relates that S. Joseph did not so much as wait for the morning to obey, but there and then arose and took the Child and His Mother by night and went into the land of Egypt.

Here they remained (and there is no very clear tradition as to the exact duration of their sojourn), awaiting the return of the Angel to intimate to them the promised permission to return. When Herod was dead the Angel returned, and again the same prompt obedience on the part of S. Joseph. He

---

desyr to ffulfyle I schall assay sekyrly." But on making the attempt he finds the cherries out of his reach, "ffor the tre is so hy." So he returns, and with a certain reproach as to the impossibility of Mary's request, that even if dissonant to our ears, contains what to an age of faith was a welcome, plain-spoken acknowledgment of the miraculous nature of her pregnancy, he says that the cherries could only be gathered by a miracle worked by the same Divine power to which she owed her then existing condition. When, to Joseph's great wonder and awe, the miracle thus brusquely challenged is there and then worked, and the tree bows itself down to Mary, S. Joseph is represented as fearing that he had offended "God i' Trinyte," by being so bold as to have thus unthinkingly challenged a miracle, and he at once humbles himself. We may surely, considering the ocean of unbelief in which we live, have humility enough not to be

arose, and came into the land of Israel.   It would seem that
his wish was to return to the domicile in Bethlehem which
they had so abruptly quitted to escape into Egypt; but the
Angel appeared to him for the fourth time.   He was warned
in his sleep of the insecurity of being so near to Herod's son,
Archelaus, and again, for the fourth time, he immediately
complies and comes back to Nazareth, where he is believed to
have dwelt for the rest of his life.

It is thus we may well rejoice to see, not without the light
of wisdom from above, that the Holy Church opposes to the
cavilling and disbelieving spirit of the later ages of the
world, the example of the promptest and most unresisting
obedience to the least clear intimation of the will of God, of
the holy patriarch Joseph, spouse of the Blessed Virgin, and
Patron of the Universal Church.   Let us hope that the zeal
which, perhaps, we have ourselves unintentionally somewhat
contributed to evoke, to defend the honour of S. Joseph, may
be followed most abundantly by the corresponding zeal to
study carefully and take pattern by his holy example of
prompt and unreserved obedience, even to the least clear
intimation of the adorable will of God.

---

displeased with the way in which an "age of faith" sought and found its
edification.

An age of faith, however, perhaps it should be said, is of course
only responsible for that which really belongs to it, and need not
own the precise form in which its traditions find themselves after being
orally transmitted through times of falling away from the faith.   This is
true, but on the other hand we may plead that all Catholics are piously
invited, and English Catholics are enjoined, to pray earnestly for the return
of England to the Catholic faith, and it may thus give us edification and
fresh courage in our prayers, and fresh hope of their being heard, to see a
proof of the tenacity of life with which, like the well of S. Winifred, a
beautiful Catholic legend also continues to hold its own in the minds of
the people for whose conversion we pray, in spite of the errors by which
they have been led astray.

SISTER ANNE CATHERINE EMMERICH OF DULMEN.

FROM the earliest ages of the Church, Our Blessed Lord has been pleased, for our joy and consolation, to draw aside, from time to time, in favour of a few chosen souls, the veil which hides the mysteries and glories of the invisible world. Among these we note, almost within our own times, Sister Anne Catherine Emmerich, an Augustinian nun, who lived in this century, whose visions and revelations have been published under the implicit sanction of high ecclesiastical authority. It may be well to observe that by this "implicit sanction," the Church simply allows such works to be used by the faithful, without pronouncing any decided judgment upon them, or in any way allowing them to become the guide of faith or morals. "The approbation of private revelations," as Benedict XIV. explains, "implies nothing more than this, that, after a careful examination, they are allowed to be published for the edification of the faithful." And he adds, "Although they are not entitled to the same belief as the truths of religion, we believe them with a faith merely human, according to the rules of ordinary prudence, as they are more or less probable." Thus, taking the very lowest view, these revelations may merely serve, like pious pictures or dramatic representations, as helps to meditation on the Passion; but there are few, we think, who will not rather claim the privilege of being able to believe in their supernatural origin. We purpose, then, to give a slight sketch of Sister Emmerich's life, and such extracts from her visions as are especially appropriate to the season of Lent, and bear chiefly on the five sorrowful mysteries of the Rosary and the sorrows of the Blessed Virgin.

Anne Catherine Emmerich was the child of poor peasants, and born on the 8th September, 1774, at a village near Coesfeld, in the Bishopric of Munster. Her life is full of singular beauty. From her earliest infancy she had constant intercourse with the inhabitants of the invisible world. Her Angel Guardian used to appear to her as another child; Our Blessed Lord, under the form of a shepherd, would help her while she was keeping her sheep; and Our Lady and the Saints would also come to her and receive the garlands of flowers which she used to weave on their festivals. For a long time she supposed that other children saw the same things, and she spoke freely about them. She had communications with the souls in purgatory throughout her life, and offered all her actions and penances to relieve their sufferings. Often, while very young, she used to be awakened out of her sleep by bands of suffering souls, and would follow them bare-footed on cold winters' nights, when the ground was covered with snow, the whole length of the Way of the Cross to Coes-feld. When she was twenty-seven years of her age, she was received into the Augustinian Convent at Dulmen. Four years previously she had received, during a vision, the impression on her head of a crown of thorns, from which blood frequently flowed. She was professed on the 13th September, 1803, at the age of twenty-nine. Nine years later the convent was suppressed, and the church closed; the nuns dispersed, and Anne Catherine was obliged to remain in a small lodging in the town. Here, about a year afterwards, she received the stigmas of the Passion in her hands, feet, and side. Blood frequently flowed from them for some years, and they were a cause of indescribable torment to her for the remainder of her life. She became unable to walk or rise from her bed, and, after a time, she could no longer take any food, or swallow anything but water, except, very rarely, the juice of a cherry or plum. This state continued till her death.

After a time she was removed to another room, "at the back of a public-house, where the men played at nine-pins under her window." Thus, by a singular disposition of Divine Providence, her ecstatic life became public. Great curiosity was excited, and most rigorous inquiry into her state was made by some doctors and naturalists, who caused her, at one time, to be placed all alone in a strange house for three weeks. But they made no fresh discovery, and after this she was allowed to remain in peace until her death. She had continual visions, in which she visited in spirit the holy places, and during which the whole of the history of the Old and New Testament was made known to her. "She saw," says her bio-grapher, "the signification of all the festival days of the eccle-siastical year, under both a devotional and an historical point of view. She saw and described, day by day, with the minutest detail and by name, places, persons, festivals, customs, and miracles, all that happened during the public life of Jesus till His Ascension, and the history of the Apostles for several weeks after the descent of the Holy Ghost." She had extra-ordinary love and devotion to the successive feasts of the ecclesiastical year. "The Christian Almanac was to her an

inexhaustible mine of hidden riches, since it gave her, in a
few pages, a guiding thread which led her through all time,
and by means of which she passed from mystery to mystery,
and solemnized each with the Saints." She had never read
the Old and New Testaments, and when tired of relating her
visions, she would say, "Read that in the Bible," and was
astonished to find it was not there.

By the direction of Dean Overberg, her director, and
Bp. Michael Sailer, the Bishop of Ratisbon, who had long been
her friend and adviser, the notes of her visions were taken by her
bedside from her own dictation, and arranged for publication
after her death, which occurred on the 9th of February, 1824.
A translation of her life, and such part of her visions as
relates to the Passion of Our Lord, (from which these extracts
are taken), has been published in English.*

The following is from the vision of the Agony of Our
Lord, in the Garden of the Mount of Olives, which commenced about nine o'clock in the evening :—

"Jesus went a few steps to the left, down a hill, and concealed Himself
beneath a rock, in a grotto about six feet deep, while the Apostles remained
in a species of hollow above. The earth sank gradually the further you
entered the grotto, and the plants which were hanging from the rock
screened its interior, like a curtain, from persons outside."

"When Jesus left his disciples, I saw a number of frightful figures surrounding Him in an ever-narrowing circle. His sorrow and anguish of
soul continued to increase, and he was trembling all over when he entered
the grotto to pray, like a wayworn traveller hurriedly seeking shelter from
a sudden storm; but the awful visions pursued Him even there, and became
more and more clear and distinct. Alas! this small cavern appeared to
contain the awful picture of all the sins which had been or were to be
committed, from the fall of Adam to the end of the world, and of the
punishment which they deserved. It was here, on Mount Olivet, that Adam
and Eve took refuge when driven out of Paradise, to wander homeless on
earth, and they had wept and bewailed themselves in this very grotto."

"I felt that Jesus, in delivering Himself up to Divine Justice in satisfaction for the sins of the world, caused His Divinity to return, in some
sort, into the bosom of the Holy Trinity, concentrated Himself, so to
speak, in His pure, loving, and innocent humanity, and strong only in His
ineffable love, gave it up to anguish and suffering."

"He fell on his face, overwhelmed with unspeakable sorrow, and all the
sins of the world displayed themselves before Him, under countless forms
and in all their real deformity. He took them all upon Himself, and in
His prayer offered His own adorable Person to the justice of His heavenly

* London : Burns and Oates. We earnestly recommend it to the notice
of our readers.

Father, in payment for so awful a debt. But Satan, who was enthroned amid all these horrors, and even filled with diabolical joy at the sight of them, let loose his fury against Jesus, and displayed before the eyes of His soul increasingly awful visions, at the same time addressing His adorable humanity in such words as these: 'Takest Thou even this sin upon Thyself? Art Thou willing to bear its penalty? Art Thou prepared to satisfy for all these sins?'

"And now a long ray of light, like a luminous path in the air, descended from heaven; it was a procession of angels who came up to Jesus, and strengthened and invigorated Him. The remainder of the grotto was filled with frightful visions of our crimes; Jesus took them all upon Himself, but that adorable heart, which was so filled with the most perfect love of God and man, was flooded with anguish, and overwhelmed beneath the weight of so many abominable crimes. When this huge mass of iniquities, like the waves of a fathomless ocean, had passed over His soul, Satan brought forward innumerable temptations, as he had formerly done in the desert, even daring to adduce various accusations against Him. . . . Among the sins of the world which Jesus took upon Himself, I saw also my own; and a stream, in which I distinctly beheld each of my faults, appeared to flow towards me from out of the temptations with which He was encircled. During this time my eyes were fixed on my heavenly Spouse, with Him I wept and prayed, and with Him I turned towards the consoling angels. Ah! truly did our dear Lord writhe like a worm beneath the weight of His anguish and sufferings.

"At first Jesus looked calm as He knelt down and prayed, but after a time His soul became terrified at the sight of the innumerable crimes of men, and of their ingratitude towards God, and His anguish was so great, that He trembled and shuddered as He exclaimed, '*Father, if it be possible, let this chalice pass from Me; Father, all things are possible to Thee, remove this chalice from Me.*' But the next moment He added: '*Nevertheless not My will but Thine be done.*' His will, and that of His Father were one, but now that His love had ordained that He should be left to all the weakness of his human nature, He trembled at the prospect of death.

"I saw the cavern in which He was kneeling filled with frightful figures; I saw all the sins, wickedness, vices and ingratitude of mankind torturing and crushing him to the earth; the horror of death and terror which He felt as a man at the sight of the expiatory sufferings about to come upon Him surrounded and assailed His divine person under the forms of hideous spectres. He fell from side to side, clasping His hands; His body was covered with a cold sweat, and He trembled and shuddered. He then arose, but His knees were shaking and apparently scarcely able to support Him; His countenance was pale, and quite altered in appearance, His lips white, and His hair standing on end. It was about half past ten o'clock when He arose from His knees, and, bathed in a cold sweat, directed His trembling weak footsteps towards His three Apostles."

After Our Lord's interview with the Apostles, He returned to the grotto, and had a second interior combat which lasted three-quarters of an hour. He was shown by Angels, in a series of visions, all the sufferings He was to endure in order to expiate sin, the beauty of man the image of God before the Fall, and how that beauty was destroyed and obliterated when sin entered the world :—

" They showed Him the satisfaction he would have to offer to Divine Justice, and how it would consist of a degree of suffering in His soul and body which would comprehend all the sufferings due to the concupiscence of all mankind, since the debt of the whole human race had to be paid by that humanity which alone was sinless—the humanity of the Son of God. The Angels showed Him these things under different forms, and I felt what they were saying, though I heard no voice. No tongue can describe what anguish and what horror overwhelmed the soul of Jesus at the sight of so terrible an expiation. His sufferings were so great that a bloody sweat issued forth from all the pores of His sacred body."

The angels were filled with compassion, and earnestly prayed to be allowed to console Our Lord.

" For one instant there appeared to be, as it were, a struggle between the mercy and justice of God, and that love which was sacrificing itself. I was permitted to see an image of God, not, as before, seated on a throne, but under a luminous form. I beheld the Divine nature of the Son in the Person of the Father, and, as it were, withdrawn into His bosom ; the Person of the Holy Ghost proceeded from the Father and Son ; it was, so to speak, between them, and yet the whole formed only one God ; but these things are indescribable. All this was more an inward perception than a vision under distinct forms, and it appeared to me that the Divine Will of our Lord withdrew in some sort into the Eternal Father, in order to permit all these sufferings which His human will besought His Father to spare Him, to weigh upon His humanity alone. I saw this at the time when the Angels, filled with compassion, were desiring to console Jesus, who, in fact, was slightly relieved at that moment. Then all disappeared, and the Angels retired from Our Lord, whose soul was about to sustain fresh assaults."

A most interesting description follows of what the soul of Jesus beheld with regard to the future of His Church. The sufferings and persecutions of His faithful followers, and the wickedness, malice and corruption of such an infinite number of Christians, all the sins of sacrilege, heresy, and schism, which were ever to exist, passed before His eyes.

" Jesus, the Anointed of the Lord, the Son of Man, struggled and writhed as He fell on His knees, with clasped hands, as it were annihilated beneath the weight of His suffering. So violent was the struggle which then took place between His human will and His repugnance to suffer so much for such an ungrateful race, that from every pore of His sacred body there burst forth large drops of blood, which fell trickling on the ground. In His bitter agony He looked around, as though seeking help, and appeared to take Heaven, earth, and the stars of the firmament to witness His sufferings."

Sister Emmerich saw that sacrilege and insults offered to the most Holy Sacrament had a considerable share in the agony of Our Lord. She describes the visions of these, as they appeared to her, with great power and clearness, even down to the irreverence shown by too many Catholics.

"Among the latter, the sight of whom grieved me especially, because Jesus so loved children, I saw many irreverent, ill behaved acolytes, who did not honour our Lord in the holy ceremonies in which they took part. I beheld, with terror, that many priests, some of whom even fancied themselves full of faith and piety, also outraged Jesus in the adorable Sacrament. I saw many who believed and taught the doctrine of the Real Presence, but did not sufficiently take it to heart, for they forgot and neglected the palace, throne, and seat of the living God; that is to say, the church, the altar, the tabernacle, the chalice, the monstrance, the vases, and ornaments; in one word, all that is used in His worship or to adorn His house. Entire neglect prevailed; things were left to moulder away in dust and filth, and the worship of God was, if not inwardly profaned, at least outwardly dishonoured. Nor did this arise from real poverty, but from indifference, sloth, preoccupation of mind about vain earthly concerns, and often also from egotism and spiritual death; for I saw neglect of this kind in churches, the pastors and congregations of which were rich, or, at least, tolerably well off. I saw many other in which worldly, tasteless, and unsuitable ornaments had replaced the magnificent adornments of a more pious age.

"I saw that often the poorest of men were better lodged in their cottages than the Master of Heaven and earth in His churches. Ah! how deeply did the inhospitality of men grieve Jesus, who had given Himself to them to be their food! . . . . This state of impurity and negligence extended even to the souls of the faithful, who left the tabernacle of their hearts unprepared and uncleansed when Jesus was about to enter them, exactly the same as they left His tabernacle or the altar.

"Were I to speak for an entire year, I could never detail all the insults offered to Jesus in the Adorable Sacrament. . . . . . I saw a great number of theologians, who had been drawn into heresy by their sins, attacking Jesus in the Holy Sacrament of His Church, and snatching out of His Heart, by their seductive words and promises, a number of souls for whom He had shed His blood. Ah! it was indeed an awful sight, for I saw the Church as the body of Christ, and all these bands of men, who were separating themselves from the Church, mangled and tore off whole pieces of His flesh. Alas! He looked at them in the most touching manner, and lamented that they should thus cause their own eternal loss. . . . . I beheld whole nations thus snatched out of His bosom, and deprived of any participation in the treasure of graces left to the Church. Finally, I saw all who were separated from the Church plunged into the depths of infidelity, superstition, heresy, and false worldly philosophy, and they gave vent to their fierce rage by joining together in large bodies to attack the Church, being urged on by the Serpent, which was disporting himself in the midst of them. Alas! it was as though Jesus Himself had been torn in a thousand pieces.

"I saw blood flowing in large drops down the pale face of our Saviour;

His hair was matted together, and His beard bloody and entangled. After the vision which I have last described, He fled, so to speak, out of the cave, and returned to His disciples. But He tottered as He walked; His appearance was that of a man covered with wounds and bending beneath a heavy burthen, and He stumbled at every step. . . . . It was then about a quarter past eleven.

" During this agony of Jesus, I saw the Blessed Virgin also overwhelmed with sorrow and anguish of soul in the house of Mary, the mother of Mark. She was with Magdalen and Mary in the garden belonging to the house, and almost prostrate from grief, with her whole body bowed down as she knelt. She fainted several times, for she beheld, in spirit, different portions of the agony of Jesus. She had sent some messengers to make inquiries concerning Him, but her deep anxiety would not suffer her to await their return, and she went with Magdalen and Salome as far as the Valley of Josaphat. She walked along with her head veiled, and her arms frequently stretched forth towards Mount Olivet; for she beheld, in spirit, Jesus bathed in a bloody sweat, and her gestures were as though she wished, with her extended hands, to wipe the face of her Son. I saw these interior movements of her soul towards Jesus, who thought of her, and turned His eyes in her direction, as if to seek her assistance. I beheld the spiritual communication which they had with each other, under the form of rays passing to and fro between them. Our Divine Lord thought also of Magdalen, was touched by her distress, and therefore recommended His Apostles to console her." . . . . . .

After this, Jesus again prayed in the grotto, and an abyss opened before Him, in which He had a vision of the first part of Limbo. He saw Adam and Eve and all the Saints of the old law awaiting His arrival with intense longing. The angels then presented to Him all the bands of Saints of future ages.

"The apostles, disciples, virgins, and holy women, the martyrs, confessors, hermits, popes, and bishops, and large bands of religious of both sexes, in one word, the entire army of the blessed, appeared before Him. All bore on their heads triumphal crowns, and the flowers of their crowns differed in form, in colour, in odour, and in perfection, according to the difference of the sufferings, labours, and victories, which had procured them eternal glory. . . . The reciprocal influence exercised by these saints upon each other, and the manner in which they all drank from one sole fountain, the Adorable Sacrament and the Passion of our Lord—formed a most touching and wonderful spectacle . . . The army of the future saints passed before the soul of our Lord, which was thus placed between the deserving patriarchs, and the triumphant band of the future blessed, and these two armies joining together, and completing one another, so to speak, surrounded the loving heart of the Saviour as with a crown of victory. This most affecting and consoling spectacle bestowed a degree of strength and comfort on the heart of Jesus . . . . As these visions referred to the future, they were diffused to a certain height in the air."

Afterwards the Angels displayed before Jesus the scenes of

His Passion, quite close to the earth, because it was near at
hand; and every part of His sufferings was shown to Him,
down to the minutest detail.   He accepted all voluntarily,
submitting to everything for the love of man :—

"When the visions of the Passion were concluded, Jesus fell on his face
like one at the point of death; the angels disappeared, and the bloody
sweat became more copious, so that I saw it had soaked His garments.
Entire darkness reigned in the cavern, when I beheld an angel descend to
Jesus . . . . He was clothed like a priest in a long floating garment, and
bore in His hands a small vase, in shape resembling the chalice used at
the last supper. At the top of this chalice was a small oval body, about
the size of a bean, which diffused a reddish light. The angel, without
touching the earth with his feet, stretched forth his right hand to Jesus,
who arose, when he placed the mysterious food in His mouth, and gave
Him to drink from the luminous chalice; then he disappeared.

"Jesus, having freely accepted the chalice of His sufferings, and received
new strength, remained some minutes longer in the grotto, absorbed in
calm meditation, and returning thanks to His Heavenly Father. He was
still in deep affliction of spirit, but supernaturally comforted to such a degree as to be able to go to His disciples without tottering as He walked,
or bending beneath the weight of His sufferings. His countenance was still
pale and altered, but His step was firm and determined. He had wiped
His face with a linen cloth, and re-arranged His hair, which hung about
His shoulders matted together and damp with blood."

(*To be continued*).

HALF-HOURS WITH THE SAINTS.—No. II.

THE STORY OF S. PATRICK.

A Legend in Verse, by the late Rev. G. MONTGOMERY, *of Wednesbury.*

[The following story, in verse, of the life of S. Patrick, here given in a somewhat abridged shape, was written in moments of leisure snatched from the laborious
duties of a missionary priest, placed in the heart of the mining and iron-working
district of South Staffordshire. Its writer had in view mainly the instruction of
the young of his flock, to whom he wished a knowledge of the history of the Patron
Saint of their native country to become a household possession. The better, as he
thought, to secure this end, he has given his lines the form of the popular ballads
often heard in the streets, sung or recited by ballad street-singers. We ask a
prayer, for the honour of S. Patrick, for the repose of the writer's soul, who is now
passed away from the scene of his former labours by a death accelerated through
the cares and troubles of his mission.]

PATRICK, our Erin's famous saint, the subject of this lay,
Was born in greater Brittany, the Church's lessons say;

Nigh years three hundred and threescore from that great day
    of mirth,
When Angels sang the Saviour born, we date Saint Patrick's
    birth.

He had not sixteen summers seen, when, lo, a pirate band,
Ruthless, on deeds of plunder bent, approached Taburnia's
    strand.
Then, marching from their mooring place, by a bold captain led,
They to Taburnia's peaceful homes with evil purpose sped.

They sacked the homes, they swept the fields, they bore the
    youths away;
They captured, with his sisters twain, our Patrick on that day.
They put to sea, this heathen crew, they gained the Irish soil;
They spread themselves along the beach, and there displayed
    their spoil.

A wealthy chieftain came to buy, to him was Patrick sold,
But what befel the little maids the legends have not told.
We trust that God, at Patrick's prayer, took up the children
    dear,
To be in joy with Saints above, safe from distress or fear.

The steward of Saint Patrick's lord now sent the lad to keep,
Upon a far wild pasturage, his master's flock of sheep.
There, heedless of the frost and snow, and of the driving rain,
He rose before the light to pray upon the open plain.

He for his people did deplore, that they in sin were found,
Whereby their homes had been despoiled and they in exile
    bound.
For he who loves, the Scripture saith, shall pardon crave for
    sin,
And so did Patrick's prayer avail the souls of men to win.

Now Patrick, by decree of God, was soon at large to be,
Yet twice again was captive ta'en, and twice again set free.
Thus oft was he by sorrow tried, as gold is tried in fire,
That from his heart God's love might burn as dross all base
    desire.

For God had chosen him to teach, and by his zeal to save,
The very Pagan race with whom he once had lived a slave.
But he who goes the faith to preach, should be with know-
    ledge fraught,
So Patrick humbly went to those by whom he might be taught.

He crossed to Gaul, he visited the great Saint Martin there,
And studied long with Saint Germain, the Bishop of Auxerre.
He learned all holy discipline, and piously he took
Most earnest care to be well versed in knowledge of God's
    book.

But Patrick knew that ere he sought the heathen's hearts to
    move,
He must commission have from Rome, at Rome his faith
    approve.
For Christ on Peter built His Church, surnaming him THE
    ROCK:
To Peter gave the keys, and said, "Thou, Simon, feed My
    Flock."

And every Christian ought to know that in the See of Rome
Peter doth ever live and speak, and ever hath a home.
So thither Patrick bent his steps, and found of Peter's line
The prince who sat on Peter's Throne, by name Pope Celestine.

This holy Pope he caused our Saint awhile in Rome to bide,
Then with full power he sent him forth a Legate from his side.
With holy haste our Saint proceeds unto Hibernia's shore,
Eager to bless the land he loved, and gift it from God's store.

'Twas on a glorious Easter Day, at Tara's famous hall,
Saint Patrick met the Irish king, the bards and chieftains all.
" I come," quoth he, " a humble man, the strong and proud
    to face,
In the Name of the Blest Trinity to bring you truth and grace.

" Let God arise, and let His foes scattered before Him be ;
Let them that hate Him, like thin smoke, at His bright pre-
    sence flee."
Chanting these words the Saint dispersed the demons of the
    air,
Who then, with purpose fell, swarmed in the Court of Leogaire.

And God was with Saint Patrick's work, and blessed all that
    he wrought,
Whereby the champion gained at last the prize for which he
    fought.
The people flocked to be baptised ; pastors o'er all the land
Were consecrated and ordained by Patrick's own right hand.

To many maids and widows, too, he gave the sacred veil,
And gathered them in order due within Religion's pale.
And by the right he had from Rome, our Saint made this
    decree,
That in the city of Armagh the primate's chair should be.

Thus he who once as slave did keep a farmer's fleecy flock,
As Prelate great for Christ did fold the faithful Irish flock.
And God in mercy granted him before his course was run,
To see his loved Hibernia for Christ and Mary won.

Satan since then has often tried, with all his force and guile,
To seize again the land he lost when Patrick blessed our isle.
But quite in vain are all his wiles to change her steadfast will,
For Ireland's heart unfailing cleaves to God and Mary still.

And Erin's faith hath well withstood the scoffer's biting gibe,
The scaffold, sword, and prison cell, and often-proffered bribe.
So let all pray that in this land, this holy faith may last,
By virtue of Saint Patrick's prayer, till time itself is past.

A LENTEN FORM OF PRAYER AND INTERCESSION FOR THE PRESERVATION OF THE SOVEREIGN PONTIFF AND THE HOLY CITY OF ROME.

A VERSION INTO ENGLISH OF A PRAYER PUBLISHED BY POPE URBAN VIII.

WE bear our guilt in thy sight, O Lord, and we have ever before us the chastisement which we have received.

If we measure the evil that we have done, less is that which we suffer, and greater is that which we deserve.

Greater are the misdeeds that we have done, and lighter the punishment that we endure.

We feel the pains which our sins have brought on us, but we do not flee from our evil doings.

By the stripes which Thou inflictest our flesh is consumed, but our iniquity is not taken away.

Our spirit is sorely tried, but our stiff neck is not bent.

Our life pineth away for grief, but we do not mend our ways.

If thou art patient and long suffering yet are we not corrected, and if thou strikest we fail.

When Thy hand lieth heavy on us we confess our evil doings, but when Thou takest it away we forget all that we have bewailed.

If Thou dost put forth Thy hand, we promise to amend; if Thou dost hold back Thy sword, we withold all that we have promised.

If Thou dost strike, we cry out to Thee to spare us; if Thou sparest us, we again provoke Thee to strike.

We confess our guilt in Thy sight, O Lord, and we acknowledge that except Thou dost mercifully forgive Thou mayest justly destroy us.

O Almighty Father, grant to us that which we ask, not deserving to obtain it, who hast made out of nothing them who ask Thee, through Jesus Christ our Lord.

V. O Eternal Shepherd, leave not Thy flock comfortless.

R. But through Thy blessed Apostles, protect us with an everlasting defence.

V. Guard Thy people, O Lord, who cry unto Thee, and who trust in the patronage of Thy Apostles.

R. Protect us with an everlasting defence.

V. Pray for us, ye holy Apostles of God.

That we may be made worthy of the promises of Christ.

Let us Pray.

Suffer us not, we beseech Thee, Almighty and Everlasting God, to be overcome by any adversities whom Thou hast firmly settled on the rock of thine Apostles' Confession of Faith.   Through our Lord, &c.

R. Amen.

Grant, O most merciful Lord, that the words of Thy holy servant, Chrysostom (who is buried in this church) may bring to us, who devoutly recite them, timely help in our need, in which he represented Thee, speaking thus with Thy holy Apostles, " Encompass and cast up a trench round about this new Sion, that is, guard, fortify, and protect it with prayers, that when my anger waxeth hot, and I shake the foundations of the earth, looking upon your burial-place that

is never to be removed, and on the bruises that you rejoice to
bear for my sake, I may overcome wrath with mercy, and
thereby give ear to your intercessions.   For when I see the
priesthood and the kingdom humbling themselves to tears,
straightway having compassion I incline to show mercy, and
I remember my promise." I will protect this city for the sake
of David, my servant, and Aaron, my holy one.—Be it thus,
O Lord.   Be it thus.   Amen.   Amen.*

THE CONVERSION TO THE CATHOLIC FAITH OF COUNT
FREDERIC LEOPOLD DE STOLBERG.

"I DO not like people who change their religion," said the
Duke of Saxe Weimar, publicly addressing one of Germany's
most distinguished men—distinguished alike for his ability as
a writer and a diplomatist, who had abjured Lutherism and
embraced Catholicity. "Nor I, my Lord," answered the noble
Count, "because, if my ancestors had not changed theirs
three hundred years ago, I should now have been spared the
trouble of changing mine." Many, perhaps, who well remember the somewhat bitter remark of the Duke and the
ready answer of him who was the object of it, have yet
no very distinct recollection, perhaps no knowledge at all, of
what manner of man he was, who, for freely exercising the
hotly contested and jealously guarded right of liberty of conscience, drew down upon himself the remark which, intended
as a public disapproval of his conduct, became instead the occasion of a display of what some called his ready wit, what
others, looking further, called his sound good sense.   Yet
Count Frederic Leopold de Stolberg ought not to be forgotten,
ought not to be unknown; but it is not merely on account
of the reputation of the youthful poet, skilful translator of
Homer, the clever writer of maturer years, the brilliant diplomatist, though here is matter quite sufficient to excite much
interest; it is not because he was the friend of Klopstock, of

---

* It will be edifying to remember that on the day of the sacrilegious
Invasion of the City of Rome by the troops of King Victor Emmanuel, the
Holy Father went down with his household into the Basilica of the Vatican
and recited this prayer before the tomb of S. Peter.

Jacobi, of Voss, the Schlegels, of Lavater, of Goethe, though here again is what would give him no mean interest in many eyes; but it is not for this or that alone that we would recall the memory of Stolberg now : there is another interest that attaches to him : the interest that does and always will attach itself to those who first break through a long-established state of things, who give the signal for a change, and turn the course of thought; in other words, to those bold men who, with intention or without, are leaders of a movement. Now when North Germany had for three hundred years been plunged in the deep sleep of Lutheranism, Fredcric Leopold de Stolberg was the first of her sons who awoke, arose, and rising, woke others, and left the dark, cold, building of the apostate monk, and was received into the Church of his forefathers. ·

On the seventh day of November, 1750, at Bramstedt in in Holstein, a child was born to the illustrious House of Stolberg, whose long line of Counts of Stolberg-Stolberg came of royal blood.   The child grew, and gave great promise: childhood passed, he fulfilled that promise ; and manhood scarce attained, Frederic Leopold de Stolberg ranked highly as a poet.   Distinguished also as a classical scholar, that he was a devoted one besides, we have ample proof in his admirable translations of the Iliad, the Tragedies of Æschylus, the poems of Ossian, and the dialogues of Plato.

Count de Stolberg began his diplomatic career as plenipotentiary minister of the Duke of Oldenberg, Prince Bishop of Lubeck, to the Court of Copenhagen.   In 1789 he became Danish Ambassador at the Court of Berlin; and finally, after having fulfilled several important missions both in Denmark and at St. Petersburg, he, shortly before his second marriage, in 1790, with Sophia Countess de Redern—his first wife had been dead two years—accepted the post of Prime Minister, embracing the offices of Minister of Finance and President of the Consistory to the Duke of Oldenburg; and this post he held for many years.   Leading an active, almost laborious life at Eutin, occupied with his ministerial duties and the education of his children, which he superintended himself, he yet found time for his literary pursuits and studies, amongst which the study of the Scriptures and the early Fathers held the foremost place.   His studies were shared by his clever sister Catherine, a woman of considerable intellectual power, and his young wife, who lacked neither mental endowments

nor judgment in the management of her family.   Brought up
from their childhood in the Lutheran Church, the three lived
together united in the same faith, united in the same studies,
and later on united in the same doubts, begotten of those
studies, concerning that sixteenth century reform whence
sprang their Church.   They began to see blots on the face
of it they had never seen, had never dreamed, were there
before.   And the blots grew larger and the doubts waxed
stronger.   They were the constant subject of their discussions:
alone and together they tried to unravel the ever-increasing
difficulties that met them on every side, and could not.   And
then they prayed, and then they strove again; and at last
help came to them in the person of the Marquise de Montagu.
The poor exile, driven from her own country by the revolution
of 1791, seeking shelter now in England, now in Switzerland,
trembling now for the safety of those nearest and dearest to
her, now learning of their imprisonment, now that "Three
generations in one day have perished," perished on the scaffold; grandmother, mother, and sister: she, the poor wan-
derer, bearing this heavy burden of sorrow, came and brought
peace and light to troubled hearts and anxious minds: she,
a delicate woman, in destitution and desolation, came and
dwelt among aliens to her Church, and taught them the
strength that is in the Catholic faith, and by example far
more than by words, though these were not wanting, led
them to embrace it.

The same revolution that drove Mme. de Montagu from
her home, drove also forty thousand of her countrymen and
countrywomen to seek shelter in Germany; and they arrived
there utterly destitute; the hour of danger had left them no
time to collect means of subsistence to carry with them; they
barely escaped with their lives.   When Mme. de Montagu
saw them, young mothers and widows, girls, old men, priests
and children, all wanting the necessaries of life, wandering
about in a strange country, without a home, without occupation, without even bread to call their own, she strained every
nerve to help them,

> "Herself not ignorant of woe,
> Compassion she had learnt to show."

But the money she earned for their relief, and she had
nothing to give them but what she earned by her own work,
was as a drop in the ocean.   She now enjoyed security from

absolute want herself, and had a house to shelter her, but she
had nothing more, and this she owed to the generosity of
Mme. de Tessé, the witty friend of Voltaire, who, also an exile,
was able, by the skilful management of her farm, situate on
the borders of the lake of Plon, not far from Eutin, to reach
a helping hand to others besides her niece de Montagu.

Grieved at the sight of so much misery, Mme. de Montagu
spared no efforts to relieve it, and at last thought of a plan by
which she would be able to relieve the wants, not only of those
who came immediately under her notice, but of all those who
she heard were spread over the country far and wide; and
it was in the execution of this plan, a plan which would certainly have daunted a less courageous heart, that she was
drawn into those relations with Count de Stolberg which
ended in the conversion of the president of the Lutheran
Consistory as well as of his family. Her scheme was this:—
to raise subscriptions throughout Europe, in Sweden, Germany, Austria, England, Russia and Spain, for the relief of
the Emigrants. According to her reckoning, to make such
relief sufficient, no less than fourteen million francs were required. Having carefully matured her plans, she laid her
scheme, before she spoke of it to anyone else, before the
Prime Minister of the Duke of Oldenburg, with whose warm,
generous nature, she was already somewhat acquainted. Struck
with the energy of this noble woman, with the strength that
could forget private sorrows, sorrows that might well have
weighed down sterner natures, with the will that could triumph
over failing health, to soften the woes and relieve the ills of
others, Count de Stolberg at once promised his help, not the help
of an offering merely, but the help of active co-operation in the
arduous labours necessary to lay the foundation of the work,
and to spread it. And a very great help his name, his position, his talents, enabled him to give. Without delay he drew
up and issued an appeal to the Danish people, which appeal
the Cabinet of Copenhagen shut their eyes to, though they
dared not authorize it for fear of the Directory. Within a
very short time it was answered by subscriptions amounting
to over two thousand dollars, and then, the subscription once
set on foot and known, money flowed in from all parts of
Europe.

NOTICE OF BOOKS.

Daily Steps to Heaven.   From the Kenmare Series of Books for Spiritual
Reading.

THIS volume is the third of a series of books for general
spiritual reading, which is every day becoming more widely
known and better appreciated. Books of this kind are the
well timed and becoming product of an age which is given to
much reading of a light and ephemeral character. Our Lord
said, Man was not made for the Sabbath, but the reverse; the
Sabbath was made for man. The same rule holds good with
books; they are things not to be made upon a theory, for the
use of an ideal public of readers, but they are to be wisely
fitted in charity for the generation of readers such as are
made by the flood of desultory and sensational reading which
now sweeps everything away in its current.

The praise, then, of having both pleased and instructed
great numbers of this class of readers, belongs, in a very high
degree, to the Kenmare Series. The very rise and growth of
such a series in the little town of Kenmare in itself contains
a beautiful lesson. The visitor to Kenmare, who approaches
it from the Killarney side, passes along a road leading over a
bleak and dark-looking mountain range, interspersed with
beautiful glimpses of lakes. As regards outward appearance,
the country might be the Highlands of Scotland; there is
nothing in particular to identify it as Ireland. Cattle graze
on the mountain-side, and turf is piled up in heaps, just as
in the Scotch Highlands. On arriving in the little town of
Kenmare, the aspect of the streets by no means fails to betoken
the absence of any very notable thrift and industry among the
inhabitants, a feature which is unhappily too common in
similar towns in Ireland. On arriving, however, at the
Franciscan Convent, the scene changes. The community has
large schools, and everything wears an aspect of tidiness, industry, cleanliness, and intelligence. The Conventual
Church is a gem of architecture, in which Minton tiles, carving,
painting, brass-work, stained glass, and all the arts of the century, vie with each other in forming a beautiful sanctuary.
In the streets outside, there is a state of things that certainly
somewhat jars with the ideas of nineteenth century progress.
But inside the precincts of the Convent all betokens the life
and intelligence of the Catholic faith, which knows no distinction of place or people. Instinct with the spirit of this

faith, the Kenmare Series of Books is able to spread itself all over the world, and to be as much at home in Great Britain and her colonies, the United States, and everywhere where the English language is spoken, as in Kenmare itself.

It is a beautiful sight, which the Catholic faith alone has the power to produce, to see how a religious community, while they largely promote by their labours the temporal and spiritual welfare of the little town of Kenmare, are also able by their labours to associate themselves with the spiritual good of others, literally in the east and the west, in the north and the south of their place of domicile.

RECORD OF EVENTS.

The wonderful activity of mind of the Holy Father remains unabated. He continues, as before, to receive the visits and addresses of his faithful subjects coming to him from all parts of the world, and always makes their visit the occasion of uttering words which are carried everywhere by the Press, and penetrate into the homes of his people in most distant lands, causing their hearts to glow with renewed hope and confidence that God, who thus speaks to the world by the mouth of His Vicar, is with His people, and does not forget them.

On Sunday, Jan. 5th, the Octave day of S. Thomas of Canterbury, a deputation, consisting of 150 Irish ladies and gentlemen, was presented to the Pope. In reply to the address, which was read by Mr. Shine Lalor, His Holiness said :—

"Your address, springing more from the heart than from the lips, is a symbol of Irish faith, of Irish devotion, and of Irish love for the Vicar of Jesus Christ. Affectionate and fervid words like these afford true consolation to my soul. I have had many pledges of the faith and piety of the Irish people, and I look upon your gifts as made, like those of the three kings to the Infant Jesus, through myself, His unworthy Vicar.

"You have enumerated our calamities and you have numbered the heavenly favours, weak instrument for the conferring of which I have been. You have marvelled at the ingratitude of men; yet this is but part of Almighty God's accustomed Providence. The world never corresponds to benefits by thankfulness. Jesus Christ Himself came down from Heaven to conquer death and reopen the gates of Paradise; He raised our nature from abject slavery and endued it with priceless attributes. Yet how monstrous was the ingratitude of the Redeemed! Men repaid Jesus Christ by nailing Him to the wood of the cross.

" No wonder that those whom we have benefited thanklessly wrong us. Let me add that Jesus Christ came not in chariots nor on horses, but *in nomine Domini.* God has willed that our warfare should not be waged with earthly weapons, but that wo should fight by preaching the Gospel of truth, by steadfastly holding to our rights. And so shall we ever continue to do. Let us praise God in all His works and ways, and let us humbly adore His inscrutable judgments.

" This reflection may serve as an answer to your beautiful words, and, acceding to your request, I now raise my hands to Heaven, and invoke a blessing upon you all. I bless you, together with your families and fatherland. I bless Ireland, and beseech Almighty God to preserve it, and to preserve in it its greatest treasure, the Catholic faith. I bless you all, with your children ; I bless your undertakings and your deeds, so that all you do may be done in the Holy Name of God. And may the blessing I in the name of God bestow upon you be such as to produce in you visible fruit of ₋oliness, visible effects of grace ! "

On the following Sunday the Holy Father received a numerous deputation composed of Germans from the German Empire. In reply to their address, His Holiness remarked :—

" With this spirit of courage and confidence in God, there can be no fear of being overcome by the forces of Satan. Such a spirit has spoken in you ; and has spoken with so much vigour and so much confidence of coming triumph, that we too must enlarge our heart with hope of the future."

The Holy Father went on to comment on the Gospel for the day, dwelling on the grief of Mary and Joseph at the loss of Jesus, and their joy at finding Him in the Temple teaching among the doctors, who were astonished at His understanding and His answers ; but who, had they known who He was, would perhaps have driven Him from the Temple as they drove out of the Synagogue the man born blind, saying : " Who art thou—thou who wast born *totus in peccatis, et doces nos ?*" The Holy Father continued :—

"This is proved by what they did when the fulness of time was come, and the world's redemption was to be begun and finished. Observe what followed. The Saviour was taken and dragged through the streets of Jerusalem. He was dragged before the High Priest and there, although His words were pacific, respectful, worthy of the Son of God, a ruffian who stood by lifted up his hand and struck a blow on that face, to look on which forms the bliss of the angels in Heaven. Jesus Christ still answered calmly and gravely : ' If I have spoken evil bear witness of the evil, but if well, why smitest thou me ?'

" Dear children, behold before you the Vicar of that same Jesus whose words I have now quoted. Vicar, unworthy as you will, incapable as you will, of worthily representing the greatness which God has placed on my shoulders, nevertheless I have a right to use the words of my Bishop, the

Bishop of my soul—*Episcopus animarum nostrarum*, and I will say to all the great ones of this world who will not understand my words: *Si male locutus sum, testimonium perhibe de malo, si autem bene, cur me cædis?* If I have told you nought but the truth, if I have alleged nothing but accomplished facts—*Cur me cædis?* Why do you suppress the Religious? Why do you usurp the churches? Why do you rob the Church of her property? Why do you pretend to that which does not belong to you? . . . . . Jesus Christ commanded that sovereigns and the rulers of the earth should be treated with respect. Yes, gentlemen, but why did Jesus Christ command this? Why did He give them the sword, why did He put power and force into their hands? It was that they might protect their subjects, that they might protect religion; not that they might become persecutors of the Church, but her patrons and protectors. Judge you if they are her protectors. The facts are before the world: every one knows them: I need say no more."

The Holy Father, in conclusion, in giving his blessing to the kneeling assembly, said :—

"I place you under the protection of Mary Immaculate, of your Guardian Angels, and of S. Boniface, Apostle of Germany, that they may keep you ever firm and constant, both you here present and those at a distance, and may preserve safe in your hearts the sacred deposit of the faith of Jesus Christ—cost what it may; cost it even your life."

The rectors of the various national colleges in Rome have united to address a joint manifesto to Signore Lanza, the President of the Council of Ministers of the Italian Government, against their intended suppression of the Roman College. The Roman College was founded by Pope Gregory XIII. in the year 1582, and its direction confided to the Society of Jesus. In it are given the lectures which the students of the various national colleges frequent in common, and the Anti-Christian Power, which it pleases God for a time to allow to be dominant in Rome, knows very well why it must aim a blow at an institution which contributes so much to the work of forming a learned body of ecclesiastics to go forth as teachers of the people in their respective nations.

The Catholic bishops of the whole world have been prepared by the wonderful working of Divine Providence for playing their part effectively in the struggle with the powers of darkness that, on all hands, appears to be thickening, at least, in the European nations. Their assembling together in Rome for conjointly passing the decrees of the Vatican Council has taught them, and the whole body of the faithful with them, the secret of *Union being strength.* The Catholic cause, on merely national grounds, is obviously very weak; but when

the Catholic cause confronts local and national *soi-disant* omnipotence, as the cause of all the people of the earth in common,
an omnipotence that is only omnipotent on one side of the river,
and nothing at all on the other side of it, appears very absurd
when it sets itself up to play the part of an offended majesty
against that which is just exactly the same on the one side of
the river as it is on the other.   The majesty that is all majesty
on one side of the river and nothing at all on the other, may
fine, torment, imprison, and render bitter the lives of its
subjects; but it can only do this like any other vulgar and
upstart tormenter that happens to have acquired power over
a victim.   It can, indeed, by physical force act the part of the
savage who dances while he is tormenting his prisoner, but
when it pretends to be a "majesty offended," then the truth
transpires, that the majesty thus offended is only majesty on
one side of the river, but the victim is one whose cause is the
common cause of all the nations alike.   But for being blinded
by the same pride of the evil one who fell from Heaven through
pride, the majesty of the one side of the river and not of the
other would exclaim in the presence of the power that is
common to all the nations alike, *Vobiscum Deus*, God is with
you, and, like Saul, from being a persecutor would become a
disciple.

We much wish space permitted us in this number to quote
from the joint pastoral letter of the Bishops of Ireland to their
people, and likewise from the manifesto of the Bishops of
Prussia.   We must endeavour to resume the subject in our
next, and, in the meantime, content ourselves with the following short extract from the former, insisting upon the dangers
to faith and morals that result from the indiscriminate reading of objectionable books, and inculcating the reading and
study of Catholic writings :—

"When you know that a book, however remarkable, or a journal, however brilliant, is openly or covertly hostile to the spirit of faith, let no weak
deference to public opinion induce you to run the risk of perusing it. And,
besides protecting, you must strengthen your faith. For this purpose, to
prayer and to constant hearing the word of God, you should add the reading of books written in defence and explanation of Catholic doctrine."

THE

Monthly Magazine of the Holy Rosary.

NEW SERIES.

No. 9.]   APRIL.   [A.D. 1873.

SISTER ANNE CATHERINE EMMERICH OF DULMEN.

VISIONS DESCRIBING THE SECOND AND THIRD SORROWFUL MYSTERIES OF THE ROSARY.

SISTER EMMERICH describes Our Lord as having been shut up in a little vaulted prison. Towards the end of the night, His enemies, having tied Him to a pillar, in the centre of the prison, left Him to the charge of two archers, who, for some time, insulted and ill-treated Him.

Being at last tired out, they left Him in peace for a short time, when He leaned against the pillar to rest, and a bright light shone around Him. "The day was beginning to dawn —the day of His passion, of our redemption—and a faint ray, penetrating the narrow vent-hole of the prison, fell upon the holy and immaculate Lamb, who had taken upon Himself the sins of the world. Jesus turned towards the ray of light, raised His fettered hands, and, in the most touching manner, returned thanks to His Heavenly Father for the dawn of that day, which had been so long desired by the prophets, and for which He himself had so ardently sighed. . . . The archers, who were dozing, woke up for a moment, and looked at Him with surprise. They said nothing, but appeared to be somewhat astonished and frightened. Our Divine Lord was confined in this prison during an hour, or thereabouts."

The following is from the vision of the scourging at the pillar:—" Jesus trembled and shuddered as He stood before the pillar, and took off His garments as quickly as He could, but His hands were bloody and swollen. The only return He made, when His brutal executioners struck and abused Him, was to pray for them in the most touching manner. He turned His face once towards His Mother, who was standing overcome with grief. . . . Jesus put His arms round the pillar, and, when His hands were thus raised, the archers fastened them to the iron ring, which was at the top of the pillar; they then dragged His arms to such a height that His feet, which were tightly bound to the base of the pillar, scarcely touched the ground. Thus was the Holy of Holies violently stretched, without a particle of clothing, on a pillar used for the punishment of the greatest criminals; and then did two furious ruffians, who were thirsting for His blood, begin, in the most barbarous manner, to scourge His sacred body from head to foot. The whips, or scourges, which they first made use of, appeared to me to be made of a species of flexible white wood, but perhaps they were composed of the sinews of the ox, or strips of leather. Our loving Lord, the Son of God, true God, and true Man, writhed as a worm under the blows of these barbarians. His mild, but deep, groans might be heard from afar: they resounded through the air, forming a kind of touching accompaniment to the hissing of the instruments of torture. These groans resembled rather a touching cry of prayer and supplication than the moans of anguish." Amidst the various sounds, might be heard the bleating of the Paschal lambs, which were being washed in the probaction pool, at no great distance from the forum. "There was something peculiarly touching in the plaintive bleating of these lambs: they appeared to unite their lamentations with the suffering moans of Our Lord. . . . The two ruffians continued to strike Our Lord, with unremitting violence, for a quarter of an hour, and were then succeeded by two others. His body was entirely covered with black, blue, and red marks; the blood was trickling down on the ground, and yet the furious cries which issued from among the assembled Jews showed that their cruelty was far from being satiated.

"The night had been extremely cold, and the morning was dark and cloudy; a little hail had fallen, and surprised every one; but, towards twelve o'clock, the day became brighter, and the sun shone forth.

"The two fresh executioners commenced scourging Jesus with the greatest possible fury; they made use of a different kind of rod—a species of thorny stick, covered with knots and splinters. The blows from these sticks tore His flesh to pieces; His blood spurted out so as to stain their arms, and He groaned, prayed, and shuddered. . . . . Two fresh executioners took the places of the last mentioned, who were beginning to flag. Their scourges were composed of small chains, or straps, covered with iron hooks, which penetrated to the bone, and tore off large pieces of flesh at every blow. . . . . The cruelty of these barbarians was, nevertheless, not yet satiated. They untied Jesus, and again fastened Him up with His back turned against the pillar. As He was totally unable to support himself in an upright position, they passed cords round His waist, under His arms, and above His knees; and, having bound His hands tightly into the rings, which were placed at the upper part of the pillar, they re-commenced scourging Him with even greater fury than before; and one among them struck Him continually on the face with a new rod. The body of Our Lord was perfectly torn to shreds—it was but one wound. He looked at His torturers, with His eyes filled with blood, as if entreating mercy; but their brutality appeared to increase, and His moans became each moment more feeble. This dreadful scourging continued, without intermission, for three quarters of an hour. . . . . Jesus fell on the ground, bathed in His blood. . . . . He raised Himself with the greatest difficulty, as His trembling limbs could scarcely support the weight of His body. They did not give Him time to put on His clothes; but threw His upper garments over His naked shoulders, and led Him from the pillar to the guard-house, where He wiped the blood which trickled down His face with the corner of His garment. . . . . I saw the blessed Virgin in a continual ecstacy during the time of the scourging of her Son. She saw and suffered with inexpressible love and grief all the torments He was enduring. She groaned feebly, and her eyes were red with weeping. A large veil covered her person, and she leant upon Mary of Heli. . . . The dress of Mary was blue; it was long, and partly covered by a cloak made of white wool, and her veil was of rather a yellow white. Magdalen was totally beside herself with grief, and her hair was floating loosely under her veil.

"When Jesus fell down at the foot of the pillar, after the flagellation, I saw Claudia Procles, the wife of Pilate, send some large pieces of linen to the Mother of God. . . . At the termination of the scourging, Mary came to herself for a time, and saw her Divine Son, all torn and mangled, being led away by the archers, after the scourging. He wiped His eyes, which were filled with blood, that He might look at His mother, and she stretched out her hands towards Him, and continued to look at the bloody traces of His footsteps. . . . . I soon after saw Mary and Magdalen approach the pillar where Jesus had been scourged. . . . . They knelt down on the ground, near the pillar, and wiped up the sacred blood with the linen which Claudia Procles had sent.

. . . . It was not more than nine o'clock a.m. when the scourging terminated."

The crowning with thorns took place in the inner court of the guard-house, the doors of which were open. A thousand Roman soldiers were drawn up in good order, and stationed there ; and, though they did not leave their ranks, they encouraged the cruel executioners by their laughter and applause.

"In the middle of the court there stood the fragment of a pillar, and on it was placed a very low stool, which these cruel men maliciously covered with sharp flints and bits of broken potsherds. Then they tore off the garments of Jesus, thereby re-opening all his wounds ; threw over His shoulders an old scarlet mantle, which barely reached His knees ; dragged Him to the seat prepared, and pushed Him roughly down upon it, having first placed the crown of thorns upon His head. The crown of thorns was made of three branches, plaited together, the greatest part of the thorns being purposely turned inwards, so as to pierce Our Lord's head. Having first placed these twisted branches on His forehead, they tied them tightly together at the back of His head, and no sooner was this accomplished to their satisfaction than they put a large reed into His hand—doing all with derisive gravity, as if they were really crowning Him king. They then seized the reed, and struck His head so violently, that His eyes were filled with blood ; they knelt before Him, derided Him, spat in His face, and buffetted Him, saying, at the same time, ' Hail, King of the Jews !' Then they threw down His stool, pulled Him up again from the ground, on which He had fallen, and re-seated Him, with the greatest possible barbarity.

"It is quite impossible to describe the cruel outrages which were thought of, and perpetrated by these monsters in human form. The sufferings of Jesus from thirst, caused by the fever which His wounds and sufferings had brought on, were intense. He trembled all over ; His flesh was torn piecemeal ; His tongue was contracted ; and the only refreshment He received was from the blood which trickled down from His head on to His parched lips. This shameful scene was protracted a full half hour."

(To be continued).

AN AUTHENTIC EXTRACT FROM THE TEXT OF THE PASSION PLAY OF OBER AMMERGAU.

To the Editors of the MONTHLY MAGAZINE OF THE HOLY ROSARY.

REVEREND FATHERS.—Your readers will readily call to mind the general interest which, in the years 1870 and 1871, drew visitors from many different nations to a little village lying at the entrance to the Bavarian Alps.   Its inhabitants have been in the habit of acting a Passion Play every ten years, having bound themselves in past times by a vow to act the play, which they have continued to act at periodical intervals as a thanksgiving for being delivered (now nearly three hundred years ago) from a terrible sickness or plague which ravaged the village and the adjacent country.

The village bore the name of Ober Ammergau, and its play will not be repeated, even if Europe continues in peace, before the year 1880.   The great attraction, which drew such multitudes to see it, was not only the wonderful skill, but the piety, with which every part of an immense drama was carried out, beginning at eight o'clock in the morning, not terminating until after four in the afternoon, and employing in its representation as many as five hundred of the villagers.

These villagers steadily refuse any assistance from those outside the village, to which, no doubt, a great deal of the decorum and pious simplicity which eminently marks their performance is due.   So determined, indeed, are they to keep everything connected with their play exclusively in their own hands, that they have resisted all attempts that have been made to persuade them to publish the text of their play and the music of the parts that are sung.   It was with no little difficulty that the present writer succeeded, in the year 1870, in begging from the retired Parish Priest Daisenberg the accompanying sample scenes of the play, which, however, he very kindly wrote out with his own hand from the MS. copy of the play that he keeps in his own custody, on the writer's earnest representation with what interest his countrymen would read them.   It would be of no advantage to relate by what accident of being mislaid the intended publicity was never, at the time, obtained.   A genuine extract from a play, the text of which is so jealously guarded, and which has attracted such universal attention, is a something that needs no apology, and quite sufficiently speaks for itself.

Your obedient servant,

A VISITOR TO OBER AMMERGAU OF 1870.

ACT THE SIXTH.—SCENE THE FIRST.

CAIPHAS, ANNAS, *Priests, and Pharisees.*

CAIPHAS. Right pleasant tidings have I to communicate,
    Venerable Fathers ; the so-called prophet
    Out of Galilee will soon be in our hands
    A prisoner. Nathan, that zealous Israelite,
    Has won over one of his followers, who is ready
    To show us the way how, in the dead of night,
    He may be seized. Both men are close at hand,
    And wait but to be called.

Several Voices.   Let them be brought in.

JOSAPHAT. I will call them.

CAIPHAS.   Yes, call them. [JOSAPHAT *leaves the room.*
                And now, my Fathers,
    What think you ? What reward assign we to the man
    For this his deed ?

NATHANIEL. (*Derisively.*)   Reward ! does not the law
    Settle this ? Are not thirty silver pieces
    The legal purchase money of a slave ?

All, in chorus, derisively.   Aye, to be sure.
    The price of a slave ! aha ! This be Messiah's worth.

"VIᵗᵉ. VORSTELLUNG.—ERSTER AUFTRITT.

KAIPHAS, ANNAS, *Priester, und Pharisaer.*

KAIPHAS. Ich hab euch frohe kunde mitzutheilen
    Ehrwurdige Vater ; Der vermeintliche
    Prophet aus Galilæa,—bald wird er
    In unsern handen sein. Gewonnen hat
    Nathan, der eifervoller Israelite,
    Von seinen schulern einen, der bereit ist,
    Den weg zu weisen, dass in dunkler nacht,
    Er uberfallen wurde. Beide manner
    Sind hier bereit, und harren nur des rufes.

Mehren. Man hole sie herein.

JOSAPHAT.   Ich will sie rufen.

KAIPHAS.   Ja! rufe sie.   [JOSAPHAT *geht ab.*
                Nur welcher Preis, o Vater !
    Was dunkt euch, ist dem mann zu bestimmen
    Fur seine that ?

NATHANIEL. (*Spottisch.*)   Nun gibt uns das Gesetz
    ' Selbst Aufschuss;' Denn auf dreissig silberlingen
    Gewerthet ist ein sclave.

Alle, mit gelachter.   Ja! oh Ja!
    Den sclavenpreis ist der Messias' werth.

SCENE THE SECOND.

The same, NATHAN *and* JUDAS.

NATHAN. O most worshipful Council, I present this man
  To the assembled Fathers ; he is resolved
  The Enemy of Moses to deliver over
  Into our hands ; he is a trusted follower
  Of the Galilean, and knows his most secret haunts.
CAIPHAS *to* JUDAS. Knowest thou the man whom this worship-
  ful assembly
  Seeks for ?
JUDAS.   Of His twelve disciples I am one.
All. Yes, O yes. He is ! We oft have seen him with Him.
CAIPHAS. What is your name ?
JUDAS.   My name ? Judas. At your service.
CAIPHAS. What is it that hath caused thee this resolve ?
  Reigns ought of disagreement 'twixt thee and thy Master ?
JUDAS. I have withdrawn myself from him.
CAIPHAS.   For what cause ?
JUDAS. (*Confused.*) There is nothing to be got with him !
  And besides . . . .

ZWEITER AUFTRITT.

Die Vorigen, NATHAN, JUDAS.

NATHAN.—Hochweiser Rath ! Ich stelle diesen mann,
  Den grossen Vatern vor. Er ist entschlossen,
  Den Feind des Moses euch zu uberliefern.
  Vertrauter ist er jenes Galiläer's
  . Und weiss desselben stillen aufenthalt.
KAIPHAS *zu* JUDAS. Kennst du den Mann nach dem der hohe Rath
  Verlangt ?
JUDAS. Ich bin aus seinen Zwolfen einer.
Alle. Ja! oh Ja! er ist's, wir sahen ihn oft bei ihm.
KAIPHAS. Wie ist deine name ?
JUDAS.   Judas heisse ich.
KAIPHAS. Was hat zu diesem schritte dich bewogen !
  Ist Zwiespalt zwischen dich und deinen Meister ?
JUDAS. Ich habe mich von ihm getrennt.
KAIPHAS.   Warum ?
JUDAS. (*Verlegen.*) Es ist nichts mehr bei ihm,—und—uberhaupt.
KAIPHAS. Bist du bereit, zu thun nach unsern wille ?
JUDAS. Was gibt ihr mir, wenn ich ihm uberliefere ?
KAIPHAS. Denn sollst du dreissig silberlingen haben,
  Sie werden allsogleich dir aufgezahlt.
NATHAN. O hore Judas, dreissig silberlingen !
  Welch ein gewinn ?

CAIPHAS. (*Interrupting.*) Art thou ready to do thy par tas we
    require from thee?

JUDAS. What will you give me if I betray Him to you?

CAIPHAS. Thou shalt have thirty pieces of silver,
    And they shall be counted down to thee this moment.

NATHAN. O, Judas, hear this! Thirty pieces of silver!
    What a fortune!

NATHANIEL.   And Judas, mark it well,
    This is not all! Dost thou thy task accomplish,
    Care shall be taken of thee.

EZECHIEL.   An honourable man,
    A great and learned man, mayst thou rise to be.

JUDAS. (*Aside.*) Now is my star in the ascendant. (*To the
    Council.*) I am ready
    For your service.

CAIPHAS.   Ho, Rabbi, here quickly bring
    The thirty silver pieces from the treasury,
    And count them out to him here in the presence
    Of this assembly. Fathers, is such your will?

All, with the exception of NICODEMUS *and* JOSAPHAT. Such is the
    will of all.

NICODEMUS.   Nay, say not of all.
    I do most loudly cry against it. No! Fathers, no!
    Far be from you such vile and shameful traffic.

To JUDAS. And O! of all men vilest and most despicable,
    Dreadest thou not thy loving Lord and Master
    Thus to betray? Be thou sure this blood-money
    Will cry aloud to Heaven for vengeance on thee.
                     [JUDAS *stands trembling and dismayed.*

NATHANIEL.   Und, Judas, merke wohl!
    Das ist noch alles nichts wenn du das werk
    Hinausfugest wird noch fernerhin auf dich
    Betracht genommen.

EZECHIEL.   Ein geehrter mann,
    Ein weiser, grosser mann kannst du noch werden.

JUDAS(. (*Fur sich.*) Jetst geht der rechte hoffnungstern mir auf.
    P*Zu den Priester.*) Ich bin zufrieden.

KAIPHAS.   Rabbi, bring sogleich
    Die dreissig silberlingen aus dem Kasten,
    Und zahle sie ihm vor in Gegenwart
    Des ganzen Rathes! Ist es euer wille?

Alle, ausser NICODEMUS *und* JOSAPHAT. Est ist der wille aller!

NICODEMUS.   Nein! nicht aller!
    Ich stimme laut dagegen. Wie! oh Vater!
    So schandlich schlecten handel konnt ihr schliessen!

JOACHIM. Nay, Judas, heed not what this foolish zealot
   Prates. A follower of the false prophet let him be,
   Thou, as a worthy follower of our leader Moses,
   Thy duty do, and give ear unto the Council.
              [The RABBI *enters with the silver pieces.*
   Now, Judas, take the silver pieces and make thyself
   A man.
        *[*JUDAS, *at the sight of the silver pieces, recovers him-*
          self, and greedily gathers up the coins as they are
          counted out to him, smiling the while.

(*Zu* JUDAS.) Und du der menschen niedertrachitgster
   Scheuest nicht, den guten Herrn und Meister
   So zu verkaufen, Wah! Dies blutgeld
   Wird um rache wider dich zum Himmel schreien!
            *[*JUDAS *steht zitternd und wie vernichtet da.*
JOACHIM. Bekummere Judas, dich nicht um die rede
   Des eiferer's! Er mag ein Junger sein
   Des trug-propheten, du, als Moses junger,
   Thust dein pflicht wenn du der obrigkeit
   Gehorchest.   *[*RABBI *eintretend.*
   Nun, Judas, nimm die silberlingen und mache dicr einen mann.
      *[*JUDAS, *beim anblicke der silberlingen einsteht sich wider auf*
        und hankelt die vorgeahlten munze lachend und begierig
        ein."

HALF-HOURS WITH THE SAINTS.—No. III.

THE MARTYR OF THE SEAL OF CONFESSION—S. JOHN NEPOMUCENE.

THE Church, at this season of the year, calls all her people to
the sacred tribunal of penance; but this tribunal has, in common with all the institutions which God, who became man,
has given to His Church, its human side. The minister who
sits in it and performs its duties is not an angel, but a human
being. It is true that the Church who appoints him to act
in the tribunal is presumed to have taken the best possible
care that he should be found furnished with the requisite
knowledge, and that he should have been prepared by suitable
training for the functions which he will be called to perform
in the tribunal; but, all this being said, the fact remains that
he is a human being and not an angel. It does, indeed, need
but a very little reflection to understand that God has in
mercy provided that the ministers of this tribunal should be
men and not angels. For their duty in it obliges them to

become the depositaries of all the criminal secrets concealed in the most secret recesses of the hearts of the people, and it is consequently necessary that they should be known to have the tenderness and sympathy for infirmity proper to those who are themselves subject to infirmity. But then it is, at least, equally necessary that they should also be known to be the inviolable and incorruptible keepers of the secrets revealed to them in the tribunal. The minister of the tribunal must be merciful and compassionate to encourage the faithful to come to the tribunal, and, that they may truly confess when there, all who come must be able to have an unshaken reliance that the sanctity of the seal of confession will be respected by the ministers of the tribunal, cost them what it may, even if they have to brave the fury and anger of kings and their courts of justice, and the worst terrors of a violent death.

The following is a history of a priest who has edified the Church by patiently resisting the bribes and unyieldingly braving the fury of the tyrant, who repeatedly tried to induce him to reveal the secrets of the confession, finally becoming the martyr of his fidelity to his sacred duty by being thrown alive into the river Moldau.

S. John, surnamed Nepomucene, from Nepomuk, in Bohemia, the place of his birth, was born of honest parentage, in humble life, in the year 1331. His parents had been for a long time childless, but, having great faith in the power and goodness of the Blessed Virgin, they went to supplicate her intercession at a celebrated shrine, which belonged to the church of a Cistercian monastery, at the foot of the Green Mountain, so called because, during a season of drought, from which the whole kingdom of Bohemia suffered, it was the first mountain that began to grow green after S. Adalbert, the Bishop of Prague, had miraculously obtained rain by his episcopal blessing. The neighbours had had their attention excited by remarkable lights, which they frequently saw, to their surprise, surrounding the humble dwelling of his parents, and, even before the birth of the infant, many were the auguries of marvellous designs of God to be worked out by the infant whose birth was shortly expected.

When the little John grew old enough to serve mass, his great delight was to run off to the Cistercian church, at the foot of the Green Mountain, to serve the masses of the Fathers there, which he did with so much regularity, modesty, and devotion, that the religious of the monastery could not help noticing the boy, and, doubtless, must have been instrumental in subsequently persuading his parents to send him to school, and to make an effort to bring him up for the priesthood. He was accordingly sent to learn Latin, at a grammar-school in the town of Zatek, from whence, when he had attained the required age, he went to Prague to be matriculated in the Caroline University of that city, so called from its founder, the Emperor Charles, who was then still living.

Here he went through his university course with great credit, and obtained a distinction in the school of philosophy, on a par with the first class degree of our times. Passing from the school of philosophy to the study of theology and canon law, in due time he obtained the degree of Doctor in both these branches of study, and, as his biographer says, " In this way, well equipped with the indispensable amount of both profane and sacred wisdom, he prepared himself for his campaign against vice, and to gain the victory over hell."

Before he presented himself to receive the priesthood, he withdrew for a whole month to a place of retirement, where he subjected himself to a severe course of preparatory spiritual exercises, and thus came, as his biographer says, like gold out of the fire. As he quickly gave proofs of possessing the gifts necessary for a preacher, it was not long after his ordination before he was appointed to a pulpit in the principal church in the city of Prague, dedicated to the Blessed Virgin, which had been occupied, in past times, by Master Conrad and John Melk, both of them orators of great fame. Notwithstanding, however, the great name his predecessors had made for themselves, the citizens of Prague soon unanimously declared that Prague had never before possessed a preacher who acquitted himself of his functions so well, and with so much knowledge and unction, as " our John Nepomucene," the name by which they loved to call him.

The fame of " our John Nepomucene " as a preacher increasing, he was often called to preach before the court, which led to the King Wenceslaus fixing upon him to fill the see of Latomisle, a bishopric in Bohemia, in possession of the most ample revenues. The humble man, however, succeeded in convincing the king that he was not fitted for such an exalted dignity ; but when, shortly after this, the king desired him to become the royal Almoner, and to accept a canonry in the cathedral of Prague, he did not know how decently to refuse,

and accepted both posts. This connection with the court led
to the Queen-Empress Jane, who had been captivated by his
preaching, fixing upon him as her confessor, and to this step she
was the more moved in consequense of the inhuman treatment
she had to endure from her husband, Wenceslaus, whose
cruelties and lawless conduct had already rendered him
odious not to Bohemia only but to the whole empire.

At this time, an event happened which became the turning
point of our Saint's career, and eventually the occasion of the
glorious martyrdom, with which he has edified the universal
Church. Wenceslaus, moved by the perversity which frequently impels vicious and degraded souls, in proportion as
they themselves desert the ways of God, to envy and persecute, with a special malice, those whom they perceive, on the
contrary, to be clinging closer to God, looked with an evil
eye on the increased devout practices of the queen. Whether
he was really blinded by a senseless jealousy, or only eager to
become possessed of some better pretext for making her life
bitter, he conceived at this time the horrible desire to extort
from our Saint a revelation of the confessions of the empress.
Fixing, therefore, upon a day when the empress had been to
her confession, he sent for her confessor, and, casually alluding
to the empress, he asked that the confessor should let him
know, as being the king and her husband, if not all, at least
a portion of what the empress had made known to him in
confession, promising him, at the same time, that his compliance with so reasonable a request should be the way to
very great promotion. The holy priest stood for a moment,
petrified at the audacity of the request, and, after a moment's
pause recovering his freedom of speech, replied that such a
demand was not only one that could not possibly be granted,
but one that could not even be made without the greatest sin.
It is always an ungracious act to refuse any request, and the
more exalted the rank of the petitioner the harder he takes
any denial of his wishes. Wenceslaus, however, for the
moment, thought it best to dissimulate his anger against his
Almoner for his refusal to comply, but inwardly determined
upon extorting compliance by and by, and with what result
we shall presently see.

"Anger," says the poet, "is a brief madness." It happened one day, shortly after this, that the cook of Wenceslaus
sent to the king's table a capon that was badly roasted, at which
the king was so incensed that he gave the barbarous order that

the delinquent cook himself should be fixed on a spit and be roasted before the fire. "Our John" hearing of this, moved with Christian horror for the crime about to be committed, sought and obtained admission to the king, and, beginning at first with mild and gentle remonstrances, he pointed out the horrible disproportion of the punishment to the offence, if, indeed, there was was in reality any offence at all; but when the king showed no signs of yielding, he proceeded to denounce the crime with the freedom of a S. John the Baptist. Such freedom of speech not being a common event in the courts of kings, all that our Saint got by it was to be thrown instantly into prison. All respect for his character as royal Almoner, and for his dignity as canon of the cathedral, was completely forgotten, and, in the midst of the tortures and ill treatment to which he was subjected in the prison, his jailor was privately instructed to let him know that he would be immediately released, and restored to favour, if he would only reasonably comply with the king's demands, and consent to reveal the confessions of the empress. Of course, this intimation remained without any effect other than that "our John" preferred to remain in his prison.

The King's mind now took one of the sudden turns not uncommon with men of violent passions; perhaps, indeed, the idea was not without its weight that it might be politic not to play too hard a game all at once with a man of such firmness of character as "our John" had unexpectedly shown himself to possess; but to try first what could be gained by flattery and cajolery. However this may be, the King sent a message, by an officer of his court, to his Almoner in the prison, to the effect that he exceedingly regretted the excesses into which his violent temper had betrayed him, and that he hoped to be favoured with the honour of his Almoner's presence at the royal table at dinner, in token of his being forgiven. Here, says his biographer, a great snare was laid for him; for, it had often been known, in the history of the Martyrs of the Roman Empire, that those, against whom the fiercest torments had availed nothing, afterwards shamefully yielded to the blandishments and civilities of their persecutors. "Our John," in pursuance of the invitation, went to the banquet, where he found himself the object of such unusual courtesy and attention on the part of the lords of the court, that in the place of being deceived by it, he was rather put on his guard, and his suspicions awakened, as to the existence of some evil purpose that he thought must

238 THE MONTHLY MAGAZINE OF THE HOLY ROSARY. [APRIL,

infallibly be concealed under it. The event only too well, as we shall see, confirmed what he suspected. The dinner being over, Wenceslaus laid aside his mask with very little ceremony, and very plainly acquainted "John" with the cause of his being invited, telling him that it was only reasonable he should comply with the desire of the king, to know the conduct of his wife, and that he should thus relieve his mind from the doubts that would leave him neither rest nor peace. "Our John," to his surprise, was not to be moved. He was ready to obey the king in all that was lawful, but his majesty, as a Christian emperor, could not but know that, though a subject of the Empire, he was bound in the first place to obey God.

The king's anger now knew no bounds; he called for his executioner, who came with his men, and hurried off "our John," to stretch him on the rack, burning his sides with heated brands, just the same as if, instead of the king being a Christian emperor, he had been a Nero, or a Domitian. There is reason to think, says his biographer, so enraged was the king, that, not satisfied with giving the order for his almoner being put to the torture, he came in person, and stood by himself, to witness its being carried into execution. The tortures failed to produce the effect the king intended, and fearing that he was going too far he suspended them, and after some days dismissed "our John" to his ordinary avocations, which he resumed, concealing what had come to pass, and uttering no complaint, just as if nothing amiss had been done.

Perceiving, however, by the light which God frequently gives to those who are eventually to glorify Him by martyrdom, that the tyrant was merely quiet for the moment, and that his fury would shortly burst out again, he went on a pilgrimage to a celebrated shrine of the Madonna, in the kingdom of Bohemia, to prepare himself for the violent death which he now clearly foresaw to be inevitable, by invoking the aid and protection of the Blessed Virgin, for whom he had ever had a most filial devotion. He preached, also, a public discourse, on the text—"A little while and you shall not see," in the Metropolitan Church, in which, to the astonishment and dismay of the people, he spoke of his approaching martyrdom, and of the calamities which were impending over the kingdom of Bohemia.

The event which he foresaw was not long in coming. Agitated afresh, with suspicions of the queen, the king one day sent suddenly for his almoner, and said to him, "Hear

you now, sir priest, know for certain that you are a dead man,
except this very moment you reveal the confessions of the
queen, and tell me everything she has at any time said to you.
I swear, by God, you shall be drowned."   "Our John" remained perfectly calm and unmoved, not indeed replying, but
showing by mute gesture that nothing the king could do
should prevail. Wenceslaus, out of himself with fury, ordered
his victim to be carried off to prison.   In the dead of the
night he was bound hand and foot, and thrown from the
principal bridge into the river Moldau, which flows through
the city. Wenceslaus flattered himself that the murder would
never transpire, but during the night the river, to his terror,
was miraculously illuminated, and the body was discovered in
the morning thrown on a dry bank, surrounded with a miraculous light, so that the whole city rang with the intelligence
of what had come to pass.   The Canons of the Church in
which "John" had his stall, casting aside all fear of the king,
went out in a body with lights and brought their martyred
comrade to the Church, where he was buried, in the midst of
an immense concourse of people, and from that day forward
the popular honour, which proclaims St. John Nepomucene a
Holy Martyr of the Seal of Confession, has never ceased.   To
this popular honour has succeeded the decree of Canonisation
by Pope Benedict XIII., A.D. 1729.

EASTER THOUGHTS, IN VERSE.

A Fragment from an unpublished Poem by the late Dr. AYLWARD, O.P.

BRIGHTER and brighter the vision grew,
Around her, and behold
There glittered now
On His radiant brow
A crown of starry gold,
And the sceptre of truth and righteousness
His royal hand controlled.
One hand upheld, like the hand of a king,
The sceptre of rule; and one
The orb whereon the precious cross,
Blest type of His victory, shone.

Still looked she on with charmed gaze,
And clearer the vision grew,
For our Lady bright,
In robes of light,
And a crown upon her brow;
Enthroned in highest majesty,
With the king upon her breast,
In golden sheen
Shone forth the Queen,
The Queen of heaven confest.
And Joseph, too, like an ancient king,
Was crowned with a diadem,
Circling around his silver grey hairs,
And shining with many a gem.

Brighter and brighter the vision grew
On the maiden's strengthening eye;
And, lo! in the rays
Of that glory-blaze
She now can plain descry,
The spirits blest,
Whose homes of rest
Lie far beyond the sky.
Myriads and myriads of angels are there,
Vested, and plumed, and crowned,
They shine in the rays,
Of the central blaze,
In circling order round.
Sphere after sphere, the crowded host
Gleam forth on every side,
Till they dimly fade on the stretching eye,
Lost far in the distant void.

"A GRACE OF NOTRE DAME DE LOURDES;"

or, How in France the Believers in the Miracles of Notre Dame of Lourdes publicly challenge the Unbelievers to Deny them.

When S. Francis of Assisi appeared before the Sultan and his Court in Egypt, instead of asking for the grant of a public dispute with the champion who might be chosen to represent the doctrines of the Koran, he asked that two large fires should be lighted, into one of which he proposed to go and stand, with a copy of the Gospels, while the rival Mahometan champion was to go and stand, with a copy of the Koran, in the other. But there being no one found among the learned Mahometans who was willing to expose himself to this test, S. Francis was, without contradiction, allowed freedom to go about unrestrained to preach to all who were willing to listen to him.

A good Catholic in France has challenged the cavillers who speak against the honour of the Sanctuary of Our Lady at Lourdes to submit to not exactly the same kind of test, but to something not so extremely dissimilar, namely : The deposit on both sides of a sum of money, in the hands of a public notary, to await the decision of a jury of professional men, who are to award the entire sum, either to the side asserting the truth of certain miraculous cures alleged to have been worked by the Water of the Fountain in the Grotto of Lourdes, or to the person of their denier, according to the success or failure of the proof of the miracles to be brought before the jury in question.

The challenge has been given, and the sum of money publicly deposited, by a Mr. E. Artus, and the circumstances that led to this being done, briefly related, are as follows :—

Mr. Artus had a sister married to a retired sea captain, M. Fournier, and during the war with the Prussians the sister, with her husband and three children, retired to Bordeaux. Here her daughter Juliet, then about 14 years of age, fell away into a state of paralysis of the limbs, such that she could not lie down to sleep, but was obliged to take her rest in a sitting position. Two medical men of the town of Bordeaux, M. Coignet and M. Denuce, gave as their opinion of her condition, that it was next to hopeless, and that, in any case, no amendment was to be expected until some more years were passed to enable her to outgrow the complaint. In the meantime M. Denuce prescribed certain tonic medicines, and recommended the treatment of the water cure.

During the summer heats the family took a little cottage at the hamlet of Bouscat, outside the town, and a donkey was procured, on which Juliet rode, at stated times, to the Hydropathic Institute, where she went through the prescribed water applications, until the neighbours began to take note of the group as they passed slowly along, many shrugging their shoulders, when they were gone by, to express their perceptions of a case that appeared to them to be beyond the reach of remedy.

Matters were going on thus, when "The History of the Apparition of Our Lady at Lourdes," by M. Henri Lasserre, fell into the hands of Juliet Fournier's uncle, E. Artus, and he was so much struck with the account of the sudden gushing forth of the fountain, and of the miracles said to be worked by it, that he wrote to his sister, Mme. Fournier, to say that she must at once have recourse to Our Lady of Lourdes, and that he had written for a bottle of the water to be sent to her.

To make our story a short one, after some delay the water came, and Mme. Fournier, Juliet, and her younger brother Albert, alternating between doubts and hopes, set themselves to the work of supplicating for the cure. The old sea captain and the eldest son Ernest looked on, without raising any opposition, but treating what the others were doing as having very little importance.

All the preliminaries accomplished, the 14th of June was fixed upon as the day for asking the favour of the cure, which, by coincidence, turned out to be the day following the anniversary of Juliet's first Communion. The Curé of Bouscat had celebrated Mass for Juliet at the Blessed Virgin's Altar, and the invalid had caused herself to be carried to the church. She went to Communion, and after having received it, and having made her thanksgiving, her mother gave her some of the water of Lourdes, which she drank. Juliet became quite pale, and there was a moment of silence. "Well, my child!" said the mother. "Well, mother," said Juliet, "I am not any better; I am not cured!"

Sad and sorrowful they returned home, and Mme. Fournier wrote to her brother, to relieve her mind by giving vent to her sorrow at the failure of her hopes. "What shall I do," she wrote; "I am worn out with grief and look like a spectre, but this is nothing compared to my child. She has not had a moment of rest, and is constantly lamenting. For two days she has taken nothing. Holy and merciful Mary pray for us. We are very unhappy. Once, again, what will become of us?"

Night came, and Juliet, her mother, and Albert had finished their prayer. Juliet was tranquil and collected, and as for the old sea captain, he had retired to his room, and not being inclined for sleep, he had taken his newspaper, La Gironde, with him, and was sitting up reading it.

"Mamma," said Juliet, pointing to the bottle of water from Lourdes, "give me some of that water; I am certain I am going to be cured." Mme. Fournier, her mind full of the disappointment of her hopes in the morning, said, "My poor child, if the Blessed Virgin had meant to cure you she would have cured you this morning." Juliet insisted. "But, at least, wait till to-morrow, and rest quiet for to-night." "No," said Juliet; "give me some of the water now. I am certain I am going to be cured." Little Albert, who had been kneeling at his prayers, said, "Mamma, give her some of the water, for I am sure also she is going to be cured. Mamma, mamma, I know she will be cured!" Mme. Fournier rose up and went for the bottle; there was a moment of silence and suspense. She poured out a glass of water, which Juliet received and drank, having first made the sign of the Cross. Then laying the glass on one side, she raised her eyes upwards, and began breathing with great eagerness. The chest appeared, as it were, to rise and expand, and Mme. Fournier was for a moment mute with surprise at witnessing the free and unrestrained breathing succeed the painful and wheezing sounds which they had so long been used to hear.

"The Blessed Virgin has cured me," cried Juliet. "Give me a towel; I must wash myself and bathe my chest and side where I have been so ill." Mme. Fournier hesitated for a moment, but as Juliet insisted, they were forced to comply; and, as they undressed her, she rubbed herself over with the water, crying out, "Mamma, all my pains disappear one after the other. I seem to wipe them away as if with a sponge."

At the end of this scene the little Albert rushed out of the door into the corridors, crying out with all his might, "Juliet is cured! Juliet is cured!" M. Fournier hearing the sound, but not distinguishing the words, came out to know what was the matter, and as he entered the room he saw Juliet stretching out her arms to him, saying, at the same time, "Papa, the Blessed Virgin has cured me." "Cured you?" faltered her father, letting fall his paper. "Yes, you may see quite plain the Blessed Virgin has cured me." The old sea captain had gone through many a shock in his time, but nothing like what the sweet and clear voice of his daughter, uttering the above words, occasioned him.

All the servants and people of the house had now come to Albert's cries, and their amazement and stupefaction is not to be described. However, they were all, after a while, put out of the room. Neither the father nor mother went to bed that night, but sat up, looking at their daughter peacefully sleeping and breathing with ease and freedom, and frequently the eyes of the old seafaring man were suffused with tears, tears of religion and piety, which God was looking for to bestow his blessing upon them.

Juliet's cure was complete. A singular circumstance, however, happened in connection with it, which we must not omit to relate, M. Denuce, the medical man, admitted the cure to be perfect, and that his mode of treatment had no share in bringing it about, but fearing a relapse, he directed that it should, nevertheless, be continued, in which, it should be said, he was not obeyed. Madame Fournier, however, having still a number of subscription tickets to the Water Cure Institute, thought that the ride on the donkey and the use of the baths of the Institute might be beneficial to Juliet, who was still feeble; so it was agreed that she should take her usual ride on the donkey to the baths.

Strange, however, to relate, this animal, hitherto so quiet and sedate, and which appeared to have been for years unconscious of even so much as a trot, no sooner had Juliet mounted, no longer as before lifted into the saddle, than it began to plunge and rear, setting off at a gallop, and throwing the terrified Juliet on to the ground, along which she was dragged for some distance, her foot entangled in the stirrup. This was enough; the warning was taken, it appearing as clear as if it had been Balaam's ass that had spoken, and all thought of having any more recourse to human remedies was abandoned.

The sequel was that the old seafaring captain quickly abandoned his unbelief, went with his wife and children to Lourdes, to return thanks to the Blessed Virgin for the miracle that she had been pleased to work for them, and there reconciled himself to the Church.

The history of this miraculous cure, which is only one among a very great number, does not stop here.

Some time after, Juliet's uncle, Mr. E. Artus, wrote a letter which was published in the journal of the *Univers*, challenging the cavillers and freethinkers of France to a test of the truth of the miraculous cures worked at Lourdes. He said that however philosophers might dispute respecting the possibility of miracles in the abstract, there could be nothing impossible in a jury of competent professional men giving their verdict upon evidence brought forward to show, that such and such persons were well known to have been for a length of time previous in such and such a state of suffering, reputed to be incurable, and that they were' suddenly restored to perfect health, by the use of the water from the spring at Lourdes. He, therefore, deposited a sum of money, 10,000 francs (£400), in the hands of a public notary, M. Turquet, N. 6, Rue de Hanovre, Paris, to be met by a similar sum on the part of the accepter of the challenge, and the whole reserved (a certain additional sum being provided for the jury) to await their verdict on the truth or falsehood of the alleged cures. The cases of alleged cure which were open to this challenge were to be all those related in the volume written by M. Henri Lassere.

To this challenge none of the freethinkers of France have as yet dared to make any reply. The only person who has made a show of having some confidence in his disbelief has been a certain M. Caseaux, at Cauterets in the south of France, who wrote to make a parade of accepting the challenge, on an issue that had not been proposed. Even here M. Caseaux, took the precaution to disguise himself under the assumed name of A. M. V. de Marcadeau, and purposely ignoring that the test proposed was to be the truth or falsehood of the alleged miraculous cures related by Henri Lasserre, he proposed to accept the challenge on the question whether the appearance of the spring at Lourdes was anything more than the hitherto existing various small streams exuding from the rock artificially brought together into one current.

To the careful reply of Mr. Artus, no answer was ever returned by the fictitious A. M. V. de Morcadeau, and to this day the challenge has found no freethinker bold enough to accept it. Juliet Fournier was cured on the 14th of June, 1871, and the challenge of Mr. E. Artus has thus been before the freethinking world of France for more than' twelve months.

We sometimes hear expressions of surprise, in the midst of which an exclamation is made, " How is it that the Blessed Virgin confines the favours of her miraculous apparitions so exclusively to France. The Holy Virgin, we fear it must be said, is the *"most prudent Virgin,"* and prudent people go upon the rule of only trusting themselves in company where they will meet with the respect that is their due. With all honour to the faith of France, it must be owned, that while cavillers and unbelievers are by no means wanting in it, there is to be found a trenchant vigour of faith among the Catholics, on which the Blessed Virgin appears to know that she can rely, and the event also appears fully to justify her reliance. If we in Great Britain and Ireland were seriously to desire to share in these favours, we certainly ought first to go to school to learn a lesson in the same trenchant and vigorous faith, and be able to show that we have removed ourselves from all remains of the awe and fear sometimes known to have been inspired by the *Times* newspaper and other organs of public unbelief.

A BRIEF BIOGRAPHICAL NOTICE OF THE LATE ALEXANDER JANDEL,

MASTER GENERAL OF THE DOMINICAN ORDER.

ALEXANDER JANDEL was born on the 18th of July, 1810, in the village of Champey, in the diocese of Nancy, not far from the city of Lunéville, in Lorraine. He was brought up to assist his father in his business, in which he showed great aptitude, particularly for the study of mathematics; but evincing, after a time, a strong desire for the ecclesiastical state, he was allowed to follow the bent of his disposition, and was placed in the *petit seminaire* of the diocese. From thence he went to study for a time at the university of Freiburg (Baden), until he was ordained priest by the Bishop of Metz. As he gave great edification by his conduct, and showed that he was largely possessed of prudence, he was shortly appointed Professor of Sacred Scripture, and subsequently President, at the *petit seminaire* of the diocese of Nancy, in the town called "Pont a Mousson," and in the year 1829 he was made honorary Canon of the dioceses of Nancy and Tulle.

Whilst he was engaged in discharging the duties of the office above named, he felt the call to a higher way of life. Entering into relations of great intimacy with the celebrated Henri Lacordaire, who had just then joined the Dominican Order, and shortly after laboured so successfully for its restoration in France, he resolved to embrace the same way of life. Renouncing, therefore, the way to honours and preferments, he came out from his country and kindred and removed to Italy, where he was clothed with the Dominican habit, in the Monastery of Santa Maria al Querco, near Viterbo, in the year 1840, and, in due time, was there solemnly professed. After his profession, he returned to France, and settled in Nancy, from whence he went out to preach in the neighbouring towns, drawing great concourses of people ; on one occasion being called to preach in Rome. This practice of preaching, however, he was obliged to discontinue, from being afflicted with an affection in the throat. He was subsequently Prior in the houses of the Order newly established at Cales and Flavigny, and lastly he was sent to Paris, to be professor of theology for the junior members.

While he was thus, in great humility, engaged in his duties, little thinking that he had any reputation that could possibly have passed beyond the walls of the cloister, he was unexpectedly called to Rome, in the year 1850, by the command of Pope Pius, to assume the government of the whole Order, by a decree of the Sacred Congregation, under the title of Vicar General, for which the same Pontiff, by an act of his own authority, in 1855, substituted the higher title of "Master General." It availed him nothing that he pleaded his inexperience and comparatively recent entrance into the Order, as reasons for declining the dignity sought to be imposed upon him. The Pope required his obedience, and he consequently entered upon the task of the supreme government of the Order, amply fulfilling in the event the high expectations that had been already conceived of him.

"Constituted high in office, he never regarded," says Fr. San Vito, his successor, who occupies his place with the title of Vicar General, "his power as an opportunity for domineering over others, but as a means of rendering them charitable service. He felt that, with whatever powers of mind he might be endowed, they would be the more profitably used for the advancement of the Order the more they were united to the study of piety towards God ; and, although he was already eminent for this virtue, he never omitted to labour to improve himself in it; and, to this end, he frequently made spiritual retreats in the course of the year, that he might obtain from them new vigour and strength for his duties. He well understood, and even laboured to have this sentence of Divine wisdom continually before his eyes, 'that their power was given to men in authority from the Most High, *who will enquire into their works, and search their secret thoughts*.' (Wisd. c. VI.) On which account he cultivated the virtue of piety towards God with even greater assiduity than the other virtues, as the best protection in the affairs of his government. With what devotion did he not celebrate the Holy Mass; how deeply did he not contemplate the eternal truths; with what humility did he not keep his daily watch before the Blessed Sacrament. Who was a more strict observer of the laws by which he knew himself to be bound in virtue of his vows of religion? In a word, what shall we say of his humility, of his contempt for pleasures, of his pity for the distressed, of his regular attendance at the offices of the choir, of his self-denial, and his attachment to the Holy See? What shall we say of his kindness, who, though a vigorous champion of justice, when occasion required, yet was always more ready to grant a favour than others were to ask it. Thus, as S. Paul says, he showed himself an example of good works, for he was well aware that in this manner rulers best infuse a religious spirit into the minds of their subjects, who are naturally disposed to follow the example that is placed before them."

In the year 1862 he was unanimously chosen the seventy-third Master General of the Order, and his period of office was prolonged, by a decree of the Sacred Congregation, to twelve years. During the term of his administration, he undertook long journeys to visit many of the distant provinces, during the course of which he came to visit Great Britain, and made himself personally known to the Fathers of the Order in this province.

His last sickness, as we have already related, left but little hope of a recovery, and he died in peace, as we have said, in the Convent of the Minerva, in Rome, in the twenty-third year of his government of the Order.

A CATECHISM OF THE HOLY ROSARY.

By the Rev. HENRY FORMBY. London: BURNS & OATES.

S. PAUL gives us warning of a time to come, when men will not endure sound doctrine, but will turn away their hearing from the truth to give themselves up greedily to tales and romances. There is quite enough to make us serious, when we consider—first, how rapidly the Catholics are learning, from the example of the corrupt society in the midst of which they live, to have their share in the prevailing greedy appetite for tales and romances; secondly, that the Apostle says, if such an appetite be indulged, it will bring with it the consequence that " the hearing will be turned away from the truth."

This desire for the garbage and offal of useless idle tales that teach nothing good, which are very frequently as wicked and antichristian as they are full of follies, extravagancies, and sensational horrors, is to be regarded as a mark of a very great growing degeneracy on the part of Catholics, who ought to know much better than to give way to such a contemptible taste; and it behoves all who have the care of youth to set their faces firmly against the growth and the indulgence of such a degrading taste among those under their charge.

If it is at all times the wisdom of the instructor to try to make knowledge pleasing and acceptible to the learner, much more is it so now, in the presence of the reigning diseased craving for fictitious tales and stories. We know, from experience, that, however needful the learning the Christian doctrine in the ordinary way may be, as a part of education, it is seldom found to be a very acceptable task to youth to be made to learn it.

Now the wisdom of God has given us a very great treasure in the " Rosary." There is a course of simple and beautiful doctrinal instruction connected with its fifteen mysteries, which no one will for a moment deny, but that it would be an admirable thing if every pupil receiving a Catholic education were required to learn as a necessary part of their education. But this is far from the whole of the treasure. The peculiar prerogative of the Holy Rosary, is that it has the gift of making its course of instruction pleasant and acceptable to the learners as they advance. There is an immediate use in the devotion of the Rosary for each piece of knowledge as it comes to be acquired. A pupil, for example, learns the lesson on any one of the mysteries,—say the " Presentation in the Temple," the next time when the Rosary is said by all the scholars in common, and the title of the mystery the " Presentation in the Temple," is given out, there arises in the mind an immediate satisfaction from the consciousness of knowing something clear and definite about the mystery, and this satisfaction is renewed each time the Rosary is said, when the mystery that is well understood recurs. When all the mysteries have come up their turn to be equally well understood, each time the Rosary is said the little stock of knowledge that has been acquired is called into play with a satisfaction that can never wear out. In this way to acquire doctrinal know-

ledge in connection with the Rosary becomes not a burden
but a pleasure to the pupil.

We hope we have said enough to induce great numbers to
try whether some of the advantages above described cannot be
obtained by the use of the catechism above named.

RECORD OF EVENTS.

The audiences at the Vatican still continue, and the Pope
continues to make them the occasion of uttering those words
the sound of which reaches to the ends of the world.

The ladies of Rome have formed themselves into associations
" circoli " for visiting the poor in various districts of the city,
and giving aid to the deserving poor women. They were
received to an audience on the week of Septuagesima Sunday,
and the Marquis Cavaltti read an address to the Pope on their
behalf setting forth the objects of their association. The
Pope, in his reply, spoke to all who were present as follows :—

"In the Gospel of last Sunday Our Lord Jesus Christ spoke a parable
for our instruction. He said that the master of a household wished to
cultivate his vineyard, and had not the labourers necessary for that purpose,
and that therefore he began to walk through the streets, and arrived at the
Forum, or market-place, where he found labourers standing idle, and said,
'Why are ye here all the day idle?' Naturally they replied that it was
because no one had called them. But this is a second part on which I shall
not touch; I will speak only of the first, that is, of the place in which the
idle workmen stood. They stood then in the market-place, and the Fathers
are all agreed that this signifies the world. Whosoever then in the world
amid so many dangers stands idle, incurs great risks, and from idleness,
in truth, springs a series of a thousand iniquities. Indeed there is even
a Pagan poet who says, 'Otia si tollas periere cupidinis arcus.' Therefore
idleness is the parent of this and all other vices. But you, my children,
are entirely contrary to this; you desire not to be idle but to do good,
because you know that to you Our Lord has said, 'Go into My vineyard.'
We are all His labourers—I first, then all the Bishops, then the priesthood,
then all good Christian men and women—so that all should occupy themselves with doing good, especially now, when God says, 'Go, go into My
vineyard, and what is just I will pay you.' And His pay is life eternal—in
paradise. You then, my daughters, have listened to the voice of God; you
have gone to labour in His vineyard, and you give this proof of it in con-
secrating yourselves to the help of so many poor women who need your aid,
your guidance, and your comfort. In this, too, you have the example of the
first ages of the Church, when so many maidens and matrons consecrated
their lives entirely to God. And, in fact, where did S. Peter rest when he
first came to Rome? History tells us it was in the house of Pudens, the
Senator, whose daughters aided S. Peter and other Christians, and who

went about secretly comforting the weak and giving alms to the poor. And
here I may remark by the way what a depositary of the offerings of the
daughters of God and of all the good Christians of that time was
S. Laurence, who fearing that the *agents* of those days should go and
carry everything away, distributed all among the poor, and when they came
to ask where were the treasures of the Church, replied, 'I have placed them
all in the hands of the poor,' and in truth this is the safest ark in which to
deposit them. Note, an example for the men. In those days a Roman
Senator did a thing hitherto unheard of, he founded a hospital. More, he,
a Roman Senator, washed the feet of the poor inmates. You know his
name, even better than I do. It was S. Gallicanus, and you have still a
hospital and church so entitled. And returning to speak to the women, I
will recall that some years ago I went outside the gate of S. John Lateran
to see a basilica then underground, and but recently discovered. At present
I do not know what has become of it, they cannot put the marble columns
in their pockets, and I hope that no hand has touched it. But who built
this basilica of the fourth century? A Roman lady, S. Demetrias. These
are the noble examples of antiquity, and I see that you have the will to
follow them. Take courage, then, and labour as much you can, and allow
me to repeat a word or two of a Psalm, *Tempus faciendi, Domine,
dissipaverunt legem tuam.'* Oh this is not the time to stay with the hands
idle, it is the time to work, *tempus faciendi,* for the enemies of God are
going about destroying what is most sacred and holy, *dissippverunt legem
tuam,* and, therefore, it behoves us to oppose ourselves to the utmost to the
torrent of iniquity. I bless then the societies (*circoli*) now present, and I
encourage you all to continue all the good you have begun; may God guide
you in your good thoughts, your angel guardian accompany you in all your
works, and the Mother of Mercy, Mary Immaculate, protect you and obtain
from God the necessary counsel, the firmness, the courage, and whatever is
desirable for yourselves, your families, and the souls of which you have
undertaken the care in this valley of tears.—*Benedictio, &c.*"

The Holy Father after this received the Lent preachers to
an audience. They were assembled in the tapestry gallery,
(*galleria degl' arazzi*) and afterwards proceeded to the throne
room. The Pope spoke to them at length on the duties of
their office, and exhorted them to acquit themselves like men.
Amongst other things he uttered the following words;—

"But there is another most wonderful circumstance of Our Lord's life,
wonderful to us all. He permitted the devil to *tempt* Him; to tempt Him
by vanity, by appetite, and by pride, 'All this will I give Thee if Thou
wilt fall down and worship me.' Of these provinces, of these kingdoms and
empires Christ was already the rightful lord and master. And yet, 'the
devil tempted Him.' Let us say in passing: Tell me then—to sit in a
usurped throne, to hold it some way or other, though but for a time, to
take that which does not belong to us—may we for this bend our knee to
the devil?—'if falling down thou wilt worship me.' There are upon thrones
. . . but enough. But Jesus Christ after having suffered the temptation
of the devil said, 'Vade retro Satanas,' Get thee behind Me Satan. And
then what happened? The Angels descended from Heaven and ministered
to Him, for the human nature He had taken upon Him required th's

consolation and support. And why should not We also hope, I do not say for the presence of angels, but for that courage which is the forerunner and pledge of tranquillity and peace, 'Come to me all ye who labour and are heavy laden.' This is the Angel, the voice of Christ, that should resound in our ears. Come, and doubt not.'"

The carnival in Rome having been the occasion of a very shameful and immoral exhibition, which the "Liberta" the official paper, in describing, says, that the Piazza Navona was transformed into a true "Pandemonium," some seven hundred of the respectable women of Rome assembled themselves in the Sala Ducale to express to the Pope their grief that the holy city should have been subjected to such profanation. The Sala Ducale was consequently well filled, notwithstanding its immense dimensions, when the Holy Father entered. He was received with every manifestation of profound respect, and addressed his hearers some touching words on the mission of woman in society, and on her power to do good.

THE ARCH-CONFRATERNITY OF OUR LADY OF THE ANGELS.

OUR readers will be pleased to learn that we have received trustworthy intelligence of the Abbé de Bray, the founder and director of the above confraternity, having been admitted to an audience with the Holy Father. The audience was fixed for Wednesday the 19th of February, at six o'clock in the evening. "The Pope," to quote a sentence from our informant's letter, "received him with the greatest kindness, and called him 'Mon cher ami mon, cher enfant.' He asked to see his brief, and returning it to him, told him to go on with his work, with the exception of the diocese of Toulouse, as the archbishop was opposed to him."

From this it appears, adds our correspondent, that the Holy Father has given the Abbé a distinct injunction to go on with the holy work of which he acknowledges no other director but the Abbé de Bray. The same information in substance is contained in a letter written by the Abbé de Bray himself, of which a copy has been sent to us, relating to a friend in France the circumstances of the interview in detail. "The Pope has directed him to seek as early as possible a diocese, the bishop of which will allow him to build a church, from which church the work of the confraternity is then to be prosecuted as soon as the foundation stone be laid." Limited by space we must reserve further particulars for another opportunity.

THE

𝕸onthly 𝕸agazine of the 𝕳oly 𝕽osary.

NEW SERIES.

No. 10.]   **MAY.**   [A.D. 1873.

No. I.—SACRUM SEPTENARIUM;

OR, THE BLESSED VIRGIN, THE MOTHER OF THE CHRISTIAN FAMILY, GIVING HER CHILDREN A PERFECT EXAMPLE OF THE SEVEN GIFTS OF THE HOLY GHOST DIRECTING THE DAILY ACTIONS OF LIFE.

No. 1.—THE SOVEREIGN IMPORTANCE OF THE EXAMPLE OF THE GREAT MOTHER OF THE CHRISTIAN FAMILY.

WE have no wish to open a series of popular instructions on a subject which cannot fail to be most near and dear to the hearts of all the children of the great Christian family, otherwise than in the simplest and the least pretentious manner. Every one may easily know that God has formed His world on the plan that the children of the families, by which He provides for the increase and multiplying of His creation, should look up in each family or household to their father and mother for an example by which to take pattern, and that they should learn to form themselves by copying and imitating the model thus provided and set before them. "Honour thy father and thy mother," as S. Paul insists, is the first commandment to which any promised reward is annexed, viz., "that thy days may be long in the land which the Lord thy God hath given thee." The honour paid by the children to father and mother was never meant to be the mere obedience of dependence to superior power, but that it should proceed from the willing belief, on the part of the children, that both parents, in their respective spheres, are what they should always endeavour to be, viz., suitable models of conduct, which it is a privilege and a delight for the children to be able to study and to do their best to follow. In infancy and in the early years of childhood the example of the mother must necessarily, by force of circumstances, go for much more in the formation of the character and the understanding of the child than the example of the father. The father is supposed to be the greater part of the day away from the house, busy at his daily work, by which he provides for the maintenance and support of his household; and the children consequently are much more the constant companions of the mother, as she is supposed to be continually in her house with the children by her side, who are hourly learning all their early ideas and knowledge, either directly from her, or under her immediate eye. Even as the family grows up, the daughters will always naturally look up much more to the example of the mother, as more akin to the condition of their sex, and as abounding much more in the kind of direction as to the various incidents of their life on which they need the light and guidance of an example.

The pattern, therefore, of the mother in the family, according to the Divine plan originally established under the natural law of creation and confirmed under the covenant of Redemption in Jesus Christ, may be easily perceived to be one of sovereign importance to the well-being of the children. The care, indeed, of both parents for the children is by Divine appointment, and the honour of the children for both of them has the sanction of one and the same Divine law. And parental care is, moreover, of that kind for which no adequate substitute can be found. For, when children are deprived by death of the care of their parents, inasmuch as there exists no other human care that can adequately replace what they have lost, we see that God Himself acknowledges the loss as irreparable, and does not disdain Himself to step in and to take the care of the orphan child into His own hands. "Orphano Tu eris adjutor" ("Thou art the aid of the orphan,") says the Psalmist. Not a sparrow falls to the ground except with the knowledge of God, and certainly not a parent is withdrawn from the care of children except by the act of God. We may thus easily perceive how great and precious that parental care must be, which on being withdrawn by the act of God from the children, God Himself deigns to declare that He takes the orphans under His own protection.

From this we easily come to learn the truth, that when God condescended to open a new covenant of mercy to all the children of Adam without any exception through the merits of the sacrifice of Jesus Christ on the cross, He would not undo the original plan of His creation. If there was to be a new universal Christian brotherhood, uniting all the tribes and kindreds of the whole earth in the new household of the Faith, and in the unity of the one Catholic Church, that is in other words, in the bosom of the great Christian family of all the nations, there was manifestly needed for this great family, in accordance with the Divine

plan, the example of the mother. In short, we may very
easily perceive this example of the mother to be indispensable,
except God is to be understood to have formed the restored
order of Redemption upon a totally changed plan from His
original order of the creation. But this is impossible, for
with God, says the Scripture, there is neither changing nor
shadow of change. "Thou art the same," says the Psalmist,
and "thy years do not fail." It could not be tolerated for a
moment that the holy Apostle should speak of the "household of faith," and that the Church should speak of herself
in her Liturgies as a family, unless a certain verity and truth
of genuine and real family life in the Church, requiring the
presence of the mother, were found manifested in it. There
must plainly, therefore, be in the Church the presence and
power of one chosen pre-eminent mother of the great Christian
family, to whom every eye can be incessantly turned from every
quarter of the globe, whose will is law to her children, and to
study to conform to whose holy pattern and example is not only
the very best of discipline and education, but the most direct
path to honour and well-being in this present life, and to
eternal glory and bliss in the next. In a word, we cannot
have the one great Christian family as the universal brotherhood of all the nations of the earth, without the living presence, influence, and example of the one elect mother, whom
all generations are to call blessed.

The task, then, that now opens itself before us will be
specially to consider the function of the Holy Virgin Mother
of Jesus in the economy of the Christian Redemption, as
affording to all generations the elect example which it is
fitting that the mother of the great Christian family of all
people should set before all her children for their imitation in
every age, nation, and clime of the earth. Now, nothing is
more familiarly within the experience of all known families
than that the example of the mother should always be perfectly level to the capacity of the children to study and
imitate. But all is far from said, when we assert that by the
order of God's natural creation, the example of the mother is
in a pre-eminent degree given to the children to take pattern
by. This example is both prior in order of time in being the
first with which they become familiarly acquainted, and prior
also in the affection of the children, from the very much
greater debt which God has placed all children under to their
mother, for the constant care and nursing so indispensable to

their state of helplessness in infancy, which they receive at her hands. If then seeing that by the Divine order of creation, the mother's example is in a special degree the gift of God for the formation of the character of the children, it is of incalculable importance that her example should be not only holy and irreproachable, but also able wisely to adapt itself to the capacities of the children. What, then, must we not have to declare with regard to the sovereign value of the maternal pattern which is to be set before the whole family of the redeemed out of every nation, tribe, and kindred for their imitation? And in what words shall we be able worthily to speak of the chosen example of the elect Lady, whom Jesus Christ having first given Himself to her as her Son, has afterwards given to be a mother to all collectively and to each singly of the great widely spread Christian family of His redeemed, comprising all generations, all times, and all nations and kindreds of the whole earth.

What, indeed, are we to say of this surpassing example, except that while it possesses a sublimity proper to itself that is without a parallel, its sublimity notwithstanding brings no prejudice to the homeliness whereby the mother's example always condescends to the infirmity of her children, and adapts itself to them, so as to be perfectly capable of being studied, loved, and imitated by them.

It is manifestly one thing to tread the heights of sanctity in such an exalted way that the ordinary beholder, becoming amazed and bewildered by his perception of the sublimity that has been attained, finds all thought of the example being one that is presented for his own study and imitation at once extinguished; and it is another to combine the sublimity of the example with the homeliness, simplicity, and affection of the mother of the family, who perfectly knows that her children are looking up to her and understands with the admirable discernment proper only to the mother, how to make her example at once perfect for the sake of the improvement of her children, and homely and attainable for the sake of their encouragement. For to repeat what we have above said; that which children require before all things in an example is to be filled with the thought of its being within their reach, that they may so be the more moved in consequence to try to imitate it. Peerless perfection in the example by itself alone would fail of its end, for the children would then say, " Which of us can climb thus up to heaven to bring this down to us, that we may hear and

perform it in act" (Deut. xxx. 12).   And if homeliness were its
sole characteristic, as need not be said, this would fail to
command universal respect.   What the great Christian family
plainly requires is that sublimity should combine and unite
itself with homeliness, so that while we admire we may both
desire to imitate, and also be possessed with the encouraging
belief that the example is one which is completely within
our reach, and perfectly level to our capacity.

Now, S. Peter Damian says, that, as there could have been
no Redemption, except the Son of God had been born of a
Virgin, so it was indispensable that the Virgin herself should
first be born, from whom the Eternal Word might become
flesh.   It was necessary, therefore, that the house should first
be built, into which the Heavenly King might deign to come
down and sojourn; that house namely, he says, of which
Solomon speaks.   'Wisdom hath built herself a house, and
hath hewn out seven pillars' (Prov. ix. 1).   Thus this
Virginal house has stood propped up with seven pillars, for
the venerable mother of the Lord was endowed with the
seven gifts of the Holy Ghost, that is with the gifts of—

1. Wisdom.
2. Understanding.
3. Counsel.
4. Fortitude.
5. Knowledge.
6. Piety.
7. The fear of the Lord."
(S. Peter Damian.   Sermon on the Nativity)

The above words of S. Peter Damian explain to us the secret
of the combined sublimity and simplicity of the example
given by the Holy Virgin Mother to her children of the great
Christian family of all nations.   In our next instruction we
shall labour to show briefly how God, by a wonderful provision of His mercy and wisdom, through the Sacrament of
Confirmation gives to all the Christian people the same seven
gifts of the Holy Ghost, and we shall explain how He thereby
provides the children of His great Christian family with the
power and capacity to imitate at once the perfect and simple
example of the Virgin mother which He has set before them.
To this end we shall in our next number betake ourselves to
S. Thomas of Aquin to learn from him as briefly as may be,
what it is principally needful to know relatively to these gifts
of the Holy Ghost.   And in the meantime, we commend our

undertaking to the patronage of the Holy Mother, the "Seat of Wisdom," and in the humble spirit becoming her children we present the first beginning of it to her as an offering for her own beautiful month of May.

(To be continued).

No. II.—THE CONVERSION TO THE CATHOLIC FAITH OF COUNT STOLBERG.

(Concluded from the Number for March.)

THE organization and carrying out of this scheme naturally necessitated frequent intercourse between its author and Count de Stolberg. Madame de Montagu was now a frequent and a welcome guest at Eutin; her goodness, her gentle winning ways won the love of wife, sister, and children, she had a warm friend in the Countess Sophia; and when they came to know her in her daily life, and saw her always the same: forgetful of self, full of thought for others, firm and cheerful in adversity, loving God and serving Him with heart and soul, admiration, mingling with their love, insensibly they yielded to the influence of living faith, and, paying tribute to her virtue, were drawn to Catholicity. It was a long time, however, before they spoke to her openly of their doubts, their difficulties, their new-born hopes; it was a long time before the subject of religion was touched upon between them. It was brought about in the following manner:—One day when Madame de Montagu had received very bad news of her sister, Madame de la Fayette, then a prisoner at Olmutz, she was so depressed that she could not shake off the sadness it occasioned her; this did not escape the notice of her friends. They asked her the cause of it, and having told them she was led on to speak of her heroic sister, of her long captivity in France, of her following her husband to Olmutz, there to become the voluntary sharer of his imprisonment; and then they gently urged her, and she spoke of the other sorrows of her family, of the captivity of her mother, her grandmother, her sister; of the courageous Abbé Carrichon, who followed them to the scaffold; of the absolution given during the dreadful thunderstorm that arose as the victims were borne on their way to execution; of the last blessing pronounced as each, with noble calm, laid down the life so fiercely claimed. . . . . She left them weeping; she wept herself, poor thing; and when she returned to them shortly after, the Count approached her, and anxiously asked if living as she did amongst heretics did not distress her sorely; then without waiting for an answer, he added, "We are almost Catholics, though; indeed, we were Catholics just now whilst listening to you. Oh! what a religion yours is! What minds it forms! What a source of strength, what consolation it gives," and he told her how since she came amongst them he had learned to love her faith, and had thought upon it much, and how he longed to say, I believe, and could not. "But once," he continued, "its truth appears without a cloud, nothing shall stop me from embracing it;" and he begged her to pray for him, for them all.

From that day forth the most perfect confidence existed between them; freely and frequently did they discuss the subject of religion; but though always ready to hear discussion, Madame de Montagu never forced it; she endeavoured by particular study to inform herself on certain points they laid, or were likely to lay, before her; but she depended on prayer far more than on discussion to help them; and when objections were raised which she could not satisfy, or questions were asked which she could not solve, unembarrassed, she frankly confessed her inability, and prayed all the harder. Her task was no easy one; she had to deal with acute, highly educated minds, and though she herself was more than well grounded in her religion, and had a knowledge of Scripture, and a power of applying that knowledge as occasion required, that often filled her Lutheran friends with wonder, yet there were many points of controversy between the two Churches, the Catholic and Lutheran, that were quite new to her; she could not answer them herself, neither could she find others to answer them for her. This made her anxious: it troubled her, knowing them so near, to see them so far from enjoying the peace on earth promised to men of good will. The Count would often compare himself to the blind man in the Gospel, who groped his way after our Lord, praying him to restore his sight; in his heart he felt the Catholic Church to be the true Church; but he dared not act upon the feeling simply, whilst so many controverted points remained unanswered: he could yield only to the most complete and absolute evidence.

At last Madame de Montagu thought of applying to the Bishop of Saint Pol de Léon to come and finish her work, then to her old friend the Abbé Edgeworth, he who accompanied Louis XVI. to the scaffold. "Do not suppose, dear Pauline," wrote the Count de Stolberg to her, 31st December, 1797, referring to the last invitation, "that your Eutinois are blind as to the real motive which makes you so anxious that M. Edgeworth should come and spend some time with us. No doubt, you are desirous that he should have repose after his illness; that he should take breath on his journey, I understand this perfectly; but at the same time it is we, rather than he, who are the objects of your ingenious, ardent charity. And so my dear, generous friend, as I fully enter into all your views, I have just written to him to press him to come myself." Unfortunately the Abbé, like the Bishop, could not come; but assistance came, and it came from a quarter she never thought of: from her sister Madame de la Fayette.

The prisoner of Olmutz was set at liberty for awhile, and at once hastened to her sister in Holstein. Introduced to the family at Eutin, it was not long before the influence of her sound judgment and vigorous intellect were felt. She gave herself up with a will to the good work that was set her, and having heard all they had to say, she drew up a full, clear statement of the various difficulties and controverted points that yet remained unanswered, and sent copies of it, one to Monseigneur de la Luzerne, Bishop of Langres; one to Monseigneur Asseline, Bishop of Boulogne.

This led to a regular controversy, carried on through the medium of Madame de Montagu, between the Bishop of Boulogne and Count de Stolberg: the correspondence, forming a complete treatise on the truths of religion rejected or denied by the Lutheran Church, may be found in the "Oeuvres choisies" of Monseigneur Asseline.

Thus, step by step we see them led forward; the crooked was made straight and the rough plain; clouds were dispersed, and the uncertain, flickering light grew clear and steady; and now just when Madame de Montagu was on the point of seeing the realization of all her hopes and anxious prayers she is recalled to France. Her work is done in Germany, and it has been a good five years' work. She must leave it; she must leave it, e'er she has seen the coping stone, the only one now wanting to complete it, set upon the slowly built up edifice of faith she has daily watched and helped in building. She left it; and scarce arrived in Paris, a letter came to her, from the Count himself, telling that he and his wife had been received into the Catholic Church, May, 1800.

In his own country the news of his conversion was the signal for persecution. Count de Stolberg was deprived of his public offices, and was abandoned by his dearest friends; or more correctly, he was not abandoned by them, but was made the object of their fiercest invective. All this, however, did not prevent his example being followed by others: once he had taken the step, many were found ready to follow him. Indeed, the very violence of the first feeling against him brought about a reaction in his favour, and not a few cried shame on Jean Henri Voss, when, forgetful alike of gratitude and friendship, he exceeded all in violent and unjust abuse of his old friend and benefactor.

Amidst all the disturbance occasioned by his conversion, De Stolberg alone was calm. He felt, and keenly too, the pain of separation, the severing of old ties, the turning aside of old friends. Who would not? He tasted the cup of persecution, and found it bitter. Who that has did not? But it did not destroy his calm; in fact, it was the price of inward peace, and he willingly paid it. Relieved of his public duties, he left the angry scene at Eutin, retired to the neighbourhood of Munster, and devoted himself entirely to literary pursuits.

It was during this period—his intellect now at its best, matured by years of deep thought and study—that he wrote his " History of the Religion of Jesus Christ." His perfect knowledge of Holy Scripture, and his wide research into the various religions of Asia, are strikingly displayed in his particular treatment of the doctrine of atonement, and lend rare interest to his demonstration of the universal tradition, amongst all peoples of the earth, of the original Fall. The work, comprising fifteen volumes, was translated, by order of the Sovereign Pontiff, from the German into the Italian. Speaking of it, at considerable length, and with warm admiration, in her celebrated book on Germany, Mme. De Staël says that it cannot fail to win the admiration of Christians of every communion.

By degrees failing health compelled M. De Stolberg to

relinquish his heavier labours; but he was still hard at work on his treatise on "The Love of God" when his last illness came upon him.

The year 1819 had been a year of great suffering to him, and in November of the same year his state of health was such as to excite the gravest fears of his family. The end had come; and the end was like the life that had been before it. God, God's Word, had been his constant thought in life: in death, life's thought is with him still, and makes him long to die. "Ah! what sharp pain," he cries; "the hour of dissolution must be near; God calls those to Him who suffer and are heavy burdened." "Come, Lord Jesus, come," murmured the priest's voice, helping him; and then the dying man said, "How beautiful it is to find the Holy Scriptures, which give us such a perfect picture of our sinfulness and of the Divine mercy, ending with these words: 'Come, Lord Jesus, come!' God, so great, begins the enumeration of his benefits, and says, 'In the beginning God created heaven and earth.' So good, he ends by saying, 'I come quickly!' Come, Lord Jesus (Gen. i. 1.; Apoc. xxii. 20). *Pater Noster, Ave Maria,*" and so he prayed.

In life surrounded with his family, they had been the object of his unceasing care; in death they still are with him, to tend him now and comfort him, to pray for him.

In life ever active, yet ever calm, *in labore requies*, he had never known what sloth was—sloth that in its many forms lays such subtle snares to catch the unwary—and now in death he still is active, still is calm; finds time to work for God, for those he leaves behind, and for himself; and if dark fears of God's dread judgment will now and then oppress and agitate him, his old friend Dean Kellerman stands by, and, speaking of Christ's great mercy, lays them, and brings back peace.

The days dragged on; December came, there was an interlude, the sharp pain and sickness ceased awhile, sleep came, hope thrilled the anxious, loving hearts around him; but it was only an interlude, a pause as if to give him time to gather strength for the approaching agony; he alone was not deceived by it. He called them all around him, made his acts of faith, hope, and charity aloud, asked pardon for all scandal he had given, begged them never to forget God, and then his voice failed him, death seemed very near, the agony was fearful. Presently he asked for the litany for a happy death, and said it with one of his daughters, his voice alone ringing clear and firm as they came to the last response.

Towards evening a slight delirium set in; he still spoke of God, and wanted to get up, as if about to prepare for a long journey. This passed away, and he turned to the doctor and asked him, "Do you think I shall last over to-morrow, or the day after?" The doctor told him he did not think he would last till midnight. "Praise be to God," he said, taking both the doctor's hands in his. "Thank you, thank you! I thank you with all my heart! Praised be Jesus Christ." And with these words lingering on his lips, he bowed his head and died, December 5, 1819.

A. L.

THE FEAST OF THE PATRONAGE OF S. JOSEPH.

Patron of the Church, S. Joseph,
Safe amid the tempest's rage,
Peter's bark hold in thy keeping
E'en in this cold, faithless age.

Thou hast known a pilgrim's sorrows,
But thy day of toil is o'er.
Help us while we journey onwards,
Speed us to the far-off shore.

He whom thou didst take to Egypt,
Is by countless saints adored,
Prostrate angels in his presence,
Sing hosannas to their Lord.

And to thee no gift refusing,
Jesus stoops to hear thy prayer,
Then, dear Saint, from thy bright dwelling
Give to us a Father's care.

Jesus, shelt'ring in thy bosom,
Feared not Herod's lifted arm,
Keep His Church and us thy children
Safe 'mid danger and alarm.

E. M. D.

A HOMILY FOR THE PASCHAL SEASON.

How Jesus honours the Daily Labour of the Christian People.

Simon Peter saith to them, "I go a fishing." They said to him, "We come with thee" (John xxi. 3.)

At first sight it cannot but strike us that what is here recorded of S. Peter belongs altogether to the order of every-day doings. What indeed can well be a more ordinary every-day kind of thing than that those who belong to any particular trade, or way of life, should say among themselves that they are going to set about the work of their particular trade or calling. S. Peter was originally a fisherman by trade, and those to whom he spoke were fishermen also. When, therefore, one fisherman says to his mates of the like trade, "I go a fishing," he manifestly only says the most natural thing that a man who is a fisherman possibly could say, and when they say in return, "We go with you," they also say the most natural every-day kind of thing that they possibly could be expected to say. But if a Holy Evangelist, notwithstanding the extreme every-day character that attaches to what he says, is inspired by the Holy Ghost to put into the sacred record of the acts and deeds of the Son of God made man, that S. Peter once said to his associates the most natural thing a fisherman possibly could say, viz., "I go a fishing," and that they in reply said, "We go with you," we are most reasonably set a thinking as to what can be the particular lesson which it is intended should be inculcated by a piece of such very commonplace, every-day kind of life, thus prominently introduced into the sacred record.

Every sensible and well-meaning Christian is prepared beforehand to accept the truth that the Holy Evangelist can have recorded nothing except that from which some very instructive lesson follows. Our task accordingly resolves itself into the labour of trying to discover what is the particular lesson which is inculcated in what is here recorded of S. Peter, that he said, "I go a fishing," and that his fellow disciples also said, "We go with you."

God, it clearly appears, intended that His creation of the human family should have their daily life fully and adequately employed. Industry of some kind was to be for them the order of their day, as these days should succeed each other throughout their life. In a word, it was the Divine plan for the life of the world, which God had made, that, all in their degree, the men, women, and children, should each have their suitable and fitting daily employment provided for them, and that there should consequently be no such thing as idleness known in the world, according to the plan that God had marked out for it.

In the Book of Genesis, when the Sacred Historian passes the course of the Work of Creation for the second time in review, adding some few particulars that had been omitted in his first account, he speaks of the formation and the condition of the plants and herbs previous to the falling of rain, and to their reproduction and growth from seed, and what is to be observed here is, that in determining this to a time previous to the creation of man, he does not simply say that he is speaking of a time before man was made; but he says pointedly, that it was before man was made to *work* the earth. So although God provided for man when he made him a special abode, which He planted Himself and formed into a paradise of pleasure, still He placed him in it " to dress it and to keep it," and not to be in any way idle or unemployed in it but to find ample daily employment for his time in the labour of "dressing it and keeping it."   When, therefore, Adam had sinned and was to receive the sentence of his punishment, this came to him, not in the way of a putting an end to the ease and charms of idleness by substituting penal labour in its place, but in creating for him the necessity for a hard and penal day's work, in the place of the day's work which was both easy and agreeable.   There was to be no longer the dressing and keeping of the pleasant garden, but the labour in the sweat of the brow to subdue the earth, which was thereupon laid under a curse, and commanded "to bear thorns and thistles to thee."   The rule itself of daily employment for time suffered no change.   It remained intact. What however was changed in it was, in place of the easy agreeable employment of providing by pleasant labour the delights and ornaments of life, the substitution of the hard and laborious occupation of contending with the earth that had been placed under a curse, to compel it to produce what urgent need should henceforth require to be produced.

It is a matter of the greatest importance to a right understanding and appreciation of our condition here, that we should most clearly know, that equally in the state of innocence, as in the fallen state, God intended that His creation of the human family should awake each morning from their sleep, to find themselves with their legitimate day's work before them. "Man," says the Psalmist, "shall go forth to his work until the evening." "The young lions shall move to and fro, roaring, that they may seek food for themselves from God. The sun is risen, and they shall gather themselves together and lie down in their lairs." Not so man. When the sun rises "He shall go forth to his work until the evening." (Ps. ciii. 25.)

So it was in the world before the flood; of such a thing as idleness, that is to say of people who have nothing to do when the sun rises, there is not a trace. Cain was a tiller of the earth, Abel was a shepherd of sheep. Cain, even when he went forth from the face of the Lord, nevertheless built a city. Of Jubal, it is said, that he was a master musician, of Jubal Cain, that he was a master workman, "a hammerer and mechanic in all works of brass and iron." Our Lord says of the world before the flood, that they bought and sold and planted vineyards, married and gave in marriage. The sun rises, and "man goes forth to his work until the evening." The world of men is a busy world, and God made it to be a busy world, and intended that every one should on the rising of the sun find his day's work laid out before him, that he might have nothing before him but to go forth to do it until the evening.

Of course the more men obeyed the Divine command given to them in the outset of creation, "to increase and multiply and subdue the earth" and the more numerous they became, naturally the more diversified would become the callings and employments, according to which the day's labour was to be determined. "This only have I found, says the wise man, that God made man upright, but he has mixed himself up with infinite questionings" (Eccles. vii. 50). Everything then betokens a busy world, in other words a world where daily labour is the order of the day, and idleness a thing so abominable as not to be contemplated, and to be in fact something totally foreign to the plan of creation.

When our Lord came into the world thus made, of His own free will He subjected Himself to its law of daily labour. "My Father, He says, worketh hitherto, and I work;" and as it was part of the plan of His work that He should associate others with Himself, it is to be carefully observed that He chose none but such men as those who had their regular day's work marked out for them. He called

S. Peter and his brother Andrew to leave their nets and become His disciples, while they were in the very act of pursuing their daily labour in casting their nets. S. John and S. James, the sons of Zebedee, in like manner. S. Matthew He called while he was doing his regular day's work, sitting at the receipt of custom, engaged in collecting the toll. Hereafter all whom He associated to Himself were to become men of toil and labour in the new order of labours which He intended to assign to them, and their day's work was to have a new form given to it, for which He was about to fit and prepare them; but from the very beginning He held familiar experience in the accepting and bearing the yoke of the first law of creation, the duty of regular daily labour, to be the indispensable condition for forming one of His company.

We are now approaching the lesson contained in S. Peter's words. The man who is accustomed to the life of daily labour, and who understands that his daily labour is his debt of duty under the Divine order of the creation, cannot bear to be idle. He reproaches himself for being idle, and says to himself what am I doing, folding my hands and wasting the precious time that God has given me to be turned to some good account. "Remember," says the wise man, "whatever your hand findeth to do, that you do it with all your might, for there is no knowledge or wisdom in the grave whither thou hastenest." S. Peter then was in this kind of predicament. He had been a man long used to do his day's work. For the three years and more he had been in the school of his Master, he had doubtless had his former experience of daily labour well confirmed and strengthened in the daily toil of accompanying his Master and of doing his bidding and learning from Him. But now, to all appearance, all this had come to a sudden end. His Master had been put to an ignominious public death, from which He had not to all outward seeming been able to deliver Himself. It is true that there was up to a certain point evidence of His having risen from the dead, and S. Peter, with his fellow disciples, had left Jerusalem and had come to the lake of Tiberias in Galilee, in compliance with a command sent to them by their Master since His rising from the dead, viz.: "That they should go there to meet Him." So far there doubtless were ample grounds for expectation, that they might even yet come to receive the commission which would restore to them their accustomed daily employment in their Master's service; but then there was, so to speak, as yet nothing positive for them to do.

In this state of expectation then, but without anything definite to do, the sight of the lake,—the self-same lake on which he had hitherto always found his day's work,—appears to revive in S. Peter the good, honourable and laudable love of being employed so natural to every honest and industrious man to whom to do his day's work, is to honour the Divine law of labour which God in the first beginning gave to His creation, and he accordingly says, "I go a fishing." No sooner are his words spoken than they appear to revive the same honourable spirit of industry that loves the day's work in the other disciples, and they immediately say, "We go with you."

While they were intent on their day's work (and how very intent they were upon it quite sufficiently appears from the fact that they had continued at it, not only through the day, but all through the night also, though they had caught nothing), Jesus came and stood on the shore. We do not find that He expresses any surprise as to how they could be so unspiritual, as to be intent on catching fish, when they had been brought into such near contact with the surpassing miracle of His resurrection from the dead. He recognizes on the contrary the lawfulness of their occupation, and asks them if they are able to offer Him anything to eat out of what they have caught. They reply that they have unfortunately not succeeded in catching anything. Then, He says to them, "Cast your nets on the right side of the boat, and you shall find fish." They did so, and the multitude of fishes which their net enclosed led S. Peter at once to discover that it was no other than their Master who had spoken to them.

Thus we see how it pleased Jesus highly to honour the honest daily toil of men, which is the first law of creation and the only good and honourable condition of human life. He who in the laudable spirit of honouring the Divine law of daily labour said, "I go a fishing," was shortly after this, when the commission was given to him to say, "I go a fishing" in another sense for the souls of men; but in this he was to change not the law of daily labour, but the form of it; and his colleagues were also to do the same by saying in another sense, "We go with you," to labour, to instruct, convert, teach, and gather into the Church the souls of men.

Let us then, in whatever state of life we are, learn to love and to honour the law of daily labour, which Jesus Christ, as we have seen, has honoured in so marked and signal a manner. Away with the wicked delusion, that happiness is to be found in shameful idling and trifling away the precious time God has given to us to be employed in honest labour, to say nothing of what is so much worse still sottish and drunken enjoyments. "The sun is risen, and man shall go forth to his labour till the evening." In the evening comes the rest of a few peaceful hours, and on the Sunday comes a holy day of religious rest, and this rest from daily toil is an earnest of the blessed rest that is reserved, as the Apostle says, for the people of God.

SACRILEGE AND ITS RETRIBUTION.

WE have many instances in the history of the Church of the signal way in which God has punished acts of sacrilege and blasphemy, not only when directed immediately against Himself, but also those that have been perpetrated against His Saints and Angels, and above all against His Blessed Mother. The following example, which happened in the time of the first Napoleon, is one in which the retributive justice of God was in a special way manifested. It was at the commencement of that disastrous expedition against Spain, which Napoleon undertook for the purpose of setting a member of his own family on the throne. Three French conscripts on their way to join the Emperor's army happened one day to be passing a small country Church in the South of France. Over the door of this Church was an image of the Blessed Mother of God. Such was the depth of irreligion in the hearts of Napoleon's soldiers, that one of these three proposed they should each have a shot at the holy image. Another of them who was less wicked than the other two, shrinking from such a sacrilegious proposal, tried to dissuade them from their purpose. They, however, only laughed at him for his scruples. The first soldier raising his musket, fired, and the ball struck the forehead of the image. The second following his example also fired ; and the ball struck the breast. The third not wishing to fire, but being overcome by human respect and the continued bantering of his comrades, fired with an unsteady hand and turning aside his head as he did so ; and his ball struck the image below the knee.   As they continued their journey they expressed their misgivings about their impious exploit. These three men went through the whole of that campaign without a wound; and they were making the best of their way back to France with other stragglers, and were within three days march of their own country, the Guerilla bands hanging in their rear picking off all they could. That evening, as they were seated around their bivouac fire, a ball whizzed through the air—no one saw from whence it came, and struck the soldier, who had fired first at our Lady's Image in the forehead and killed him on the spot.   This caused the other two soldiers to exchange silent but significant looks. Next evening, a ball from an invisible hand struck the soldier who had fired second at the Image on his breast and pierced his heart.   On the third day, just before arriving at the frontier, a stray ball struck the third soldier who had fired unwillingly at the Image on his leg.   The surgeon on dressing it, pronounced it only a slight flesh wound; but three days after on removing the bandage expecting to find it well-nigh healed, to his surprise found it a terrible wound full of worms.   The wounded man reached his own home, and lived for some years after, but the wound in his leg could never be healed; it was always a frightful running sore which bred worms.   Skilful surgeons tried in vain to heal it, and the sufferer visited the different famous mineral springs in France to try to obtain a cure, but equally in vain.   The good Mother of Mercy, however, had pity on him and he became converted, and henceforth lived a Christian life; but he went down to his grave with this mark of God's just, though to him, merciful vengeance for the blasphemous act perpetrated against the Image of His ever Blessed Mother.

SPREAD OF THE DEVOTION TO OUR LADY QUEEN OF THE ANGELS.

REMARKABLE ORIGIN OF A MIRACULOUS PRAYER.

A PIOUS priest of the Diocese of Bayonne, the Abbé Cestac, is the founder of two religious congregations in the aforesaid city, viz., the Servants of Mary, who devote themselves to the work of the Sisters of the Good Shepherd, without being cloistered; and the Bernardines, who are contemplatives.

To one of these latter devout religions the Blessed Virgin
deigned to make the communication an account, of which is
contained in the following letter from the Abbé Cestac to
M. Dupont of Tours.

"Anglet, near Bayonne.

" SIR,

    " It is not exactly correct to say that the Blessed Virgin appeared
to a good, simple person of the Community, but rather, I should say, that
this soul received a supernatural communication from this Divine Mother,
or at any rate conceived she had received such communication from on
high. She was at prayer, when a ray of divine light illumined her soul.
She saw in spirit the vast desolation caused by the devil throughout the
world, and at the same time she heard the Divine Mother telling her that
it was true that hell had been let loose upon the earth ; but that the time
had come when we were to pray to her as Queen of Angels, and when we
were to ask of her the assistance of the heavenly legions to fight against
these deadly foes of God and of men.

    " ' But, my Good Mother,' answered this soul, ' you who are so kind,
could you not send them without our asking you ? '

    " ' No,' she answered : ' because prayer is one of the conditions required
by God himself for obtaining favours.'

    " And the soul believed she heard the prayer I send you. Naturally, I
was made the depository of this prayer, and my first duty was to submit
it to my Bishop, who has deigned to approve of it. It was then that our
Lady made known to me that I should get it printed, and distribute it
gratis. Since that time, this prayer has received the approbation of their
Lordships the Archbishop of Tours and the Bishops of Toulouse, of
Besançon and of Tarbes. It is being translated into Spanish, and is being
spread far and wide.

    (Signed)   " CESTAC,
    " Priest of the Diocese of Bayonne."

It would appear that the devil was terribly enraged at the
publication of this prayer, for the Abbé Cestac in a recent
letter to M. Dupont tells him that the very day on which he
sent to Tours 20,000 copies, with an offering of 300 francs
for the tomb of S. Martin (sent to him for that purpose), a
large building three storeys high, was cast to the ground;
while a similar misfortune befel the same Community at
another of their establishments, some distance off. In
neither case, however, was anyone hurt! This occurred on
the 11th of November, 1863, Feast of S. Martin of Tours.
The Abbé Cestac adds that Providence came to the aid of the
good religious, and enabled them to restore their injured
property.

THE MIRACULOUS PRAYER.

August Queen of Heaven! Sovereign Mistress of the
Angels! Thou, who from the beginning hast received from

God the power and mission to crush the head of Satan; we humbly beseech thee to send thy holy legions that, under thy command and by thy power, they may pursue the evil spirits; encounter them on every side; resist their bold attacks, and drive them hence into the abyss of everlasting woe. Amen.

"𝔚𝔥𝔬 is like unto 𝔊𝔬𝔡!"

An Indulgence of 40 days is attached to the devout recital of this prayer.

✝ ETIENNE, Bishop of Lausanne.

RECORD OF EVENTS.

THE Papal audiences still continue. In the month of March the Catholics of the United States of America presented their address to the Pope, by a deputation which was introduced by the Very Rev. Dr. Chatard, rector of the American College. An advocate of New York, Mr. Glover, read the address, to which his Holiness replied in French as follows :—

"I am greatly consoled by the kind expressions which I have just heard, the more that they represent, not only the sentiments of the circle here present but those of all American Catholics; and in truth these protestations of sincere affection and devotion render me greatly indebted to the nation that offers them. I feel myself under the obligations of gratitude and of prayer for a country particularly blessed by God with fertility of soil and with prosperity of industry, both sources of great wealth; I pray that God may increase all these good things and render them fruitful, but I also wish that they may not be the only desire of those who possess them. North America is the richest country on the earth, but riches ought not to be her only treasure. In the gospel of this morning Jesus Christ says, 'Where your treasure is there will be your heart also.' The American nation is one given to commerce and merchandise of all descriptions; so far, so good, for to all men it is necessary to provide for the wants of this life, and to all it is permitted to trade honestly in the things that God has given. It is just and proper also that heads of families should educate and maintain their children according to the exigencies of their condition of life, but we must not have an overweening love of riches, we must not attach ourselves too much to them, lest we set our hearts on them, for this is reproved by Jesus Christ. He too had his little purse, and moreover the administrator of it—Judas, and we know how this man finished from his too great love of money. Then, there may be possessions, and even great possessions, but we must not put our hearts in them. This is the only reflection I shall now make, praying God to protect you and to give us all strength and courage in all trials and difficulties. Here we live on a volcano, here we have a Government which is the crater of a volcano, but God is sufficient to save us." The Pope then gave his blessing and the deputation took their leave.

On the 8th of March an important international deputation received an audience from the Pope, consisting of the representatives from Great Britain and Ireland, Austria, France, Belgium, Prussia, Spain, the United States of America, and from Switzerland. Their object was to place in the hands of the Holy Father a united protest against the contemplated act of the Piedmontese Government in its projected law for the suppression and spoliation of the religious orders.

Their united address was read to the Pope in the Hall of the Consistory, by the Prince Alfred of Lichtenstein, and amid many expressions of uncompromising loyalty to the person and authority of the successor of S. Peter, fearlessly denounced the intended iniquitous projects of the Italian Government using the following remarkable words, " *With the enemies that rage around you, Holy Father, no conciliation is possible, and war with such enemies is not to be feared. It is only peace that is dangerous.*"

The Pope then rose and replied as follows :—

"The sentiments you have manifested towards me command my gratitude. There are truths expressed in your address, harsh truths, but still truths. In reply, I will take the words of the first Vicar of Jesus Christ, I will take the words of S. Peter. The Prince of the Apostles addressed himself to various cities, to various nations. He wrote to those of Pontus, of Galatia, of Bithynia, and of Asia, and to them all he addressed one letter. You in one respect represent the object of this letter, for to your different nationalities and languages I reply only this once. I receive your words, and I reply with the Apostle *Gratia vobis et pax multiplicetur*; May the grace of God always dwell in your souls, and the peace of Christ be multiplied in your hearts. 'I know well, even I,' proceeded the Apostle, 'that this peace cannot be lasting; that peace will always be accompanied by conflicts and wars as it was in the case of the Divine Master of whom it is written, *Prophetaverunt Prophetæ passiones Christi et glorias posteriores.* So that we must hope that after we have participated in troubles and sorrows, you with me, and I with you and those whom you represent, we may sing of the mercies of God and the hosannas and glories of the Church of Christ.'

"This was the faith of S. Peter and ought to be ours. Faith was the grand characteristic of the Prince of the Apostles. It was faith which taught him to say when Jesus asked, 'Whom do men say that I am? Thou art the Christ, the Son of the living God.' This it was that merited the reply which hailed him Blessed : *Beatus tu, Simon Barjona, quia caro et sanguis non revelavit tibi*—Blessed art thou, not because flesh and blood has revealed to thee the doctrine of my Divinity, but because thus the Eternal Father has inspired thee.—*Non quia caro et sanguis revelavit tibi, sed Pater meus qui in cœlis est.*

"From this arises that Peter is the foundation of the Church. It is true that the foundation thereof is Jesus Christ, the chief corner-stone on which is raised this majestic temple, but Jesus Christ was pleased to associate with Himself His Vicar, and in the contact of these two stones S. Peter has followed in part the greatness of Christ, and has himself become great by virtue of Jesus Christ—*Quæ mihi sunt potestate propria, hæc tibi participatione communia.* Thus says the holy Pontiff S. Leo."

The Pope then remarked upon the folly of the Government, which indulged in the delusion that they could educate the clergy of the Church on their own pattern, and revive the Byzantine Cæsarism, which had become ridiculous before it was destroyed by an infidel power.

"Let us hope," he said in conclusion, "that this union between Christians and their Clergy, between the Clergy and their Bishops, between the Bishops and the Sovereign Pontiff may form a compact phalanx that need never fear the fury of the adversary.—Benedictio, &c."

On the following day the Pope received a deputation of the Central Committee of the Italian Catholic Union, whose spokesman, Count Grassi, read an address. The Holy Father in the course of his reply spoke as follows :—

"Here is another manifestation that you make in union with the good and pious Catholics who have come to represent the faith of so many nations. Here is another demonstration that the enemies of God and His Church may see, and know that you are not ashamed of being true Christians, followers and imitators of Jesus Christ. And note that Jesus Christ, when there was a question of confessing before his enemies His Divinity, feared not to do so. When he was asked, '*Art thou the Son of the Living God ?*' he replied '*I am.*' He knew that this confession would take Him to Calvary and the Cross, yet He hesitated not a moment to declare who He was ; and this was to teach us the courage we ought to have in similar circumstances, reminding us that men may kill the body but not the soul ; they may have power over the temporal life, but cannot deprive us of the eternal one."

The Bishops of the immediate neighbourhood of Rome sought an audience of the Pope, and presented him with an address protesting against the projected laws of the Italian kingdom. The Holy Father counselled them to follow the counsel of the Holy Ghost. "Waste not words where there is no hearing," and not to apply for justice to those who, ruling Italy at the present time, trample justice under foot.

We find the following remarkable warning from a sermon by a Protestant preacher, a Mr. Nevins, quoted from a

London journal, in the *Propagateur de la devotion à S. Joseph*, for April. "You wealthy citizens of the towns in England, you rich bankers, you proprietors of great domains, you proud and prosperous merchants, tremble. Your hearts beat with joy at the suppression of the religious orders in Rome, and of the Jesuits in Germany. What will you say when the fanatic communists and socialists shall declare that capitalists are the enemies of nations. Bitter, but too late will be your regrets for having hastened on those days of disaster, by aiding the man you are pleased to call the great Bismark to persecute and expel the sons of S. Ignatius of Loyola."

THE DOWNFALL OF THE GLADSTONE GODLESS UNIVERSITY SCHEME.—The unbelieving politicians of our nineteenth century, whose ignorance and pride combine to fill their minds with the notion that they hold in their own hands the power to build up and construct society after their own pattern by their public legislation and command of the public revenues, have had an opportunity for reflexion furnished to them by the sudden downfall of the Godless University Scheme, constructed, with great labour and thoughtful study, by the Gladstone ministry.

This ministry said, "Come, let us make a University," but apparently they failed sufficiently to take into account what would be the effect of the "confusion of tongues" on their design. The event has turned out to be a perfect repetition, on a small scale, of the attempt to build the Tower of Babel. Their University was planned after the pattern of a certain tower, the top of which was to reach to heaven; that is to say, it was to undertake to form the minds of its scholars in the highest branches of knowledge that remain after omitting the knowledge of God and such branches of history in which the works of God are especially recorded, and the treatises of philosophy which border upon the knowledge of God. Their plan was to make a tower reaching to heaven without these, the confusion of tongues, however, has completely upset their scheme, "et cessaverunt ædificare civitatem." Mr. Gladstone has been compelled for the moment to desist from building "his tower," but the warning of his fall, notwithstanding, appears to be lost upon others.

The Psalmist says of God, "*Thou teachest man knowledge*," and Jesus Christ has sent those into all nations, to whom He said, "*Go ye and teach all nations.*" Catholics, consequently, who believe in these words can have no University which is not erected in virtue of power obtained from the Vicar of Jesus Christ. All other attempts to construct a University like the one that has just broken down, will only repeat the confusion of tongues that must always accompany each successive attempt to build a new Tower of Babel. The moral of what has happened is easily read by Catholics in the verse of the Psalm, "Except the Lord build the house, the labour of them that build it is in vain."

An instructive little work has been written by a zealous Catholic, on the pattern of Pope's "Essay on Man," in easy verse, treating of the Education Question.* It sums up the objections of the Catholics to the unbelieving plan of a state University in the following terse words :—

> It must not come, 'fore God and man,
> We one and all reject a plan
> Designed to blight our sainted soil,
> And make it part of Satan's spoil.
> It must not come; you toil in vain,
> To rot our heart, to sap our brain.

Out of evil God brings good. The weakness of the Catholic side in all times and places has its root in our own failings and shortcomings. "O, Israel," says the prophet, "thou hast destroyed thyself." The enemies will infallibly say, "You Catholics do nothing but act the part of the dog in the manger." What you do to educate yourselves is little or nothing, and when any one else is willing to come to the rescue, you raise the cry of "Wolf," "Wolf," "the faith is in danger." We must remember the Pope's words : "Tempus faciendi, Domine, dissipaverunt legem tuam." Our own independent exertions to teach and improve our own people is what is needed as our one great safeguard. We ought to say, "Let us alone to do our own work; we understand it better than you," and our enemy should not be able to say, "No, we cannot let you alone, for if we were to let you alone, you would not do your work, and your people would continue, as they have been, to be left to live and die in their ignorance."

---

* *Essay on the Education Question*, viewed in relation to the danger of placing Catholic youths with Protestant or infidel teachers. By U. C. G., Dublin: McGlashan & Gill. London: Burns, Oates, & Co.

MIRACULOUS CURES IN PARIS.

(We copy the following from the *Guardian*, April 2.)

In this week's *Semaine Religieuse*, a publication of at least diocesan authority, a narrative, under the head of *Deux guérisons miraculeuses, d Batignolles*, is given with such marked circumstantiality of detail as "offering all the character of miracles" as to seem to require some notice. Batignolles, as is well known, is a northern suburb of Paris. An upholsterer's child there, of thirteen years old, Armand Wallet by name, 36, Rue Truffault, had, after three years of suffering from rheumatism, become a complete cripple, subject to violent nervous convulsions. On the 18th of February last, at 8 a.m., after a violent attack, the child exclaimed to his mother, who came to him with remedies, "Mother, I see the Blessed Virgin there on the window-sill." The mother said, "Perhaps she has come to heal you." And, in fact, the cure followed instantaneously. The doctor (name and address given) was called in, and substantiated the fact. The apparition was visible to the child for six days and nights successively, under any light or no light. The figure was "only about a palm in height, but animated, making signs to the child to kneel, or to take a chaplet when offered to him." Sometimes it carried the Infant Jesus, sometimes assumed the attitude of the Immaculate Conception. The apparition was seen by many others, especially children (names given, with that of the Abbé de la Perche, vicar of S. Mary's, who interrogated the several children, and found them all to agree in details, &c.) "Also Mdme. Lemercier, a grave person, who saw the Blessed Virgin twice."

Another child in the same quarter, Alfred Fontès, a scholar at the Petit-Séminaire, was taken ill—at the point of death, in fact, as certified by two doctors (names and addresses given). On the 16th of this month, the Abbé Bourgeat, also a vicar at S. Mary's, on visiting the child *in extremis*, "felt himself compelled to say to its mother, on leaving, 'Your child will be suddenly cured.' He was thinking of the cure of Armand Wallet." On the 17th, the child suddenly cried out to its mother, "I am cured. I have seen the Blessed Virgin." The vision was that of "the Immaculate Virgin, clad in blue and white, and of surpassing brilliancy. The features were visible, but not the eyes." The cure was complete and instantaneous. "The enormous swelling of the stomach had entirely disappeared. The excessively emaciated limbs had recovered their full size and flesh. Pain and sickness had disappeared, and health was perfect. The child got up and eat heartily." The certificate of Dr. Crestey is given, and concludes thus:—" These facts were certified by me on the very same day; and I affirm, on my soul and conscience, that they are the result of a miracle, no scientific reasons being capable of explaining such a state of things."

The above narratives, observes the *Guardian*, are evidently inserted to challenge and defy all inquiry. They are accompanied by minute details of names, addresses, diseases, witnesses, authorities of every kind, in marked and pretentious display; and are now published in a religious journal holding almost acknowledged official rank within the diocese of Paris.

The above is purposely quoted from the pages of the *Guardian* Newspaper, an organ in high favour with the large majority of the Clergy and people of the established Church, that we may derive fresh courage in our prayers for the Conversion of our Country. It is but a short time since that it was almost as much a dogma in the Established Church as anything else that miracles had long ago ceased. The above narrative is a proof, at least, that this false prepossession is losing its hold. May God in his mercy grant the still more rapid falling away of this and the many other similar false prepossessions that stand in the way of the conversion we pray for.

RELIGIOUS PILGRIMAGES IN BELGIUM FOR THE DELIVER- ANCE OF THE POPE.

THE Catholics in Belgium are foremost in setting an example to their brethren of other countries. On Easter Monday an immense crowd of devout worshippers repaired to the celebrated Sanctuary of the Blessed Virgin in Walcourt, in the Diocese of Namur; The Bishop of Namur preached to the multitude assembled; he drew a forcible picture of the evils of society and said that the cause of all these evils was the conspiracy of men without faith to cast Jesus Christ out, and to govern their respective nations, without taking into account what Jesus Christ has revealed respecting the eternal destinies of men.

Our Lord Jesus Christ cannot permit a design of the kind to be carried into effect, but as nations and their governments appear unwilling to hear any voice of warning, God seems decided to let events convey the warning. Here the respected prelate pointedly referred to the downfall of the French Napoleonic Empire, a punishment which it richly deserved for its felonies against the Papacy, to the sufferings of the city of Paris, and to the continually deteriorating condition of Italy.

THE MIRACULOUS CONVERSION OF MARY DOLORES ELLEN PLUMLEY,

MEMBER OF THE CONFRATERNITY OF THE HOLY ROSARY (DECEASED APRIL 7TH, 1873.) RELATED BY HER SURVIVING SISTER.

IN gratitude to Almighty God I the only surviving sister of the above, desire, for the sake of edification and the confirmation of others in their faith, to make known the miracle by which my sister was brought to the Catholic Church.   As soon as she reached womanhood she was, by God's mercy, fully awakened to the necessity of knowing with certainty what to believe. In her first inquiries she was assisted by a priest now retired from active service.   One by one the various difficulties commonly experienced by Protestants gave way, and the diligent attendance on the offices of the month of Mary, at St. George's Cathedral, led her to seek an interview with the Rev. Dr. Doyle.   She remained under his instruction till the Feast of Corpus Christi came.   All along the mystery of the real presence had been her great difficulty ; and when she entered the cathedral on the feast day, and saw the lights, the flowers, and decorations of the altar, she thought, " Oh, my God, if the Holy Eucharist be indeed what Catholics say it is, how insufficient are all the beauty and reverence that men can bring to celebrate so great a miracle; but if it be all a delusion, what a mockery is all I now look on."   She then knelt, humbly praying for some answer to her fervent petition that Almighty God would vouchsafe to enlighten her in this matter.

Having thus prayed, she rose from her knees, and her

attention became fixed on the details of the ceremony; she did not, as she afterwards said, think the music suitable, and as, by-and-by, the procession came down the church, her eye was caught by the sight of the flamers that were scattered before the sacred Host, and also by the guttering of the tapers used.

I mention these things that none may say her imagination was in an excited state; at that time (more than twenty years ago), there were very few worshippers present, and little in the ceremony itself to speak to the senses of the spectators.   But, be it remembered, Ellen had fervently prayed for light, and now behold the mercy of God to her! As the procession drew near, she covered her face and knelt, and a voice, real, and clear, and distinct, a voice from heaven itself, then said in her ear, " Jesus of Nazareth passeth by." Thus, in the very words of Holy Scripture was her prayer miraculously answered.   She was received into the Church the next day, and has lived a holy life worthy of such a beginning.

Her path has been one of sorrow and suffering, but she has had the grace of offering it all to God in union with the sufferings of Christ Jesus.   As I leant over her just as her soul departed to compose her limbs for the tomb, a fragrant odour, as of violets, greeted my nostrils; and her sweet face, as she lay in death, seemed to the loving and charitable souls who looked on it already to bear the seal of the perfect peace, which through the sacrifice and merits of Christ is the reward promised to those who are faithful to the end.

M. F. A. P.

2, Henstridge Villas,
St. John's Wood, N.W.
April 14th, 1873.

THE

𝔐onthly 𝔐agazine of the 𝔥oly 𝔐osary.

NEW SERIES.

No. 11.]   JUNE.   [A.D. 1873.

No. II.—SACRUM SEPTENARIUM: A WHITSUNTIDE INSTRUCTION;

OR, THE BLESSED VIRGIN, THE MOTHER GIVEN BY GOD TO THE CHRISTIAN FAMILY, SHOWING TO HER CHILDREN THE FAULTLESS PATTERN OF A PERFECT CORRESPONDENCE WITH THE SEVEN GIFTS OF THE HOLY GHOST.

IN our preceding instruction we shall find that we have come clearly in view of three very important truths, each in their degree calculated to exert an extremely practical influence on our entire conduct throughout life. The first is,—

I. That in the economy of the Christian Redemption, the Holy Virgin Mother of Jesus has been given as a mother to the whole of the great Christian family, to place before her children a true and perfect mother's example, for their imitation and guidance.

II. That, being herself endowed with the seven gifts of the Holy Ghost, she has set her children the special example of a perfect correspondence with these gifts, and of the manner in which the actions of daily life ought to be perfectly controlled and directed by them.

III. That God in the riches of His grace, and desiring that all men should be saved and come to the knowledge of the truth, has given to all the children of the Christian family, in the holy Sacrament of Confirmation, the same seven gifts of the Holy Ghost; through which they receive the capacity of profiting by the example which their great Mother has placed before them of a perfect correspondence with these gifts.

If proof could be supposed to be needed, that God gives these seven gifts of the Holy Ghost—the Sacrum Septenarium for which the Church prays at the season of Pentecost—to all without reserve, it will only be necessary to seek our proof from the office for the administration of the sacrament of Confirmation.

(Rubric.) Then the Bishop, with his hands extended towards the persons to be confirmed, says—

Let us pray.

Almighty and Everlasting God, who hast vouchsafed to regenerate these Thy servants by water and the Holy Ghost, and hast given unto them the remission of all their sins, send forth upon them Thy Sevenfold Spirit, the Holy Paraclete, from heaven.—Amen.

V. The Spirit of Wisdom and Understanding.—*R.* Amen.

V. The Spirit of Counsel and Fortitude.—*R.* Amen.

V. The Spirit of Knowledge and of Piety.—*R.* Amen.

Replenish them with the Spirit of Thy fear; and sign them with the sign of the Cross in Thy mercy unto life eternal, &c. (*From the Roman Pontifical.*)

Passing, then, from the words of the office of the administration of the sacrament, we proceed to learn as briefly as possible what is necessary to be known respecting these seven gifts of the Holy Ghost from the words of the Angelic Doctor S. Thomas of Aquin.

S. Thomas's method of treating his subjects, we perhaps ought to observe, will possibly appear a little peculiar at the present day. It consists in opening the question under consideration by a statement of the principal reasons which appear to make against his real doctrine; which being done, he brings forward some brief statement in a contrary sense, commonly taken either from the Holy Scripture or from some great and distinguished Father of the Church; after which he proceeds to unfold his own doctrine, concluding with an appropriate solution of the difficulties that he had raised against it in the beginning.

S. Thomas then first raises the doubt whether it may not be said that the gifts of the Holy Ghost are not distinguishable from many of the virtues, and that they are in fact only the Christian virtues under other names. Having met this and other difficulties by a citation from S. Gregory the Great, he proceeds to unfold his own doctrine, from which we quote the following words:—"And, therefore, in order to distinguish the Gifts from the Virtues, we shall do well to adhere to the mode of naming them which we find in the Scripture, where they are spoken of not as gifts, but as 'spirits.' Thus it is said in Isaias, 'There shall rest upon Him the Spirit of Wisdom and Understanding,' &c., from which words it is manifestly given to be understood that these seven gifts are there enumerated according as they are in us by Divine inspiration; for the word inspiration points to some moving power that acts from without. It is to be considered, indeed, that there is a twofold moving principle in man, one internal to himself, which is his reason; the other external to him, which is God. But it is manifest that everything which is moved should be rightly disposed to the power by which it is moved, and the perfection of the thing moved, in so far as it is a thing capable of being moved, is the disposition by which it is disposed to be rightly moved by the power that moves it. The more exalted, therefore, the moving power, the more necessary it is that the thing moved should be rightly disposed towards it, as we see that the scholar must be more perfectly disposed towards his master in proportion as he is to receive a higher doctrine from him. But it is manifest that the human virtues perfect the man, according as he is born to be moved by his reason in everything that he may do either outwardly or inwardly. It is necessary, therefore, that there should be in man a higher order of perfection, according to which he becomes properly disposed to be moved by God. And these perfections are called ' Gifts,' not solely because they are infused by God, but for the reason that by them a man is made prompt to be moved by the Divine Inspiration, as it is said (Isaias l.), ' The Lord hath opened mine ear and I do not gainsay, neither have I gone back.'"

From the above words of S. Thomas, we shall easily gather what his answer will be to the question, "*Are these Seven Gifts of the Holy Ghost necessary to a man for his salvation ?*"

After stating some arguments which appear to prove that the seven gifts of the Holy Ghost are not necessary to salvation, S. Thomas says: " (*Sed contra est*) But against this it is to be considered, that among the gifts, Wisdom appears to be the first in order, and the fear of the Lord the last; but both of these are necessary to salvation, for of Wisdom it is said, ' that God loveth no one except those who dwell with wisdom' (Wisd. vii.) ; and of Fear it is said, that ' he who is without fear cannot be justified' (Eccles. i.); therefore the other intermediate gifts also are necessary to salvation.

" I answer, then," S. Thomas says, " that the gifts, being, as we have said, a certain perfecting of the man, by which he is rightly disposed to hearken to the Divine inspiration, it follows that for those things for which the instinct of reason does not suffice, but an inspiration of the Holy Ghost is required, the gifts become necessary. But the human reason is perfected in two ways by God—first by natural perfection,

that is by a perfection that is according to the natural light
of reason ; and, secondly, by a certain supernatural perfection
through the theological virtues. And although this second
perfection is in itself greater than the first, the first perfection
is had by a man in a more complete manner than the second,
for the first is had by a man after the manner of a full and
entire possession, whereas the second is possessed only imperfectly, for we love and know God only imperfectly. But
it is manifest that whatsoever possesses *perfectly* either its
nature, form, or power, can act by itself in accordance with
these (not, indeed, to the exclusion of the working of God, who
inwardly works in every nature and intelligent will), whereas
that which possesses only imperfectly any nature, form, or
power, cannot so act except it be moved by another. Thus
the sun can give light by itself because it is perfectly bright
in itself ; while the moon, being imperfect in this respect, can
only give light in so far as it receives light itself; the
physician also, who perfectly knows his art, can act by
himself, whereas his pupil, who is not as yet fully initiated,
cannot act by himself, but needs to be directed how to act.
In the same manner, therefore, so far as those things are
concerned which are by nature properly subject to human
reason, a man may act by the dictate of his reason, and
if herein he receives any additional aid from God by some
special inspiration, this is to be understood to come from the
superabounding goodness of God.

" But in order to the final supernatural end to which even our
natural reason moves us, in so far as it is after a fashion
imperfectly informed by the theological virtues, the movement of our natural reason does not of itself suffice, except
there be also besides a movement and an inspiration of the
Holy Ghost, according to what is said by the Apostle, 'They
who are moved by the Spirit of God, these are the sons of
God and heirs ' (Rom. viii.) ; and in the Psalms, 'Thy Spirit
shall lead me into the right land' (Ps. cxlii.) ; the reason being
that none can come to the inheritance of that land of the
blessed except he be moved and guided by the Holy Ghost.
Hence, in order to the attainment of this final supernatural
end, it is *necessary* for a man to have the gifts of the Holy
Ghost."

S. Thomas then proceeds to treat in a similar manner
several other questions relative to these seven gifts of the
Holy Ghost, but as it is not indispensable to our subject that

we should burden our readers with his weighty words, the close reasoning of which must appear in rather strong contrast with the light kind of reading with which our own times are familiar, we shall forbear. All that our present purpose absolutely needs is gained when we have shown what the great Doctor of the Church says respecting the sovereign dignity and value of these gifts of the Holy Ghost for the purposes of Christian life, and the important part they are appointed to fulfil in rightly directing us in the work of obtaining our salvation.

Plainly nothing can be more manifest than that the gifts of God the Holy Ghost, which, as we have seen, are freely given to all in the Sacrament of Confirmation, are intended to be used and turned to good account in all humility and submissive gratitude to the Divine Giver by those who are made receivers of them. But it is clear also that they are by no means of a nature to force their efficacy upon any of those who receive them, independently of their own grateful acceptance and co-operation with them. No one by these gifts is made either pious or brave, intelligent or wise, against his will; on the contrary, our diligent co-operation with them, or, in S. Thomas's words, our disposition to be moved by them is an indispensable condition of their having their due effect. Since, then, nothing is more consonant to the very first provision of God for the bringing of His creation to perfection, than that the children of the family should be taught by the example of their Mother, it is not easy to see how there can be any one thing more beneficently devised by the mercy of God for the good of all the children of the wide-spread Christian family, than that the great Mother of this family should be known to set an example to her children for their imitation of a perfect co-operation with the seven gifts of the Holy Ghost, of which gifts we are able to affirm, on the authority of the great Doctor of the Church, that they are necessary for every Christian in order to the work of his or her salvation.

The case, to sum up in brief what we have said, stands thus : God gives to all the Christian people in the Sacrament of Confirmation the seven gifts of the Holy Ghost, and these gifts are not of a nature to force their efficacy upon even the careless or the indifferent, to say nothing of the irreverent and the scorners. In order for us to benefit by them in the work of our salvation, for which they are necessary aids, we are required to do our part to cultivate them and co-operate with them, and we must diligently dispose ourselves to be moved by them. But in the order of God's creation He has appointed, as the first law of creation, that the children should first of all begin to learn from their mother's example. What, therefore, will not be the priceless value to the Christian family of the example of their great Mother, showing them the faultless pattern of a perfect correspondence with the seven gifts of God the Holy Ghost, which by the grace and bounty of God are given freely to every member of the great Christian household, as the necessary Divine aids to assist us all in the labour of working out our salvation?

Although, then, the sacred records appear to be even sparing rather than abundant in what they have related respecting the Blessed Virgin, who has been given as Mother to the Christian family, our task will be strictly limited to gathering from them the requisite proofs of the blessed Virgin having given to her children this chosen and elect pattern of a perfect correspondence with the seven gifts of the Holy Ghost, and of her having perfectly exemplified for their guidance and imitation the effect which these gifts ought to have upon the actions of our daily life.

Should any new honour hereby accrue to the Holy Mother, whom all generations are to vie with each other in calling Blessed, whom can we find who is more worthy such honour? And if her example becomes by what we are about to say in any respect, to their exceeding great benefit, either dearer and more valued, or better understood and better appreciated by her children, "non nobis, Domine, non nobis, sed Nomini tuo da gloriam" ("Not unto us, O Lord, not unto us, but to Thy Name give the glory"). "Servi inutiles sumus" ("We are unprofitable servants").

As Cardinal Bellarmine represents the seven gifts of the Holy Ghost under the figure of a ladder, the lowest step of which, the Spirit of the Fear of the Lord, rests on the earth, and the highest, the Spirit of Wisdom, leans upon heaven, we propose at an early opportunity to commence, so to speak, our ascent of the ladder thus uniting earth and heaven, and to show how our Holy Mother gives her children the faultless example of a perfect correspondence in the first place with the gift of the Spirit of the FEAR OF THE LORD.

H. F.

(To be continued.)

FATHER IGNATIUS SPENCER, PASSIONIST,
The Apostle of Prayer for the Conversion of England.

On the 21st December, 1805, a great event happened to a
little boy. He was the child of noble parents, one on whom
the choicest gifts of rank and fortune, with all the advantages
this world can give, had been showered from earliest infancy
with an unsparing hand. But it was not till this day, his birthday, on which he reached the age of six years, that he was
considered old enough to be told, for the first time, that there
was an Almighty God, who had made him and all things, and
an eternity of rewards or punishments. When the child
became an old man, he could still recall the very room in his
home into which he had been taken by his kind Swiss
governess when she made this great announcement; and the
tender words and gracious expressions with which it was
accompanied were never afterwards obliterated from his
memory. This child was the Honourable George Spencer,
youngest son of Earl Spencer, and his early years were spent
at the family seat at Althorp, in Northamptonshire.

Two or three years later we have a different picture. He
and his brother Frederick, who was a little older than himself, are now at Eton, living at the house of a tutor, the Rev.
Richard Godley. The poor children are running the gauntlet
of the crowded playing-fields, on their way home from school.
They incur the wrath of the elder cricketers if they refuse
to fag for them and stop their balls, while the prospect of
Mr. Godley's anger if they are a few minutes late is still
more terrible. This miserable ordeal occurs, not once only,
but several times each day. They are obliged to appear
publicly with the other boys at school, chapel, and at least
every three hours during the day, and these unhappy playing-
fields have to be passed through each time. They are the
only boys obliged to return home without delay, and a set of
big bullies make it their business to watch and torment them.
No wonder they felt "in an enemy's country, obliged to guard
against danger on all sides," and that "shrinking and skulk-
-ing beyond the ordinary lot of little schoolboys" became
inevitable.*

Mr. Godley was "a conscientious and deeply religious
man," who, considering the eternal welfare of his pupils as

---

* Fr. Spencer's Autobiography of his Early Life, in his "Life," by Rev.
Father Pius, Passionist.

his chief concern with them, judged that their innocence
could only be guarded by cutting off all communication with
the other boys out of school hours.   Stern as was his discipline, it had the effect, "which those who know what our
public schools are will reckon almost incredible," of preserving
George during the first four years of his Eton life from the evil
and contamination with which he was surrounded.   During
the last of these years Frederick went to sea, and Mr. Godley
attached himself strongly to the desolate child who was now
his only pupil.   Under his influence George began decidedly
to love and take pleasure in religion.   He had not, indeed,
any definite understanding of the great doctrines of revelation,
but he believed implicitly what he was taught; took great
delight in hearing Mr. Godley talk, as he continually did, on
religious subjects; had a great horror of sin; and thought
with pleasure that he was intended himself to be a clergyman.
These dispositions were greatly increased by his accompanying
Mr. Godley on a visit of six weeks to his mother and sisters,
who lived at Chester.   These ladies showed him much kindness, and recommended him various books, such as "The
Pilgrim's Progress," which made a great impression upon
him.   He returned to Eton full of ardent desire to keep
himself untainted by sin, and to shun all those boys whom
he knew to be mockers of religion.   From that time, and
during the first part of the summer holidays, he knew no
delight like that of being by himself at prayer.   But his
parents did not approve of his thus imbibing Mr. Godley's
views of religion, which were not what is usually called
"orthodox Church of England religion."   They therefore determined to remove him to the care of a fresh tutor, also a
clergyman, when he returned to Eton.

His new experience of school life began in September,
1812.   Here, he says, I was "effectually to be untaught what
there might be unsound about my religion, by being quickly
stripped of it altogether."   This house contained about ten or
twelve boys, and, "dreadful as was its moral condition, it was
respectable in comparison to others."   Here for the first time
he had to submit to domestic fagging, "which consisted in
performing to one or more of the fifth or sixth form boys in
the house almost all the duties of a footman or a waiter at an
inn."   This was, however, a minor evil.   The younger boys,
who were quiet and good-natured, received him kindly, but
he soon found that to get on with them he must abandon

devotion, and sacrifice his principles by joining in their pilfering excursions, which caused him perfect misery, both from his natural timidity and tender conscience. " One day we went to pick up walnuts in a park near Eton; another day to steal beans and turnips, or the like, from fields and gardens; those more bold, to take ducks and chickens from farmyards." For in this great public school, where the flower of the youth of England are popularly supposed to be educated to a standard unattainable in any other system, a boy " for robbing orchards and farmyards would be honoured and extolled, and so much the more if, in doing it, one or two or three together had violently beaten the farmer's boy, or even himself." A boy would not even be blamed for stealing his schoolfellows' books, though to take money was considered highly disgraceful.

But it is only Father Spencer's own words that can adequately describe the Eton boy of his day : " My ignorance in the mysteries of iniquity was soon apparent. However much I strove to keep my countenance firm, I could not hear immodesties without blushing. I was on this account a choice object of fun to some of the boys, who took delight in forcing me to hear instructions in iniquity. One evening after another, I well remember, the quarters would be invaded where I and my companions were established; all our little employments would be interrupted, our rooms filled with dirt, our beds, perhaps, tossed about, and a noisy row kept up for hours, of which sometimes one and sometimes another of our set was the principal butt. I was set up as a choice object, of course, on account of my simplicity and inexperience in their ways, so that some of the partners of these plagues with me would blame me for being so silly as to pretend ignorance of what their foul expressions meant; for they could not believe it possible that I should really be so simple as not to understand them. I maintained for some time a weak conflict in my soul against all this flood of evil. For a little time I found one short space of comfort through the day, when, at length, after an evening thus spent, I got to bed, and in secret wept and prayed myself to sleep; but the trial was too strong and too often repeated. I had no kind friend to speak to.

"Mr. Godley still lived at the Wharf, and, though he seemed to think it right not to press himself upon me, he asked me to come and dine when I pleased. Two or three times I went to dine with him, and these were my last really happy days, when for an hour or two I could give my mind liberty to feel at ease, and recollect my former feelings in his kindly company.   But I could not, I dared not, tell him all I was now exposed to, and so I was left to stand my ground alone. . . .   It might be, perhaps, ten days after my arrival at Mr. ——'s when I gave up all attempt to pray; and I think I did not say one word of prayer for the two years and more that I afterwards continued there."

It was, perhaps, happy for George Spencer that the negligence of the Eton masters for the advancement of their pupils in learning was equal to their carelessness of their morals. It led to his being placed under the care of Mr. Blomfield, afterwards Protestant Bishop of London, whom Earl Spencer had recently presented to a living in his gift at Dunton, in Buckinghamshire.   He spent here the two last years before entering Cambridge.   The change was of great advantage. The regular habits and moral tone of the family, the daily prayers and prominence of religious instruction, revived much of his early inclination to good.   It was, as he says, a little breathing-time before the "second cruel and more ruinous devastation" he was to undergo in his college career.   He prepared seriously for Confirmation at Easter, 1816; resolved to approach the Sacrament from time to time, and resumed many of his old practices of private devotion.   He bought a manual of prayer, and spent much time in "self-examination over the table of sins in the book, which was similar to our Catholic Preparation for Confession."   These devout habits ceased at his entrance into the University of Cambridge, where he was entered fellow commoner of Trinity in the spring of 1817, and for some years every kind of religious impression or influence seems to have wholly ceased and faded away from his mind.

His university career was, however, highly creditable.   The real love of study and learning with which Mr. Blomfield had inspired him now stood him in stead, and preserved him from much of the dissipation around him, and it enabled him to pass through his course with honour.   One great defect in his character—a great weakness in the point of human respect—was counteracted by that extraordinary susceptibility to good influence which with him, as with so many who are destined largely to influence others, was a marked feature.   We have a charming glimpse of an evening spent in London with his elder brother Robert, a commander in the navy, who warned him, as a parting advice, "never to laugh or look pleased when forced to hear immoral conversation." These few words, coming, as they did, from a gay, gallant, young officer, were, he says, of "infinite service" to him. He began his college life with many good purposes of leading a moral life, and persevered for a long time in keeping clear of the dissipation which prevailed among his companions, though any intimation of disapproval of what others did, on moral or religious grounds, would not have been tolerated. "The crying, universal, and most frightful evil of the place was open immorality." For a time his horror of vice made him struggle manfully, but in the end the "fashion of iniquity" became too strong for him, and his dread of being unlike others made him fall from many of his good purposes. Still the mercy of God seemed to hold him back, as it were, at the very brink of the precipice, and he was preserved from great and irretrievable excesses. His university career closed with great honour, and he received his degree as Master of Arts, from the Duke of Gloucester, in 1819. He had attended twenty-five divinity lectures, and obtained the certificate necessary for ordination whenever he chose to apply for it.

His time was now spent chiefly with his parents, who introduced him into the best London society, which he greatly enjoyed. He was a graceful, handsome young man, nearly six feet high; a great dandy, fond of balls and flirtations, and with an enthusiastic love for all athletic sports. Still his old tendency to melancholy and morbid human respect caused him at times much suffering. He travelled with his parents for a twelvemonth on the Continent. They were at Rome for Holy Week and wintered at Naples. But the sights and sounds of a Catholic land had no charms for him, except as mere spectacles of curiosity and amusement. A doubt that the Catholic religion might be the true one never so much as crossed his mind. It is truly marvellous to find that positively the only direct religious impression he could remember at this time was a great fear of hell and of the judgments of God which seized him at the spectacle of Don Giovanni being carried into the lower regions by a troop of devils, at the opera-house in Paris!

When he was of age he began to think of his future ordination. Though his religious opinions were wholly unformed, he looked forward with pleasure to being a clergyman, as the means of leading a good and useful life. He began to write a sermon, which he finished in six months, and consulted the diocesan examiner as to what books he should study; but that gentleman most graciously assured him that, with his talents and good qualities, he should not think of subjecting him to an examination except as a matter of form. Certainly, his preparation for Orders was not of a laborious character.

George Spencer was ordained deacon by the Protestant Bishop of Peterborough on the 22nd December, 1822. Though he regarded this event in a cool, business-like manner, and one requiring no special religious preparation, yet we now trace the beginning of the great change which was to lead to conversion and sanctification.

He was a man who gave himself wholly to whatever he undertook; and the same energy and single-mindedness with which he had pursued his studies, his field-sports, and other amusements, were now brought to bear, with undivided force, on the duties of his profession. Above all, he soon became absorbed in visiting the poor; and it is interesting to find that he tried at once to bring them to the long-neglected Sacraments. During the first fortnight of his clerical life he baptized the nine children of the village blacksmith. "On the first Easter Sunday of his ministry he gives thanks to God and prays against pride, at having 130 communicants." But the number of Dissenters in his parish caused him much annoyance, and doubts and difficulties of mind as to religion first began to occur to him. He prepared, however, with care for his ordination—refused to play at whist with the bishop " and the other clergy and their ladies on the evening before," felt strongly what he calls the " awful tie of the priesthood," and devoted himself most solemnly to the service of his Divine Master. The ceremony took place on the 13th of June, 1824, and he was inducted to the excellent family living of Brington n the beginning of the next year.
i

(*To be continued.*)

THE FEAST OF SS. PETER AND PAUL, June 29, 1873.
ROMA CAPTA.*

DOES the senseless world imagine
　　That the deathless Church is dead,
That her ancient crown is broken,
　　And her former glory fled?
True it is the Holy City
　　Is abandoned to the world,
And the standards of rebellion
　　Round her ramparts float unfurled.

What, though Sion lies downtrodden,
　　And the brilliant star has set
On your gallant deeds of daring,
　　Allet, Kanzler, and Charette—
Never shall the Rock be broken,
　　Never shall the earth prevail,
Where the very gates infernal
　　In their strong endeavour fail.

God on high, thy Church is like Thee,
　　Always peaceful and secure,
Hated by the sons of darkness,
　　For they know that she is pure.
And she stands and fights unflinching,
　　Bearing up the bloodstained sign,
Which, till all the worlds are shattered,
　　Shall not lose its power divine.

And she sees her mighty empire
　　Growing like the Psalmist's tree,
Shading with fresh living branches
　　All the rivers and the sea.
Far away amid the Indies,
　　There her voice is feared and known,
On the shores of Austral Asia
　　Hearts are found her power to own.

On the barbarous Corea
　　Hundreds of her sons have bled,
And the life-blood of her martyrs
　　Stains the coast of China red.

Rushing comes she back to England,
  Like a vast, resistless wave.
(Never to the Tudor princes
  Christ the keys eternal gave.)

With the wandering child of Erin
  She hath crossed the Atlantic foam,
On the shores of pale Missouri
  She hath founded her a home.
Wondrous in her glorious union,
  Binding fellow man with man,
From the rocks of Connemara
  To the Islands of Japan.

Rome the new, like Rome the olden,
  To the world proclaims aloud,
I will spare the meek and contrite,
  But I war against the proud.
What the men of Babel could not
  In their strange confusion do,
I, in my more wondrous concord,
  Did, and have established too.

On the Cross I found the Latin,
  And I spread that changeless tongue
Either side the Western Ocean,
  All the barbarous tribes among,
Till my children lisped my language,
  And, with durance all their own,
Built my heavenward-pointing palace,
  Slowly piling stone on stone.

It hath altars for foundations,
  And the battlements are bright,
Far above in holy places,
  In the uncreated light.
Hither come and rest, ye nations,
  Lay your weary weapons down,
To the proud I deal destruction,
  But, to all who weep, a crown.

                          A. W. EDGELL.

No. III.—THE SOCIAL DEVOTION OF THE ROSARY:

A SCHOOL OF CHRISTIAN IMPROVEMENT FOR ALL CATHOLIC PEOPLE,
BOTH RICH AND POOR.

No. II.—FREE CONSENT ON THE PART OF THE SUBJECT THE
NECESSARY CONDITION OF ALL HOPE OF IMPROVEMENT.

WE have been proposing the social devotion of the Rosary as
a very effective school of Christian improvement for all classes.
Now, the one principle from which alone any improvement
can come, in the case of rational beings, is their own consent
to be improved. "You may expel Nature with a fork (i.e.,
an instrument of torture), but it will always come back
again," says the Roman poet. We cure the brute creation of
their vices and make them amenable to the service of their
owners, by discipline more or less severe, according to the
needs of the particular case, and this without asking their
consent or consulting them in any way. The brute creatures
must either be made to serve the will of their owners or be
put to death. But, if men need improvement, the first requisite in leading them on to improvement is to obtain their
consent to come to be improved. God Almighty, who
is Lord of all, may, and by no means unfrequently actually
does, administer the rod of correction to men, using for this
purpose persecutors of the Church, wars, pestilences, famines,
and a vast variety of visitations, both upon whole people as
also upon individuals; but He, usually speaking, reserves the
application of the rod of correction in the ways above-mentioned entirely to Himself. The labour of His Church on
earth, in bringing about the improvement of His people, must
always have for its groundwork the willing consent of those
who come to be improved.

Now, when we claim for the social devotion of the Rosary
that it should be valued as a very effective school of improvement, at least it is plain that it clearly possesses the first and
foremost condition, that is in other words the indispensable
groundwork, upon which alone improvement is possible—viz.,
the free consent of those who come to be improved. We
cannot impose the assembling for the recitation of Rosary in
common upon anyone as an ordinary obligation. By way of
a salutary penance, it may, indeed, for particular reasons, be
imposed for a limited time upon this or that person; but even
then this has its root in the free will of the person who has
come to the sacred tribunal; to the multitude it must always

remain a matter of their own free choice whether they are pleased to come or to stay away.

Happily, however, for the welfare of the society of the faithful, there is in the very nature of humanity, which God has made, a feeling and instinct that human life is essentially a social thing, and that for the defence, as well as for the enjoyment of even natural life, it is indispensable for human creatures to do the very best they can to live in the vicinity of each other, and to try to punish and repress the vices and acts of injustice which render such society with each other impossible.   This natural feeling of the need of society one with another passes over into the domain of faith, and becomes, under Divine grace, a holy motive power, leading the Christian people to love to frequent the assemblies that are held for the purposes of public prayer and their own sanctification, and to find comfort and consolation in being able to associate with each other in acts of worship, praise and intercessory prayer.   There is, therefore, in every locality where a number of Catholics live within practicable reach of a sanctuary or a place of assembly for prayer in common, a kind of moral guarantee or reasonable certainty that a sufficient number will always be disposed to avail themselves of the opportunities that are put in their way for assembling themselves together for purposes of prayer; and as they come willingly, so they bring with them, as we have above said, the first condition and groundwork of all capacity for improvement—namely, their own consent to the improving and ameliorating influences within the reach of which they are willing to place themselves.

So far, then, all promises well; and as all the usual authorised prayers cannot fail to be good and excellent in their degree, here is the Christian school of improvement opened, and in active operation, by the simple assembling of the people together for prayer in common; and it is evidently the Apostle's earnest exhortation that the Christian people should be abundantly furnished with such opportunities for their assembling together, and for thus helping each other for their mutual comfort, encouragement, and benefit.

But ours is a special purpose, in particular, with the devotion of the Rosary, whose cause we desire to plead as a something that has a speciality and a leading part of its own to take in the improvement which may be hoped for from such frequent voluntary assemblies, and we must proceed to set forth the reasons why we thus regard it.

It will not be difficult to recall to life, in the minds of those who come to it, the knowledge which must be already there, that the Rosary is the special devotion of the Holy Mother, whose care is over all and whom those who assemble in the church for the recital of the Rosary in common undoubtedly intend to honour in a special manner. With this for a foundation, it will not be difficult to remind all who are attracted to it of the words in which the Church addresses the Blessed Virgin in the season of Advent: " *Succurre cadenti surgere qui curat populo* " ("Succour the falling people who manifest the desire to rise.") The charitable monitor will thus be able to say to these people, "Now, you see, good people, the Blessed Virgin Mother has her eyes open and takes account how her children conduct themselves, and what the dispositions are that they manifest. To gain a title to her favour and help, you must show on your side a real desire to rise; you must not helplessly give yourself over to settle and sink down in your bad habits, you must make an effort, like men and Christians, to rise up out of your evil ways. You can at once ask for and obtain her help, if you do your part. For example, if you make up your mind, for the honour of the Blessed Virgin, that you will break off from the companions who lead you away, drinking on the Saturday night after you have had your reckoning; that you will take home all your wages to your wife, and that you will begin and get your clothes out of pawn, and return to your duty as Christians, by commencing to go again to Mass on a Sunday ; that you will set yourself to get your wife and children decent clothing that they may begin to go to Mass also, that you will begin to see that your children are at least sent to learn their catechism on the Sunday. If you make up your mind to do this, in order to honour the Blessed Mother of God, you will plainly then manifest a very praiseworthy disposition to rise, and then the whole Church in the Advent season diligently invokes the Blessed Virgin to take you under her especial care, because, though it may be true that you have fallen into a bad way, still you are manifesting a sincere desire to rise, and in this case the whole Church calls on the Mother of God to help you."

Thus we may claim to show cause why it must always be a very special act of mercy and charity, on behalf of a large and numerous class, to place within their reach the oppor-

tunity for assembling themselves for the recitation of the
Rosary. As to how these assemblies may be still further
improved for their benefit we will reserve for another
number.

(To be continued.)

S. WINIFRED'S WELL, IN FLINTSHIRE, NORTH WALES,
AND ITS MIRACULOUS CURES.

IN our number for April we gave a narrative of a remarkable
miraculous cure that had been effected by the water from the
fountain that burst suddenly from the earth in the grotto at
Lourdes, in the South of France, after the apparition of the
Blessed Virgin there to the girl Bernadette Soubirons, and
of the challenge publicly given to the unbelievers of France
by a M. Edmund Artus to stake a considerable sum of money
(£400 a side) on the question whether the miraculous cures
related in the work of M. Henri Laserre could be proved upon
evidence to the satisfaction of an international jury of scientific
men. Our readers will be pleased to learn, from the following
narratives, that we are not entirely strangers to the working
of miracles in our own land. When the Evil One, profiting
as he is always on the watch to do by the sins of the people
of God, prevailed against the cause of faith in England in the
reign of Henry VIII., with the instinct of the implacable
enemy that he always is and will be, his first use of his power
as conqueror was to destroy the sacred relics of the saints and
their shrines at which miraculous cures were continually
worked. The two chief places in England at that time where
miraculous cures were most abundant were the respective
shrines of S. Thomas Becket, archbishop and martyr, in
Canterbury, and of S. Cuthbert, bishop and confessor, in
Durham. S. Thomas Becket's shrine was rifled, and his
relics were publicly burnt in the market-place in Canterbury,
and his canonization was cancelled as far as any impious
legal mock proceeding could be of any avail; and the shrine
of S. Cuthbert was in like manner destroyed, though the
precious relics themselves were providentially preserved; the
secret of their resting-place continuing to be transmitted in
the Benedictine Order. Such were the immediate conse-

quences, to the working of miraculous cures, of the victory of
the Evil One in England; but though his destroying power
extended over the relics of saints, the custody of which then
came into his hands, he did not find it quite as easy a matter
to dispose to his satisfaction of the holy wells which existed
in different parts of the country.

"Rusticus expectat dum defluat amnis," says the poet
("The countryman waits for the water in the river to flow
dry; but it continues to flow on for ever"). The relics could
be impiously destroyed and were so; but the holy wells have
gone on flowing the same as before, quite regardless of the
Evil One's dislike to them.

Of these holy wells, that of S. Winifred, in Flintshire, is,
for many reasons, the most remarkable. The tourist to North
Wales, as the train stops at a moderately well-built station on
the Chester and Holyhead line, hears the name "Holywell!"
cried out. To the ordinary passenger it is the name of a place,
like any other, and nothing more; yet its name—Holywell—is
neither more nor less than the continuance of the original
name—the holy well of S. Winifred—the same which burst
forth, at the moment of her martyrdom, from the spot on which
her head fell under the sword of her murderer. What is remarkable in it is that up to the time of the bursting forth of the well
the valley was popularly known as the Dry Valley. But such
is the wonderful volume of its water, not affected by any length
of dry seasons, bursting forth from the earth, that within a
few yards from its source it turns the large mill-wheel of a
factory, which is the building immediately adjoining, and
there and then forms a waterfall of considerable size. It was
by the moss growing at the side of this well that the miraculous cure which we are about to relate was worked, and we
are in duty required to add that the account is made public
under the express sanction of the Bishop of the Diocese.

"Mary Ann Wood was born, 1759, in the parish of Bushbury, about
four miles from Wolverhampton, in Staffordshire, of honest and laborious
parents, of the Roman Catholic religion. She lived several years house-
maid in the family of Mr. Whitgrave, at Mosely; and from thence removed to Mr. Weld's, of Lulworth Castle, where she was first in the same
employment as at Mosely, and afterwards nursery-maid. Almighty God calling her to a religious life, she, by the recommendation of the last-mentioned
family, was received as a lay-sister in the community of the English
Religious of the Third Order of S. Francis, at Princenhoff, Bruges, in the
Austrian Netherlands, and took the habit in the year 1791. On the 15th
of March last, while employed in washing, she went to open a sash-window
in the washhouse to let out the steam, and unfortunately run her left hand

and arm through a pane of glass, by which the arm was cut to a great depth ; the muscles and nearly the whole of the tendons that lead to the hand were divided ; she suffered the most acute pain, and till the 6th of August the hand and arm remained entirely useless. This loss of power, as the surgeon remarked, must of course have arisen from the division of the muscles and tendons. The hand and arm were for some time fomented and poulticed, and the wound itself treated in the usual way. It was quite healed over in three weeks after the accident. The swelling contined much longer, but in proportion as it abated the mischief done became more apparent. The arm and hand semed withered and somewhat contracted, and the ends of one tendon visibly two inches asunder. She still continued to suffer much pain, which inclined the surgeon to think that small pieces of glass had penetrated the tendons and remained in them, though he could not trace them. He gave little or no hopes of her ever again having the use of her hand, only saying in some years nature might give her some little use of it, which was considered by her Superior as a mere delusive comfort. The good sister, despairing of further human assistance towards her cure, determined, with the approbation of her Superior, to have recourse to God through the intercession of S. Winifred, by making a Novena in her honour. She had no idea of asking a miracle, but confidently hoped and believed that He who had made her arm would restore to her through the prayers of the Saint some small use of it. On the 6th of August she put a piece of moss from S. Winifred's Well on her arm. She suffered after this such excruciating pain for a little while that she was inclined to take it off again, till she reasoned with herself that the moss could not naturally occasion it. She continued particularly recollected all the evening and praying mentally without taking notice of her arm ; and, to her great surprise, when she got up the next morning she found that she could dress herself, put her arm behind her, put it to her head, &c., &c. As soon as she could she informed the Superior of what had happened, but she wished to verify the fact a few days before she would inform the Community, and ordered her to conceal the difference until the 10th. This act of obedience cost her much, for her joy and gratitude were so great she had hard work to conceal it. Finding that she continued perfectly cured, the Superior, on the Feast of S. Laurence, informed the Community, and on the 16th—the last day of the Novena— the Religious sang a solemn *Te Deum*. The Superior sent, the same day, for the surgeon, who had not seen the arm since the month of July, after having asked his opinion concerning it, and received no hopes from him of a perfect cure, and very little of her ever having even the least use of it. She sent for his patient and shewed him the arm and hand, which he thoroughly examined and tried, and was so affected at the sight and the recital of how it had happened as to shed tears, and in the first emotion to exclaim it was a miracle, a special interposition of Divine Providence to show the efficacy of faith and prayer. He was not told of the application of the moss. Since the 6th of August she has continued to have the free use of and the full strength in that hand and arm, and does all the laborious work of her station. The scar remains, and the ends of the tendon, two inches asunder, are still visible.

"The Lodge, Taunton, Nov. 19, 1809."

The above miraculous cure is one all but belonging to a

past century, and, of course, the power of working miracles is not circumscribed by limits of time. To a narrative, therefore, of a date such as the above it will be quite suitable to add one from the mouth of a witness now living.

Mr. Arthur Oldfield Hammond, of S. Mary's Lodge, Croom's Hill, Blackheath, writes the following letter :—

> "The King's Head Hotel, Holywell,
> "October 23, 1871.

"My wife, Julia Hammond, has been low and weak ever since her confinement, in October, 1867. She suffered greatly from an internal burning pain, rendering her unable to walk. Indeed, since March last she has scarcely been able to take any exercise, and a visit to the sea-side at Brighton this summer was not of the least benefit to her. During the month before she came hither she scarcely ever left the house, except in a carriage to go to church, which is only the width of three houses distant. She had conceived a great desire for a long time to bathe in S. Winifred's Well, and felt sure she would be cured there.

"On the evening of the 6th instant we came to this town, and on Saturday, the 7th, she rode down to the Well, and immediately after entering the water the pain left her and has never returned. She is in good health and spirits, and was able to walk immediately. She came back from the Well on foot; and some days this week she has gone for a walk of between four and five miles at least, without feeling any unusual fatigue. In this case it cannot be said that mere bathing has effected the cure, for my wife has been in the daily habit of taking a cold bath.

"Truly God is wonderful in His Saints.

> "ARTHUR OLDFIELD HAMMOND.

"S. Mary's Lodge, Croom's Hill, Blackheath."

Emma Fletcher, living at 106, Wallgate, Wigan, suffered from fits, having had twenty, twenty-two, and even twenty-seven in a single day. She was anointed and given up for death. She, however, asked to be carried to Holywell, and on the 6th of July, 1869 (in her own words, taken from the record book kept by Fr. di Pietro, S.J., the Priest of the Mission), "*I bathed in S. Winifred's Well for the first time; thanks be to our good God, S. Winifred, and our Lady of the Sacred Heart, I have never had one since.*" Emma Fletcher comes every year to Holywell, on the 6th of July, to thank S. Winifred for her cure, and to make an offering to the Hospice.*

---

* The following letter, from the Earl of Denbigh to the *Tablet* newspaper, will be read with general interest :—

"Sir,—Those of your readers who have a devotion to S. Winifred will be glad to hear that through the spirited exertions of the Rev. J. B. di Pietro, S.J., of Holywell, the management of the Well and Baths attached to it has been secured in Catholic hands for three years. Those who have been as pilgrims to bathe there will know what an advantage this

It would be natural to suppose that the people of Holywell are proud of possessing so great a treasure as this well, and that they would be among the foremost to glorify S. Winifred for the many striking miracles worked at it. When a voice from Heaven once bore testimony to Jesus Christ in the presence of a multitude of the Jews, many only said "*it thundered.*" The moss of the Well has, they say in Holywell, natural medicinal properties, and the water holds minerals in solution. Those who believe recognize the power given to S. Winifred, and it is they who obtain the favours of the miraculous cures.

NATIONAL DESIRES FOR SPIRITUAL GRACES.
LETTER OF A ROSARIAN.

SIR,—May I ask permission through your pages to throw out an idea that doubtless has been presented to the minds of many of your readers who have been interested, like myself, in the accounts during some years past from France of the apparitions of our Blessed Lady in that her favoured country? They may have wondered why England was not also equally honoured, and have thought that there must be some cause that has made our Blessed Mother fight so shy of our shores. England was once the Isle of Saints; the Divine Emmanuel had long made his loving home on our cherished altars, and Mary, Mother of our Eucharistic Lord, was then also loved and honoured amongst us. The terrible Reformation came, and

---

will be to all such. This has not, however, been accomplished without incurring much risk. The revenue of the Well, &c., last year amounted to £170 in Protestant hands. Fr. di Pietro has engaged to pay the Local Board of Holywell £162 per annum. Besides this he has to pay his Well-keeper £1 per week, and the purchase of furniture, bathing-dresses, and cost of coals, gas, &c., will run the expenditure to about £250. I earnestly hope that many, when they read this, will consent to send him some little donation towards defraying these expenses, so that he may not in his charity be a loser by this undertaking. The Hospice is now, I am happy to say, doing well, and it has been of great value to those respectable pilgrims who are above the common lodging-houses, and yet cannot afford to pay for separate lodgings. The assiduous care shown them by the good Sisters who have charge of the establishment is admirable.—I am, Sir, yours faithfully,   "DENBIGH.

"Newnham Paddox, Feb. 17, 1873."

we cast off the bright, living faith of centuries for the cold,
dead negations of Protestantism. Our altars were overturned,
and the Eucharistic Victim and His glorious Mother alike
denied, dethroned and banished ; our Mother particularly
feeling the weight of Protestant hatred in being even set up
as a barrier against her Divine Son. Does not such a public
universal outrage demand some public universal reparation ?
Catholicity has once again spread her golden threads over the
land, but the faith that bids us ask that we may receive in
order that our joy may be full is perhaps dimmed by too
great a deference to Protestant prejudice. Might it not
almost be said that Catholics in England are somewhat
afraid to give utterance to the honour and veneration due to
Mary as the Mother of God, though, doubtless, there are
numerous hearts most sincerely attached to her service and
who find their joy and comfort in her devotion ? The month
of our Blessed Mother will soon dawn upon us : could we not
make some reparation for the past and some amends for the
present indifference ? Could not all her devoted children,
with one voice and soul, send to Heaven, from every English
altar and from every Catholic home, a prayer for pardon ?
Could we not then invite her to return once more to the
cherished England of old, and ask her to choose a spot where
she could reign as Queen of Mercy, and open a fountain of
blessings which would draw all minds to admit her wonderful
power with her Divine Son, and compel the most reluctant
heart to submit to her love ? Let us remind her how prodigal
she has been in affection to our sister country, and let us tell
her how grieved our love will be if she continues to hide
herself from us. Let us ask her to look at the innumerable
heresies, sects, and divisions leading daily astray those im-
mortal souls for whom her Divine Son shed His precious
blood. Would it not be a worthy object to propose to the
piety of the Rosarians ? Could it not be proposed that every
child of Mary should unite together in prayer for this purpose
during the beautiful month of May ? We may be sure that
our union of prayers will bring down a fertilising shower of
heavenly blessings upon ourselves and our country.—I remain,
sir, your obedient servant,

A ROSARIAN.

We gladly give insertion to the foregoing letter, notwithstanding that it reached us far too late for insertion in our

May number, for which it will be seen that it was specially intended. The special acts of reparation which our correspondent suggests, though most gracefully appropriate to the month of May, are by no means things necessarily to be limited to the month of May exclusively. There is every reason why the other months of the year should partake with the month of May in the kind of service our correspondent suggests.

However, it may be well to temper the pious desire that the Blessed Virgin should honour the shores of Great Britain with the grace of an apparition with a little sober reflection as to what may be among the reasons why for the present it appears to be her pleasure principally to confine these favours to the soil of France. S. Paul says "that where sin abounded, there did grace much more abound." The purpose of the Blessed Virgin in her apparitions is something far more serious than merely to pay a compliment to the people of any particular country. In France faith and unbelief, piety and impiety, are opposed to each other in an incomparably more decided and extreme manner than is the case with ourselves or most other countries; and, without in the least seeking to detract from the merit of French faith and piety, it will be easy to perceive that in a country where the faithful have to endure in so much higher a degree the penalties of open mockery and contempt on the part of undisguised scoffers, with the many evils superadded that can be inflicted by a bitter dominant infidel legislation, the Blessed Virgin may there be moved to grant to the many who believe the grace of frequent apparitions as the "Mater Misericordiæ," to console, comfort, and encourage those who do believe under their sufferings. Where, therefore, the same urgent or pressing reasons for such graces do not exist, there is not the same reason why the pious persons of other countries, who are not exposed to the same trials in an equal degree, should be too clamorous for the same graces being immediately granted to them.

Again, it is also true that there is at the present time an "internationality" in good as well as in evil. The nations of the world are not to be looked upon as wholly or irredeemably given up to the evil designs of the hateful conspiracy which calls itself the "International Society." The benefits, for example, which have flowed from the apparition of the Blessed Virgin at Lourdes, in France, continue to be graciously extended to the people of other countries, and the water of the fountain at Lourdes does not require for its wonder-working efficacy either the nationality or the air of France.   The Mother of the whole Christian family, though for excellent reasons she has chosen Lourdes, in France, for the scene of her apparition, by no means intends that her graces conveyed by it should be subjected to any local or national restrictions.

But all this notwithstanding, it will undoubtedly be extremely becoming for all who are devout clients of Mary, especially Rosarians, to possess themselves fully with the idea that reigns in our correspondent's mind—namely, that we in England have all an important debt of shortcoming and defect to retrieve in respect of our undue deference to Protestant prejudice.   The ways to retrieve this debt, however, can be made very numerous, and are in no way to be confined to the month of May.   If we are seen to be diligent in endeavouring to retrieve this debt in the ways that are open to us, perhaps in due time we may be rewarded in the particular manner our correspondent desires.   The great religious need of our fellow-countrymen is that they should come to be better informed and better furnished with knowledge.   The vast majority, though possibly in a very self-willed way of their own, nevertheless it is true, sincerely desire to be Christians. We would suggest, then, to all good Rosarians who sympathise with our correspondent not to be above setting in their own persons an example of making a beginning in a good direction.   The more humble, practical, and unpretentious their beginning, the better will it be entitled to a blessing from above.   Let all such, then, at once begin to look out for those to whom it will be a great work of mercy and charity to teach the doctrine of the Fifteen Mysteries of the Rosary. There are vast—enormously vast—numbers of such to be found.

NOTICES OF BOOKS.

THE MONTH OF THE SACRED HEART (June), by the authoress of the "Book of the Dedication of Ireland to the Sacred Heart."   .

OUR readers will be gratified to learn that they are once more indebted to the praiseworthy zeal and industry of the Community at Kenmare for another eminently popular spiritual book, "The Month of the Sacred Heart."   It is a nicely printed small volume of more than a hundred pages, and contains a short appropriate reflection for every day of the month, followed by Novenas of prayer for the feasts of Corpus Christi and of the Sacred Heart. Subjoined is a welcome specimen of the book, forming the meditation for the thirtieth day.

The Heart of Jesus teaches us to seek for the Joys of Heaven.

SHORT REFLECTION.

The reason we think so little of death is that we are afraid of it. This pain is great indeed, and it is not wrong, if we do not allow it to become excessive. Death is a punishment, and God intends us to feel when He punishes us; but God has also given us great consolations, if we would only receive them. We think of death as if it were shutting us out for ever from all pleasure and happiness, and from all whom we love. Whereas, on the contrary, if we die a holy death, our real pleasure and happiness is all before us; for we can suffer no care or sorrow, or grief, or pain in Heaven. Heaven is our true home, and we ought to teach ourselves to care for it, and to think of it more than we do. We ought to think of it so much, that we should long for it and desire it; and yet how few there are who really desire Heaven; how few there are who if they had their desire, would not rather stay on in this world of misery than go to their God, and the blessed Heaven He has prepared for them.

Oh! Sacred and wise Heart of our Jesus, teach us, we beseech Thee, to love our Heavenly home, and to long for it, and to desire it with our whole heart. Teach us to prepare for it, and that we may become fit for that blessed place where no sin can defile us, and where no sorrow can give us pain. Teach us also how to desire it, because when we are once there, we shall never grieve Thy Sacred Heart again, and shall dwell with Thee for ever and ever.

RECORD OF EVENTS.

DURING the past month the London and other newspapers have been doing their best to create a sensation and panic by the publication of sundry alarming telegrams with reference to the health of the Holy Father. The chief result of all which has only been to furnish a rather remarkable, though quite unintentional testimony, proving how indispensable the old man at the Vatican, though despoiled by fraud and violence of his regal state, continues to be to the peace and well-being of the people of Europe; even on the showing of his worst enemies.

If the Catholic Church were in reality nothing more than the sacristy and ceremonial affair which Continental infidel scoffers say it is, it is not very intelligible how, on their own showing, the state of health of its supreme head, who is now fully past the term of fourscore years, should be a thing about which the busy world of politicians has any very clear call or need to trouble itself. One old man more or less in the world, whose business is only with ceremonies, cannot particularly signify, one would naturally think, to the makers of laws, and rulers of the destinies of kingdoms. *Mentita est iniquita' sibi*, says Divine Inspiration, "Injustice tell lies to itself.' That the telegrams respecting the Pope's health should turn out to be little else than lies is just what may be reasonably expected from the source from which they come; but this is not the whole of the story. The authors of these telegrams not only tell us their lies, who it is to be hoped are slow to believe them, but they likewise lie to themselves. In one and the same breath they speak of the Papacy as a worn-out institution, and they industriously fill the whole world with news respecting the Pope, as the one thing above all others that is of the greatest importance and concern to it. *Mentita est iniquitas sibi*.

The sole material out of which the above-mentioned alarming telegrams have been fabricated at various times has been that the Pope has suffered during the latter part of April and the past month of May from occasional attacks of rheumatism, which at his advanced age have rendered it a matter of prudence that he should enjoy greater intervals of rest and retirement from the never-ceasing round of business interviews, and the granting of daily audiences, in the midst of which he has now for so long a time spent his whole life.

The Italian Government is showing how it understands "liberty" in a sense quite different from the meaning usually attributed to the word in great ignorance, by issuing orders to place every kind of obstacle in the way of the religious pilgrimages. The police has been employed in more than one instance to disperse such pilgrimages where they were known to be Christian and religious.

"Every sign of religion appears to be an offence," says a Correspondent of the *Tablet*, from which journal we quote the account, "as a pilgrim from Massa Carrara has discovered this week to his cost. Whoever has been in past years in Rome during Holy Week must have seen pilgrims, male and female, arriving in the brown habit, the cockle-shell, the broad-brimmed hat, and the staff surmounted by a cross. The costume is no novelty in Rome, and could have been seen in every street. A young man, thus attired, arrived in Rome last week, and though walking inoffensively across the Piazza Colonna, was insulted by a set of lads and young men. It is not for one moment pretended that he impeded the traffic. On the contrary, finding himself hissed and hooted, he escaped into the Church of S. Maria in Aquiro. Hither he was followed by one of the questurini, without his having committed any offence whatever—he had not begged, though begging is far from being prohibited here: he was lodged in gaol. Some gentlemen, sorry for the poor young man, went to the Questura and interceded for him, requesting at least to know why he was to be sent to prison. The officer replied, and it is said in anything but a polite manner, that he was not obliged to give his reasons: and the next day the young man was sent back to his home in North Italy, accompanied by a policeman; all inquirers after him having been informed that it was because he was of unsound mind. There has been at least no medical evidence to that effect published, and those Romans who conversed with him observed no traces of mental alienation either in his manner or language. The young man had been to Loretto and Assisi, and proposed going to Jerusalem. No one can conceive by what right he has been forcibly conveyed to Massa Carrara. But this is ' liberty.' "

A little instance has occurred in Rome, tending to prove that punishment does not in all cases follow so very slowly upon the offence. The master locksmith, who, at the bidding of the Government, broke open the doors of the Pope's palace of the Quirinal was rewarded by the distinction of being made captain in the national guard. His workshop is now closed, and he has run away from his creditors, though up to the time in question he was known as a well-to-do man among his artizan class.

On the 5th of May the Pope granted several audiences, and amongst others he received a company of French pilgrims to Rome, headed by the Vicomte de Damas, who read an address to the Holy Father, from which we extract the following words:—"Most Holy Father, Pilgrimages are part of our customs. We required a patron to lead us, and your Holiness has given us one; the exemplar of our peaceful manifestations is our countryman Benedict Joseph Labre, the great pilgrim of these modern times. He went from sanctuary to sanctuary; he prayed, he protested, he suffered. On the threshold of the Vatican he finished his course, and from the same threshold of the Vatican we begin ours." The Holy Father was evidently much moved by the enthusiastic cheer, and replied in French, which he spoke with great ease and fluency.

THE

Monthly Magazine of the Holy Rosary.

NEW SERIES.

| No. 12.] | JULY. | [A.D. 1873. |

THE FIRST SUNDAY OF JULY.
THE FESTIVAL OF THE MOST PRECIOUS BLOOD.

THE brief of the present reigning sovereign Pontiff, in which
he has appointed the first Sunday in July to be kept as a
solemn memorial festival of the shedding of the most precious
blood of the Divine Victim for an atonement for the sins of
men, assigns a particular reason for his instituting this festival, which we may study with great profit, in connection
with the solemnity which we shall so shortly celebrate. The
Pope says, that, in view of the great and deplorable increase
of human crime and of sins against the laws of God, it will be
most profitable for the faithful to have their minds called to
meditate on the shedding of the most precious blood of Jesus
Christ, as the price at which forgiveness of sin and admission
to the grace and mercies of the Christian covenant was
bought for them by our Lord and Saviour.

The value of a privilege is commonly estimated according
to the price at which it is known to have been purchased.
Consequently the more we live in the habitual practice of
piously fixing our minds on the thought of the great price,
which was paid for our admission to the grace of our redemption—viz.: the life-blood of the Divine Victim for the sins of
men—the more effectually we, doubtless, must be inwardly
admonished of the value of what we have gained. The more
likewise we shall nourish a holy fear and dread of ever
coming to forfeit, by our own carelessness about falling into
sins, the grace and privilege of our admission to the Christian covenant, when we confess that this has been bought for
us at the so great a price of this same precious blood.

The precious blood, therefore, of Jesus Christ undoubtedly
ought, as a matter of duty and gratitude, to have, as it were,
an habitual place of its own in our minds. In either one way
or another, the thoughts of a good Christian should never be
allowed to be empty of the memory of the blood of Jesus
Christ : he should never be without the consciousness that it

was no less than the great price of this blood of the Son of God which was paid for all the Christian privileges which he enjoys.

But that which should, as we have said, have an habitual resting-place of its own in the minds of Christians, with the very greatest fitness, calls on us not to remain in an unbecoming ignorance of the knowledge which cannot but appertain to an event so intimately concerning the whole Being of the world of man, as that the blood of the Very Eternal Son of God made Man, should have been shed in it. That the history of the world of men should know even of such an event as that the Son of God entering into it as Man, this by itself is a sufficient marvel, but that He should have been made to suffer a blood-stained death at the hands of men ; here is indeed matter for religious meditation. We shall hope in our way to foster the spirit in which the holy reigning Pontiff desires the festival which he has instituted to be kept, by presenting our readers, on the occasion of the festival, with a brief summary of the knowledge, which it is certainly becoming that all Christians should possess, respecting the most precious Blood itself by which the world has been redeemed.

The Church, then, we should know, honours the most precious blood of Jesus Christ in three different ways. The first, which is the highest as being universal—that is to say, as being the common ordinary duty of all Christians throughout the whole Catholic Church, is the worship which is paid to Jesus Christ as well in the Holy Sacrifice of the Mass as in the Holy Eucharist, which as the Sacrament of both His precious body and blood, is the gracious fulfilment of His promise, "Behold, I am with you all days even to the end of the world."

But besides this, it is becoming to know that the Providence of God has likewise permitted certain relics of the true and real blood which was gathered from the very body of the Divine Victim himself, as He suffered under the lashes of the scourgers at the pillar and as He bled on the cross, to be preserved in particular localities, as most precious and sacred memorials of His passion and death, for the comfort of the faithful, and to bear their peculiar witness for all ages to the truth of His most sacred passion. These sacred relics of which but a very few survive the wreck of time, possessing the requisite attestations, are known as the " Sang Real," or " real blood," to distinguish them from another class of sacred

relics, consisting of the drops of blood that at various times
have miraculously exuded from consecrated Hosts and crucifixes,
as, for example, that of the famous Crucifix of Beyrout.

It has, indeed, been at one time doubted whether it has
been given to the faithful on earth to possess any relics at all
of the most sacred blood of Christ; and the early schoolmen,
reasoning on their conclusion that the Incarnate Word had
never parted with any portion of His sacred humanity to
which he had been substantially united, affirmed that it was a
heresy to say that we possessed any relic of the real blood of
our Lord upon the earth. This, according to them, was the
same as separating the Eternal Word from His Humanity.
Pope Pius II., however, in the year 1459, at the provincial
Council of Mantua, permitted the question to be argued in
his presence, and decided that it was open to all to maintain,
free from the least suspicion of heresy, that our Lord had left
portions of His sacred blood upon earth.

This decision was founded on the showing that it is a thing
of every-day experience that men may part with a portion of
the blood in their bodies without any prejudice to their
identity, and that nothing was more in accordance with the
universal practice of the faithful, at all times, than to preserve relics of the blood of those who underwent death as
martyrs. Thus, when the body of S. Stephen, who suffered
death by stoning only a few weeks after the death of Jesus
Christ, was discovered, it is recorded that a phial, containing
his blood, was found with the body, carefully sealed up; and S.
Augustine speaks of many miracles which were wrought by
it. But if the blood of S. Stephen was thus treasured up,
how much more would the Sacred Blood of Jesus have been
gathered up and religiously preserved.

A Bishop of Lincoln, pronouncing a discourse at a Nationa
Council, which was held in the year 1247, thus sums up the
ecclesiastical tradition with reference to the sacred blood
gathered from contemporary narratives, commonly known as
the Apochryphal Gospels, and which, though they are entirely
without authority in all matters of doctrine, nevertheless
enjoy a large degree of credit, as bearing witness to what was
the general belief of the first Christians:—

"After the death of Jesus, Joseph of Arimathea, laying all
fear aside, went boldly and asked for the body of Jesus, and
he obtained it, for he was a man believed to possess great influence. Not caring for the discontent of the Jews, he took

down from the cross, with honour and veneration, the most
sacred body of Jesus, covered with wounds and bruises. In
order not to touch irreverently this blessed body, he had
girded himself about with a linen towel. He wiped in succession, with great devotion, all the wounds, which were still
moist and covered with blood together with the extremities
of the cross where the nails had caused the feet and hands
to send forth blood. Having carried the sacred body to the
tomb, he washed it, and preserved with the greatest care, in
a vessel carefully cleansed, the water of which he had made
use and which had been discoloured with the blood of the
wounds. He kept, however, with even still greater veneration the blood itself which had come from the hands and the
feet. He looked upon both one and the other as an inappre-
ciable treasure for himself and his successors."

The constant and invariable practice of the faithful, in all
ages, in making every exertion to obtain and to preserve the
blood of the martyrs as a most precious relic, appears inex-
plicable, except for precisely the same reasons which would
lead S. Joseph of Arimathea and the holy women to gather
together and preserve the blood of Jesus Christ; and this
view is confirmed by the frequent mention, which occurs in
ecclesiastical traditions, of relics of the precious blood being in
the possession of certain churches and of miracles being
worked by them. Thus, for example, the Eastern Church
mentions a certain pious hermit, Barypsabas, who had in his
possession a relic of the sacred blood that had trickled from
the cross, and who worked miracles with it. He is thus
spoken of in a summary of the lives of the Saints, called the
"Synaxarium," which used to be read on Sundays in the
churches :—" Which the heathens observing (viz., the miracles
that he worked), certain persons who had no fear of God, and
who thought that by murdering the hermit they should gain
possession of the treasure by which he worked the miracles,
and thus greatly enrich themselves, attacked him by night,
and murdered him. But, by the disposition of Divine Providence, their expectations were disappointed, for Barypsabas
had already entrusted the precious deposit to the keeping of
one of his followers, and after a lapse of time it was given to
the great city (Constantinople)."

George, Archbishop of Nicodemia, who lived in the ninth
century, expresses himself as follows, in one of his sermons
to the people :—" She (Mary) kissed His sacred feet, and the

wounds caused by the nails, and, looking with a tender affectionate compassion upon the Lord, she collected the blood and water that flowed from His side, and received it with the greatest veneration." The above are but samples of the numerous testimonies that our limited space, of course, precludes us from attempting to give at length, in which the ecclesiastical writers bear testimony to the truth that relics of the sacred blood of our Lord were permitted to be preserved in various places as memorials of his passion.

Again, the medieval poets, particularly those of the Breton race, frequently made the Holy Blood the theme of their verses, under the name of " Sangraal," which Tennyson renders as the " Holy Grail," though, in reality, the name " Sangraal " only indicates, as we have said above, the distinction between the relics of the real sacred blood (sang real), preserved from the actual body of our Lord, and the relics of blood miraculously obtained from certain Crucifixes and sacred Hosts.*

The principal relic we may mention of the sacred blood (sang real) that is now in Europe is that possessed by the town of Bruges, in Flanders, to which city it was brought, in

---

* The following extract from the poet Laureat's poem of the " Holy Grail," will give a notion of the way in which the theme of the· " Holy Blood " used to belong to poetry, as inspired by faith. The poetic tradition is seen even yet to survive the wreck of faith :—

    " 'Tell me, what drove thee from the table round,
    My brother? Was it earthly passion crost?'
    ' Nay,' said the knight, ' for no such passion mine,
    But the sweet vision of the Holy Grail,
    Drove me from all vain glories, rivalries.'

    *   *   *   *

    To whom the monk: ' The Holy Grail!

    *   *   *   *

    Yet, one of your own knights, a guest of ours,
    Told us of this in our refectory ;
    But spake with such a sadness, and so low,
    We heard not half he said. What is it ?
    The phantom of a cup, that comes and goes ?'
    ' Nay, monk! What phantom ?' answered Percival.

the year 1148, by Leo, the Abbot of St. Bertin, as the gift of Baldwin, King of Jerusalem, to Thierry, Count of Flanders; and this relic has been preserved with the greatest veneration in that town ever since, being publicly exposed with the greatest solemnity to the veneration of the faithful every year.

God, we may then perceive, continues to plead with the Christian people, as He did with the former Israel: "What is there that I could have done for my vineyard that I have not done for it? Wherefore, then, when I looked, that it should bring forth sweet grapes, brought it forth sour grapes?" All things, says the inspired writer, are double, and set one against another: "Against evil stands good, and against death life" (Ecclus xxxiii., 15). The Blood of the Son of God continues to be set against the sins by which the Christian people are daily bringing themselves to ruin and misery in this world, and to everlasting perdition in the next. To endeavour to enter, then, into the spirit of the holy solemnity of the Feast of the Most Precious Blood, which the reigning Pope has given to the Church, let us be careful to learn from it that, by our calling as Christians, we must not only "flee from sin ourselves as from the face of a serpent," but vigorously oppose it in others, and with great charity and patience labour to turn them away from it.

'The cup, the cup itself, from which our Lord
Drank, at the last sad supper, with His own.
This, from the blessed land of Aromat—
After the day of darkness, when the dead
Went wandering o'er Moriah—the good Saint,
Arimathæan Joseph, journeying brought
To Glastonbury, where the winter thorn
Blossoms at Christmas, mindful of our Lord.
And there awhile it bode; and if a man
Could touch or see it, he was healed at once,
By faith, of all his ills. But then the times
Grew to such evil that the holy cup
Was caught away to Heaven, and disappeared.'"

—TENNYSON, *from the Idylls of the King—"The Holy Grail."*

The poem supposes that it was a devotion of the knights of King Arthur to go wandering in quest of the lost treasure of the "Holy Grail."

No. II. FATHER IGNATIUS SPENCER.

In a worldly point of view, few positions could have been more advantageous than that of Mr. Spencer, as Rector of Brington. He had a good living, and a fine income; he was near a delightful family circle, where he could enjoy the varied charms of social and intellectual intercourse of the highest order; he had the prestige of rank and station, and the influence of his parents was sure to obtain for him the highest dignities of the Church in due time. But none of these things could satisfy a soul which was beginning to seek the love and service of God above all things. He had still to tread thorny by-paths and to drink of many muddy streams, but he never wavered, nor consciously turned aside from what had gradually become the engrossing aim of his life.

He had begun his clerical life with High Church prin-principles, and was sorely exercised with the multitude of Dissenting sects in his parish. It happened one day, while yet only a deacon, that he was expatiating on this subject to a distinguished clergyman in whom he had great confidence. He explained to him his views and methods of warfare against the Dissenters, fully expecting to meet with encouraging sympathy. "These would be very convenient doctrines if we could make use of them," replied Dr. Elmsley, "but they are available only for Roman Catholics. They will not serve us." In a moment the truth of this answer struck his mind. "I went away," he says, "with my High Churchism mortally wounded in the very prime of its vigour and youth, to die for ever to the character of an Anglican High Churchman." He had now to set to work in a new direction, to endeavour to open the doors of the Establishment as widely as he could, so as to embrace as many religious sects as possible. The Athanasian Creed became a source of great scruple and anxiety, which was never quite set at rest until he became a Catholic.

Mr. Spencer began his new life as a Rector with redoubled labours in his parish. He had gradually given up worldly amusements, and he now increased his ascetic habits, and devoted himself to the service of the poor. He had for some time adopted the practice of fasting, and he increased it in spite of his Evangelical views. As he frequently tasted nothing till six o'clock in the evening, it caused him much bodily pain, and he made many unavailing efforts to conceal his abstinence from food from his housekeeper.

An incident, almost pathetic in its grotesqueness, was soon to change the current of his spiritual life. By the so-called doctrine of *Election*, the believers in Calvinism are supposed to receive an inward assurance of salvation, which marks the elect from the reprobate; fixes the very hour and moment of conversion, and is declared to be permanent in its effect. Mr. Spencer had not yet clearly understood this doctrine, but a poor woman, whom he met one day in Northampton, undertook to enlighten him. She put together the various texts of the New Testament, which are perverted in support of this tenet, with such success, that Mr. Spencer felt himself "assured" or "justified" on the very spot! Those who are acquainted with old-fashioned Evangelical literature will hardly be surprised at this circumstance. Nothing is more common than to read of similar conversions effected by a few words from a "believer" of lowly station. Little children even, in the words of the *Quarterly Review,* "keep open death-beds for the conversion of their parents and relatives," by this means, in such publications. It is needless to say that spiritual pride and self-complacency are the prevailing features of this strange distortion of religion, and they were not without effect on Mr. Spencer, who was so delighted with his new spiritual experience that he set to work with the greatest zeal to convert all his relatives and friends, and all whom he could in any way influence. His sole interest was in the state of the souls of others, and they afforded him very little comfort; only two or three persons who were immediately dependent upon him for alms or employment, came up to his spiritual standard. He wrote to all the clergymen he knew, and tried hard to convert his Bishop. In the ways of providence, this personal experience of the vagaries of private judgment gave him a deep knowledge of the hearts of his fellow countrymen. He could enter into the simplicity and earnestness of their delusion with profound sympathy, and it probably laid the foundation of his burning zeal for their conversion, and *his faith in its possibility.* When, in after-years, his brethren were disposed to laugh at some of his anecdotes, bearing on this point, he would become serious, and say, "They are really in earnest, poor things, and we ought not to laugh at them, only to pray that their conversion may be properly directed."

His own success was not encouraging. After more than a year's labour in spreading these peculiar views in his parish, it appears from his journal, at the end of 1826, that there was only one person, and that an old woman, of whom he could say, "She seems fully established in grace." (She afterwards became a Catholic.) In vain he distributed "Bibles and blankets, prayer-books and porridge;" his converts had a bad habit of lapsing into their old ways, when they ceased to require his alms, and three of the most hopeful went mad.

There is one melancholy entry in his journal, in which he describes calling at every house except one, in Nobottle; "Alas! I found *not one soul* over whom I could rejoice as a true child of Christ." It is possible that he became in some degree discouraged, for he begins his journal for the New Year, 1827, with these words—"I have found my mind so far from settled that I never saw myself more in need of God's grace. But I shall find it."

In the course of this year he was settled in the new house he had built, which was excellently furnished by the taste of his mother and other friends. His Calvinistic views had long given the greatest pain and uneasiness to his family, totally opposed as they were to their own decorous and respectable religious opinions, besides being likely to prove a complete bar to Episcopal honours. Now that he had so delightful a house, it was thought that if he could only be induced to marry, he might quietly settle down like his neighbours, and forget all his spiritual crotchets. A plan was arranged for this purpose, and it must be supposed that his old friend Dr. Blomfield was in the secret, for during the following October, while Mr. Spencer was accompanying him on a visitation of the diocese of Chester, he was asked by the Rector of Warrington to preach at his Church, and, to his great surprise, he found that Miss A——, a young lady he had formerly greatly admired, was to be one of his hearers. "He walked with her to Church, and was delighted with her company; he used to say he never preached with greater satisfaction than on that day." In his diary he says—"I begin this volume with one of the most interesting Sundays I have ever spent. After breakfast with Mr. ——'s family, we went to Church, about half a mile from the house, when I preached the first sermon which it has been given me to preach in this diocese; and I am pleased that it should be in this Church, and before N. N., among other hearers, with whom I now converse as

pleasingly as in former times, but on higher subjects. With
her and her sister I walked home, and again to evening service, when I read prayers, and Mr. —— preached." We now
come to a great crisis in his history. He was actually in his
carriage, driving to Althorp to ask his father's consent to
propose to this young lady! We cannot help speculating on the
difference it would have made to the future of England if that
carriage had reached its destination. But on his way, the
words of St. Paul, "*He that is unmarried careth for the things
that belong to the Lord, how he may please the Lord,*" flashed
before his mind. The conflict may have been sharp, but it
was a short one. "When near to the door, he called to the
driver to stop, and turn to the Rectory. He had just formed
the resolution *never to marry.*" No after-attempts had any
effect upon him, and we may well consider this as the turning-
point of his life.

Mr. Spencer's charities so far exceeded his very liberal
income at this time that he had to reduce his personal expenses to the lowest limits, giving up wine and sweet things
at his table, amongst other things. We have a lively picture
from his housekeeper of the crowds of poor and sick people
who used to come for miles to him for relief. He would first
give them all the money he had, and then strip himself of his
clothes—thanking God when he had nothing left but His
holy truth to impart. He would dress their loathsome sores;
his house was open to all the distressed, and he often longed
to turn it into an hospital. He often walked to Northampton
with a knapsack containing his clothes on his shoulders,
smiling at the jeers with which he was greeted; and he would
visit the lowest dens of the dissolute, and try to reclaim them.
He was the father of the poor, and the peacemaker among all.
These heroic acts were soon to pave the way for his conversion, for the beautiful words of Faber, that "*To many the
touch of the poor is the real presence of the Lord,*" may be eminently applied to George Spencer.

So far was he yet, however, from Catholic opinions, that
his father, who was a staunch advocate of Emancipation,
was oblige to rebuke him for the violence of a sermon he
preached on the Catholic question. But his scruples about
the Athanasian Creed revived, and, after some time, he gave
notice to his bishop that he should no longer read it in the
Church service; to which he received no reply.

Shortly before this he had received an anonymous letter,

purporting to be from a gentleman at Lille, "who was grievously troubled about the arguments for Popery," to which Mr. Spencer sent a long controversial answer. This incident made him anxious to find out what kind of people Catholics really were. It happened that he was one day at the barracks at Northampton, when the Catholic priest entered to look after the soldiers under his care. Mr. Spencer accosted him, and introduced him very kindly to one of the officers. A few days after, he met the priest, who thanked him, and said he had been sent there by Providence at that time, as the good reception he had procured him had assisted him in the discharge of his duty. That "these Papists should believe in Providence," startled Mr. Spencer, and made him suspect that he might have misjudged them in other matters. He was still more shaken by a second controversial letter from Lille; a few days afterwards he dined at Lady Throckmorton's, and met the celebrated Dr. Fletcher, with whom he had much conversation. His comment in his journal is, "I am thankful for the kindness of both these Papists. The Lord reward them by showing them His truth!" A third letter from Lille so far changed his opinions that he no longer desired to keep his correspondent in the communion of the Protestant Church, but promised that if he would send his name, and pause before being received into the Church, he would himself follow up the same inquiries with him. To this he received no answer, and it was not till a year after his own conversion that he found out that his correspondent was a lady—Miss Dolling. She had never seen Mr. Spencer, but had been moved to pray for him, and had written the first letter just after having been received into the Church herself. She died at Paris about a year before he became a Catholic, just as she was about to take the veil as a nun of the Sacred Heart. The immediate effect of her letters was to inspire him with a great hope for unity between Catholics and Protestants, and a desire to forward this project by intercourse with them. Towards the end of the year 1829 he became acquainted with Ambrose Lisle Phillipps, then a recent convert to the Catholic faith, who took a warm interest in Mr. Spencer, and obtained prayers for him from several religious communities. The zeal and piety of this young man had a great effect upon him, and he became "more than ever inflamed with desire to be united in communion with persons in whom he saw such strong signs of the Spirit of God." On Sunday, the 24th

January, 1830, he preached in his church, and took leave of
his family to spend a week with young Phillipps at Garendon,
his father's place, to meet the Bishop of Peterborough.
Many distinguished clergymen were of the party, and he was
much impressed with seeing that Phillipps, then only a youth
of 17, had always the advantage over them in argument.   The
result of this week was his having an interview with Father
Caestrick, the priest at Leicester, on the following Saturday.
The joy of his friend Philipps may be imagined when, on
their return to the hotel, he made up his mind not to go
back to his parish, but to wait at Leicester to be received.
"God alone knows," he says, "the peace and joy with which
I laid me down to rest that night.   The next day, at nine
o'clock, the Church received me as her child."

AN APPARITION OF THE BLESSED VIRGIN IN THE VALE OF EVESHAM IN THE EIGHTH CENTURY.

AT a time when so much attention has been drawn to accounts
of similar manifestations in France, it may prove acceptable
to our readers to be presented with a passage of our own
history, illustrating the belief of Catholics in our own country
with regard to such visitations from the unseen world.

The Abbey of S. Mary and S. Egwin of Evesham, situated
upon the Avon, of which, with the exception of the bell-
tower, scarce a vestige now remains, was one of the largest
and most stately in the kingdom.   It was founded by S. Egwin,
third Bishop of Worcester, and first Abbot of Evesham, who
died in 717, and was buried in the Abbey Church.   The origin
of this foundation is recorded as follows in an ancient life of ·
S. Egwin :—

"During the reigns of Ethelred and Kenred his successor,
kings of the Mercians, there lived in the Worcester country a
religious named Egwin, of royal descent.   In his youth,
renouncing all worldly pleasures and ambitions, he espoused
voluntary poverty, and in order the better to serve God, gave
himself up wholly to the ecclesiastical life and divine offices;
and so through successive steps being called to the priesthood,
occupied his whole time in prayer and divine contemplation.

" On the See of Worcester becoming vacant, both clergy
and people demanded that the holy man should be raised to
the episcopal dignity; and yielding at length with great
reluctance to their wish and to the entreaties, not to say
commands, of King Ethelred, he consented to become Bishop
of the aforesaid city. In this holy estate he lived most
excellently, doing all that in him lay, by preaching and other
devout labours, to promote the good of his people. But, by
his zeal and severity in reproving some yet remaining Pagan
customs, having angered certain of his flock, a persecution
was raised against him, wherefrom he took occasion to make
a penitential pilgrimage to Rome. Here he was with much
honour received by Constantine, the Pope of that day; and
his cause being approved, he returned, with the Apostolic
benediction to his own See. Not long after his return, the
foundation of Evesham Abbey took place in this wise.

" In those days there was a district in the Worcester
country, all forest and dense thickets, then called Haum,
but now Eovesham. This district blessed Egwin asked for
and obtained from King Ethelred, and appointed over it
four men in charge of the flocks and herds it maintained.
One of these, Eoves by name, happened to wander on a time
into the deeper recesses of the forest, and lo and behold, there
appears to him in a retired spot a Virgin exceeding bright,
standing between two other maidens. Her beauty surpassed
all the beauty of this world, and such was the splendour of
her glory that the sun itself could not bear comparison with
it. In her hands she held a book, and, with the two sacred
virgins beside her, was engaged in singing some celestial
canticle. Astonished at so brilliant an apparition, and unable
to endure the sight, Eoves, silent and trembling, returned home,
and going to the holy Bishop carefully narrated to him what
he had seen. Whereupon the man of God, considering the
matter over within himself, after much fasting and prayer,
proceeded, attended by three companions, his feet bare, with
psalms and devout supplications, to the forest; and leaving
the others on the outskirts, advanced alone into the interior,
where, lying for a long time on the earth he implored with
groans and tears the loving mercy of our Redeemer.

" On rising from prayer, the three virgins presented themselves to him, in no less splendour and glory than when seen
by Eoves. Of these, she who stood in the middle was tallest
and most radiant. Fairer than the lily she seemed, more

blooming than the rose, and breathed a fragrance around her exceeding the most precious odours of earth. Before her she held a book, and a glistening gold cross ; and while the good Bishop was saying to himself that this must be the Mother of God : the most excellent Virgin, as though favouring so pious a judgment, held forward the cross and blessed him with it as he bowed down before her, and with such valediction evanished. Thereupon the holy man, being filled with joy and giving thanks to God, understood it to be the Divine will that the spot thus honoured should be consecrated to Christian worship, and dedicated to the Blessed Mother of God. For he had already vowed, under the stress of various trials, that if his desire were prospered he would build a temple to the Lord. Accordingly he straightway had the land cleared, and began the work of building an Abbey."

To the Abbey thus commenced, an endowment in the form of estates in land was above all things necessary, and this need was amply supplied by Egwin's two royal friends, Kenred and Offa, both of whom later on renounced their temporal principalities, to become monks, as indeed Ethelred himself had done before them.

In company with his two royal benefactors, Kenred and Offa, S. Egwin now made a second journey to Rome, in order to obtain a confirmation of his work from the Holy See. He returned with a Brief authorizing and strongly recommending the devout object he had in view.

On his return from Rome, Egwin, thus supported by the authority of the Holy See, proceeded with the building of his Abbey; and it was probably at this time that the site was consecrated by S. Wilfrid, on occasion of the assembly of bishops and others whose names were mentioned in the Brief which he had obtained.

The church itself, it would seem, was not dedicated till 714, five years later, on which occasion S. Egwin wrote as follows :—

LETTER OF S. EGWIN TO THE FAITHFUL ON THE COMPLETION OF HIS MONASTERY.

"I, Egwin, poor Bishop of Worcester, desire to make known to all the faithful in Christ, how that by inspiration of the Holy Ghost, and by many and great visions, it was shown unto me that I must build a house to the praise and glory of Almighty God, and of S. Mary and all the elect of Christ, and to my own eternal recompense. While, therefore, Ethelred was yet reigning in his kingdom, I besought of him as a gift a certain district named Haum ; and there the Holy and Ever-virgin Mary first of all appeared

unto a certain shepherd and herdsman named Eoves, and afterwards to me
also, between two virgins, holding a book in her hand. For this cause I
cleared the forest ground, and began to build a Church and Abbey thereon,
and by the grace of the most good God have brought the work to an end.
Now, therefore, I desire to show to all generations to come what lands I
have obtained in the district aforesaid, in endowment of the said Abbey,
and how that I have freed these estates from all demands and exactions of
all persons whatsoever, and have caused the same to be confirmed by
charters, privileges and royal edicts, to the end that Brethren may be able
to live there undisturbed according to the rule of S. Benedict, serving God
in that place. And here I give the names of the several estates, all which,
having justly obtained and made freehold, I have offered to God and Holy
Mary. [Here follows a description of the various properties forming the
endowment of the Monastery corresponding with the description of the
same lands in the charter of Kenred and Offa.] Written in the year of the
Lord's Incarnation 714."

The site and demesnes of the Abbey thus carefully founded
and endowed are termed in Domesday Book, compiled in the
reign of William the Conqueror, *Terra sanctæ Mariæ de
Evesham*—"The land of S. Mary of Evesham."

For eight hundred years, through all the eventful changes
of England's history, the Monastery continued to fulfil the
sacred object of its founder, and at the period of the so-called
Reformation its church is described as a noble building, of
more than ordinary length, with a cloister at the south end,
and containing altogether a hundred and sixty-four pillars,
which were gilt. The church had fifteen altars, besides the
High Altar; namely, those of the Blessed Virgin, of the
Twelve Apostles, of Pope Constantine and of S. Egwin, each
with their several chapels. We learn from its sacristy-records
that a lamp was kept burning continually before the tomb of
S. Egwin, and a wax candle and lamp before the altar of our
Lady, where also High Mass was daily celebrated with
incense, and with twenty-four lighted wax tapers and thirty-
three lamps.

The ancient seal of the Abbey shows on the principal side
S. Egwin on his knees in the wood before three virgins, with
Eoves in the lower part tending swine, and the abbey church
in the background. Round the whole runs the following
inscription :—SIGILLUM SANCTÆ MARIÆ ET SANCTI EGWINI, "The
seal of S. Mary and S. Egwin." Under the abbey church
are the words ECCE LOCUM QUEM ELEGI, "Behold the place
which I have chosen;" and surrounding Eoves an inscription
in Saxon :—EOVES HER WENEDE MIT WAS SWIN. ECGWIN CLEPET

VIS EOVISHOM, "Here Eoves wended with his swine; Egwin named the place Eovishom."

Of this particular local devotion of our forefathers to the Holy Mother of God scarce a vestige remains, yet the faith which gave birth to it is still the same. "*Veritas Domini manet in æternum.*" May it be granted to us to emulate the good deeds of those who have gone before us.

No. IV.—HALF-HOURS WITH THE SAINTS.
PARIS SAVED BY S. GENEVIEVE.

IN the fifth century, the Huns, a barbarous people from the extremity of Tartary, appeared in Europe, destroying and ravaging all the countries through which they passed. Their chief was the fierce Attila, who was called "the Scourge of God." They were everywhere victorious. No rivers, mountains, nor strength of walls, could arrest their progress, and Attila used to say that the grass could not grow until his horse had passed.

Five hundred burned villages had marked their entrance into Gaul, when they drew near to Paris. At the news of their approach, the inhabitants of the city were filled with despair. Relying little on their walls, they determined to fly, carrying away with them their most precious treasures, and retire into some better-fortified place. Only S. Geneviève, then a simple shepherdess, remained perfectly calm and without fear. She endeavoured to reassure the Parisians, boldly announcing that, if they would have recourse to prayer, God would protect their city, and that the towns where they had thought to find shelter would be themselves sacked and pillaged. She entreated them to do penance, promising, in answer to their prayers and supplications, the succour of heaven. Her inspired look and the force of her words reanimated hope in their hearts. The churches were filled with throngs of people, all uniting in heartfelt petitions for the safety of Paris. Geneviève herself, followed by some pious women, shut themselves up in the church of S. Jean le Rond, where they passed several days and nights in prayer.

The promises of the Saint, however, did not seem as if they

were about to be fulfilled. The Huns still continued their
devastating march, and were quite close to the city. The
enemies of Geneviève turned anew against her. Their rage,
which for some time had been suppressed, rekindled and burst
forth into a blaze. The same people who a few days before
had thrown themselves at her feet, now treated her as a
visionary and false prophetess. They accused the Saint of
having an understanding with the enemy, and said it was for
that reason she had preovnted the citizens from flying whilst
there was yet time. The fury of the populace increased
every minute : at last they determined to put her to death.
Great disputes then arose as to the mode of execution, some
wishing her to be drowned, others desiring that she should be
stoned, whilst again some insisted on her being burnt.

Geneviève, meanwhile, patient and resigned, prayed for her
enemies and offered the sacrifice of her life to God, who,
however, was not going to permit His faithful servant to
perish. He sent to her succour the Archdeacon of Auxerre,
who arrived suddenly from Italy. The people told him of
the designs of vengeance they were about to execute on the
Saint. Animated with a holy zeal, he exclaimed, " Citizens !
what are you about to do ? Beware of bringing down on
yourselves the vengeance of God by the commission of such
a crime. She whom you condemn to death has been declared
by Germanus our holy bishop to have been blessed by God
from her birth, and behold the gifts I bring from him for her
acceptance." These presents consisted of blessed things
which were sent in those times as a sign of communion and
friendship.

The words of the Archdeacon calmed the fury of the mob.
The opinion of Germanus, that illustrious prelate whose name
was so much venerated and whose authority so much respected, produced a great and instantaneous change in the
feelings of the people. They no longer sought to take the
Saint's life, and Geneviève, saved from so great a peril,
adored that protecting Hand of God which, though invisible,
is always present in the hour of danger to protect those who
put their confidence and their strength in Him alone.

Events justified the predictions of Geneviève. The Scourge
of God soon learnt that he was powerless where there were
to be found true servants of God who by their prayers
appeased the anger of heaven. He suddenly withdrew his
army from Paris without daring to strike a single blow.

This change, when all had seemed lost—this extraordinary retreat of the Huns, when victory would have been so easy to them—filled the Parisians with joy and astonishment. They saw clearly in this miracle the work of Providence, and, not hesitating to acknowledge that they owed their safety to the prayers of Geneviève, they gave her from that time continual proofs of their love and gratitude.

THE FEAST OF THE VISITATION. (JULY 2.)
THE SECOND JOYFUL MYSTERY OF THE ROSARY.

Sweet the lesson, Maiden Mother,
　Which thou teachest us to-day,
Courteous kindness to each other,
　As we journey on life's way.

O'er Judea's mountains wending,
　With the Eternal Son thy guest,
Bliss, all earthly joy transcending,
　Fills thy pure and humble breast.

Not to tell thy wondrous story,
　Not to claim thy kindred's praise,
Didst thou journey—though thy glory
　Fills e'en angels with amaze.

No! Thy mission to that dwelling
　Was another's joy to share,
All a mother's fears dispelling
　By thy blessed presence there.

Sweetest mother, earth is dreary
　Bring us Jesus here to-day,
Bravest hearts are sometimes weary
　Come to cheer the rugged way.

Come to teach us tender Mother,
　Thou canst teach us best of all,
Kind compassion for each other
　Pity for the frail who fall.

E.M.D.

MIRACULOUS CURES, AT THE HOLY GROTTO OF OUR BLESSED
LADY OF LOURDES, ON THE 1ST OF MAY, 1873.

Atherstone, May 5, 1873.

THE following account is from a private letter (sent from
Bagneres de Bigories, France) to St. Scholasticas Priory,
Atherstone, and is from the mother and sister of one of the
community. Its authenticity can therefore be safely attested.

C. D. BOWEN, Chaplain.

"To-day, the 1st of May, 1873, there was a pilgrimage from
La Vendée. We went to Lourdes for the day. There had
been three cures that we know of for certain. The first was
that of a girl of 24, who had not walked without crutches since
she was three years old. This morning, having drunk some
of the water, while she was praying in the Grotto, *she suddenly felt she was cured, gave her crutches* to the parish priest,
and walked quite alone. We saw the crutches hanging up,
tied together with the scarf she had worn as a child of Mary."
A servant of a great friend of ours saw her cured. This
servant when we were there went into the Grotto and brought
her to the Grille (or iron grating in front of the Grotto),
to speak to us. When she came out, everyone saluted and
welcomed her; shook hands with her. She then walked
quite alone to the railway station. Except that she limped
from one leg being shorter than the other, you would not
have known that she had ever been lame. The second cure
was that of a child of six years, who had not walked since she
was born. A lady told us that she *herself* had seen her cured
that morning. The third we saw ourselves : it was that of a
girl of 26 years of age (who had lost her voice). She had
not been able to speak above a whisper for twelve years.
She drank some of the water to-day, and was saying the
Rosary. Everybody kept telling her to say *Mary*, and to invoke
our Lady. At first she could not; nor for some time was
she able; but at last she suddenly roused herself and said,
quite aloud, "Mary!" Then they all began exclaiming and
crying and saying "Vive Notre Dame de Lourdes," "All
honour to our Lady of Lourdes." The poor girl was so overcome that they had to walk her up and down in the fresh air.
She looked so good and recollected, and so happy. We saw
another girl come out of the Grotto, who was cured on the
8th of December last. She was dressed all in blue."

THE OCTAVE OF SS. PETER AND PAUL.*

The mighty bell upon the Capitol
Sudden gives forth to Rome its signal sound.
And lo ! the myriad lesser bells around
Throughout the air their deep vibrations roll.
As though they sought—where'er are Christians found
Where'er are those who own faith's sweet control——
To warm, to rouse, to elevate the soul.
For one whole hour continuously resound
Their notes, announcing to the throngs of Rome,
City eternal, all true Christians' home,
That the great Octave hath e'en now begun ;
That till eight days their course complete have run,
The Apostles twain, who hold the keys and sword,
Who ever plead for Rome before their Lord,
Shall with undying honours honoured be,
And ages yet unborn shall bless their memory.   (E. F.)

MISCELLANEOUS ANECDOTES.

AN ANECDOTE OF LACORDAIRE AND HIS TIMES.

"ARCHBISHOP DE QUELEN was not acquainted with my project for re-establishing the Dominican order in France, and I was obliged to go and inform him. After having listened to me, he replied, rather coldly, 'These sort of things are in the hands of God, and He has not as yet, in any way, manifested His will.' 'Perhaps it is you,' resumed the Archbishop, 'who is going to make my dream come true ?' What dream, your Grace ? 'I had been appointed,' he replied, 'coadjutor to the Archbishop of Paris, and in 1820 I went to occupy an apartment in the Archbishop's house. In the night of the 3rd or 4th of August, the eve of the Feast of S. Dominic, I thought in my dream I was being carried into the gardens of the palace. The sky was clear, and without clouds, but the sun was covered with a thick veil of vapour, through which its rays appeared to come the colour of blood. Its course was

---

* On the Vigil of SS. Peter and Paul the bells of the entire City are rung for one whole hour in the afternoon, to announce that the first vespers of the Feast have begun.

very rapid, and it seemed almost to precipitate itself towards the horizon. In a very short time it totally disappeared. I then saw the waters of the Seine swollen as it were by a tide pouring in from the sea. Certain sea-monsters coming up with the flood, appeared to stop opposite Notre Dame and the Archbishopric and to make efforts to climb over from the stream upon the quay. After, this I was carried to a convent of religious, where I remained a long time. The Archbishop's palace had disappeared, and in its place was an open space covered with flowers. After this, I thought I saw ten men, clothed in white, who plunged their hands into the Seine and brought out numbers of sea-monsters, which they transformed into lambs as they laid them down on the grass. You see this dream of 1820 has, for the most part, turned out true. The Monarchy, represented by the sun covered with a dark veil, has fallen suddenly in the midst of the public rejoicings at the taking of Algiers. The populace has risen up and attacked Notre Dame and my palace. The palace has been destroyed, and on its site is now an open space planted with trees. I have had rooms for a long time as you see, and still occupy them, in a convent of religious clothed in black. What remains then for my dream to have its complete fulfilment but to see at Paris these men clothed in white occupied in labouring to convert the people. Perhaps it may be you who will bring them into it." A little time after Lacordaire had put on the habit of the Friars Preachers the Archbishop died.

A Blasphemer Killed by his own Dog.

AMONG the things which people call "*accidents and nothing more*," an Italian journal ('*Il Buon Pastore*,' published in Naples) contained the following :—" An inhabitant of Francavilla, in the province of Lecca, in the extreme South of Italy, out of sacrilegious contempt for the person and office of PIUS IX., had given his dog the name of "PIO NONO" (Pius IX.) One day, in the month of July, happening to be alone in his room, he called in his dog to amuse himself according to custom with him, making him stand up against the wall in soldier fashion. Here, venting his usual gibes and jests against the Pope, suddenly, as if indignant against such insults, the dog flew in a rage at his master and, seizing him by the throat, pulled him down, bit him, and disappeared. The unhappy man could with difficulty cry out for help. He

was found by his wife and children, who ran to his cries,
covered with blood, and it was with great difficulty that he
was able to tell them how it had happened. He died shortly
afterwards, without the rites of the Church."

RELIGIOUS PILGRIMAGES IN FRANCE.
A NATIONAL PILGRIMAGE TO THE SHRINE OF OUR LADY OF CHARTRES.
(Abridged from the Narrative of a Correspondent.)

AN amusing incident furnishes a remarkable proof of the zeal
with which pilgrimages are carried out in France.

"One of the *Rouge* party, on receiving the news of the fall of M. Thiers's
Government, exclaimed, 'That's all the effect of these d——d pilgrimages'
—an act of faith on the part of this disappointed Republican which greatly
entertained the Bishops to whom I heard the story told. And certainly
the recent revival, on so large a scale, of this mediæval practice is one of
the most remarkable phenomena of the day, well deserving the thoughtful
attention both of statesmen and of ecclesiastics. Of course the ordinary
race of Protestant journalists only see in it proofs of political conspiracies
on the part of 'the clerical party.' One of the more respectable of them,
writing a description of the pilgrimage to Notre Dame de Chartres, from
which I have just returned, lays it down that these processions 'are got up
as a taunt and a defiance to the anti-clerical party, with a view to provoke
a conflict or disturbance;' and then he goes on to show his intimate
acquaintance with the subject by conjecturing that 'the reason why
Chartres was selected was probably owing to its proximity, which actually
enabled some of her pious pilgrims to pay their devotions at the shrine of
Notre Dame and return to Paris in high time for luncheon.' There is no
doubt that there is a great difference in this particular between ancient and
modern pilgrimages; few pilgrims run any great risk now-a-days of 'vexa-
tion and trouble by outrageous long living on the sea, dangers and perils
by long continued winds and exceeding great storms, great weariness
because of the beasts that we rode upon,' as Sir Richard Guildforde tells
us of his own pilgrimage to the Holy Land in 1506. But surely it is easy
to see that these were always the accidents and not the essentials of a
pilgrimage—unavoidable accidents, because of the conditions of travelling
in those days, and not without their use as a salutary penance to this or
that pilgrim in particular.

"I think it may be worth while to point out one benefit of these vast
national pilgrimages that have lately sprung up on the Continent, viz.,
the increased strength they must give to all good men, by teaching them
in a most vivid manner that they are not solitary stragglers, but are enrolled in a mighty army scattered all over the country, identified with
themselves in principles and interests. Protestants might read with profit
a sermon of the late Mr. Robertson, of Brighton, which handles well this

subject of 'association for reciprocated strength ; the thrilling thought of numbers engaged in the same object, the idea of our own feelings reciprocated back to us and reflected from many hearts, other aspirations mingling with our own,' &c. They would then be enabled to make a juster estimate of what is going on in this matter in France and Italy, which at present they so strangely misunderstand. The Cathedral of Chartres has been famous for centuries as the rendezvous of all devout lovers of Mary ; it has been called her *palais de preference*, and it claims to be the very oldest of her shrines, and devotion to her began there even before Christianity itself. This statement will sound at first as a ridiculous anachronism ; but there is a great deal more to be said for it than I have now time to write, or you space to print. I will only remind your readers of what several of them will once have read in their school-days, viz. : that it was in the territory of Chartres (*in finibus Carnutum*) that the great annual meeting of the Druids was held in a sacred grove (*in luco consecrato*). And nobody who has ever visited the place and marked how the hill on which the Cathedral stands rises above an immense expanse of level country on every side, can doubt but that the Druids would have chosen just such a spot as this as a favourite place for their worship. I must not stop to quote either Protestant or Catholic authors, who have collected evidence as to the existence among various Pagan nations of a certain kind of belief in a Virgin-Mother, and consequent worship of her. I will only refer to two : M. Auguste Nicholas, in his work on Our Blessed Lady, who has shown this specially about the Gauls, and Stanley Faber, in his Origin of Pagan Idolatry, who maintains that the Druids were originally from Persia and disciples of the Magi, states that they brought with them from the East the prophecy of Balaam and that of Isaias too. However this may be, to the student of Pagan literature there is certainly nothing ridiculous, but, on the contrary, a very respectable amount of probability, in the tradition to which the good citizens of Chartres so affectionately cling, that our Blessed Lady was there honoured by anticipation, even before the birth of Our Lord. They say that, as at Athens, S. Paul found an altar 'to the Unknown God,' and made it the occasion of preaching the truth, so at Chartres there was an altar *Virgini Parituræ*, and that the first Apostles of Christianity in this country took advantage of it, exactly as S. Paul had done, saying, 'What therefore you worship, without knowing it, that I preach to you.' Hence Charles VII., in the fifteenth century, granting certain privileges to the Cathedral of Chartres, calls it, 'the most ancient Church of my Kingdom, founded by *prophecy*, and in which the Glorious Virgin was honoured whilst yet alive.' And at a later period, M. Olier dedicated the Seminary of S. Sulpice to N. D. de Chartres, calling it "a holy privileged place, the first of the whole world in point of antiquity for devotion to Our Blessed Lady, since it was built by prophecy.' It is not to be wondered at then that pilgrimages to N. D. de Chartres should have long been of annual recurrence, especially during the month of May. I had however been kindly invited to assist at a pilgrimage, which was to be of exceptional magnitude and interest. It was to be not merely a parochial, or diocesan, but a *national* pilgrimage : men and women were invited to come from all parts of France, to forge the link (as another Capuchin preacher well expressed it in his discourse in the Cathedral on a crowded congregation on the same Sunday evening) that should reunite modern times to the traditions of ancient times. The invitation was issued a month or six weeks before, and a mixed Committee of laymen and clerics had held frequent meetings to make all the necessary preparations. It was an anxious question whether it would prove a success or a failure, but the good Bishop and people of Chartres were determined that nothing should be wanting on their parts to make it a success. So arrangements were made with all the public establishments, and especially the Religious Houses, of the town that they should provide lodging, each for a certain number of pilgrims, according to their capacities. It need hardly be said that this could not be done without great sacrifices on the part of the Communities, but *how* great those sacrifices were, none can tell but those who had special opportunities of peeping behind the scenes. I visited two or three houses in the town, belonging to one Religious Order, on the eve of the pilgrimage, and found 150 beds prepared in one, 100 in another, and so on. And even so, the demand exceeded the supply, where five priests were expected, fifteen were received; where 150 were provided for, 200 were received, and so on. On Tuesday, the first day of the great pilgrimage, 2,000 arrived by train, and probably an equal number on foot or in other ways. At half-past ten, several hundreds of the clergy were assembled at the episcopal residence adjoining the Cathedral—the curés and vicaires, in the garden; canons and prelates from other dioceses, in the entrance-hall, and some ten or twelve Bishops, with their attendants, in the inner apartments of the palace. Everything was admirably arranged, and it was but a few minutes after the appointed hour, when the procession advanced through a most dense, but most orderly crowd, to the Cathedral, where they defiled into the choir until it was completely packed. Mgr. Forcade, Bishop of Treves, but now Archbishop-Elect of Aix, sang the Mass; and, after the Credo, a sermon was preached by one of the two Capuchin Friars from Versailles, who had been conducting the May devotions during the whole month. Every corner of the Cathedral was crammed; so it was useless to attempt to get down into the cave to hear the preacher. From our places in the choir we could just see an animated figure in the pulpit, and catch an occasional scream of a human voice; but that was all. However, the pilgrimage had now been solemnly inaugurated by the High Mass; and the subsequent proceedings, both of this day and the next, were of a more varied and popular character. At two o'clock, six or eight of the Bishops in copes, mitres, and crosiers, appeared at the top of one of the towers, just at the base of the beautiful steeple, and, from thence, gave their blessing (simultaneously) to the assembled multitudes beneath. This was followed by vespers, Mgr. Forcade again officiating, and a sermon from Mgr. Marguerye, who has lately retired from the See of Autun. And after the sermon came the event of the day, the procession of our Blessed Lady's statue, N. D. du Pilier, through some of the streets of the town. The civil authorities had at first deprecated this as highly imprudent, calculated to promote a breach of the peace, and so forth; but finding the ecclesiastical authorities firm in their purpose, no hindrance was attempted, not a single cry, or gesture, could be detected amid the countless multitudes that were assembled, to justify the apprehensions of M. le Maire. On the contrary, the crowd was most respectful and reverent in its demeanour, so far as I could see; even young men, gathered at the doors of the cafes, made the sign of the Cross as the statue was borne before them. The procession was very long, and as I took part in it, I could of course only see a small portion of it, but it was the grandest portion; the statue, carried by six ecclesiastics, chosen from different bodies of the clergy, who relieved one another at intervals, and eight or ten Bishops who followed it. Unfortunately, the rain began to fall in very heavy drops as we came in sight of the Cathedral on our return, which caused a sudden development of umbrellas, and a sudden disappearance of divers crosses, blue ribands, and other decorations which had shone on the tippets of some of the canons and prelates. We were glad to gain the friendly shelter of the Cathedral, and after walking all round it, we descended into the subterranean crypt, or rather the subterranean gallery, which runs right round the church, underlying the aisles. This contains the original cave, supposed to be a part of the *lucus consecratus* of the Druids, where there is a modern statue, intended to replace the ancient one *Virgini Pariturœ*, destroyed in the great revolution. The whole of this subterranean has been restored of late years, or rather is still in course of restoration, in very excellent taste; and as we descended the stairs and the long vista broke on our sight, beautifully illuminated from end to end, and the longest section of the procession we had yet had an opportunity of seeing slowly defiling through it, the *tout ensemble* was really perfect. I don't think a single Frenchman, as far as my observation went, refrained from exclaiming, as first he caught sight of this, "*Ah! comme il est beau.*" Rows of candles and lamps hung all the way down on each side, and in the last five or six bays, towards the end where the altar was, all the lines of architecture in the groined roof were similarly picked out by rows of small lamps, whilst the altar itself before the statue was, of course, one blaze of light. We passed this, and went down the other subterranean aisle, where every chapel was filled with the students of some school, the members of some pious confraternity, or other privileged individuals; and then we emerged into the Cathedral again, where we visited N. D. du Pilier, sang the *Regina Cœli*, and then dispersed. The procession must have lasted two or three hours, and some of the Bishops must have been somewhat fatigued; nevertheless this did not prevent their being very excellent company at the Evéché in the evening, where the venerable Bishop of Chartres, delighted with the success of his first day, entertained about thirty guests, including the Archbishop of Paris, the Bishops of Evreux, of Poitiers, of S. Brieux, of Canton, &c. At eight o'clock in the evening there were the usual devotions of the month of May, with a sermon from a Capuchin Friar, followed by interminable *cantiques*, sung successively by various bodies of pilgrims all the night through. For the Bishop, fearing lest some should find it impossible to procure lodgings, had ordered that the Cathedral should be thoroughly illuminated both inside and out, and the doors remain open all night. For the accommodation also both of the priests and people, leave was given that Masses should be begun immediately after midnight, and I was told that they went on uninterruptedly at all the altars, both above and below, till mid-day. It was said that 1,500 Masses were celebrated.

J. S. N.

CURRENT EVENTS.

ROME AND THE POPE.—The health of the Pope is now so
well re-established that the newspapers have ceased to spread
their false alarms. He has returned to his ordinary occupation, and continues, as usual, to receive great numbers of
persons to private audiences. Amongst other distinguished
persons, the Empress of Russia has been presented to His
Holiness. His Holiness has also received in audience a deputation of the most distinguished advocates of all Italy, who
had united in an address showing that blasphemies against
Christ, such as have appeared in the *Capitale*, ought by the
laws of the land to have been suppressed and punished; and
that the letter of the Procurator (Attorney-General) upon the
Cardinal-Vicar's protest against the publication of those most
profane articles, was utterly wrong, both on the letter and
the principle of the law as it actually stands. On the same
day the Commendatore Margotti, representing the Turin
paper the *Unità Cattolica*, of which his brother, Dom T. Margotti, is the well-known editor, presented 200,000 lire, and
also twelve volumes of signatures, protesting against the
above-mentioned blasphemies published in the *Capitale*. Mgr.
Bodoira, of Turin, also read an address in his character of
LL.D. To the three addresses the Holy Father replied:—
" All that I have just listened to confirms me in the persuasion
that the filial piety of Italy to this Holy See and the purity
of faith is not diminished, but rather increases with the contradiction opposed to them. For this God be praised. Not
many days since I read in a so-called 'officious' journal
some words quoted that I had used. I had said that God was
with us, and 'if God be with us, who shall be against us';
and the writer had the hardihood to say, ' God is not with the
Pope, but rather with Italy.' This impudent assertion is
contrary to the facts, and I say first that if Italy is with God,
it must also be with His Vicar. Distinguishing the true from
the false Italy, I say that the first is immensely more numerous than the latter. You, and the immense number of those
associated with you, are a proof of the union with God
and with me of that Italy which you represent; and whilst
this Italy opens her hand to acts of filial piety, she lifts up her
heart in the Divine presence to implore the favours of God,
within the walls of the temples, in devout pilgrimages, in
honouring the memory of the saints, and especially in this
present month in fervent supplications to the Mother of Divine

Mercy, Mary. Here, in Rome also, I have the consolation of knowing that the churches are crowded, and that with extra-ordinary fervour the Roman people call upon Mary to aid the assailed Church. God is with His people, with the people that multiplies works of piety, that labours in so many ways to excite to all good the young, who generously respond to the appeal that endeavours to arrest the corruption sown by the enemies of Italy, and that remains faithful in its opposition to the blinded obstinacy of the enemies of God. This is the Italy that is with God and His Vicar. But God is not with that smaller part of Italy which oppresses the Church, and which makes itself an instrument of corruption and infidelity. No; God is not with that part of Italy which robs the Church and dis-perses the Religious Orders. He is not with those who persecute the ministers of the Sanctuary and the spouses of Christ, who se-duce into the way of unbelief so many souls that were redeemed at an infinite price, and who will one day have to render an ac-count of all those to whose eternal loss they have contributed. With this Italy God is not; but this Italy which causes the loss of souls also engages the true Italy, the greater majority of Italians, to oppose with firmness all the works of wickedness. The Church to-day (Feast of S. Gregory VII.) commemorates one of the greatest of my predecessors, and asks him to obtain from God, courage, fortitude, and strength to fight and over-come the enemies of God. *Deus in te sperantium fortitudo.* God is the strength of all those who hope in Him, and the intercession of this great Saint will obtain for us constancy and strength to overcome the enemies who make war upon us. Recollect that we are in the Octave of the Feast of the Ascen-sion. Let us turn ourselves to Jesus Christ who returns to heaven whence He came, and let us ask His blessing. Stand-ing in the midst of His Apostles, 'lifting up His hands he blessed them.' I lift up my hands to bless you, and desire that it may fill you with joy, comfort, and consolation. *Ele-vatis manibus,* I bless you, and I implore the Lord to sustain my weakness, so that, strengthened and supported by His grace, I may bless those only who are worthy to be blessed by Him, receiving with this benediction comfort, guidance, and strength. May this benediction remain with you, your families, and colleagues. Finally, for that portion of Italy that refuses to be united with me, I pray that God may con-cede those graces and those lights that may show her the way she ought to go, issuing forth from the darkness and shadow of death in which at present she abides." Benedictio, &c.

THE NEW CATHEDRAL OF THE DIOCESE OF WESTMINSTER.—
Among the events of public interest which should not be
passed over are the preparations which are at least in progress for obtaining a Cathedral Church and Episcopal residence for the See of Westminster.   Considering that London
is the chief city of the British Empire, and in many respects
the principal commercial market of all the nations of the
world, that the Catholic Church should possess in London a
Cathedral Church proportionate to the rank and dignity of
the city, among the other cities of the world, is a question
of very much more than merely diocesan and local interest. A
site has been purchased in the limits of Westminster for the
sum of £36,500, which is perfectly adequate to the erection
of a Cathedral Church fully as large as that of Westminster
Abbey. To the property thus acquired there has been recently
added a third purchase of an adjacent site, with a house
standing upon it, that had been built in 1866 by the officers
of the Guards as an institute for their men.   This house
furnishes a spacious and convenient Episcopal residence, and
it has already undergone a large portion of the alterations.
and fittings necessary to render it serviceable for the purposes
of the diocese.   Suitable plans have been prepared by Mr.
Clutton for the erection of the Cathedral on a scale befitting the
extent of the site.   The whole work of these plans, which have
been successively designed, with most elaborate care, according as the acquisition of increased extent in the site called for
increased proportions to the buildings, have been given
gratuitously by Mr. Clutton as his contribution to the funds
of the Cathedral.   The work, consequently, of the new
Cathedral has been formally inaugurated, and will appeal,
possibly for years to come, to all to whom God may give the
gift of a zeal for the glory of His House.

INDEX

www.ingramcontent.com/pod-product-compliance
Lightning Source LLC
Chambersburg PA
CBHW021118270326
41929CB00009B/939